Methodologies of Affective Experimentation

Britta Timm Knudsen
Mads Krogh • Carsten Stage
Editors

Methodologies of Affective Experimentation

palgrave
macmillan

Editors
Britta Timm Knudsen
School of Communication and Culture
Aarhus University
Aarhus, Denmark

Mads Krogh
School of Communication and Culture
Aarhus University
Aarhus, Denmark

Carsten Stage
School of Communication and Culture
Aarhus University
Aarhus, Denmark

ISBN 978-3-030-96271-5   ISBN 978-3-030-96272-2   (eBook)
https://doi.org/10.1007/978-3-030-96272-2

CONTENTS

NOTES ON CONTRIBUTORS

Rebecca Coleman is a professor at the Bristol Digital Futures Institute, University of Bristol, UK, where her research focuses on the everyday life of digital media, presents and futures, affect and materiality and inventive methodologies.

Natalie Ann Hendry is a senior lecturer at the Melbourne Graduate School of Education, The University of Melbourne, Australia. Natalie's research investigates the relationship between education, health and media, with a focus on the pedagogical role of social media and digital well-being and finance cultures.

Julian Henriques is a professor in the Department of Media, Communications and Cultural Studies at Goldsmiths, University of London, UK. His research deals with the field of street technologies and cultures (particularly reggae dancehall sound systems) and sound studies.

Sophie Hope is Senior Lecturer in Arts Policy and Management at Birkbeck, University of London, UK. Her practice-based research explores political, economic and social histories of cultural democracy and socially engaged art, physical and emotional experiences of work and the ethics of employability in the creative industries.

Christina Jerne is a postdoctoral researcher at the Centre for Global Criminology, University of Copenhagen, Denmark. Her research interests lie in the fields of political economy and organized crime. She is a member of the Community Economies Institute, a non-profit that fosters thought and practice to help communities survive well together.

Kilian Jörg works at the multimedial interfaces between philosophy and art. He employs the expression of text as well as those of installation, performance and music. He is a founder of the collective Philosophy Unbound and operates in Vienna, Berlin and Brussels. His main field of research is that of ecological epistemology.

Christoffer Kølvraa is Associate Professor of European Studies in the Department of Global Studies at Aarhus University, Denmark. His current research is focused on the ideological, affective and political aspects of the rise of far-right populism and neofascism in the contemporary context of what has been called 'late postmodernity'.

Mads Krogh is Associate Professor of Popular Music Culture at the School of Communication and Culture, Aarhus University, Denmark. His research deals with issues of practice, mediation and genre in popular music culture combining perspectives from new materialism (ANT, assemblage theory, affect theory) with cultural sociology.

Susanna Paasonen is Professor of Media Studies at University of Turku, Finland, and most recently the author of *Dependent, Distracted, Bored: Affective Formations in Networked Media* (2021).

Sverre Raffnsøe is Professor of Philosophy and Leadership at Copenhagen Business School, Denmark, and editor-in-chief of the international journal *Foucault Studies*. His main interests lie in affirmative critique, self-management and humans at the edge of the Anthropocene. He is a fellow at the Institute of Advanced Study, Collegium de Lyon 2020–2021 and recipient of the Carlsberg Foundation's Semper Ardens Monograph Fellowship.

Paul Schütze is a research assistant in the *Ethics of AI* group at the Institute of Cognitive Science, Osnabrück, Germany. In his work, he currently focuses on the functioning of digital capitalism and its connections to the climate crisis. His research fields are social philosophy, critical theory, phenomenology and affect theory.

Jan Slaby is Professor of Philosophy of Mind and Philosophy of Emotion at Free University of Berlin, Germany. His areas of expertise are philosophy of mind (construed broadly), philosophy of emotion, phenomenology, social philosophy, affect theory and philosophical methodology.

Carsten Stage is Professor of Culture and Media at School of Communication and Culture, Aarhus University, Denmark. His research explores digital illness narratives, social media, affect and participation. Recent books include *Quantified Storytelling* (Palgrave Macmillan, 2020) and *The Language of Illness and Death on Social Media: An Affective Approach* (2018).

Dorthe Staunæs is Professor of Social Psychology at the Danish School of Education, Aarhus University, Denmark. Her methodological approach lies at the intersection of affect studies, black feminist studies and feminist new materialism. She is currently leading the projects Diversity Work as Mood Work and Affective Investments in Diversity Work in STEM at Danish Universities.

Britta Timm Knudsen is Professor of Culture, Media and Experience Economy at School of Communication and Culture, Aarhus University, Denmark. Her research focuses on difficult heritage, futures, affect and event studies, tourism and digital media.

Signe Uldbjerg is a PhD from Aarhus University and holds currently a post-doc position at University of Southern Denmark. Her research investigates the use of experimental, participatory and activist methods, recently, in a PhD project on victim experiences of sexual violence, but also in a number of other writing experiments within youth, educational and mental health contexts.

Phillip Vannini and April Vannini teach in the Faculty of Social and Applied Sciences and in the School of Communication & Culture at Royal Roads University, Victoria, British Columbia, Canada. Together they are the authors of *Wilderness* (2016), *Inhabited* (2021) and *In the Name of Wild* (2022). Phillip's research over the years has focused on mobilities, the senses and renewable energy. He works at the intersection of human geography, cultural studies and the environmental humanities. April holds a PhD in Philosophy, Art and Social Thought from the European Graduate School. Her work spans the fields of social and cultural geography, continental philosophy, research creation and ecological place-based education.

Imke von Maur is Postdoc in Philosophy at the Institute for Cognitive Science, Osnabrück, Germany. Her research areas are philosophy of mind and emotions, (social) epistemology and (post-)phenomenology, with the main interest in the societal and political relevance of understanding processes.

LIST OF FIGURES

CHAPTER 1

Introduction: Methodologies of Affective Experimentation

Britta Timm Knudsen, Mads Krogh, and Carsten Stage

THE TIME TO EXPERIMENT?

We live in an era of experimentation—both if we take a look at the broader social world of politics, media and art and at the narrower context of academic knowledge production. The claim of this book is that experiments are inherently affective due to their ability to produce sensuous events that enable more or less intense shifts in attention and involve participants in orchestrated yet unpredictable processes that activate the body's ability to relate to, sense and imagine the world in new ways. Experiments are, in other words, affective per default by enacting the body as entangled with and attuned by a particular setting—and maybe even by drawing attention to the body's ability to become affectively entangled with the world in the first place. In this introduction we offer a heuristic aimed at qualifying the analysis of both 'found' examples of affective experimentation and research

B. Timm Knudsen (✉) • M. Krogh • C. Stage
School of Communication and Culture, Aarhus University,
Aarhus, Denmark
e-mail: norbtk@cc.au.dk; musmk@cc.au.dk; norcs@cc.au.dk

© The Author(s), under exclusive license to Springer Nature
Switzerland AG 2022
B. Timm Knudsen et al. (eds.), *Methodologies of Affective
Experimentation*, https://doi.org/10.1007/978-3-030-96272-2_1

1

processes or methods that are themselves experimental. The heuristic unfolds three dimensions of what affective experiments fundamentally do: they reveal unrecognized aspects of the social, they engage with unpredictable and transgressive processes and they enact a future in the making. Our claim is that all experiments to be called affective engage with these three dimensions.

In understanding experiments as situations that make the body affectively aware of its entanglement with a setting—and of its potential for being involved in and distributed by entanglements—we are inspired by Lisa Blackman. According to her, practices of experimentation can be described "as inventive strategies for producing particular forms of entanglement. This is in line with work taken up across the sciences and humanities, which approaches experimentation as performative, and where the technical framing of an experimental event provides the setting for dynamic processes of enactment to take form" (Blackman 2012, p. 144). Following this line of thinking, experimentation is a force of sensuous transformation and intensification that simultaneously 'touches' the body as a defined or subjectively felt entity and enacts that very same body as dispersed and distributed in relation to a setting. In that way experimentation also stresses and produces awareness about how "we extend into our environments and yet paradoxically are required to live this extension as interiority" (p. 151). This edited collection offers 14 chapters that develop various strategies for empirically exploring experiments as affective and performative events of sensuous entanglement—both in relation to experiments as 'affective strategies' enacted by non-researchers (e.g., cultural producers, as in the chapter by Julian Henriques, or activists, as in the chapter by Paul Schütze, Kilian Jörg, Imke von Maur and Jan Slaby) and as research methods. That is, experiments strategically devised and methodologically reflected by researchers in order to explore affective aspects of the world (as with the creative-writing workshops developed by Natalie Ann Hendry and Signe Uldbjerg or the virtual reality installation devised by Britta Timm Knudsen in order to explore wind as elementary attraction).

The collection responds to a pressing need to understand the intersection between affect, experimentation and sociocultural change by offering analytical strategies that enable researchers to explore just how and with what consequences experimentation is affective. The chapters of the collection address the field of affect studies in different ways, but they share an analytical interest in how experiments produce, modulate and circulate experiential intensity, shifts in attention and movements between bodily states (Anderson 2014; Brennan 2004; Massumi 2002)—even if this does not necessarily make experiments transformative per se, as they can also reproduce affective economies and hierarchies (Ahmed 2004; Berlant 2011; Ngai 2005). The chapters in the volume also share an interest in affective experimentation as a practice that is at once inherently unpredictable, vested with the ability to open up new (but not necessarily progressive) futures, but which may also give otherwise hidden or invisible social logics a visceral form. In keeping with these communalities, we aim in this introduction to stake out an understanding of affective experiments as linked to overlapping processes of unpredictability, potentiality and (re)presentation enacted or put into motion through bodily entangling events. Simultaneously, we wish to underline that the affective intensity of experiments are produced by their ability to engender spectacles (on widely varying scales) and experiences of immersion and 'showing-not-telling' that in themselves hold a potential of experiencing world-making and futurity for participants and witnesses. Indeed, we consider this world-making capacity a key aspect of affective experimentation, in keeping with the performativity noted by Blackman.

Let's consider an all-too-present and pressing example to help set the intended direction. Besides its far reaching and catastrophic consequences, the outbreak in 2019/20 of COVID-19 encompassed all sorts of experiments. The virus itself could already be regarded as a non-human force of constant experimentation-through-mutation. However, in its global rupture of routines, the pandemic also triggered a dire need to experiment on multiple levels, for example, as regards vaccine development, cross-national research collaboration, production and dissemination of protective gear, establishment of test centres, upscaling of treatment facilities and so forth. In the highly unpredictable, experimental processes, set off to accommodate these various needs, economic inequalities were quickly exposed, especially in relation to the world's poor for whom lockdown measures (even something as simple as washing one's hands several times a day with soap) were a luxury beyond reach. In the French media, two doctors suggested a very specific experiment: Africa should be used as a testing ground for the efficacy of vaccines. This provoked a furious backlash, notably from leading African and Afro-European football stars. Also in politics, the crisis opened a space for experimentation with dramatic consequences—for example, the return of authoritarian political logics legitimized by a permanent state of emergency, biopolitical remedies to govern and survey bodies, lockdowns, border closings, giant sums of subsidy—all examples that either fuelled hopes for political alternatives to capitalism or just confirmed already existing inequalities. Even culturally and in the arts, lockdown and demands of social distance inspired new forms of expression and performance—for example, balcony singing (spreading via social media from Italy in March 2020), drive-in concerts, online theatre performances and museum visits that transformed into take-home-kits allowing audiences to interact with cultural institutions (e.g., the National Gallery of Denmark) from their homes.

These experimental ways of doing science, politics, culture (and of intertwining these spheres) bore the mark of crisis or emergency in the sense that normal procedures seemed indefinitely suspended. New cultural forms and new online formats, as well as a burgeoning hope for the pandemic to be an event capable of mobilizing populations for long-lasting change or for rediscovering more progressive uses of new media, were produced as a response to the lack of efficient everyday routines (see Susanna Paasonen's chapter in this book). However, fear, anxiety and anger also occurred as pronounced, affective reactions to the medical, economic, political, social and cultural crises created by a global pandemic that to a large extent re-affirmed global power-geometries and nationalist agendas. Here, again, it is important to stress that an interest in understanding affective intensities in their collective, relational and unpredictable unfoldings does not prevent us from considering the sociocultural and political implications, stabilisations and hierarchies of affective processes. The latter focus could, for instance (as in the chapters by Christoffer Kølvraa and Schütze et al. in this book), stress the inherent magnetism of the status quo as a structure of feeling or populist political discourse as an efficient evacuation of 'what could be' replaced by a sentimental celebration of 'what is'.

Looking beyond COVID-19, a wider array of developments in media, arts and politics is easily identified, which reinforces the need to understand the social ramifications of affective experimentation. Examples could be media formats, where, for example, reality TV of the 1990s sparked a persistent wave of lifestyle experiments (Dovey 2000; Black 2002; Jerslev 2004), or the cultural industries, where liveness and the possibility of immersing oneself into a staged environment that trigger affects are constantly probed—whether in contexts of museums, tourism, festivals or consumer branding (Pine and Gilmore 1999; Klingmann 2007; Knudsen 2011a, b; Bjerregaard 2015; Daugbjerg et al. 2016). Another example is how experimental approaches from the arts travel to the world of healthcare to engage with and affect illness experiences (Charon 2006; Sampson 2004) or to contexts of social media, where reading and writing experiments (steered by researchers) may counter issues of assault and solitude (Mortensen 2020). Also in politics, experiments aimed at performing power and decision-making differently draw on affective dynamics in the enactment of alternative and temporary forms of radical democracy—as in the case of place-based social movements such as Los Indignados, Madrid 2011, and Les Nuits Debout, Paris 2016 (Romanos 2016; Guichou 2016). In various scholarly contexts, we also perceive a rising methodological interest in experimental and creative approaches to doing research, where methods are not approached as routinized procedures, but rather as performative tools for producing knowledge and relations between researcher and research participants in new ways (Bergold and Thomas 2012; Hope 2016; Kara 2015; Mannay 2016; Markham and Pereira 2019).

Research on the affective, emotional and intensive aspects of contemporary culture has been flourishing for two decades, but the development of methodological approaches and devices for understanding the importance of affect is still a burgeoning research agenda. Existing contributions to this methodological challenge have tended to aim at either tracking or documenting affective aspects through the retuning of established qualitative methods of social and cultural research (e.g., Kahl 2019; Knudsen and Stage 2015) or unfolding how methods cannot represent but must instead create or produce affective attunements due to the inherited performativity of methods (Vannini 2015; Clough 2009; Law 2004). This edited collection suggests instead to develop a different trajectory—one that tries to transgress the dichotomy of understanding methods as being either representative or performative (see also Lury 2021)—by approaching the academic exploration of affects through the lens of experimentation. Moreover, as indicated, we consider affective experiments to be both actual strategies of social agencies that must be explored to understand crucial aspects of contemporary culture and society (Fleig and Scheve 2021) and as research methods able to not only produce but also give insight into and reveal existing social and affective logics. This difference structures the collection's bipartite organization.

The edited collection *Affective Methodologies* (Knudsen and Stage 2015), in line with other timely attempts to take up the methodological challenge of studying processuality and affect (see Lury and Wakeford 2012; Coleman and Ringrose 2013; Anderson 2014; Vannini 2015; Kahl 2019; Fleig and Scheve 2021), positioned inventive experiments as one of three constructive meta-strategies for producing empirical material for affect research. In that volume, the experiment was characterized as double-edged: on the one hand, it unfolds as staged events within which it is possible to produce academic knowledge; on the other hand, the experiment was understood as intentional attempts to produce affective forces offering open-ended opportunities for multiple encounters and responses to take place (Knudsen and Stage 2015). In terms of affect studies, our methodological take in that collection was based on the premise of moving away from focusing primarily on what affect is and its relationship to other concepts like 'discourse' and 'cognition' (e.g., Massumi 2002; Brennan 2004) in favour of focusing more on ways of investigating how affective intensity is (re)produced, circulated and rewired in and by particular experimental settings (Anderson 2014).

In keeping with these earlier efforts and the double interest in affective experimentation as both social phenomenon and research method, this collection aims at offering methodological approaches that allow researchers to address the increasing importance of experimentation for contemporary culture, media and politics but also to develop new creative research methodologies that engage in co-constructing and re-sensibilizing to the sociomaterial world through experimentation. Thus, we understand 'methodology' in the overall sense of comprising the reflective design of a research process in order to be able to answer to a particular knowledge problem. Particular approaches (or methods) range from specific ways of engaging sites and practices of affective experimentation (e.g., via field work, interviews, text analysis), through analytical strategies for exploring such practices and the importance of affective experimentation in contemporary culture, to researcher-initiated arrangements that produce social situations where research can take place (e.g., in the form of events, interventions, workshops, creative communication endeavours). In this way the collection simultaneously develops ways of methodologically exploring existing societal logics of affective experimentation and of potentially changing these logics by means of affective experimentation. The impetus for bringing these different methodological strands together in the same collection is that their combination can help us identify and reflect on the various ways affective experimentation matters for contemporary culture and sociopolitical change.

In the following, we take some preliminary steps towards unfolding the concept of experimentation before presenting the analytical heuristic for studying affective implications of experiments in their various forms and functions. Finally, we briefly present the collection of articles.

The History and Politics of Experimentation

To advocate a performative understanding of affective experimentation calls for some historical elaboration. As epitomized by the natural sciences, experimentation is traditionally aimed at trying or testing theories. This requires strict procedures—protocols, instruments, standards and so forth—and the seclusion of factors (traditionally in terms of the laboratory) to ensure trust in the conducted trial (Franklin and Perovic 2021; Gooding et al. 1989). A linear idea of efficient causes governs this idea of the experiment both in terms of how observations confirm or dismiss theories and as regards the reproducibility of results, and even if the positivist tenet of such thinking was long ago revised by science and technology studies scholars, among others, trust in experimental research prevails—by way of networks of scientific institutions, publications, norms and interests, media, technologies and so forth. That is, a broad range of (f)actors enrolled to make experiments work as a 'convincing' and 'reliable' mode of knowledge production. Even in the humanities and social sciences, the idea of the laboratory has been adopted as a privileged space for doing experiments to transfer into real-world settings (i.e., field sites for testing interventions), 'real-life experiments' or living labs (implementing scientific knowledge or technology and infrastructural innovation in urban environments), without dispensing with ideals of theory testing, procedural strictness, the seclusion of effective factors and so on (Krohn and Weyer 1994; Bruun Jensen and Morita 2017).

Understanding experiments as performative emphatically counterposes traditional, positivist ideals. But, in fact, we find, in a closer inspection of the history of the scientific experiment, indications that support a performative and affective approach to what experiments do. Indeed, it seems that the scientific experiment was born to be affectively compelling. Staying within a Eurocentric frame of scientific knowledge production, one of the ideological pioneers of experimental science was Francis Bacon and his *Novum Organon* from 1620 (Bagrie 2004). This philosophical work, concerning how knowledge is generated in the natural sciences, refers to Aristotle's *Organon* and presents a new, more inductive and empirically grounded method still based on logics. Bacon's focus on new discoveries was dependent on the travels to and explorations of 'new' territories as a part of European colonial endeavours in the seventeenth century. In the *Novum Organon*, Bacon was hoping to discover something about the natural world and not only to deduce something from already established principles. Even though the Aristotelian approach was also based on the human sensing of a natural world, Bacon claimed that the general principles of nature according to the Aristotelian method were not based sufficiently on empirical knowledge (Bacon [1620] n.d., p. 3). The new methodological procedures, according to Bacon, had to be inductive. They should be embedded in the human sensing of nature and according to principles that nature acknowledges as its own (p. 4). However, Bacon distinguishes between an immediate sensing of the world that we cannot rely upon and a mediated experience of the world enacted through experiments and their devices capable of correcting sensuous errors along the way (Bagrie 2004, p. 65). In other words, Bacon supported the idea that mediation and, in a wider sense, the staging of an intentional, experimental situation—as a distributed environment of knowledge production— can be a way of moving closer or of immersing oneself into an (affective) experience of the world, creating awareness about otherwise hidden aspects of that world.

Similar indications of affective implications in the trajectory of the scientific experiment can be found by looking to another champion of experimental research, co-founder of the Royal Society of London for Improving Natural Knowledge, Robert Boyle. In Steven Shapin's reading (1984), experiments' reliability as valid sources of knowledge came with the work of Boyle to depend on three technologies: a material technology of demonstration (such as the air-pump in Boyle's experiments with pneumatics), tempered by collective labour and disciplined by artificial devices (additional tools or machinery); a literary technology by means of which the phenomena could spread to larger audiences than the ones directly witnessing demonstrations; and a social technology (Shapin 1984, p. 484) pointing to how the social solidarity of the experimental community was created. Apart from the fact that the experiment was born as a spectacle with eye-witnesses present to attest to the matter-of-factness of discoveries, the striking feature of the scientific experiment from the seventeenth century, according to Shapin, is that its aim was to enlarge the witnessing public beyond the immediacy of the actual experimental event. Literary technologies should facilitate replications, which depended on extensive use of visual representations but also on thorough considerations of how to write scientific prose to affect audiences (see, e.g., Vannini and Vannini,

Chap. 13 in this volume). Elaborate sentences with circumstantial details were understood as being able to mimic the immediacy of pictorial representations (Shapin 1984, p. 493) and detailed accounts of failed experiments and modesty in relation to the position of the researcher—including the claims made—heightened the credibility of the researcher and increased the interest of wider publics. Adding to the mediated sensory engagement, which Bacon emphasized as a means to 'revelation', with Boyle, in other words, we find produced attention and immediacy in the spectacular liveness of the experiment, capturing witnesses, and in the technological—pictorial and literary—ways of rendering this liveness in order to engage and excite wider publics.

Recognizing these affective implications in the historical meaning of experimentation is important, not least considering the spreading of scientific ideas to other fields such as experiments in the sociopolitical realm. As a tragic example, consider the initiative in 1951 of sending 22 Greenlandish children to Denmark as part of a 'civilizing mission'. The goal of this mission was to create a bilingual Greenlandish elite and the forced removal was at that time understood and framed explicitly as a social experiment. The delimited group of specially chosen children and variables in terms of ethno-national and socioeconomic circumstances for their upbringing constituted a sense of a laboratory condition aimed to test the significance of such variables for advancing a process of Greenlandish modernization. Certainly, notions of linearity governed the experiment, as regards the 'good' to follow from relocating children, just as specifying criteria of selection and circumstantial variables could afford replication.

More than half a century later, the Danish state is still experimenting, now with initiatives—since 2010—in the officially labelled 'ghettos', which are problem-ridden (according to official statistical criteria) but also affordable housing areas in the suburbs of bigger cities in Denmark. With the aim of countering "parallel societies" or "failed integration" (Simonsen 2016), these areas are either partly demolished or encumbered with so many restrictive rules regarding income levels, levels of education, unemployment levels, criminal rates and percentage of non-Western immigrants and descendants that large groups of minority-religious or minority-cultural groups are forced to move away from their network and from earlier social initiatives that have been beneficial to the areas. The decision to reduce the affordable housing stock in 'areas of parallel societies' will cost around 11,000 citizens their homes before 2030. Critics have called this and related initiatives one of the most significant social welfare experiments—based on racialized housing politics—in recent history (Bach 2019; Soei 2021). Moreover, initiatives are also in this case conducted in a limited space designated by demographic, socioeconomic and ethnic variables with explicit effects to be tested, that is, according to a real-life notion of the laboratory echoing scientific experimental ideals.

The affective implications of these cases from recent Danish history merge scientific logics with political gesture. Indeed, this has, arguably, added to their destructive character. The spectacular character of the experiment may be amplified through forcefulness or the 'radical' nature of measures—as with removing children by force and demolishing homes—in order to engage and arouse publics far beyond the scientific community. The mediated distribution of the experiment may, and perhaps inevitably will, translate into politicized representation. Indeed, in this respect, our examples fall in tragic line with the way "experimental subjects" in politics have often been "vile bodies" (Guerrini 2016), such as prisoners, prostitutes, orphans, people with disabilities, the mentally ill, hospital patients, slaves and the colonized. In the mentioned cases we see colonized citizens and Muslim minorities in the role of 'vile bodies'. Also, representations of social experiments may play to moral panics enticed by and, reciprocally, enticing radial measures. Public flows of fear, anxiety and perhaps dreams of another state—a 'better' future for Greenland or less 'parallel societies'—converge, in this respect, with the sense of efficient linearity vested in the experiment. Indeed, the affective experimental strategies employed by Danish officials could be said to reinforce dominant forms of governance—protend established power relations—via feelings of fear, repulsion and anxiety for the majority population.

By exploring these kinds of experiments, consisting in governmental interpellation to particular ethnic groups, an ethics of affective experimentation becomes clear. It should be possible not to participate in—and to exit (Kelty et al. 2014)—the experiment in order to counterbalance the affectively compelling nature of the experiment. The collaborative and participatory modes of doing fieldwork that are explored by Carsten Stage, Sophie Hope, Signe Uldbjerg and Natalie Ann Hendry in this volume are one way of proceeding to further empower participants in experiments; a point also thematized in the tradition of experimental ethnography (Estalella and Criado 2018; Torfing and Ansell 2021). Another is to grant all actors involved—also the non-human—the ethical agency to refuse involvement as Dorthe Staunæs and Sverre Raffnsøe propose in their chapter on equine-assisted leadership courses.

Of course, science and politics are not the only fields to have significantly influenced the trajectories and, thus, current uses of experimentation. As noted, developments in culture, media and the arts also involve experiments as has been the case historically. Perhaps the open-endedness or unpredictability we argue are central to affective experiments have been most directly cultivated by the arts—for example, through the strong connections between experimental approaches and avant-garde movements in the aesthetic field throughout the twentieth century (Bürger 1984; Ferrari 2020). After the First World War, dadaism invented the experimental subject as a reaction to the progressive mechanization of life and the inhuman horrors of the war. Within an organized apparatus of experimentation, techniques such as automatic writing and drawing, ready-mades and collages reframe agency (Hookway 2020). In the 1960s, merging of social movements and arts—'happenings' and 'performances'—often violated commonly accepted social rules to explore how people react—to expose self-evident social rules and to anticipate new and utopian social orders (Klimke and Scharloth 2009). This aesthetic trajectory enables ludic or unplanned happenings, without much care for standards and protocols, in the pursuit of non-linear development or affective lines of flight (Deleuze and Guattari 1994) where interventions are 'tried out', iterated and creatively tweaked without always knowing exactly what the outcome will be (Markham and Pereira 2019; Probyn 2004). And this is even if, as in the arts, minute planning, elaborate staging and the assistance of an entire artworld may be required to translate chance into artistic expression. The relationship between postmodernism—in the 1980s—and avant-gardism is stressed by Jean-François Lyotard, who considers postmodernism to be the avant-garde impulse within modernism (Lyotard 1979), but also by Brian McHale, who explores the world-modelling processes of artistic experiments in a way similar to what happened in the 1960s (McHale 2012). The difference between the attacks on the social order in the 1960s and the ones in 1980s postmodernism relates to the difference between having multiple perspectives on one reality and a turn to ontology that posits the existence of multiple worlds, a pluriversality (Escobar 2016; Mignolo 2018).

After outlining and discussing some of the many historical trajectories of experimentation in various fields, like science, politics and aesthetics, we will now proceed by describing how the concept of affective experimentation is put to analytical use in this edited collection.

ANALYSING AFFECTIVE EXPERIMENTATION

To analyse affective experimentation is to enquire into the dynamic shifts and sensory entanglement of both found and researcher-initiated experiments. If experiments create shifts in attention, then how does this happen exactly? When attention shifts, what is brought to the fore? What kind of event or spectacle is enacted? And simultaneously, how are subjects immersed; in other words, which sensory or other entanglements afford affective dynamics to be felt and to, potentially, produce experience or action?

Thinking about scientific and artistic lineages, we understand the experiment as played out in the tension between being planned and unpredictable. Also, this in-between can be analytically explored. Guided by a performative interest in what the experiment does, affective dynamics can be considered strategically produced, that is, planned and executed with some degree of linearity or, indeed, co-producing some sense that desired forces may be preconceived, arranged and brought into effect. Simultaneously, affective experiments may also probe the indeterminacy of encounters, unexpected forces or, in other words, a sense of multiplicity and non-linearity arising from the experimental apparatus. In both cases, by way of its procedures (or deliberate lack thereof), the experiment (re)presents particular affective dynamics—arrested, exposed and prospected on the performative terms of the experimental setting, however distributed. Moreover, from the perspective of Spinozist-Deleuzian affect theory, the in-between—of strategically planned effects and unexpected happenings, conceived linearity and aleatory indeterminacy—may be regarded as an intensive state, only preliminarily configured in and by the experiment. Indeed, to stage and analytically navigate this in-between in terms of actual experiments is, simultaneously, to draw attention to a virtual reservoir of intensive flows as a potential for further experimentation.

Noortje Marres, in her discussion of the 'living experiment', strikes a related perspective. She stresses the material and affective aspect of experiments as crucial for testing the future sustainability of provisional milieus. Here experiments are understood as "a format or 'protocol' for exploring and testing forms of life" (Marres 2012, p. 76). Through the construction of particular arrangements, these are, however, aimed at giving the non- or not-yet-existent an interim existence, which can be felt, tried out and engaged with. In that sense, experiments also offer their participants the opportunity to sense, understand and connect with potential, future or virtual versions of the world (Knudsen et al. 2019) and thus maybe to modify their habits or ways of understanding. Experiments are in that way vested in a particular relationship with temporality and the future. By staging subjunctive zones where distinctions between the non-existing and the existing, the felt and the imagined are complicated, they also expose the relationship between actual affective dynamics and virtual potentials for these to change—again, as a subject for analysis.

To accommodate these perspectives, we propose that an analysis of affective experimentation should focus its attention on how affects are produced and circulated in specific experimental practices that (1) intentionally craft milieus aimed at (re)presenting hitherto hidden or unnoticed aspects of the social world; (2) engage with unpredictability in non-linear (e.g., playful) ways; or (3) imagine, test or in other ways give the future a provisional form. In other words, an analysis of affective experimentation would want to take into account how affects come into being through found or researcher-initiated processes of converging (re)presentation, unpredictability and potentiality. Relatedly, we offer the following overall understanding of experimentation as a social, and sometimes researcher-controlled, practice involved in overlapping processes of revealing, playing with and testing the futural potential of life forms, entanglements and social worlds (Blackman 2012; Knudsen et al. 2019; Marres 2012). We propose to consider (re)presentation, unpredictability and potentiality as the three key points of orientation within an analytical framework—a heuristic that can be used to create awareness of different knowledge-producing dimensions of an experimental setting and to focus on the affective implications of the entanglements produced. The heuristic is aimed at both qualifying the analysis of found examples of affective experimentation and understanding the aims and results of research initiatives that are themselves experimental. In the following we unfold the three dimensions relating briefly to some examples from the book:

Experimentation Aims at (Re)presenting Unrecognized Aspects of the Social

Whether testing theoretical hypotheses or aiming at creating novel artistic expressions or forms of social encounter, experiments may be primarily oriented towards revealing or (re)presenting otherwise unnoticed aspects of the world—for example, in Mads Krogh's chapter on how streaming services and users navigate a sense of simultaneous openness and closure in musical mood management. Maybe the revealed reality shows itself due to the researcher's discursive and affect theoretical focus—as in Christina Jerne's piece on social and political limits as both sad and joyful creative obstructions for research. Maybe the reality is not immediately accessible because it evades direct perception, lack of awareness or falls outside norms, hegemonic or established categories—as in Britta Timm Knudsen's chapter on an artistic VR experiment situated in the dunes of the Danish West Coast that made the elemental movements of the wind visible and 'sense-able' for the users. By understanding experimentation as (re)presentation we become aware of how experiments are vehicles for an expanded mediation of and knowledge about the social world in its affective dimensions.

Representation itself could also be considered an aspect of social dynamics—as in decolonial efforts of bringing 'other' voices, other epistemologies of knowledge to the fore by experimenting with academic forms and their methodological underpinnings, which may be de-territorialized or 'otherwise' performed. Several of the chapters in the book—for example, those by Julian Henriques, Rebecca Coleman, Signe Uldbjerg and Natalie Ann Hendry, and Carsten Stage—experiment exactly with how to give voice and lend ears and bodies to otherwise silenced (e.g., material) perspectives through processes of experimentation. As mentioned, this political ambition does not make affective experimentation progressive in and of itself. Indeed, creating awareness in certain respects, for example, about political resentment or anger among marginalized groups, may bolster established social relations, for instance, by affording anger dynamics to be used to enforce political othering and marginalization. Still, this calls for analysis.

Experimentation Engages with the Non-linear and Unpredictable

Affective experiments are often designed to transgress common ways of doing research or of achieving other goals (e.g., of communication, politics or education). To this aim, open, playful, transgressive ways of acting may be set against established or proven ways. Thus, experimentation translates methodologically into creative, ludic or spontaneous manners of trying something out or into (e.g., everyday) practices of trial-and-error in which the process itself is prioritized over the formulation of predefined results. Moreover, the contingent, illimitable excess, which is also often regarded as a key aspect of relational dynamics, links affective experimentation to play, pleasurable inventions, disruptions and ambivalences as in Susanna Paasonen's piece investigating the ambivalent dynamics of boredom and interest and as in Christoffer Kølvraa's chapter on populist parapolitics that at one and the same time is to be considered transgressive and reactionary. The creativity of less controlled and non-linear processes seems key to this understanding of the experiment, even if creativity by design and deliberate loss of control may in fact take minute planning. In this respect, affective experimentation is also a matter of navigating the ambivalence of non-/linearity. This navigation is clearly present in Sophie Hope's chapter that—besides making relations and past experiences present as an explicit topic of convivial interaction among the participants in her experiments—plays with formalized processes like card games and dinner conversation to 'see what happens' in the specific assemblage of each experimental situation and with no strong aim in terms of what the outcome of these processes should be.

Experimentation Produces Scenes of Provisional Future-Making

In the tradition of the sciences, experiments forecast the future by testing general claims. In the understanding adopted here, this forecasting is performed on par with other aspects of the production of scientific facts. Still, the potential of engendering a sense of linearity, of assurance or trust in what the future brings remains an important aspect of the conceptual heritance of the experiment. It resonates in methodological considerations verging on the trope of generality, for example, in terms of repeatable measures—'the same' experiment reproduced in different sites or with different participants, via protocols or some idea of laboratory conditions—to allow comparison of observations. As performed, the sense of linearity achieved by experimentation will always be preliminary or provisional, even if it may sediment as fact continually reproduced by, for example, technological and institutional arrangements.

However, the point of experiments may also be less about forecasting and more about trying out possible visions or even producing merely a prospective sense of openness—as a forward projection of the aforementioned sense of non-linearity. As a political tool, experiments can, for example, be investigated as specific strategies and outlines of utopia launched to evoke affective investment, repulsion, resonance and circuit. Experiments may, in other words, function as catalysts or media of change and/or as vehicles to sense and feel the world's capacity to move and be moved. A future-oriented politics of change saturates many experiments in their capacity to offer participants the opportunity to sense, understand and connect to potential, future or virtual versions of the world. When experiments are enacted by individual researchers or artists, in response to, for example, major global challenges such as climate change, sexual, racial and ethnic/religious inequalities or economic imbalances, they often seem invested with the capacity to give future worlds such a provisional existence. The notion of building a different future is, for instance, present in Phillip and April Vannini's chapter in this book. Here they produce an ethnographic allegory that unfolds the lives of glaciers in Los Glaciares National Park, Argentina, aiming to foster new affective bonds through narratively enhanced reader experiences of empathy for other species. The experiment thus—more or less explicitly—points to the potential of a future characterized by multispecies kinship and flat ontologies, quite similar to the piece by Dorthe Staunæs and Sverre Raffnsøe that introduces the reader to leadership programmes with horses and their affective impact.

To sum up, we suggest approaching affective experimentation analytically as processes that (re)present existing dynamics/investments and engage with issues of non-linearity with the potential of opening up the present through the enactment of provisional futures. These aspects of the experimental may be variously probed in analyses, for example, by focusing more directly on exposing existing dynamics than on futural imagination. The processual interplay and variations in analytic emphasis is amply demonstrated by the contributions to this collected volume.

STRUCTURE OF THE BOOK

As mentioned, the collection consists of two sections. Part I, 'Understanding Affective Experimentation as a Method of the Social', offers chapters analysing found examples of affective experimentations, while the chapters in Part II, 'Understanding Affective Experimentation as a Research Method', share more researcher-initiated and often participatory affective experiments (Mannay 2016). In the following we will describe the contributions of each chapter in both sections.

Chapter 2 in Part I, titled 'Affect as Disruption: Affective Experimentation, Automobility, and the Ecological Crisis' by Paul Schütze, Kilian Jörg, Imke von Maur and Jan Slaby, looks at affective experimentation as a method of disruption to counter the conservative power and affective grounding of existing social formations. The case in point is the supremacy of the automobile arrangement and affective milieu—saturated by associations of progress, freedom and privacy—at the heart of the Western capitalist social order. It is argued that political activism towards automobiles—such as the flattening of SUV tyres—is capable of challenging the established affective fabric around cars exactly because the ideology and culture upholding it becomes strikingly evident in these micro-political actions.

Populism understood as a playful form of 'as if' politics is argued to perform itself along the lines of affective experimentation in Christoffer Kølvraa's chapter (Chap. 3), 'Populism as Para-politics: Play, Affect, Simulation'. Here the specificity of the populist para-political gesture lies in its ability to create situations in which opponents cannot 'not respond'. The images of the future that reveal themselves in populist experimentation are never fully invested in by the followers, but are, according to Kølvraa, to be understood as fantasies of the non-followers' dystopia. Reduced to play the role of the affective host to a populist parasite, the critics of populism are constantly compelled to react to the outrageous nature of the populist sketches of world-making as 'fake open-ended' versions of futures.

Chapter 4, 'Interspecies Pedagogies: More-than-Human Experiments with Leadership in/of the Anthropocene', by Dorthe Staunæs and Sverre Raffnsøe performs an autoethnographic study of equine-assisted leadership programmes that hope to help future leaders respond adequately to global grand challenges and pressing issues. These programmes cultivate non-human-centric sensibilities that try to reconfigure the interspecies relations anew by letting the animal be the educator. Staunæs and Raffnsøe argue that the affective output of these horse-laboratories is a strong sense of attunement to the mutual encounter between human and non-human actors, an acute awareness of oneself being affected as well as an interspecies ethics of care that also gives all parties in the encounter the freedom to not respond to the invitation to enter into a relationship.

Julian Henriques, in Chap. 5 'Engines of Affect: Experimenting with Auditory Intensities in the Jamaican Sound System Session' on the street music scene in Jamaica, outlines three ways of working with affective experimentation by looking at how the sound engineers in the streets of Kingston and their ways of knowing are building the 'vibe'; how the sound assemblage on the streets attunes the crowd and how a theoretical thinking-through-vibrations might be a way of approaching affect.

Henriques demonstrates that the sound engineers possess a non-epistemic way of knowing that is experienced through immersion into sonic dominance and through atmospheres of vibrational intensities that merge the listener and the listened-to.

Music streaming and its capacity for mood management in the context of everyday listening is the phenomenon examined in Mads Krogh's chapter (Chap. 6) 'Experimentation in and with the Stream: Music, Mood Management and Affect'. A multivalent notion of affect combined with a simultaneous sense of experimental openness and (teleological) closure are traced across platform procedures and user practices. Moreover, a methodological experiment is evoked to probe this ambivalence—a series of workshops with students at Aarhus University exploring the affective charge of data-based listener profiles—who am I?—and music categories—what am I listening to? Being a user of streaming services predicts and captures affects as well as it provides an experience of eventual openness.

The global COVID-19 pandemic as a 'natural experiment' causing primarily the flat affect of boredom is what Susanna Paasonen examines in Chap. 7 'Experimentations in Pandemic Boredom'. There it is argued that boredom's inherent ties to the historical experience of modernity and in particular to networked media and social media as machines of boredom are questionable. Instead, she shows that networked media during the pandemic shifted discursively to act as cures against boredom. Seeing social media users as boredom managers, she advocates for an ambiguous understanding of boredom tied to fascination and excitement, and she puts forward the attempt to hold on to irreconcilable tensions as an ideal for critical thought.

Part II on researcher-initiated affective experiments is commenced by Rebecca Coleman's chapter (Chap. 8), 'Worlding with Glitter: Vibrancy, Enchantment and Wonder', that examines how glitter—considered through a new materialism lens and Jane Bennett's concept of thing-power in particular—can open up future worlds. On the basis of two collage workshops with 13–14-year-old teenage girls from racially and ethnically diverse groups, it is argued that methods make worlds and thereby futures capable of composing and curating 'the wonderful' through specific materials and affects. We, as readers, are also directly addressed in Coleman's text (through inserted questions) and thus prompted to consider how our own research practices can make enchantment and wonder happen through affective experimentation.

Signe Uldbjerg and Natalie Ann Hendry present a comparative study of online creative workshop experiments with graduate research students from Australia and Denmark during the global COVID-19 lockdowns in Chap. 9 'Affective Writing Experiments'. The 'therapy-like' workshop assemblages enabled through the Zoom interface—that at one and the same time accommodates and alleviates depression—produced an affective solidarity of being stuck together during lockdowns. The creative-writing processes were in that way capable of producing affectively accurate depictions of participants' feelings. The authors furthermore argue that affective experimentation first and foremost has to facilitate participants' experiences of themselves as being productive and capable.

Carsten Stage has set up a partnership-based research experiment—in the form of a theme week—with persons with chronic conditions to investigate their shared stories of shame on social media. In Chap. 10 'Problematising Shame: Affective Experimentation on Social Media', the understanding of experiment is double: on the one hand, the experiment reveals that shame is a fundamental affect in the real or imaginary encounter with derogatory gazes from significant others and loved ones, and, on the other hand, the experiment is capable of repositioning shame amongst chronically ill persons as a collective and structural affect. Furthermore, Stage argues that the research experiment also gives voice to those who reject shame as a relevant framework for understanding life with chronic illnesses.

Sophie Hope's chapter (Chap. 11), 'Affective Experiments: Card Games, Blind Dates and Dinner Parties', presents a range of methods to produce socially engaged art and critical enquiry through different experimental formats. They include staged encounters between strangers on a reflection on memories of a year in history, 1984 Dinners, or they set up Blind Dates between project-partners who have never met, or they invite colleagues who are familiar with each other to critically join Cards on the Table to reflect on ideals and agendas in common projects. Hope argues that assumed knowledge and stereotypes are less used in these experiments and that they are instead characterized by analytical conviviality, at one and the same time peaceful and conflictual interaction. Furthermore, they create awareness of interpersonal dependency and offer possibilities of empathizing with the perspectives of others.

Chapter 12, 'Wind as Elementary Attraction: An Avant-Garde Experiment on the West Coast of Jutland, Denmark', presents an artistic experiment of wind at a coastal tourism destination of Denmark. The project was supposed to try out subtle and locally sustainable attractions capable of problematizing well-known divisions between natural and cultural heritage and between locals and tourists. Visualizing wind through a pair of VR glasses, the facilitators hoped to be able to attune bodies to the landscape through joy and enchantment instead of through moral imperatives. Britta Timm Knudsen argues that the quite open-ended affective experiment cultivated both a kin-centric affective ecological attunement to the particular landscape and a general sensibility towards creativity as such in nature, in technology and in artistry.

Chapter 13, 'The Tombstones that Cried the Night Away: An Allegory', by Phillip and April Vannini presents their affective experiment partly in the form of an ethnographic allegory based on fieldwork in Patagonia around glaciers, which is part of a larger multi-site project on natural heritage and wildness. The authors use the allegory as an experimental worldmaking literary device to give voice to the icebergs' complaints, sorrows and political mobilization against uncaring humans. In that way the chapter fosters a speculative ontology challenging Western binary oppositions between inanimate and animate objects. In the meta-reflexive part of the chapter, it is argued that the allegory allows new futures of multispecies kinship to be sensed and that it invokes old and forgotten ways of coping with limits of knowledge, but also that the allegorical form is a way of exerting the affective responsibility of researchers to the general public and to stress the affective capacity of ethnographic knowledge to the research community.

In Chap. 14 'Activating Limit as Method: An affective Experiment in Ethnographic Criminology', Christina Jerne performs a thought experiment and argues that the methodological affordances of limits function as affective dispositions capable of steering bodies and processes during a research process. Studying minority gangs as enterprises, Jerne proposes three ways of understanding limits that constrain and produce research—oscillating between sad, passive passions and joyful, active passions in the sense of Spinoza—in the arena of crime: the more general limits (e.g., juridical) ruling in a field of research, the limits that others put to your actions through their own actions and the limits one experiences as a researcher being in the field in question.

This rich collection of chapters, written by both established and junior researchers in the field of affect studies, in various ways show that experiments are affective because they enact intense attentive shifts, while entangling bodies in particular settings. Experiments can do this through planned procedures, strategic design and attempted control but also—and sometimes simultaneously—playful, transgressive or unpredictable forms. Hereby, they navigate the in-between of linearity and non-linearity, of openness and provisional closure from where a sense of world-making and future-ability may emerge. Experiments can—as shown in several of the chapters—disappoint, be flawed or neutralized by culturally sedimented discourses, economic logics and hierarchies. They can also, however, and it may be that here lies their most fundamental attraction, enable spaces of transformation, where other voices and invisible or forgotten aspects of the world can suddenly be heard, seen and felt.

REFERENCES

Ahmed, S. (2004). *The cultural politics of emotion.* Edinburgh University Press.
Anderson, B. (2014). *Encountering affect: Capacities, apparatuses, conditions.* Ashgate.
Bach, S. J. (2019). Demolition blues: Resistance against demolitions plans in a Danish disadvantaged affordable housing estate. *Archivio Antropologico Mediteraneo,* Anno XXII, 21 (2). https://doi.org/10.4000/aam.2250
Bacon, F. (n.d.). *Novum Organum* (New Method). Freeditorial Publishing House. (Original work published 1620).
Bagrie, B. S. (2004). *Scientific revolutions, primary texts in the history of science.* Pearson Education.
Bergold, J., & Thomas, S. (2012). Participatory research methods: A methodological approach in motion. *Forum: Qualitative Social Research,* 13(1). Retrieved December 23, 2021, from http://www.qualitative-research.net/index.php/fqs/article/view/1801/3334#g48
Berlant, L. (2011). *Cruel optimism.* Duke University Press.
Bjerregaard, P. (2015). Dissolving objects: Museums, atmosphere and the creation of presence. *Emotion, Space and Society,* 15, 74–81. https://doi.org/10.1016/j.emospa.2014.05.002
Black, J. (2002). *The reality effect: Film culture and the graphic imperative.* Routledge.
Blackman, L. (2012). *Immaterial bodies: Affect, embodiment, mediation.* Sage.
Brennan, T. (2004). *The transmission of affect.* Cornell University Press.
Bruun Jensen, C., & Morita, A. (2017). Introduction: Infrastructures as ontological experiments. *Ethnos: Journal of Anthropology,* 82(4), 615–626.
Bürger, P. (1984). *Theory of the Avant-Garde.* University of Minnesota Press.
Charon, R. (2006). *Narrative medicine: Honoring the stories of illness.* Oxford University Press.

Clough, P. T. (Ed.) (2009). *The affective turn: Theorizing the social.* Duke University Press.

Coleman, R., & Ringrose, J. (Eds.) (2013). *Deleuze and research methodologies.* Edinburgh University Press.

Daugbjerg, M., Eisner R. S., & Knudsen, B. T. (2016). Re-enacting the past: Vivifying heritage 'again'. In M. Daubjerg, R. S. Eisner, & B. T. Knudsen (Eds.), *Re-enacting the past: Heritage, materiality and performance* (pp. 1–7). Routledge.

Deleuze, G., & Guattari, F. (1994). *What is philosophy?* Verso.

Dovey, J. (2000). *Freakshow: First person media and factual television.* Pluto Press.

Escobar, A. (2016). Thinking-feeling with the Earth: Territorial struggles and the ontological dimension of the epistemologies of the south. *Rev. Antropol. Iberoam,* 11(1), 11–32.

Estalella, A., & Criado, T. S. (Eds.) (2018). *Experimental collaborations: Ethnography through fieldwork devices.* Berghahn Books.

Ferrari, R. (2020). On the pluriversality of the avant-garde. A response to "The future of avant-garde studies: A European roundtable." *Journal of Avant-Garde Studies,* 1–3. https://www.academia.edu/43678173/On_the_Pluriversality_of_the_Avant_Garde

Fleig, A. & Scheve, C. (2021). *Public spheres of resonance: Constellations of affect and language.* Routledge.

Franklin, A., & Perovic, S. (2021). Experiment in physics. In E. N. Zalta (Ed.), *The Stanford encyclopedia of philosophy* (Summer 2021 Edition). Retrieved December 23, 2021, https://plato.stanford.edu/archives/sum2021/entries/physics-experiment/

Gooding, D., Pinch, T., & Schaffer, S. (1989). Introduction: Some uses of experiment. In D. Gooding, T. Pinch, & S. Schaffer, *The uses of experiment: Studies in the natural sciences* (pp. 1–28). Cambridge University Press.

Guerrini, A. (2016). The human experimental subject. In B. Lightman (Ed.), *A companion to the history of science* (pp. 126–138). John Wiley & Sons.

Guichou, A. (2016). Nuit debout et les "mouvements des places" désenchantement et ensauvagement de la démocratie. *Les Temps Modernes,* 691, 30–60.

Hookway, Branden. 2020. The making of the experimental subject: Apparatus, automatism, and the anxiety of the early avant-garde. *Theory, Culture & Society,* 37(7–8), 115–132.

Hope, S. (2016). Bursting paradigms: A colour wheel of practice-research. *Cultural Trends,* 25(2), 74–86.

Jerslev, A. (2004). *Vi ses på TV: Medier og Intimitet.* Gyldendal.

Kara, H. (2015). *Creative research methods in the social sciences.* Policy Press.

Kahl, A. (Ed.) (2019). *Analyzing affective societies.* Routledge.

Kelty, C., Panofsky, A., Erickson, S., Currie, M., Crooks, R., Wood, S., Garcia, P., & Wartenbe, M. (2014). Seven dimensions of contemporary participation disentangled. *Journal of the Association for Information Science and Technology,* 66, 474–488.

Klimke, M, & Scharloth, J. (2009). Utopia in practice: The discovery of performativity in sixties' protest, arts and sciences. *Historein,* 9, 46–56, https://doi.org/10.12681/historein.21

Klingmann, A. (2007). *Brandscapes: Architecture in the experience economy.* MIT Press.

Knudsen, B. T. (2011a). Thanatourism: Witnessing difficult pasts. *Tourist Studies,* 11(1), 55–72.

Knudsen, B. T. (2011b). Deportation day: Live history lesson. *Museum International,* 63(1–2), 109–119. https://doi.org/10.1111/j.1468-0033.2012.01769.x

Knudsen, B. T., & Stage, C. (Eds.) (2015). *Affective methodologies: Developing cultural research strategies for the study of affect.* Palgrave Macmillan.

Knudsen, B. T., Stage, C., & Zandersen, M. (2019). Interspecies park life: Participatory experiments and micro-utopian landscaping to increase urban biodiverse entanglement. *Space and Culture.* https://doi.org/10.1177/1206331219863312

Krohn, W., & Weyer, J. (1994). Real-life experiments. *Science and Public Policy,* 21(3), 173–183.

Law, J. (2004). *After method: Mess in social science research.* Routledge.

Lury, C. (2021) *Problem spaces.* Polity Press.

Lury, C., & Wakeford, N. (2012). *Inventive methods: The happening of the social.* Routledge.

Lyotard, J-F. (1979). *La condition postmoderne.* Les Editions de Minuit.

Mannay, D. (2016). *Visual, narrative and creative research methods.* Routledge.

Markham, A., & Pereira, G. (2019). Analyzing public interventions through the lens of experimentalism: The case of the museum of random memory. *Digital Creativity,* 30(4), 235–256.

Massumi, B. (2002). *Parables for the virtual.* Duke University Press.

Marres, N. (2012). The experiment in living. In C. Lury & N. Wakeford (Eds.), *Inventive methods: The happening of the social* (pp. 76–95). Routledge.

McHale, B. (2012). Postmodernism and experiment. In J. Barady, A. Gibbons, & B. McHale (Eds.), *The Routledge companion to experimental literature* (pp. 141–153). Routledge.

Mignolo, Walter D. (2018). Foreword: On pluriversality and multipolarity. In B. Reiter (Ed.), *Constructing the pluriverse: The geopolitics of knowledge* (pp. ix–xv). Duke University Press.

Mortensen, S. U. (2020). Defying shame. *Mediekultur,* 36(67), 100–120.

Ngai, S. (2005). *Ugly feelings.* Harvard University Press.

Pine, B. J., & Gilmore, J. H. (1999). *The experience economy: Work is theatre & every business a stage.* Harvard Business School Press.

Probyn, E. (2004). Everyday shame. *Cultural Studies,* 18(2–3), 328–349.

Romanos, E. (2016). Late neoliberalism and its indignados: Contention in austerity Spain. In Della Porta, D. et al. (Eds.). *Late neoliberalism and its discontents in the economic crisis* (pp. 131–167). Palgrave Macmillan.

Sampson, F. (Ed.) (2004). *Creative writing in health and social care.* Jessica Kingsley Publishers.

Shapin, S. (1984). Pump and circumstance: Robert Boyle's literary technology. *Social Studies of Science,* 14(4), 481–520.

Simonsen, K. B. (2016). Ghetto-Society-Problem: A discourse analysis of nationalist othering. *Studies in Ethnicity and Nationalism,* 16(1), 83–99.

Soei, A. (2021, December 4). Boligpolitikken bliver stadig mere racialiseret og kafkask. *Politiken,* Sektion 2 (Debat), p. 3.

Torfing, J., & Ansell, C. (2021). Co-creation: The new kid on the block in public governance. *Policy and Politics,* 49(2), 211–230.

Vannini, P. (Ed.). (2015). *Non-representational methodologies: Re-envisioning research.* Routledge.

PART I

Understanding Affective Experimentation as a Method of the Social

Affect as Disruption: Affective Experimentation, Automobility, and the Ecological Crisis

Paul Schütze, Kilian Jörg, Imke von Maur, and Jan Slaby

In this chapter we explore affect as a means of disruption. Can affect be deployed to disturb, fracture, and break ossified social formations, practices, and patterns? In asking this question we take up but also diverge from a central motive in affect studies. Commonly, affect in the tradition of Baruch Spinoza, Gilles Deleuze, and later Brian Massumi is thought of in terms of a dynamic relationality, as the capacity of bodies affecting and being affected by each other (see, e.g., Deleuze 1988; Gregg and Seigworth 2010; Mühlhoff 2018; Slaby and Mühlhoff 2019). There is a promise attached to this articulation of affect that it is immanently transformative, open, and continuously prone to change bodies in their

P. Schütze (✉) • I. von Maur
Universität Osnabrück, Osnabrück, Germany
e-mail: paul.schuetze@uos.de; imke.von.maur@uos.de

K. Jörg • J. Slaby
Freie Universität, Berlin, Germany
e-mail: kilian@jorg.at; slaby@zedat.fu-berlin.de

B. Timm Knudsen et al. (eds.), *Methodologies of Affective Experimentation*, https://doi.org/10.1007/978-3-030-96272-2_2

27

composition and relationality (Anderson 2010, p. 162). Hence, much work on affect has focused on the potentials within this dynamic relationality, on the possibility of a "creative opening to an outside in moments of rupture [and] instances of discontinuity" (p. 166).

In contrast to some of these prevailing conceptions of affect, we argue that affect is in fact not a predominantly transformative force. Affect operates equally as a conservator of established structures, as a 'dynamic glue' that holds things in place. While affect indeed implies a potentiality, for "you do not know beforehand what a body or a mind can do, in a given encounter, a given arrangement, a given combination" (Deleuze 1988, p. 125), this potentiality is not necessarily transformative, but it also implies that relational dynamics may solidify and lock into relatively stable formations. In other words, affect facilitates territorialization, consolidation, and a routinization of (social) life as much as it offers potentialities for breaking out. Accordingly, it is a difficult, non-trivial task to actualize affect's transformative potential given the grip of consolidated patterns of affecting and being affected. In this chapter, we argue that this actualization implies a willingness for affective experimentation, to explore ways in real-life scenarios in which affect can intentionally be mobilized as a disruptive force.

Instead of contemplating the transformative possibilities of affect, instead of getting lost in potentialities and a virtuality of 'what could be', we propose to first reflect and deconstruct the old solidified affective formations. In that way, we draw on the concepts *affective arrangement* and *affective milieu* to show affect as a bearer of the old and as a force preserving the past. In surveying this apprehension of affect, we direct our attention towards the ecological crisis. Using the case of automobile supremacy, we discuss a paradigmatic affective formation that keeps many of us deadlocked in a continuous loop of business as usual. We then turn towards prospects of obstruction within these affective tangles, leaning on affective experimentation as a method of disruption, exploring how and under what conditions affect might be mobilized in such an experimental way.

THE IRON GRIP OF AFFECT

In 2020, the COVID-19 pandemic forced an overarching pause upon societies across the globe when cultural as well as large parts of economic life came to a sudden halt. As hard as this pause has hit many people, it simultaneously represented a unique chance for a collective new start.

Questions about the distribution of the pandemic's costs, the best support for workers and the most affected economic segments, or about the worthy payment of care work, brought with them the discussion about the very fundamentals of the societal order. And so, for a short period of time, a possible social and ecological transformation seemed to lie within reach. An unprecedented break in the continuous loop of business as usual made conceivable a turn towards a sustainable and social economy. But so far, none of this has occurred. Instead, Western societies find themselves deadlocked in their old routines and any thought of 'the new' is yet again buried under the pressure of daily routines as a distant utopian ideal.

The reasons for this overwhelming inertia and, it seems, mesmerizing magnetism of the status quo are varied. Some are plainly economic, some political, others reflect locked-in infrastructures and practices whose reform or abolishment seems unthinkable to many. Yet, there is more to the swiftness with which alternatives to the prevailing condition are time and time again side-lined in favour of nothing but the ordinary. Central to the tenacity of established ways of doing and thinking is their affective grounding. Social formations are anchored and manifested in sustained and enduring affective patterns. These affect dynamics have settled and solidified over long periods, laying down dispositions and modes of attachment that make up the texture of social life. Accordingly, these affective patterns and structures of feeling are unlikely to change just like that. In many of its prevailing social forms, affect operates as a sluggish glue or even an iron grip that holds practices and social routines in place. From this perspective, it is not surprising at all that the concreted social structures persevered.

A Nation of Automobility: On Affective Arrangement and Affective Milieus

Now, in view of the typical tendency within affect theory to focus on the transformative character and openness of affect (e.g., Gregg and Seigworth 2010; Lim 2007; Massumi 2015), our assumption that affect is foremost a conservative force in social life might be puzzling to the reader. However, we do not contradict the fact that affect bears much potential for change (see, e.g., Massumi 2015, p. ix). In fact, it is the very aim of the current text to probe ways in which this potential can be brought out and be utilized in ways that succeed in initiating actual, lasting change. Thus, we concur that any dynamic of affecting and being affected is initially indeterminate and therefore immanently malleable (Lim 2007, p. 55; see also Massumi 2015, p. 3). Nonetheless, we hold that affect's potential for transformation is not always converted. To the contrary, in the current societal order this potentiality for change rarely manifests.

Recent years have brought to light the remarkable "resilience of modernity" (Jörg 2020). There is a lot of new evidence about the fundamental immovability of much of the Western status quo, not only in terms of failures to meaningfully address the climate crisis, but also with regard to racism, economic inequality, exploitation of the global south, and much else. In view of these recent (non)-developments, a celebratory insistence on affect's transformative potentials, while not wrong in a theoretical sense, begins to ring hollow and out of touch with the present moment.

Accordingly, we deem it an important task to focus on the conservative thrust of affect. Relations of affecting and being affected are always manifestations of historical trajectories. On the surface of social life—that is, feelings, emotions, or modes of attachment—they have to be understood against a rich backdrop of formative affective dynamics and socio-material relatedness. In that sense, affect is a matter of material efficacy that goes along with a discursive and mental dimension: characteristic talk and text on the societal level, thoughts, feelings, imaginations on the part of individuals enmeshed in these relations (see Slaby et al. 2019). As such, what we call the conservative power of affect is grounded in the tendency that affective relations tend to reproduce their prevailing patterns and clusters into stable constellations at the discursive level, while habituating individuals into characteristic modes of relatedness and attachment. In fact, 'the lure of the familiar' might be the single most effective force when it comes to affect's conservative thrust. It ensures that affect relations often reinforce and sustain specific historical trajectories.[1]

The conservative thrust of affect is strikingly evident in Western responses to the ecological crisis. The alarming effects of climate change are all over the media, and they can increasingly be felt. Still, the answers remain utterly inadequate. Even though there is a rising awareness regarding climate issues, for instance in the discussions on policies for environmental protection or in the public discourse regarding CO_2

---

[1] We keep this theoretical starting point brief, as our text has a different focus. For a detailed development of the affect theoretic position, see Mühlhoff (2018). Slaby and Mühlhoff (2019) also provide an abbreviated take.

emissions, this discursive change seems to be deadlocked in old and inadequate problem-solving approaches. So here we are, the sea levels are rising, the forests are burning, the soil is ravaged, and the air around us is polluted (von Redecker 2020, p. 83). Still, Western society keeps on driving forward.

This widespread failure to acknowledge the extent and urgency of the ecological catastrophe is a paramount instance of affect maintaining an iron grip on society and it characteristically shows why a disruption of current modes of attachment and affective practices is urgently needed, while immensely difficult to pull off. In the following, we focus on a condition that is paradigmatic for Western societies' ignorance of climate change, namely the *supremacy of the automobile*.[2] We find this supremacy at the heart of the Western capitalist social order. This is not only because the car is arguably "the single most important cause of environmental resource-use" given the sheer scale of materials, space, and power consumed to produce cars and the infrastructures needed to sustain them (Urry 2004, p. 26). But this is also because the automobile is characteristic of a culture of consumption, progress, and individuality, which essentially constitutes forms of life that are at the root of the ecological crisis.

The Automobile Supremacy

The automobile is a central component of the Western world. In a country like Germany, cars are everywhere[3]; cities are crammed with them. In rural areas they are often the only feasible means of transportation, and the countryside is scarred by highways congested with traffic day and night. It is nearly impossible to find a place where one does not see or at least hear a car. The entire infrastructure of the country is built for and around it. Moreover, the automobile industry is central to the growth of the German economy, entire industrial sectors only exist because of the car, and many livelihoods depend on it. This attachment to the automobile has led to what we call *automobile supremacy*—the dominant position of the car in the economy, in society, and even within culture. The automobile is the

---

[2] The considerations on the automobile are in part based on the text "Autoregime" (Jörg 2020).

[3] Being from Germany and Austria ourselves, the German context is for us, experientially and discursively, most salient. However, on a global scale, the United States is surely the paradigmatic nation built around the car, the haven of automobile supremacy (not to mention some other malign supremacies).

epitome of industrial late capitalism and it has long represented progress as well as technological dominance.

The automobile has established itself at the centre of an entire mechanistic network built around it, sustaining and reproducing itself. This network functions as an autopoietic system that only works because of its relationality: Material elements (such as the automobile infrastructure consisting of roads, parking lots, workshops, oil companies, and gas stations) and socio-cultural elements (such as automobile clubs and lobby groups, cultures of consumption and social status, perceptions of property and individuality, and the idea of a good life) are all reciprocally related in virtue of the car (see Mattioli et al. 2020; Urry 2004; Sheller and Urry 2000). Together, these material, social, and discursive components make up a system of relations, which itself works like a well-oiled engine. The car is indispensable; it is the centre of a material as well as a symbolic universe.

This formation continuously modulates its elements all the while drawing in new ones and submitting them to its rhythms. Ensuing from the Western world, the automobile makes even the remotest lands available to the needs of consumption. Ahead of the car's desire to move ever forward, the world is straightened and tamed. In this way, the car is the central player in 'modern land equalization' and it marks the social standard for getting around: villages, shopping centres, and warehouses can only be reached by automobile (see Jörg 2020, pp. 75–76). Sitting in a car, marching forward into the flattened and uniform landscapes, the Western individual travels towards the future.

Owning a car provides an individual with flexibility of movement, temporal freedom, security, and privacy, and it even feeds back into a sense of individuality that it helps to produce and hold in place. Moving around in an expensive and supposedly aesthetic vehicle distinguishes drivers from others on the road, not only in terms of size and occupied space, but also in regard to safety and the price tag attached to the car. In other words, the automobile has attached to it a socio-material arrangement—a heterogeneous ensemble united in its relationality—by which car owners as well as non-users are affected. This formation is central to the Western way of living—integrating drivers and non-users, consuming spaces and flooding cities, accumulating capital and fuelling consumption, shaping cultures, and creating ideals of individuality and privacy.

The Automobile Arrangement

The complex around the car is not a mere technological formation, but it is essentially a tangle of affect relations, an *affective arrangement* manifested in various dynamics on different levels (see Slaby et al. 2019). This arrangement has an idiosyncratic affective texture, and it can exemplarily be observed in the middle-class SUV driver. Behind the windscreens of the SUVs sit the complacent drivers, their expression blank and looking ahead, isolated, and undisturbed by the smell and noise the automobile produces. They are sitting high above the road in a pleasantly climate-controlled ambiance, surrounded by their own music, protected from the airstreams and turbulences outside—the car as a private space, an isolated cocoon keeping the hostile outside at bay (Mattioli et al. 2020, p. 11). While driving individuals feel autonomous and free, moving wherever they please in their well-maintained and unspoiled machines, they also detach themselves from the outside world (see Jörg 2020, pp. 77–78). This automobile space is not only a material space, for example, the car as a physical cocoon. But this also manifests in a uniquely textured affective space: *the automobile arrangement.*

Cars require users to change their behaviour, attitudes, and expectations. The affect relations surrounding the automobile literally hold individuals captive—unknowingly and without force, by integrating them into their web. Owning an SUV will, for instance, demand a frequent schedule of maintenance at the workshop, as the expensive and aesthetic character of the car wants to be sustained. This may be accompanied by the constant worry of whether the car will be stolen or damaged, producing a habit of finding just the right parking spot. However, not only are such habits and practices transformed, but the entire bodily awareness of the driver is adapted to the car. The SUV facilitates a certain driving style and affords a unique bodily feeling—quick acceleration and high speed while being comfortably cushioned from the road. In that sense, the driver's affective repertoire is shaped by the car; the proud SUV owner feels particularly violated when being cut off, after all, he is sitting in the superior car, and his time schedule is especially important (see, e.g., Katz 2015, pp. 14–48). And so, car owners think, talk, and behave towards and around their cars in a unique manner, resulting, for instance, in a "discursive bias that motorists exhibit towards car use" (Mattioli et al. 2020, p. 11). The negative sides of automobile culture, such as the massive environmental damage caused by it, "are seen as distant, theoretical, and ultimately negotiable" by large parts of the population (Mattioli et al. 2020, p. 11). The automobile arrangement claims a territory that pertains not only to car users but to non-users as well. When walking through any city, an overwhelming presence of steel, noise, and smell testifies to the dominance of cars and makes any living being aware of their presence. Parking cars enclose pedestrians wherever they go, shiny machines occupy public space while embodying modern perceptions of private property. Just as car owners are painstakingly focused on protecting their car, non-users are always aware that their surfaces must not be touched, no scratch, no dent must disfigure them (see Jörg 2020, pp. 76–77). Moreover, cyclists and pedestrians encounter cars not only as a waste of space, but as dangerous objects. The habituated glance to the left and right is a permanent companion in city life—or rather, a vital necessity. And so, for non-users automobiles anonymously pass by, almost as living entities accompanied by an aura of discomfort and fear. The car is a vehicle of domination that manifests in affect relations, submitting cities and landscapes, threatening and restricting its non-users, and paving the way for its owners.

The Automobile Milieu

However, the automobile supremacy is not only substantiated in the automobile arrangement, but it stretches far beyond constellations surrounding automobility. At heart, this complex is built on and facilitated by the expansion of Western industrial capitalism in the twentieth century (see, e.g., Mattioli et al. 2020). The automobile is paradigmatic for a capitalist mode of production in which the environment and its resources are equalized and made accessible (see Jörg 2020). The car may move freely while capitalist production may expand and grow without bounds or interruptions. Where roads and automobiles conquer and straighten the landscapes, they leave behind places of accessibility, turned into commodities, shrouded in exhaust fumes, and seamed by piles of debris. Likewise, where the capitalist wheel starts turning, it transforms landscapes into accessible resources, and resources into profitable commodities, only to leave behind dust clouds above polluted and consumed places (von Redecker 2020, pp. 49–64).

In essence, the Western societal order is an automobility-based, capitalist culture paradigmatically represented in the Western middle-class construct. This construct is inherently entangled with the functionining of fossil fuel capitalism (see, e.g., Malm and Hornborg, 2014), and attached to the authority of the automobile. In terms of affect dynamics, this means that the relations of the automobile arrangement are not merely tied to the localities of the car, as shown in the section above, but they reach out and permeate society on an extensive scale. They form a deep affective complex of capitalist Western culture that is cemented—literally: made concrete—in society with the help of the car and can be observed particularly well in the affective underpinnings of the middle-class construct. The nature of this affective formation can be captured in terms of what we have elsewhere called an *affective milieu* (Schuetze 2021).[4]

The notion of affective milieus illustrates how the social sphere at large is fundamentally influenced and moulded by affect relations. An affective milieu describes a uniquely textured territory in the social universe where specific affect dynamics are at play (see Schuetze 2021, pp. 6–9). This means that the capitalist-fuelled middle-class construct is essentially etched into peculiar affect relations that take shape in an affective milieu: *the Western middle-class milieu*, or in brief, *the automobile milieu*. Different from the tangible automobile arrangement, which can concretely be felt and observed in local and material patterns anchored by the car itself, the automobile milieu describes a larger societal constellation attached to the car. At heart, this constellation is characterized by liberal ideas of freedom and opportunity, a longing for money and social status, a need for control and regulations, as well as an affirmative vision of progress and technology. This substantiates in the attachment to, for instance, unfettered traffic routes, such as the autobahn without speed limits, or specific practices of urban planning and construction, such as sprawling car parks and multi-lane roads.

Moreover, the automobile milieu is the result of historically grown and sedimented processes of exclusion and domination manifested in particular affect relations. These relations come together and create "a racialized, androcentric, and class-based hierarchy of knowing and being" (Schulz 2017, p. 47; see also Malm and Hornborg 2014; Moore 2015; Todd 2015, p. 247). This creates a milieu that is characterized by a kind of masculinity "which is formed in the context of class and race as well as gender

---

[4] Our use of the term 'milieu' is in part inspired by Deleuze and Guattari (1987) as well as Merleau-Ponty ([1945] 2012). However, we are closer to a sociological conception of social milieus (such as, e.g., in Bourdieu; for a discussion of this, see Schuetze [2021]). A deeper engagement with these conceptual issues is unfortunately beyond the scope of this chapter.

domination" (Plumwood 1993, p. 26) and which is at the core of a cultural development of peculiar middle-class and masculine-governed processes of societal becoming (Plumwood 1993, p. 23; see also Scholz 1992).

Thus, even though the car is a central component of Western culture and as such it is widely accessible, the affective meaning attached to it is distinctively entangled with this smaller social space—the automobile milieu. This illustrates the unique and paradoxical character of the car. On the one hand, the automobile is designed for the masses; it is available for all and an important part for the independence of many people. On the other hand, it is an integrative force attaching people to a way of living that developed emanating from a small group of people, from the middle-class milieu.

Now, the above provides a tentative grip on the fundamental affective formation that facilitates the culture of automobility. This is a culture of isolated subjects that construct and conceive their autonomy depending on various degrees of privacy and materiality. At the centre of this culture is the need to continuously move forward, fuelled by neoliberal ideals of freedom and progress, and fantasies of everybody being given the ability to freely impose their exhaust fumes and noise on the environment (e.g., Plumwood 1993, pp. 20–27). Of course, these ideals are not only characteristic of the automobile milieu, but historically, these dynamics have developed for and around it.

In sum, we have seen that the middle-class milieu and the automobile arrangement are the affective formations that underlie the automobile supremacy. They manifest not only in affect relations around the car, but they also materialize in the affective underbody of the Western middle-class construct. Distinct affective formations on different scales come together, feed into each other, and thus support as well as reproduce each other. This comes about as a web of affective threads running through society, where one thread supports the other, resulting in a thick, tear-resistant fabric that holds habits, practices, and ways of knowing and being in place.

Disruption

Before we can move beyond the automobile supremacy, we need to disrupt the underlying affect relations that uphold and reproduce it. Moving beyond the authority of the car requires more than a transformation of technological or cultural structures. The affective underpinnings of this socio-material formation need to be disrupted in order to enable sustainable changes. However, affect is not a paramount, progressive, and transformative power that readily enables new beginnings. The automobile arrangement and its affective milieu are dynamic patterns that form individuals; they form what individuals can perceive, what they can see, what they can feel, what they desire, and what they can think or imagine. These formations are the affective fabric of the automobile-based capitalist culture.

Our bodies are products of powerful affect relations stretching from the past to the present. These relations mould and constitute us (see von Maur 2021a). As Eva von Redecker nicely puts it, they are like "ingrown walls" enclosing our being (von Redecker 2020, p. 32)—just like parked cars frame the streets. These walls are manifestations of the past and they sit heavily on the present. To move towards something truly otherwise, one cannot just build on or transform already existing walls, for this inevitably inherits their constraints. Taking this seriously means to grapple with the walls that enclose us; it calls for a recognition of their toxicity and for an appreciation of their radical, world-preserving influence. Here is where a disruption of these walls, a rupture in the affective fabric, is needed. However, since many of us are affectively, economically, and socially invested in this way of being, bringing about such a disruption is immensely difficult. To overcome this entanglement with a toxic lifestyle, a subtle and yet effective deep transformative disruption is called for.[5]

Disrupting the Automobile Supremacy

How can the affective underpinnings of the automobile supremacy be disrupted? In his book *How to Blow Up a Pipeline*, Andreas Malm (2021) illustrates a case of disrupting the well-oiled machine of the automobile supremacy. Targeting one of the richest neighbourhoods in Stockholm, Malm and a group of activists took action and deflated the tyres of about 60 SUVs. They moved in at night and 'disarmed' the cars by opening their valves, flattening the tyres without damaging the car. To make the owners

---

[5] This thought is developed in von Maur (2018, ch. 5) with more of an emphasis on the individual and the epistemic dimension of conservative affect. Importantly, the habitualized schemata through which an individual makes sense of the world are socio-culturally specific and need to be brought to awareness as something contingent and thus changeable. This is made possible through affective disruption.

aware of what had happened at night, they put leaflets on the windscreens of the SUVs, preventing the owners from driving off with a flat tyre and informing them about the reasons for the sabotage (Malm 2021, pp. 79–81). "Don't take it personally. It's your SUV we dislike" (p. 80). Now, this is a prime example of a disruption of the car on the material level as the functioning of the technological and cultural automobile complex is brought to a halt. However, this is not only a break on the socio-material level, that is, stopping SUVs from moving, but this is also a disturbance of ingrained affect relations.

Even though, the deflating of the tyres did not actually damage the SUVs—the material disruption was limited to the loss of air—the action evoked vigorous personal, public, and medial responses. The group even received death threats: "If I would have seen you 'in action' I would have killed you" (Malm 2021, p. 82). For a moment the entire automobile arrangement was revealed to be vulnerable. While the media reception of the action was mainly negative, the success lay in making visible, tangible, and therefore debatable what usually goes by unnoticed and unseen: the catastrophic status quo of the automobile supremacy and our entanglement with it. The drivers and a shocked media-society witnessed a rupture in their well-attuned affect relations. An immobilization of the SUVs not only prevented some—in fact very few—individuals from driving, but it meant an obstruction of a hegemonic affective regime of producing individuality, privacy, social status, and freedom. A minor material sabotage that would warrant annoyance at most did elicit a massive affective and media reaction revealing a deeper structure of our toxic and beloved lifestyles.

Immediately after the action, various counter-movements emerged, revealing the persistence and depth of the affect relations emanating from the car. Not only were these people concerned with the sabotage of their cars, but they were irritated by a disruption of the capitalist Western culture. Now suddenly compromised, the background conditions that had always been in place became abruptly felt. As a consequence, the automobile milieu was defended with slogans such as "The air in my tires is private property—deflation is an assault on democracy" (Malm 2021, p. 83). And after some more nightly actions of deflating tyres, the SUVs were even guarded by "grim men in dark clothes" ready to violently preserve their authority (p. 83). It was no longer about preventing sabotage to cars, but the automobile milieu felt the need to defend itself.

Even though the above is a prime example of what it means to grapple with the walls that enclose us, it also demonstrates how prevailing patterns of affective relationality resist, tighten, and keep us in their toxic grip. One affective thread supports the other, the threads interlock, if one fails the others maintain their grip. But then, if such disruptions of the old affective formations are immediately fought off by the status quo, should we rather pursue a consensus-based, slow transformation? And how can we actually apprehend affect as a disruptor after all, if affect seems so deeply implicated as a conservator of the old?

Affect as Disruption

Firstly, our emphasis on disruption, as opposed to transformation, aims at forestalling visions of glorified new worlds in front of us. Regarding the ecological crisis, the "boat had sailed on gradual change" already back in 2013 (Klein 2013). Secondly, our focus on disruption is based on the assumption that we cannot simply build new ways of knowing and being on top of the existing majoritarian ones. It matters from where this world-making starts, from where we start moving (Haraway 2016, p. 35). As the critical Indigenous feminist Zoe Todd puts it, we need to ask: "What other story could be told here? What other language is not being heard? Whose space is this, and who is *not* here?" (Todd 2015, p. 244). Change is not a matter of looking ahead, but of struggling with the troublesome present (see Haraway 2016).

Yet, how can affect be understood as a disruptor if it is the very reason for the immense staying power of current structures of knowing and being? First of all, a disruption of current affective formations does not necessitate a singular heroic sacrifice, nor does it demand a grand tipping point (see von Redecker 2020, p. 147). There is no single action that can overthrow the automobile arrangement, let alone the middle-class milieu. Rather, moments of disruption are small-scale openings that abruptly, unexpectedly, and momentarily bring to a standstill the affect relations that were running smoothly before. The plain action of deflating the tyres of a handful of SUVs briefly halted the autopoietic system attached to the car, and all of a sudden, this brought to light the deep affective connectedness of the automobile supremacy. A point of disruption is therefore first of all a disturbance of well-oiled affective machineries (von Maur 2021b; see also von Maur 2018, pp. 241–258).

Exactly this is where an understanding of affect as a disruptor comes to fruition. Deflating the tyres of an SUV temporarily halted the automobile arrangement, and it might even have created a break in the Western middle-class milieu. For a brief moment, a small-scale action became a momentary disruptor—a break occurred, a moment of standstill, if only briefly. When the pathways in which affect usually flows are interrupted, the usual routes these flows constitute are shaken. What before were ossified affect relations reproducing themselves are suddenly inoperable symbols of what, from one moment to the other, begins to look suspiciously like a soon to be overcome past.

Relatedly, Walter Benjamin writes that "where thinking suddenly comes to a stop in a constellation saturated with tensions, it gives that constellation a shock, by which thinking is crystallized" (Benjamin [1940] 2003, p. 396). In the context of affect this means that where the frictionless functioning of affect is interrupted, it suddenly becomes crystallized and thereby visible. The texture of the entire fabric changes, it appears in a new light: what was formerly obvious now seems peculiar, strange, and oddly alien—the formation thus literally 'gives us pause'. It is this unforeseen standstill of the automobile arrangement that makes it possible to capture and highlight the affect relations that usually run in its background. This is not to say that this opportunity is actually seized and surely not by those immediately affected. Yet, this pause is a tangible experience for the drivers who are immediately halted in their routines, as well as for a broader social collective, such as pedestrians becoming aware of a changing status quo in their street. From the vantage point of public reception—media reporting, social media commenting, attention-grabbing political discussions, follow-up engagements by other activists, and so forth—the sabotage of an SUV brings to light the far-reaching attachment of the car to Western capitalist culture. The point is that dynamics that are normally hidden during ongoing business only become distinguishable in a moment of disruption; a moment in which affect stops flowing in its customary manner, in which its smooth operation is abruptly and noticeably interrupted. Such moments of discontinuance open the prevailing order to various ways of challenging it, of continuing differently, or questioning it fundamentally (see von Maur 2018, pp. 241–245).

This may well be illustrated with an example from a different social context. Suppose a workplace meeting where your boss unjustly shames a female colleague for a mistake that did not provoke this level of ire when male colleagues had made it before. It makes a huge difference, obviously, whether co-workers in the meeting sit silently and wait for the tense moment to pass, or whether some colleagues stand up and object sharply to that unfair treatment, thereby transcending their role and status position. Responding to a toxic workplace routine by intervening and confronting those up in the hierarchy is a prime moment of affective disruption. The entire procedure halts, irritation turns from latent to manifest, and what was a flowing routine suddenly gives way to a juncture of collective reckoning. It is not certain that the situation will change for the better, but a brief moment of aversive standstill renders a workplace culture or ideology strikingly evident. Seizing this opportunity might initiate processes of contestation, resistance, or opposition. Even if the initial occasion might be fended off by those in charge, that one brief moment of disruption might provide inspiration and a shared rallying point. Without that initial disruptive moment, the toxic status quo would have continued unperturbed, its toxicity likely unnoticed by many in the room.

Such unexpected disruptions, small as they may be at first, can become the seeds for further disruptive interventions, encourage others to join the effort, or come up with movements of their own. They can prompt a moment of reckoning: sudden heightened attention on the prevailing practice with the potential to alter the discursive and symbolic landscape. The stage has changed; disestablishing the reigning status quo is suddenly thinkable, even tangible. Where affect is unable to operate as it had been prearranged, it can be turned into the proverbial sand in its own gears. A moment of affective disruption is therefore not an isolated instance, in which an individual may become aware of their involvement in toxic routines. Rather, it is a starting point from which the established affective fabric can be challenged.

Such moments of disruption, crystallization, and discontinuity are an essential dimension of affective relationality. However, since their outcome is more than unclear, such moments need to be initiated over and over again; they need to be experimented with. Not every rupture brings about genuine and lasting change, and so, this calls for a certain creativity in fabricating these moments. Trying out and experimenting with the disruption of habituated affective dynamics is essential in finding ruptures that stick. Thus, creatively playing with these moments creates a foundation on which a radical change of affective formations may rest.

Outlook

Every third Friday in September the yearly PARKing day takes place. During this day, people all over the world are encouraged to occupy parking lots in their city centre by converting these spaces into playgrounds, improvised gardens, or places for social gathering. The goal is to unsettle the dominant cityscape, to disrupt the everyday stream of automobility flowing through the city, and to create a break in the space-devouring omnipresence of the car. In order to join the movement, participants simply seize a parking lot of their choice and set up camp for the day. In some cities the PARKing day is so popular that entire streets and neighbourhoods change into busy and colourful places freed from the usual overbearing presence of steel, noise, and smell.

However, what should offer a liberated and above all varied sight is not perceived so by all. While the participants and passing pedestrians enjoy their newly gained territory, automobiles and their drivers rush by, perturbed by the fact that their usually granted spaces on the side of the road do not readily present themselves. Sitting in one's converted parking lot, one is even yelled at angrily by some particularly agitated individuals in their automobiles, looking for a space to place their machines. Other drivers honk their horns, and a slight aggression strikes the peacefully seated. A peculiar situation: objects that are usually welcomed—gardens as green oases in an otherwise grey city, or playgrounds as gathering spaces and recreational areas—suddenly become obstacles disrupting the automobiles in their free movement. As soon as the daily flow is disrupted, cracks open up and the relations within the automobile arrangement crystallize. For a moment, it becomes tangible that the freedom and taken-for-grantedness of automobility is built on the constraints imposed on others. When the side of the road is occupied by something other than the car, this is perceived as irritating, whether positively or negatively, because in truth this territory only belongs to the automobile arrangement. One might even call it the property of the middle-class milieu. So here, in a situation of organized disruption, we once more see how prior background relations suddenly come to the fore and emerge as available positions.

Now, when we consider disobedient acts of affective disruption as instances of experimentation, we are not adhering to a cynical neoliberal idea of trying out policy measures in real-world settings. In contrast, we focus on more daring interventions into an ossified status quo. It is characteristic that such affective disruptions oppose dominant formations and might accordingly seem like lost causes at first. Yet, as we hope to have shown, these interventions can initiate transformative processes. Moments of disruption in which the smooth functioning of affect comes to a halt and the background affect relations crystallize present an opening. These moments begin to unsettle symbolic and discursive landscapes, shake up established hierarchies of knowing and being, and put aside the habits and routines normally employed without asking. In short, these moments are the disruptive seeds necessary for true transformation.

The conception of affect that has inspired the field of cultural affect theory understands affective relations as a web of dynamic forces that coalesce into local ecologies shaping the conditions of existence for all the entities and actors involved in these settings. In such a field of immanence, there is no external vantage point from which one can neutrally assess the relational fold. All actors—including decision-makers in policy, research-ers, practitioners, and activists—are thoroughly involved and immersed. What they do, how they react, what they feel and imagine inevitably con-tributes to the ongoing tangle of relations of affecting and being affected. An intervention into the majoritarian formations, such as the automobile arrangement or the middle-class milieu, has the potential to ramify throughout the whole fabric. Yet, the direction, magnitude, and sustain-ability of these changes are impossible to predict. That is why such inter-ventions are a form of affective experimentation: disruptions of established affective ecologies happen under opaque conditions; they are wagers on a future that is not yet tangible. The art of deploying affect disruptively is an art of reading social situations in order to choose a promising mode of intervention, after which the events run their course. Affective experimen-tation, as an activist political practice, concerns such disruptive interven-tions and the balancing of their ramifications. There is always also an acute awareness of alternatives that are already present in minoritarian forma-tions, or in the virtual undertow of surrounding affective spheres. Thus, what we mean by affective experimentation always involves a point where potentially new dynamic constellation and angles of disruption unfold—opportunities to intensify or adjust one's initial interventions. This requires a playful, risk-seeking ethos and a refined sensibility for tonalities and nuances within prevailing affective ecologies.

Furthermore, when we speak of these disruptions as forms of affective experimentation, we do so in view of an important connection between affect deployed as a means of disruption and affect as the focal point of a type of research and scholarship. Given the immanence of affective ecologies, scholars are themselves immersed within the domains under study, and thus affected and conditioned by affective milieus and their affective arrangements. The study of affect itself involves an element of experimentation even where it is theoretical and discursive in nature. Writing on affect is an experimental intervention into an affective milieu with the potential to alter habitual modes of perception, reasoning, and imagination. In light of this, our message is twofold: Given the stability and historical depth of dominant affective formations and their power to modulate subjects, we should never underestimate the permanence and change-resistance of the status quo. Yet, we should likewise not underestimate the potential of affective interventions to disrupt the dominant affective milieus, even if the ramifications of affective disruptions seem miniscule initially.

REFERENCES

Anderson, B. (2010). Modulating the excess of affect. In M. Gregg & G. J. Seigworth (Eds.), *The Affect Theory Reader* (pp. 161–185). Duke University Press.
Benjamin, W. (2003). On the concept of history. In M. W. Jennings & H. Eiland (Eds.), *Selected Writings 1938–1940,* vol. 4 (pp. 389–400). Harvard University Press. (Original work published 1940).
Deleuze, G. (1988). *Spinoza: Practical philosophy.* City Light Books.
Deleuze, G., & Guattari, F. (1987). *A thousand plateaus capitalism and schizophrenia* (B. Massumi, Trans.). University of Minnesota Press.
Gregg, M., & Seigworth, G. J. (Eds.). (2010). *The affect theory reader.* Duke University Press.
Haraway, D. J. (2016). *Staying with the trouble: Making kin in the Chthulucene.* Duke University Press.
Jörg, K. (2020). Autoregime. In K. Jörg, *Backlash: Essays zur Resilienz der Moderne* (pp. 75–103). Textem Verlag.
Katz, J. (2015). *Über ausrastende Autofahrer und das Weinen* (H. Knoblauch, Ed., & H. Knoblauch, Trans.). Springer VS.
Klein, N. (2013, October 29). How science is telling us all to revolt. *New Statesman.* Retrieved April 1, 2021, from https://www.newstatesman.com/2013/10/science-says-revolt
Lim, J. (2007). Queer critique and the politics of affect. In K. Browne, J. Lim, & G. Brown (Eds.), *Geographies of sexualities: Theory, practices, and politics* (pp. 53–67). Ashgate.

Malm, A. (2021). *How to blow up a pipeline*. Verso.

Malm, A., & Hornborg, A. (2014). The geology of mankind? A critique of the Anthropocene narrative. *The Anthropocene Review*, 1(1), 62–69.

Massumi, B. (2015). *Politics of Affect*. Polity.

Mattioli, G., Roberts, C., Steinberger, J. K., & Brown, A. (2020). The political economy of car dependence: A systems of provision approach. Energy Research & Social Science, 66, https://doi.org/10.1016/j.erss.2020.101486

Merleau-Ponty, M. (2012). *Phenomenology of Perception*. (D. A. Landes, Trans.). Routledge. (Original work published 1945).

Moore, J. W. (2015). Putting nature to work. In C. Wee, J. Schönenbach, & O. Arndt (Eds.), *Supramarkt: A micro-toolkit for disobedient consumers, or how to frack the fatal forces of the Capitalocene* (pp. 69–117). Irene Books.

Mühlhoff, R. (2018). *Immersive Macht: Affekttheorie nach Spinoza und Foucault*. Campus Verlag.

Plumwood, V. (1993). *Feminism and the mastery of nature*. Routledge.

Scholz, R. (1992). Der Wert ist der Mann. *Krisis*, 12, 19–52.

Schuetze, P. (2021). From affective arrangements to affective milieus. *Frontiers in Psychology*, 11, https://doi.org/10.3389/fpsyg.2020.611827

Schulz, K. A. (2017). Decolonising the Anthropocene: The mytho-politics of human mastery. In M. Woons, & S. Weier (Eds.), *Critical epistemologies of global politics*. E-International Relations Publishing.

Sheller, M., & Urry, J. (2000). The city and the car*. *International Journal of Urban and Regional Research*, 24(4), 737–757.

Slaby, J., & Mühlhoff, R. (2019). Affect. In J. Slaby, & C. von Scheve (Eds.), *Affective societies: Key concepts* (pp. 27–41). Routledge.

Slaby, J., Mühlhoff, R., & Wüschner, P. (2019). Affective arrangements. *Emotion Review*, 11(1), 2–12.

Todd, Z. (2015). Indigenizing the Anthropocene. In H. Davis & E. Turpin (Eds.), *Art in the Anthropocene: Encounters among aesthetics, politics, environments and epistemologies* (pp. 241–255). Open Humanities Press.

Urry, J. (2004). Automobility and its self-expansion. *Theory, Culture & Society*, 21, 25–39.

von Maur, I. (2018). *Die Epistemische Relevanz des Fühlens*. Retrieved July 1, 2019, from https://repositorium.ub.uni-osnabrueck.de/handle/urn:nbn:de:gbv:700-20180807502

von Maur, I. (2021a). Taking situatedness seriously: Embedding affective intentionality in forms of living. *Frontiers in Psychology*, 11, https://doi.org/10.3389/fpsyg.2021.599939

von Maur, I. (2021b). The Epistemic Value of Affective Disruptability. *Topoi*, https://doi.org/10.1007/s11245-021-09788-5

von Redecker, E. (2020). *Revolution für das Leben*. S. Fischer Verlag.

CHAPTER 3

Populism as Para-politics: Play, Affect, Simulation

Christoffer Kølvraa

Just Playing

"I promise not to do this to Greenland!" Donald Trump had coyly tweeted as a comment on the Instagram post by his son Eric in which a massive golden Trump Tower had been Photoshopped onto a small Greenlandic village with the caption 'Greenland in 10 years'. A few days earlier the *Wall Street Journal* had revealed that Trump had "with varying degrees of seriousness" expressed an interest in buying Greenland from Denmark (Salama et al. 2019). The international press debacle that followed was distinctly 'Trumpian' because it was a political spectacle in which the central question was 'Is he serious?' It can therefore be a means to explore Trump's political performativity and curious 'un-seriousness' or indeed 'experimental playfulness' which I will claim is central to understanding both its political discourse and affective dynamic. While here I focus on Trump as an accelerated and thus eminently illustrative instance of such

C. Kølvraa (✉)
Aarhus University, Aarhus, Denmark
e-mail: eurock@cas.au.dk

B. Timm Knudsen et al. (eds.), *Methodologies of Affective Experimentation*, https://doi.org/10.1007/978-3-030-96272-2_3

para-political or 'playful' populism, many European populist figures could be described in the same vein. Figures such as Matteo Salvini in Italy, Björn Höcke in Germany, Nigel Farage or Boris Johnson in the United Kingdom, Geert Wilders in the Netherlands, Marine Le Pen in France, or Jair Bolsonaro in Brazil not only testify to the continued presence of this kind of populism post-Trump, but in many cases were also the first to employ a political discourse characterized by the kind of 'playful experimentation' that ultimately makes contemporary (Trumpian) populism a distinct political phenomenon.

By 'experimenting' I mean a specific kind of gesture towards the future, a moment of prospective world building, something imagined or 'tried out' without any obligation or responsibility to persist in the endeavour, nor with any belief that this practice signifies a deep truth about the world or the subject engaging in it. It is *just* an experiment—a mode of action where we are 'just playing around'. The problem with the tendency recently to simply and swiftly reduce Trumpian populism to fascism is therefore not that it is 'too harsh', rather, it is that simply to accuse Trump of 'fascist lies' (Snyder 2021) allows one to sidestep the much more complicated task of understanding a mode of politics that—as in Harry Frankfurt's philosophical conceptualization of 'bullshit' (Frankfurt 2005)—does not simply lie, but is, in its unserious, playful way, strangely immune to the restraints of 'factual truth'. By reducing populism to fascism one can instead simply replay the twentieth century's core narrative of a political struggle between two different, yet both 'serious', modes of politics—the revolutionary meta-politics of fascism and the deliberative pragma-politics of liberal democracy—thereby overlooking the possibility that populism represents something new beyond this duality: an 'unserious', indeed playful, *para-politics* operating as a kind of parasite inside it.

It is important to note from the beginning that the Greenland purchase was never 'seriously' realistic. Greenland is a self-governing entity within the Kingdom of Denmark, and thus very far from something 'essentially owned' by Denmark and potentially the object of 'a large real estate deal' as Trump had put it. But what is curious about the Greenland idea is that not even Trump seemed to take it entirely seriously. Already the *Wall Street Journal* story quoted sources to the effect that it might simply be "a joke meant to indicate 'I'm so powerful I could buy a country'" (Salama et al. 2019). And yet, many commentators pointed out early on that this had all the signs of something deliberately leaked to the press. If so, one could read the obviously 'unrealistic', 'half-baked', even 'unserious' nature of this idea not as signifying the deficiency of the content, but as the actual point of the political performance surrounding it; the point was never to actually buy Greenland, only to 'play' with the idea—and to make the press and the opposition play along as well. What might be called a para-sitical reading could start from such a suspicion that what is significant here is not so much what is said, but the distance enacted between the statement and the agent of its articulation. For Michel Serres, parasitism is exactly defined not by substance, but by a certain distance, by a certain kind of position: "[t]o parasite means to eat next to" (Serres 2007, p. 7). Parasitism is to maintain this position of 'being apart and yet attached to', benefiting from the fact that "[t]he one who plays the position will always beat the one who plays the contents", in that "[t]he one who plays the position plays the relations between subjects" (p. 38). Playfulness is in a similar way a mode of speech or action that is separated from 'serious' content, and yet simultaneously connected to it, feeding off it. As J. L. Austin noted, performatives framed as play are "used not seriously, but *parasitic* upon its normal use" (Austin 1962, p. 22). Core to most definitions of play is what Johan Huizinga called the 'magic circle', its separateness or distance from ordinary life (Huizinga [1950] 2014, p. 10). It was this that allowed the subject to invest in playing, taking it *affectively* serious exactly because it was not serious in terms of having direct conse-quences in real life. That "play is non-seriousness" is thus not equivalent to "play is not serious" (p. 5). The opposite of play is rather "one-dimensionality or literal-mindedness" (Nachmanovitch 2009, p. 12), and its core, therefore, is not simply the rigid following of 'game rules' but rather its "intimate attitudes" (Caillois 1960, p. 154) famously seen by Bateson as ushered in through the meta-communicative frame 'This is Play' (Bateson 1972, p. 180). Play is not in what we do or say but "in the way we do it or say it, whatever it may be" (Nachmanovitch 2009, p. 3). Play in this sense—which we might simply call an invitation to playful-ness—is context and content independent, and yet it has a distinct effect on context and content. As Miguel Sicart argues, "[p]layfulness means taking over a world to see it through the lens of play, to make it shake and laugh and crack" (Sicart 2014, p. 24), because in playing we transform things "from functional or goal oriented to pleasurable or emotionally engaging" (p. 27). In this sense what is inaugurated by play(fulness) is an alternative sociality, and while this in games takes the somewhat rigid form of concrete rules, in other forms of play—for example, in role playing—it would be more precise to describe it as a collective process of world-making. The point is, however, that in either case, play is a vehicle for a distinct kind of experimental freedom. As Jean Baudrillard pointed out, submitting to the rules of play is the only way to escape the Law because "we live within the realm of the Law, even when fantasizing its abolition". But the playful space of rules operates entirely differently from that of the Law: "[o]ne neither believes nor disbelieves a rule—one observes it" (Baudrillard 1990, p. 133). Play escapes the realm of belief (in the Law) not by disbelieving but by 'make-believe'. As opposed to 'ritual', which is about 'what should be', and 'ordinary life', which is about 'what is', play speaks to 'what can be' (Handelman 1977, p. 187). Play in this sense is "in the subjunctive mood" and "subjunctivity is possibility" (Turner 1983b, pp. 222–223). Indeed, both Victor Turner and Brian Sutton-Smith in this vein saw play as much more than a frivolous pastime, because ultimately it was "a primary place for the expression of anything humanly imaginable" (Sutton-Smith 1997, p. 226), thereby serving the "liminal function of ludic recombination of familiar elements" (Turner 1983a, p. 236), and as such it became a realm apart where novel futures could first be experimentally articulated or enacted in a spirit of 'unrealistic optimism' (Sutton-Smith 1997, pp. 229–231).

One of the most famous descriptions of Trumpism remains Salena Zito's claim that "[t]he press takes him literally, but not seriously; his supporters take him seriously, but not literally" (Zito 2016). Such 'non-literal seriousness' could indeed be what is found in an attitude of playful experimentation. The question as to how anybody could seriously believe in a plan to 'buy Greenland'—or in another more famous but similar instance that he would build a wall towards Mexico and 'have Mexico pay for it'— is then from the beginning the wrong one. It was not a matter of belief, or of lying, it was about the enjoyment of 'playing along', of indulging in a ludic fantasy for its own sake and on its own fantastic merits.

Yet while many journalists have noted the 'post-truth' nature of Trumpism, most scholars of populism remain content with conceptualizing it as 'political belief', ignoring the glaring fact that if what Baudrillard in the 1980s heyday of postmodernism designated as the simulacrum, was then still something of a tech-dystopian fantasy, then today it is in many ways simply our mundane everyday (un)reality—not least as a consequence of the rise of ever denser online networks. An understanding of populism as fundamentally implicated and entangled with contemporary societies and their 'affective landscapes' (Grossberg 2018; Schmalenberger 2021) should reflect this uncomfortable and normatively ambiguous fact.

But while there is certainly an intersection between Trump's success and the communicative possibilities delivered by social media (Papacharissi 2016), and while the eventual exclusion from these platforms certainly had an impact, we should nonetheless be careful not to simply reduce Trumpism to some perverse effect of social media. It is not just that this tends to lead to a nostalgic exaggeration of the merits and importance of 'proper journalists' or to praising various tech-giants as guarantors of good democracy. Rather, the problem is that simply pointing to Trumpism's preferred communicative infrastructure does not in itself give us a full understanding of the performativity and affective dynamics this infrastructure—among others—is used to pursue.

Trump's playful or 'post-truth' theatrics is thus not simply an effect of the media through which he prefers to communicate, a smokescreen insidiously employed to mask his 'real' ideological project or an amusing idiosyncrasy which can safely be bracketed in serious political commentary. Playfulness, so to speak, 'goes all the way down' and is a kind of political performativity that aims to include rather than to fool its audience—akin to Bakhtinian carnivalesque (MacMillan 2017; Bakhtin 1984). It is in this vein that some scholars have claimed that Trump's followers are analogous to audiences of WWF wrestling. As Roland Barthes already pointed out in his analysis of the French version of such wrestling, it is "not a sport, ... the wrestler's function is not to win but to perform exactly the gestures expected of him" (Barthes 2013, p. 3). Fights are strictly choreographed, planned, and scripted—and the audience is well aware of this. Thus, the term 'kayfabe' (a pig-Latin-esque word for fake) points to how wrestling fans as 'smartdom', rather than simply fandom, can enjoy the show without being duped, appreciating instead the performativity required to produce this very faking: the choice of plotlines, the production value of the show, and the talent displayed in the performance of the stunts in the ring (Moon 2020). Thus, rather than being at the mercy of the kind of ideological delusion associated with Guy Debord's *Society of the Spectacle* (Debord 1970), Trump's smartdom is seen as engaged in a highly reflexive appreciation and co-creation of the media-event 'Donald Trump™', involving a simultaneous awareness and appreciation of an 'obvious artifice' in the vein of Susan Sontag's 'Camp' or Bertolt Brecht's alienation effects (Sontag 1966; Brecht 1964). But exactly as also in the case of these, the awareness of artifice actually leads to a deeper involvement and identification with 'the show'. Even if wrestling fans now heatedly debate not the fight itself but "how it is being constructed for their consumption" (Mazer 2018, p. 178), this still reproduces the 'affect factory' of wrestling. Just like the broader so-called Alt-Right, Trumpism as such illustrates that ideological messaging does not have to be undertaken in the declarative or indicative mood (Nagle 2017). The 'playful' subjunctive can be just as effective and can even entail a certain frustrating immunity to attack. Interrogated as to their 'ideological core' or 'actual plans', populists can easily be shown to be inconsistent, uninformed, or immoral. And yet under such 'serious' fire, populism does not collapse, but seems to dematerialize as the proverbial Cheshire cat, leaving behind only the condescending smile of a wrestling fan confronted by somebody outraged at the 'real' violence of the sport.

But while the concept of smartdom seems helpful in understanding Trumpism, the analogy to wrestling needs to be qualified in a crucial sense. As Claire Warden, Broderick Chow, and Eero Laine have argued, the 'kayfabe' of wrestling not only empties it of real brutality but transforms it into an environment of intersubjective care (Warden et al. 2018). What fans come to appreciate is not the raw enjoyment of a spectacle of aggression, but rather the attentiveness, respect, and professionalism needed between performers to allow for the appearance—the mere artifice—of violence, without ever allowing the actual event of violence. What this makes clear—and which is indeed Warden, Chow, and Laine's main point—is that even if the smartdom of wrestling can serve as a model for a more complex understanding of the collusive post-truth quality of Trumpism's relationship to its followers, the actual affective environment of professional wrestling appears to share little with that of Trumpism. Indeed as Sharon Mazer relates, Trump's actual appearance in the WWF ring—as a guest star of the 2007 Battle of the Billionaires—was cringeworthy to true fans, not simply because of his bad acting, his wooden delivery of lines, and his inability to figure out what to do with himself most of the time, but primarily because he seemed unconcerned with the safety or professional dignity of his fellow performers, often throwing real punches or appearing indifferent to agreed plotlines and scripted behaviour (Mazer 2018, pp. 188–189). Wrestling's smartdom might serve as a first model for post-delusional political followers, but what is important about Trump (and populists in general) is that he is both literally and figuratively a spectacularly bad wrestler; he and his smartdom being completely unconcerned with the dignity and safety of those against which (and with which) they are 'just playing'.

Not Playing Nice

This qualification that Trumpism is not simply like wrestling but more like bad wrestling prefigures the broader point about the connection between Trumpism and 'playful politics'. The danger here is that if Trumpism is simply made equivalent to 'playful politics', then the desire to critique the Trumpian project can all too easily flip into an outright rejection of play or playfulness in politics. It is ironic that while a dominant definition of populism speaks of it as a "moralistic imagination of politics" (Müller 2016, p. 19), a certain moralism is also present in those critics of populism who implicitly condemn any place for 'playfulness', in favour of an ideal of politics as rigidly rational, factual, professional, and above all coolly evacuated of affect. What is needed to critique Trumpism is therefore neither to misunderstand it as a serious belief, nor to grant it the undue privilege of being equivalent to playful politics as such, but instead to read it as analogous to various kinds of socially negative or abusive forms of play.

Play, however, has mostly been conceptualized in thoroughly positive terms. The supposedly "inclusive and harmonious relationality" of play (Halliday-Scher et al. 1995) is most often assumed with reference to the image of play as a completely separate and autotelic practice, carried out entirely for its own sake and thus depending entirely on the desire of the players to engage in it (see Gray 2013, pp. 139–154). In this vein the main and inalienable privilege of the player is imagined to be that "[o]ne can only be compromised by whatever one has consented to [because] withdrawal is possible as soon as desired" (Caillois 1960, p. 158). But already Brian Sutton-Smith challenged this view by insisting that children often engage in 'cruel play'—a form of play which is not actually separate from the power hierarchies and agendas of the real world and from which one has no more 'right to quit' than in normal life. Richard Schechner's and Miguel Sicart's notions of 'Dark Play' entail exactly such an intentional erasure of the border between play and 'real life', because it is a form of play in which the meta-communicative message 'This is Play' is always on the verge of subversion (Schechner 2013, pp. 118–120), resulting in a situation akin to what Cindy Poremba calls 'Brink play' in which actions "use their status as 'only a game' as a strategic gesture" and thus "embrace the contested space at the boundary of games and life—pairing 'it's just a game' with a knowing wink" (Poremba 2007, p. 772).

As a unifying concept for these strands of thought one could suggest 'para-play', a concept which has enjoyed a marginal presence mostly in zoological play-theory where it has been used variously to signify either "unsuccessful play initiation" (Hayaki 1985, p. 344) or play which involves overly aggressive behaviour and leads to real fighting (Mendoza-Granados and Sommer 1995, p. 59). Para-play would in a sense signify a form of play that is not really play, which is exactly parasitical on the expectations of a playful situation or mood, in that it cynically uses the performativity of playfulness as a cover to pursue agendas and abuses very much of the 'real world'. At the core of such a performance would be not simply the 'ambiguating of the world', which Sicart and others rightly identify at the heart of playfulness and its creative subjunctivity, but rather a quite different ambiguity, one which makes insecure the very status of play and of the other within it. If playfulness enters the world in and through the meta-communicative signal 'this is just play', then the presence of a situation of para-play would be revealed by the anxious doubt expressed in the question 'Are we still just playing?' This kind of ambiguity is in essence a form of what Gregory Bateson famously designated as the 'double bind' (Bateson et al. 1956, pp. 253–254), a situation in which the subject is unable to resolve the relation to the other harmoniously because it is confronted with a contradiction between different levels of communication. Confronted, in para-play, with the contradiction between the meta-communicative signal 'just playing' and a practice of undeniable abuse and aggression, it becomes impossible to navigate the situation without either suffering the negative consequences of its manifest content or the negative consequences of violating its meta-communicative framing. The subject is, so to speak, 'stuck' because either option would just open it up to further condemnation or other adverse consequences. Strick points to such a contradiction in the circulation of racist jokes by the extreme right. If ignored as 'just jokes', they are free to contaminate the public space, but if confronted and critiqued as racist messaging, the critic can be immediately mocked as the quintessential 'unfunny' liberal, in contrast to whom the Alt-Right appears 'transgressive', 'easy-going', or 'youthful' (Strick 2018, p. 120). But Strick also hints at a version of the double bind that turns on the production of a specific kind of white majoritarian—yet perpetually vulnerable—male subject (p. 122), and in this way on a certain kind of white identity politics in which it is the majority that constantly finds itself wounded or transgressed against by the demands of minorities (Strick 2019, p. 39). Combining such performances of hypervulnerability and an insidious provocative playfulness result in what might be termed the 'weepy-faced bully' version of the double bind, where the aggressor, when forcefully counterattacked, swiftly effectuates a kind of role-reversal, now morally berating his victim for overreacting in a situation where we were 'just playing'. Trump beautifully illustrated this when he was challenged on his misogynist language by Fox News journalist Megyn Kelly during the 2016 campaign. He initially sought to frame the statements as 'just playing'—"it's fun, it's kidding, we have a good time"—but when Kelly pushed the point the tone changed: "[H]onestly, Megyn, if you don't like it, I'm sorry. I've been very nice to you, although I could probably maybe not be, based on the way you have treated me, but I wouldn't do that" (Winberg 2017, p. 2). One may notice that the threat inserted into the middle of what is—at least formally—a kind of apology exactly illustrates Strick's point that this is a performativity of vulnerability that nonetheless reproduces a site of power.

Something almost identical unfolded in the context of the Greenland purchase after Danish Prime Minister Mette Frederiksen called the whole thing "an absurd discussion". The reaction came a few days later when Trump announced that he would cancel a planned state visit to Denmark because "I thought that the prime minister's statement was nasty. ... Greenland was just an idea, just a thought. But they say it was 'absurd' and it was said in a very nasty, very sarcastic way." Trump, now restyled as victim, could then further punish his tormentor with a series of tweets pointing at Denmark's inability to live up to its NATO defence spending obligations. Frederiksen soon deemed it necessary to appear before the world press emphasizing that the United States was Denmark's most important ally and indicating that a re-scheduled visit would be much looked forward to. What was a story about one of Trump's 'half-baked ideas' was thus potentially transformed into yet another example of him—and the United States—being accosted by a 'Nasty Woman'. I would argue, however, that even if this performance appears to be all about Trump's hurt feelings, its real purpose is to draw attention to and even retroactively overinflate the affective intensity of the other's response. Frederiksen's choice to deem the idea 'absurd' was certainly beyond normal diplomatic language, but it was equally Trump's 'hurt' performance that retroactively gave Frederiksen's comment the intensity of something 'nasty'. Such fetishization of the other's affect, of 'how much they hate us', is already linked by Richard Hofstadter to a certain 'paranoid style' in US politics (Hofstadter 1964), but beyond its stylistic particularity, it is also indicative of a certain kind of affective dynamic, which might be described as 'extractive'—or indeed by Serres as abusively parasitical.

Crucially, 'parasitic abuse' for Serres does not mean just any kind of aggression or exploitation. Parasitism is a specific kind of relationship; neither of equivalence nor of reciprocity, neither exchange-value nor use-value. Parasitism interrupts such relations being itself a matter of sheer 'abuse value' (Serres 2007, p. 75). It is fundamentally a relation in which something of the other is devoured without compensation, and thus a form in which the other is not simply an enemy or a threat, but a resource consumed, something that one 'feeds off'. It is in this sense that I want to suggest that there is an element of parasitism in the constant animosity populists seem to cultivate with their opponents. Contrary to the often-heard conventional wisdom that populism is empty of political content but full of 'feelings', populism might instead be thought of as 'affectively parasitical'; as largely dependent on affective intensity evoked and extracted from *outside* itself (see Kølvraa 2015).

This line of argument could start by considering the image of the Golden Trump Tower rising above Greenland, as what Robert Pfaller calls an 'illusion without owners'; a representation or practice, the belief in which is not fully supported by the subject engaging in it, but which can nonetheless be sustained by imagining a 'subject-supposed-to-believe' elsewhere (Pfaller 2014, p. 93). The consequence is that we can thus engage in practices on the assumption that others 'believe' in them, even if ultimately nobody does. Who then in this sense is imagined to 'believe' in the Trump Tower image? It is already disavowed by Trump's own coy promise 'not to do this to Greenland' and his smartdom is, as argued, well aware of the artifice at the heart of their enjoyment. Rather, the subjects who guarantee the image, who are imagined to, at some level, believe that it signifies a possible future (that Trump might actually attempt to do this), are of course his opponents. This image does not represent a 'Trumpian dream', but instead the nightmare that the 'liberal other' is expected to believe that Trump believes. And it is not even necessary that Trump's political opponents actually believe that he is serious (i.e., that he believes) beneath the playfulness. All that is required is the presence of enough (para-playful) ambiguity about the status of a given statement or performance for there to be a reason to fear that *someone, somewhere* might believe it. Frederiksen—and many other Danish politicians who refuted the idea aggressively—did not need to believe that Trump was serious about buying Greenland. A forceful response was necessitated simply on the grounds that there *might* be Danish or Greenlandic voters who believe in this as a true Trumpian ambition and thus need reassurance that it will not happen.

That all roads, so to speak, lead to the necessity of a forceful response might suggest that the point of para-play is not only to catch the other in the vulnerabilities of the double bind, but ultimately to elicit and put on display an affectively intense reaction; to set up a situation where one 'cannot not respond'. This is a dynamic that emerges most forcefully in acts of provocation (Kølvraa 2015), because the reflexivity of the provocateur—the necessary self-awareness that what one is doing is 'just' provocation—means that the relationality at the heart of it is necessarily one of asymmetrical affective intensity. In provocation, the affect is drawn from the other; the hope of provocation is that the affective investment of the target's response exceeds the provocateur's investment in the initiating action as much as possible. As Mason has put it, the core question of the provocateur is always 'Let's see what happens [i.e., how they react] if I do this!' (Mason 2016, p. 18). And indeed, the provocative quality of much populist discourse comes not simply from its content, but from the way the most outrageous statements seemingly lack much affective investment; when, for example, blatant racism is stated as disinterested fact, misogyny as a humorous aside, and semi-totalitarian policy ideas as pragmatic solutions. As Sicart notes in passing, Dark Play can in the same vein entail a marked withdrawal of investment signalled by the question "[W]hy are you taking this game so seriously?" (Sicart 2015, p. 110). Such a mockery of the other's 'over-investment' in what is after all 'just a game' marks the tactical advantage of not having let oneself be immersed; of maintaining and controlling the ambiguity of a playfulness that is not really play, and in which one therefore does not fully invest affectively. The affective 'heat' of para-play—as in bullying—must as such come mostly from the victim, and it is telling therefore, as Kowalski notes, that the word 'teasing' comes partly from the French *attiser*, meaning "to feed a fire with fuel" (Kowalski 2000, p. 232). In a sense the other becomes a surrogate not just at the level of belief but also at the level of affect. But beyond the 'subject-supposed-to-enjoy' theorized by Slavoj Žižek (2008), the other's 'enjoyment' is here not only assumed (to exist) but, so to speak, consumed; it becomes the object of the game to elicit and extract displays of affective intensity from the other. As para-politics, the affect enjoyed at the heart of Trumpian populism would in this way be not 'its own', but that of its outraged opponents. An affect evoked and elicited from the other through the provocative prodding of abusive (para)playfulness, and ultimately thereby seeking to compensate for its own sterility. Indeed, this could be one reason why populist visions of the future always seem so hollow and barren, so 'gimmicky' in the sense Sianne Ngai gives to the term. They are not really about the future but "[p]opped off like tiny, nonreusable fireworks [as a] kind of bad contemporaneity, akin to the 'elongated present', 'endless present' or 'perpetual present' strikingly diverse theorists use to account for the peculiar feel and situation of our contemporary moment" (Ngai 2017, p. 483). In contrast to full play's celebrated experimental subjunctivity, the two most successful populist slogans—'Take back control' and 'Make America Great Again'—inadvertently seem to admit that in the political unconscious of populism there is such a vacuity of actual ideas about the future that one has to go backwards to get to it. The 'transgressive' images of radically different futures that populism spews out constantly—new walls, new purchases, new profits—are sterile, because they are never true images of utopia, fully believed and invested in, but pernicious fantasies about the other's dystopia; less nascent social imaginaries and more empty provocative shells filled only by the eager expectation of an outraged reaction.

SIMULATING THE ALTERNATIVE

The argument so far results in a somewhat tragic image of the opponents of (Trumpian) populism: Hopelessly outplayed, provoked, abused, and reduced to a role as affective hosts for the populist parasite. These opponents almost appear to be caught in a kind of 'cruel optimism' which makes them "despite an awareness that the normative political sphere appears as shrunken [and] broken ... return periodically to its recommitment ceremonies and scenes" (Berlant 2011, p. 227). What we need to notice, however, is that this narrative relies entirely on a sharp and definite distinction between populists and non-populists. And yet the scholarship on populism has struggled to deliver on this point. Cas Mudde's still widely used definition of populism as a thin ideology centred only around the moralizing dichotomy between a 'pure people' and a 'corrupt elite' fits a variety of political discourses from the extreme left to the extreme right (Mudde 2004). As such the question raised by Jan-Werner Müller—'[I]s everyone a populist, then?'—slides uncomfortably towards the affirmative even if Müller mobilizes the curious argument that even if non-populists sometimes act and talk like populists, they 'implicitly accept' the Habermasian pluralist principles of deliberative democracy (Müller 2016, pp. 38–40).

Often the meaning of 'populism' is constituted simply by reference to a field of names: Farage, Berlusconi, Le Pen, and Trump. Always Trump. Or it is reduced to the subjectivism of obscenity: 'you know it when you see it' (see Betz 2020, p. 4). But what if the difficulty encountered when attempting to isolate populism in a distinct and clearly demarcated corner of the political field is taken as a clue to the phenomenon itself; as subtly indicating the possibility that what is important about populism is exactly that it is not just a property of distinct actors—who can then be condemned and expelled—but instead just one part in a much wider game in which the role of parasite and that of host become utterly interchangeable.

Serres also thinks of the parasite in terms of the 'noise' in communicative systems and that it is this dimension that opens up a perspective of radical, if not unlimited, parasitical implications. In fact, one might argue that Serres's ultimate agenda is to undercut any hope that the parasite could be distinctly located, isolated, or eliminated within either bodily, social, or communicative realms; indeed, to undercut any hope of a secure distinction between who is parasite and who is host. Parasitism is instead to be thought of as a "cascade" (Serres 2007, p. 5), as a chain of parasites feeding off each other. Indeed as 'noise' the parasite is not only ineradicable, but also inseparable and indispensable from the communicative flows themselves (Serres 2007, p. 79). Judging what is parasitical and what is productive, what is noise and what is communication, is simply a 'game of exclusion' which "overvalues the message and undervalues the noise" in 'dogmatically' separating "the good, the just, the true, the natural, the normal" from the insidiously parasitical (Serres 2007, p. 68). But the relationship between a systemic norm and its parasitic noise is not actually antagonistic. Rather, it entails radical implication, "[t]he counter-norm is never a noise of the norm but the same norm reversed, that is to say, its twin" (Serres 2007, p. 68), moving "a hair's breadth in either direction causes the noises to become messages and the messages, noises" (Serres 2007, p. 67). What would such a 'hair's breadth' look like in the context of discussing Trumpian populism? Certainly not a rehabilitation of it. As James Burton and Daisy Tam helpfully point out, "[a]n ethics of parasitism would not amount to an unchecked, perhaps perverse acceptance of every invasive threat, every instance of theft or corruption: rather, it would consist in the reserving of judgement on such perceived invasions, and the abandonment of the fantasy of immunization, of absolute security, order, and cleanliness" (Burton and Tam 2016, pp. 121–122). It is not about forgiving Trump's parasitism, but rather about considering the wider 'cascade' of which he might be thought to be part.

In this vein, the headache around neatly separating populists and non-populists might be resolved in a quite different way, by realising that, of course not everybody can be a populist, simply because somebody has to play the role of non-populist in the performance of the grand political struggle against populism. Serres's cascade would then take the form of a joint and integrated performativity involving both populists and their opponents. Maybe even as something akin to Baudrillard's argument that,

> Disneyland is presented as imaginary in order to make us believe that the rest is real, when in fact all of Los Angeles and the America surrounding it are no longer real, but of the order of the hyperreal and of simulation. ... Whence the debility, the infantile degeneration of this imaginary. It is meant to be an infantile world, in order to make us believe that the adults are elsewhere, in the 'real' world. (Baudrillard 2001, pp. 174–175)

What if we read the 'bad mannered', carnivalesque, and playfully provocative antics of populism as exactly such an 'infantile debility' serving to distract from a much more extensive vacuity of political space? Namely, from the fact that the political projects of non-populist 'adults' are in fact often neither particularly 'decent', 'inclusive', nor 'visionary' themselves. What would be simulated—equally well for two diverse voter-bases—is both 'populism' as the 'radical' alternative and non-populism as the 'decent' defence against it. If, as argued, populist futures in fact hold little radical promise, then, in the same manner as Baudrillard claimed to be the case with Watergate—"before, the task was to dissimulate scandal; today, the task is to conceal the fact that there is none" (Baudrillard 2001, p. 176)—the truly scandalous secret of populism is that it is not 'scandalous' in the sense of being a real challenge to the system. But if populism actually in no way constitutes a fundamental or 'dangerous' alternative to what Müller calls the good 'run of the mill democratic politicians' (Müller 2016, p. 40), then the opposite is also true; the 'good' opponents of populists are in many cases hardly their diametric opposites. Rather, such apparent radical differences between the two sides are not the cause of the struggle but instead the spectacular and equally beneficial product of it.

What was in this sense, at least from the perspective of someone familiar with Danish domestic politics, the most disconcerting effect of the Greenland debacle was how Mette Frederiksen seemed to be instantly transformed into the shining counterpoint of the 'nasty' populism embodied by Trump. If he imagined buying whole nations as though they were 'real estate', she progressively insisted that 'Greenland is not Denmark's— it belongs to the Greenlanders'; if he crazily imagined Golden Towers over the artic landscape, she rationally wanted to focus on realistic investment opportunities; if he raged on Twitter, she responded calmly in professionally managed press conferences. The most convincing performance in the whole show might in fact have been Frederiksen's delivery of 'so not Trump'.

But what the international press never took an interest in is the fact that Mette Frederiksen's own political project is only by some stretch of the imagination this stellar 'decent' alternative. Described from a different and more critical angle, one could easily argue that Frederiksen has spearheaded an utterly unpresented and radical right-wing turn both for her party, the government it leads and for public discourse in Denmark. This has involved not just an extremely aggressive anti-immigration discourse but also, as a more general cultural agenda, the rehabilitation of a pugnacious national pride; a recent poster campaign showed only her smiling face and the strangely infantile statement "Denmark is the best invention". Furthermore, Frederiksen's government and party have arguably displayed a progressively diminishing tolerance of critique whether from parliamentary opposition, 'the cultural elite', or the press; Frederiksen simply declining to participate in interviews with critical journalists and preferring to communicate 'directly to the people' via her Facebook page. All these are actions and attitudes curiously close to those elsewhere being counted among the shortcomings of 'populists'. In the international realm her government has been severely sceptical of the EU, generally dismissive about guidelines or recommendations from the UN, and has, alone in the world, insisted on repatriating Syrian refugees, singlehandedly judging parts of the country as 'safe enough'. Simultaneously, it was long the principled line of Frederiksen's government to refuse to allow not just female Danish citizens—former ISIS affiliates sitting in Kurdish prison camps—to return to Denmark for legal prosecution, but equally to refuse to allow their children who are also Danish citizens back into the country. Again, such a practice of punishing children, of refusing them the rights supposedly guaranteed by citizenship, because 'their parents have turned their backs on Denmark', would—had it been practised by one of the 'usual suspects' of populism—certainly have been described as 'typical' of the harsh and xenophobic core of that ideology. Most recently, her government has been congratulating itself on a lucrative deal struck to sell military-grade barbed wire to secure the EU's external borders against immigrants, forgetful of or indifferent to the fact that Frederiksen was not so long ago among the outraged critics of Trump's plan to 'build a wall'.

I cannot here engage in a full critical evaluation of Frederiksen's political project or its ethical merits—that judgement must be left to future historians. My point here is only to illustrate that the performance of the 'decent' alternative to populism is not (always) reliant on ideological content (or actual decency). The 'decent' alternative is—as with the 'radicality' of populism—often simulated rather than real.

We might then re-describe the aggravated back and forth between populism and its opponents. It is not a classical political antagonism, but neither is it just a case of political 'bullying' with clear aggressors and innocent victims. Rather it can be understood as something along the lines of what Serres described as a game around a 'quasi-object'; for example, in the shape of a ball being passed around in certain children's games. This is an object which "marks or designates a subject who, without it, would not be a subject" (Serres 2007, p. 225). The subject is here constituted by its continuous transformation; as the ball is passed around, new players becoming 'it', the role of aggressor and victim shift rapidly, uniting the players in a shared state of suspense, "the more the ball is passed, the more the vicariance changes, the more the crowd waits breathlessly" (Serres 2007, p. 227). This is neither community nor conflict, neither cooperation nor confrontation, but a strange kind of grudging collusion in which "we are all possible victims; we all expose ourselves to this danger and we escape it" (Serres 2007, p. 227), because only in and through this vulnerability, only by remaining in the game, remaining open to attack from the other, is there the possibility of becoming an 'I'. There is collusion here, but not care. One does not play the ball to the other in order to 'recognize' him, but to make him 'it', to designate him the 'sacrificial victim', to 'kill him'. And yet this gesture is what bestows on him subjectivity, even if only of a temporary and precarious kind, as something dangerous to be quickly passed on, indeed as something that only ultimately exists in 'being passed on'; as "a game token exchanged" (Serres 2007, p. 227). Serres's intersubjectivity is ambiguous and conflictual at its very heart; to be subject is to be victim, one attacks the other yet remains in the game in the hope that one's aggression will be reciprocated, one enjoys the status of subject only on condition that one plots to pass it on. And, in the end, there is a strange and unstable unity of purpose as "this passing, this network of passes, these vicariances of subjects weave the collection" because "[t]he 'we' is made by passing the 'I'" (Serres 2007, p. 227). What I am ultimately suggesting here is simply that this image of a collection of 'victim-aggressors' locked in a strange and unstable kind of conflictual yet ultimately collusive intersubjectivity could be a way to think about the contemporary 'populist zeitgeist' as signifying not specific actors or ideological projects but a unified simulation of political alternatives involving precisely many of those would-be non-populists. If, with Berlant we describe populism as a 'juxta-political' space of 'feeling political together' (Berlant 2011, p. 224), then it is important to note that this space is co-created by political antagonists—'populists' and 'non-populists' alike—in an opaque and perhaps only partly self-aware collusion. It is a joint para-politics securing the continued fascination and loyalty of both populist smartdom and outraged 'decent' voters who together make up Serres' 'breathless crowd'.

What is lost in this interlocking cascade, what is actually 'dis-simulated', would then be what Franco Berardi (2017) has called 'futurability', because if populist fantasies aim to articulate nothing more than their opponents' worst fears about the future, their opponents typically respond with a 'celebration of the status quo'. It is in the shadow of the horror of a future Trump Tower over Nuuk that Frederiksen can sweepingly cover over the myriad remains of Danish colonial power in Greenlandic affairs by the easy affordance that 'Greenland belongs to the Greenlanders'. Indeed, after the affair, several Danish politicians and commentators could not resist the temptation to make the point that this should remind Greenlanders that 'things could be much worse'. Such a celebration of the status quo at the heart of the non-populist 'alternative' became abundantly clear in the shadow of COVID-19 lockdowns. As many have pointed out, populists seemed—perhaps surprisingly—unable to find ideological traction in the context of the pandemic. This was certainly partly self-inflicted; many populists either holding on to the fatal fantasy that this was 'just a flu' or hopelessly mismanaging the necessary response. But we should also appreciate how the lockdowns allowed for—or were skilfully cultivated to evoke—an almost hysterical appreciation of the 'normal' or the 'everyday' now temporarily suspended, which could then through certain ideological practices and discourses be securely linked to a much wider celebration of the societal status quo. In Denmark, as in many other places, the symbolic template for a 'lockdown community' was almost immediately drawn from a collective memory of war and occupation, including most overtly the communal (televised) singing of traditional hymns and popular songs. There was a clearly nostalgic enjoyment of the re-emergence of something like a 'Blitz spirit', styled as a rediscovery of the nation's desire to 'take care of each other'. As with all nostalgia, however, the wishful idealization of a certain past implicitly entails the wishing away of groups or elements of society having been added in the meantime. This Second World War nostalgic self-image was of a more ethnically homogenous Danish community and was therefore predictably accompanied by a rising suspicion of immigrant communities as 'not doing their part' to curb the crisis. And it must be noted that this hyper-sentimentalization of traditional community, the re-invention, if you will, of a nationalism able and willing to take itself fully seriously, was by no means the invention of or primarily pushed by 'vulgar' populists. Rather it was exactly the 'decent' opponents—in Denmark no one more so than Mette Frederiksen herself—who were able to make ideological hay from the crisis. But it was not just that the ethno-cultural nation was re-booted as the unquestioned container for, and bio-political principle behind, communal 'care', but that even the most quotidian elements of our (suspended) lives—getting a haircut, going shopping, going to a bar, even going to work—were imbued with an almost mythical meaningfulness. In a way akin to how Elias Canetti saw the 'density' of an actual crowd experience as alleviating the abstract anguish of social hierarchy (Canetti 1984), political alienation was mapped onto social distancing, such that the structural condition of the former (along with any ambition to change it) could be forgotten with reference to the strictly temporary imposition of the latter. Utopia did not need to be nostalgically excavated from the past and certainly should not be found in a radically different future; it was here in the (absent) status quo. It is in a wider sense no mystery that populism struggled to find ideological traction in a situation where their own brand of playfully provocative xenophobia seemed to drown in a flood of seriously sentimental nationalism unleashed by their 'decent' opponents and where any subjunctive imagination of 'what could be' had been entirely filled by postapocalyptic viral fantasies, skilfully employed to garner a public mood of appreciation, gratefulness, and obedience. With the 'status quo' now de facto suspended in the lockdown state of exception it could be fetishized without having to claim that it was under potential threat from some 'outrageous' populist plan for the future. In the context of COVID-19, the opponents of populism were thus suddenly free to play with themselves— and as such the core and limits of the non-populist political alternative was never clearer. Whatever COVID-19 may have revealed about the deficient talents of populists such as Trump and Bolsonaro in handling a major crisis, it has in this sense also served to fully illustrate the poverty of the alternative on offer. If, indeed, the alternative to the fake utopianism of populism is no utopianism at all, then the hope to "recover some sense of the future as well as of the possibilities of genuine change" (Jameson 1998, p. 90) is exactly what the collusive simulation described serves to eliminate.

BEYOND COLLUSION?

What this points to is that projects to 'recover the future' must not only confront the para-play of populism and the extractive affective dynamic that its fake utopianism sets in motion but will also have to avoid the lure of being folded into a vacuous non-populist alternative where only an endlessly recycled and sentimentalized present is on offer. Getting caught up in the back and forth of these two camps—whether in the frenetic day-to-day simulation of political debate or in the slower rhythm beaten out by the alteration of who is government and who is opposition—is the best way to ensure that nothing happens. But in a wider scope, the danger is that playfulness or experimentation is allowed to become synonymous with actors such as Trump or the contemporary Alt-Right, and thus discredited by association. There is already a tendency that those actually seeking to articulate a truly 'anti-populist' position (whether academic, activist or parliamentary) end up doing so by rallying around a rigid and ultimately authoritarian discourse centred on the call to return to Truth, Reason, and Fact. This is why I have taken such pains here to emphasize that what populists do is not really play, but degraded and pernicious para-play. Effective opposition to populism—or more generally to the contemporary 'great turning-right show'—would in this light seem to have to both resist the provocative 'baiting' of endless protest or outrage and, perhaps more crucially, reject a wider temptation to style oneself exclusively, in an attempt at maximum contrast, through the celebration of seriously un-playful modes of political performance, such as adolescent rage, pompous self-righteousness, or a self-indulgent recourse to sweeping demonization. If, as I have argued, play is a form of experimentation, and experimentation is the way we reach for the future before it happens, then to deny that play can and should be part of a progressive mode of political agency would be a most serious mistake. The agenda for an anti-populist project today should not be to root out play in the realm of politics, but to (re)invent a mode of political playfulness that can realise the potential for creativity, inclusivity and enjoyment found in play as a unique mode of experimental world-making.

REFERENCES

Austin, J. L. (1962). *How to do things with words*. Harvard University Press.
Bakhtin, M. (1984). *Rabelais and his world*. Indiana University Press.
Barthes, R. (2013). *Mythologies*. Hill and Wang.
Bateson, G. (1972). *Steps to an ecology of mind*. Ballantine Books.
Bateson, G., Jackson, D. D., Haley, J., & Weakland, J. (1956). Toward a theory of schizophrenia. *Behavioral Science, 1*(4), 251–264.
Baudrillard, J. (1990). *Seduction: Culturetext*. Macmillan Education.
Baudrillard, J. (2001). *Selected writings* (2nd ed., revised and expanded). Stanford University Press.
Berardi, F. (2017). *Futurability: The age of impotence and the horizon of possibility*. Verso Books.
Berlant, L. (2011). *Cruel optimism*. Duke University Press.
Betz, H-G. (2020). The emotional underpinnings of radical right populist mobilization: Explaining the protracted success of radical right-wing populist parties. *CARR Research Insight*, 2, London, UK: Centre for Analysis of the Radical Right.
Brecht, B. (1964). Alienation effects in Chinese acting. In J. Willett (Ed.), *Brecht on Theatre* (pp. 91–99). Hill and Wang.
Burton, J., & Tam, D. (2016). Towards a parasitic ethics. *Theory, Culture & Society, 33*(4), 103–125.
Caillois, R. (1960). *Man and the sacred*. Free Press of Glencoe.
Canetti, E. (1984). *Crowds and power*. Penguin.
Debord, G. (1970). *Society of the Spectacle*. Black & Red.
Frankfurt, H. G. (2005). *On bullshit*. Princeton University Press.
Gray, P. (2013). *Free to learn: Why unleashing the instinct to play will make our children happier, more self-reliant, and better students for life*. Basic Books.
Grossberg, L. (2018). *Under the cover of chaos: Trump and the battle for the American right*. Pluto Press.
Halliday-Scher, K., Urberg, K. A., & Kaplan-Estrin, M. (1995). Learning to pretend: Preschoolers' use of meta-communication in sociodramatic play. *International Journal of Behavioral Development, 18*(3), 451–461.
Handelman, D. (1977). Play and Ritual: Complementary Frames of Meta-Communication. In A. J. Chapman and H. C. Foot (Eds.), *It's a Funny Thing,*

Humour: Proceedings of The International Conference on Humour and Laughter 1976 (pp. 185–192). Pergamon Press.

Hayaki, H. (1985). Social play of juvenile and adolescent chimpanzees in the Mahale Mountains National Park, Tanzania. *Primates, 26*(4): 343–360.

Hofstadter, R. (1964). *The paranoid style in American politics.* Vintage.

Huizinga, J. [1950] 2014. *Homo ludens: A study of the play-element in culture.* Roy Publishers.

Jameson, F. (1998). *The cultural turn: Selected writings on the postmodern, 1983–1998.* Verso.

Kølvraa, C. (2015). Affect, provocation, and far right rhetoric. In B. T. Knudsen and C. Stage (Eds.), *Affective Methodologies* (pp. 183–200). Palgrave Macmillan.

Kowalski, R. M. (2000). "I was only kidding!": Victims' and perpetrators' perceptions of teasing. *Personality and Social Psychology Bulletin, 26*(2), 231–241.

MacMillan, C. (2017). Welcome to the carnival? Podemos, populism and Bakhtin's carnivalesque. *Journal of Contemporary European Studies, 25*(2), 258–273.

Mason, B. (2016). *Provocation in popular culture.* Routledge.

Mazer, S. (2018). Donald Trump shoots the match. *TDR/The Drama Review, 62*(2), 175–200.

Mendoza-Granados, D., & Sommer, V. (1995). Play in chimpanzees of the Arnhem Zoo: Self-serving compromises. *Primates, 36*(1), 57–68.

Moon, D. S. (2020). Kayfabe, Smartdom and Marking out: Can pro-wrestling help us understand Donald Trump? *Political Studies Review,* November 2020, 1–15.

Mudde, C. (2004). The populist zeitgeist. *Government and opposition, 39*(4), 541–563.

Müller, J.-W. (2016). *What is populism?* University of Pennsylvania Press.

Nachmanovitch, S. (2009). This Is Play. *New Literary History, 40*(1), 1–24.

Nagle, A. (2017). *Kill all normies: Online culture wars from 4chan and Tumblr to Trump and the alt-right.* Zero Books.

Ngai, S. (2017). Theory of the gimmick. *Critical Inquiry, 43*(2), 466–505.

Papacharissi, Z. (2016). Affective publics and structures of storytelling: Sentiment, events and mediality. *Information, communication & society, 19*(3), 307–324.

Pfaller, R. (2014). *On the pleasure principle in culture: Illusions without owners.* Verso.

Poremba, C. (2007). *Critical potential on the brink of the magic circle.* Situated Play, Proceedings of DiGRA Digital Games Research Association 2007 Conference, Tokyo, Japan, 772–778.

Salama, V., Ballhaus, R., Restuccia, A., & Bender, M. C. (2019, August 15). President Trump eyes a new real-estate purchase: Greenland. *The Wall Street Journal.* August 15.

Schechner, R. (2013). *Performance studies: An introduction* (3rd ed.). Routledge.

Schmalenberger, S. (2021). Visualisierter Opfermythos: Die deutsche Neue Rechte, sozial-mediatisiertes Gedenken und das Orchestrieren rechter Affekte. In M. Futh, J. Homeyer, R. Pates, & F. Spissinger (Eds.), *Die Beharrlichkeit der Nation*. Springer VS.

Serres, M. (2007). *The parasite*, University of Minnesota Press.

Sicart, M. (2014). *Play matters: Playful thinking*. The MIT Press.

Sicart, M. (2015). Darkly playing others. In T. E. Mortensen, J. Linderoth, & A. M. L. Brown (Eds.), *The Dark Side of Game Play* (pp. 100–116). Routledge.

Snyder, T. (2021). The American abyss. *New York Times Magazine*, January 9.

Sontag, S. (1966). *Against interpretation, and other essays*. Penguin Classics.

Strick, S. (2018). Alt-Right-Affekte. Provokationen und Online-Taktiken. *Zeitschrift für Medienwissenschaft*, 10(2), 113–125.

Strick, S. (2019). Tired Trump oder: Die Ermüdung der Theorie. In L. Koch, T. Nanz, & C. Rogers (Eds.), *The great disruptor* (pp. 21–46). JB Metzler Verlag.

Sutton-Smith, B. (1997). *The ambiguity of play*. Harvard University Press.

Turner, V. (1983a). Body, brain, and culture. *Zygon*, 18(3), 221–245.

Turner, V. (1983b). Play and drama: The horns of a dilemma. In F. Manning (Ed.), *The World of Play: Proceedings of the 7th Annual Meeting of the Association of the Anthropological Study of Play* (pp. 217–224). Leisure Press.

Warden, C., Chow, B., & Laine, E. (2018). Working Loose: A Response to "Donald Trump shoots the match" by Sharon Mazer. *TDR/The Drama Review*, 62(2), 201–215.

Winberg, O. (2017). Insult politics: Donald Trump, right-wing populism, and incendiary language. *European Journal of American Studies*, 12(2), 1–16.

Zito, S. (2016). Taking Trump seriously, not literally. *The Atlantic*, September 23.

Žižek, S. (2008). *The plague of fantasies*. Verso.

CHAPTER 4

Interspecies Pedagogies: More-than-Human Experiments with Leadership in/of the Anthropocene

Dorthe Staunæs and Sverre Raffnsøe

Global warming, melting ice, poisoning of the hydro- and biospheres, pandemics, starvation, migrant flows, extinction of species, terror, racism, inequalities rooted in invented social categories of race, gender and class. The project of Western Man (that 'overrepresent himself as the human'[1]; Wynter

---

[1] The concept of Man assembled the colonization of time and space and the perfections of geometrics forms as visualized in Vetruvian Man by Leonardo de Vinci. According to Sylvia Wynter Western epistemology propels Western man and culture to be *the* human and *the* humanity. By 'overrepresentation of man' we refer to Sylvia Wynter's overall point that in the system of the modern human, Man is accepted as the generic sex, bourgeoisie as generic

---

D. Staunæs (✉)
Aarhus University, Aarhus, Denmark
e-mail: dost@edu.au.dk

S. Raffnsøe
Copenhagen Business School, Copenhagen, Denmark
e-mail: Sra.mpp@cbs.dk

© The Author(s), under exclusive license to Springer Nature
Switzerland AG 2022
B. Timm Knudsen et al. (eds.), *Methodologies of Affective
Experimentation*, https://doi.org/10.1007/978-3-030-96272-2_4

2001) and the inherited cosmogonies in this project have in the age of the Anthropocene (often characterized as the age in which the activities of the human species have influenced the Earth System in profound ways) multiplied and intensified environmental damage, human suffering and challenges that leaders of big countries as well as small ones need to care about.

New ways of dis/affecting 'Man's project' in the Anthropocene seem to be requested and needed. The question is how may leaders learn to respond to and lead in the rapidly changing material conditions of living beings in the Anthropocene? How may human leaders *un*learn the habits, epistemologies and cosmogonies that are embedded in 'Man's project'? How may human leaders learn to 'stay with the trouble' (Haraway 2016) and continue to care in precarious times?

Interestingly, the education of leaders and managers in the leadership learning laboratories already seem to have begun to respond to the indicated radical challenges to presently practised and conceived leadership in interesting ways. In certain contemporary leadership learning laboratories, one finds an ongoing and re-iterated experimentation with ways leaders may become affected not only by human beings but also by other kinds of beings and in which they may affect other kinds of beings with whom they are entangled.

As it will be developed in this chapter, this kind of interspecies intraaction permits experimentation with more than other ways of being affected and affecting across what may traditionally be perceived as sharp species divides. In addition to developing an openness and a sensitivity that transcends received human-centric interaction as well as an ability to pay serious and careful attention to other kinds of beings with whom humans intra-act (Despret 2019), the interspecies intra-action staged in contemporary leadership learning laboratories permits development of new kinds and new conceptions of leadership.

Disaffecting Man's traditional project, these new kinds of relationships and leaderships enable human leaders to move ahead in ways that affect other beings as well as themselves to behave differently (Raffnsøe 2013). Experiences with interspecies intra-action made in the leadership learning

class, Indo-European as the generic race, Christian as generic religion, homo economicus as generic genre of being human (Wynter 2001). In other words, human and Man becomes one and the same, when Columbus and other voyagers arrived in 'the New World' (Mignolo 2015).

laboratory permit the development of a capacity to be affected by and affect others, thereby making the involved parties capable to behave in ways that differ from their usual behaviour, preferably even making them able to manage to do more than they would normally do, and maybe even more than can even be predicted by any of the involved parties (Raffnsøe et al. 2019). In this way, interspecies intra-action makes it possible to make experiences with moving beyond planning, management, mere control and strategic management towards leadership in an emphatic sense of the word (Raffnsøe 2013).

The education of managers has changed to the extent that managers develop into leaders capable of registering and adjusting to alternative registers of being, thinking and feeling during leadership or self-development journeys. New experimental learning arrangements are played out on a continuum between (cognitive) training of 'the reflective leader' (see Schön 1991) and transforming leaders. These transformations make the leader emotionally affected and 'reformatted' in experiential learning labs cultivating a kind of existential and spiritual atmosphere. Meditation, fire walking, drumming or singing can bring leaders into this ambiance; however, it may also be gained while some leaders 'walk the talk' at leadership pilgrimages accompanied by minoritized boys (Raffnsøe and Staunæs 2014; Hvenegård-Lassen and Staunæs 2015) or by sleeping with penguins at outdoor camps. Yet other leaders, as the ones this chapter focuses upon, may take up the challenge of interspecies encounters and ask animals, for instance horses, simultaneously wild and domesticated, to support the development of more-than-human relationality and in this way affect human perceptiveness and attentiveness, maybe even sustain the development of a different kind of sense of the human self.

While this kind of interspecies pedagogy decentres the human as the only educator, it does not have the animal as the pedagogical target that is to be educated. Rather, the aim is to educate the human sensorium through an aesthetic intervention design. The ideal leader of this intervention design is no longer the rational, self-sufficient or a disentangled Man who has the *power over* others, but the human being radically entangled with the world and with the ability to respond and thereby the *power to do* something (Raffnsøe 2013).

OUTLINE OF THE CHAPTER

To zoom in on the specificities of how interspecies pedagogy might affect human participants, we in the following take our point of departure in three smaller written snapshots from the auto-ethnography of one of the authors of this chapter who has attended equine-human leadership laboratories. We blend her close-ups with written excerpts of lasting impressions made by former human participants in similar labs. We end the chapter by speculating about the material through the concepts of differential attunement, auto-affection and interspecies ethics.

The analysis builds on an auto-ethnography as well as documents and media representations of horses and equine-assisted leadership programmes.[2] In addition, we include observations made in 2019 at a one-day session with a group of public managers attending a course as well as the informal e-mail feedback from the participants.

To counter possible unfair prejudice and accusation that what takes place in the leadership learning laboratories can be regarded as mere exceptional exercises pursued by the few as a mainly enjoyable pastime, the chapter starts out by situating the material within a larger social and theoretical setting. The following section describes how the affective relationships developed in the leadership learning laboratories not only moves decisively beyond well-established and leading conceptions and practices of leadership but also presents a more adequate response to the Anthropocene predicament that life on Earth presently faces. The following section then further fleshes out how the interspecies entanglement in the human-equine leadership learning labs differs from traditional leadership settings and learning laboratories. Subsequently, the specific characteristics and affective potentials of the human-equine relationship as developed in the human-equine leadership learning labs is described by contrasting it, on the one hand, with other kinds of interspecies relations and learning labs and, on the other hand, with traditional relationships between humans and horses and inherited conceptions of management.

Centred on the auto-ethnographical snapshots and utterances from other participants at the labs, the following three sections provide a detailed articulation of the experiences with the affective outcome of

---

[2] Parts of the analysis have previously been published in Staunæs and Raffnsøe (2018). This chapter differs from the previous article insofar as we focus less on affects and more upon dis/affecting Man's project in the Anthropocene as well as the interspecies intra-action and its potential for leadership in the Anthropocene. This is originally developed for this book.

interspecies intra-action. While being an intervention design opening the body and amplifying the sensorium as well as allowing for connection, response and mutual interest, the leadership laboratory also emphasizes mutual entanglement and permits the participants to breathe together.

Taking the empirical experiences made in the horse-pen laboratory to the next level, the final sections ask: What may the interspecies pedagogy involving horses teach us and how may it challenge Man's project as well as established human ways of relating to and managing other beings? What are the theoretical and ethical implications of the experiences made in the horse pen?

NEW KINDS OF NON-HUMAN-CENTRED LEADERSHIP

If one departs from a broadly inclusive understanding of leadership as the ability to do or effect something, and more specifically do so by exercising power (Dahl 1957; Morriss 1987/2002) in ways that point ahead and have the capacity to affect other beings and thereby make them behave in ways different from their previous or usual behaviour (Raffnsøe 2013; Raffnsøe and Staunæs 2014), leadership can obviously be expected to have a decisive role to play in a contemporary context characterized by a number of radical and even life-threatening challenges. The right kind of leadership would be able to respond to global grand challenges as well as to other pressing issues in ways that indicate a passable way out of present predicaments (Kramer et al. 2020).

Across areas such as leadership, management, organizational studies and motivational theory change management has for more than 50 years been regarded as a crucial approach and ideal when leadership and management sought to respond adequately to the challenges presented by a constantly evolving environment and related acute experiences of shock, grief or freezing (Lewin 1948; McGregor 2006) by creating a sense of urgency (Kotter 2012). As 'the capacity to marshal resources, lay out plans, program work, and spur effort' (Hamel 2007, p. x), management and leadership is here concerned with leading a culture of change that is decisive for a nation's, an organization's, a group of people's, or an individual's ability to anticipate and stay ahead of time in a context that is already precarious and moving. In 'the age of upheaval', 'a world of accelerating change' where 'change is unrelenting, pitiless, and occasionally shocking', 'a world of unrelenting and unprecedented challenges', presently leading approaches to leadership and management thus aim to effect human responses that are 'passionate', 'resilient and daring' (Hamel and Zanini 2020, pp. 6, 14–16).

Whereas presently leading conceptions of leadership, such as change management, thus seek to rise and respond to contemporary challenges in anticipatory ways by relying on and inspiring, facilitating and developing more fully and resilient versions of the human, the very focus on creating and expanding a space for a more humane 'humanocracy' and 'putting it into action' (Hamel and Zanini 2020) implies that even the most presently prominent ideas of leadership are not sufficiently on par with the radical and monumental challenges presented by the present Anthropocene predicament.

The designation 'the Anthropocene' has increasingly won a place in geological literature. This age distinguishes itself from all previous aeons in the history of the Earth, since it is the epoch in which the impact of collective human activity has acquired paramount importance and in which human activity has decisively begun to affect geological sedimentation around Earth.

Whereas the Holocene, the most recent geological epoch during which the human species proliferated and spread worldwide for 11,700 years, seems to have been climatically the most stable period in the history of the Earth so far, the Anthropocene is characterized by a new, accentuated instability and unpredictability. As global warming renders graphic, the human significantly effects the home planet of human beings so drastically that not only heat and drought but also flooding may come. In consequence of human influence, the ground on which humankind has stood is quaking. After beginning to congratulate themselves with finally being allotted the principal part at centre stage of their local scene, humans suddenly seem to become affected and troubled as they discover that what they used to consider merely the environment of their performance begins to play an active role.

No longer to be perceived as an indulgent and stable framework for human activity, life and nature on Earth in the Anthropocene has increasingly begun to appear as a large, irritable and easily excitable physical and animated being that is susceptible, reacting and responding vehemently; may be even erupting in violent outbursts at time. While the human species has taken on a colossal size, the world has equally also taken on overarching, even unsurvivable proportions.

On closer inspection, then, the Anthropocene is not only the realization of human influence. Concomitantly, it implies an acute recognition that the lives of human beings are embedded in, constantly depend upon and only come to play a role within a continuous exchange and intra-action with a larger constantly evolving globe containing life on Earth (Raffnsøe 2015, 2022) and that human earthlings still need to come to terms with this experience, not only in general but also in particular with regard to the ways in which they seek to exercise leadership and create value (Raffnsøe 2022). Thus, the wider planetary conditions that appear with globalization, including globalized capitalism, enslavement and other implications of the realization of 'Man's project' (Wynter 2003) in the Anthropocene (Chakrabarty 2021), call for a more profound reorientation, including a confrontation with inherited anthropocentrism, in general, but also as it effects ideas and conceptions of human leadership in the Anthropocene.

When starting to think about how to understand and practise leadership as the ability to do or effect something, and more specifically do so by exercising power in ways that point ahead and have the capacity to affect other beings and thereby make them behave in ways differing from their previous or usual behaviour, human earthlings must start by thinking of themselves as acting *within* the Earth system and *with* other beings on Earth, instead of clinging to the idea that the only agency is human agency (Raffnsøe 2022).

Interspecies Leadership Pedagogies

With new ideals of responsive and responsible leadership come new signposts for the affective pedagogy upon which the training of sensing and wondering is based. Here the horse laboratorium enters as an experimental field for transforming leaders' attitudes and perception, and the experiments are meant to encourage leaders to contribute to other world-makings. Experimenting with different kinds of affective pedagogies and reconfiguring the interspecies relations are promising in this regard (Kelly 2014).

There are different intervention designs and different ways horses are supposed to help develop leadership. Some equine-assisted programmes remain more attached to anthropocentric paradigms of steering, grooming and dressage. The ability to ride on horseback and hold the reins firmly to control the horse signals power and authority; and, for centuries, princes and kings have practised horse riding to acquire the skills required for the art of ruling.

The ones we focus upon build on (more or less reflected) philosophies of Indigenous American horsemanship and different kinds of equine-assisted therapy. The aim of these labs is to benefit from cultivating the human ability to listen to the animal, learning to accept responsibility, taking care of oneself and others, showing patience, humility, pride and appreciating the joys of life.

Significantly, one does not learn to ride the horse at these labs but is taught to stand on the ground beside the horse and to stay grounded together with the horse. Rather than recurring to talks and reflexivity, which have previously been among the most utilized educational tools in management learning, the kind of equine-human experiments we explore, are supposed to adjust and recalibrate the leader's ways of sensing and perceiving the world through embodied, outdoor encounters. Encountering a horse pen as an affective pedagogical setting means to enter a space with other rules, other habits, other cosmogonies and other repertoires of how to relate to other living creatures than those an 'ordinary' leader normally meets daily. The horse, the horse pen and the round manège function as sensorial amplifiers of receptive forms of coming into being.

The leadership learning laboratory takes the form of a specific assemblage or the construction of a particular affective arrangement, which in turn serves as 'a format or "protocol" for exploring and testing forms of life' (Marres 2012). The laboratories serve as experimental arrangements in which a provisional existence can be felt, tried out and engaged with in ways that permit the invention new life forms and social worlds (Knudsen et al. 2019).

Several horse studies (Birke and Hockenhull 2015; Birke et al. 2010) challenge anthropocentric designs and decentre the human by observing and filming how the horses participate in horse-human partnerships. The experiments we have explored go beyond visual methodologies. They configure the leader as a kind of seismographic device able to be affected by the affective beats, rhythms and intensities that emerge due to the intra-action between different affective-discursive material arrangements involving different tools, soil, wind circulations, paddocks, horses, leaders, coaches, robes, voices, horsetails, skins, senses, learning objectives, grass, sun, snowsuits, philosophies, mirror-neurons and so forth.

Interspecies Companionship: Peregrines Versus Horses

As Eve K. Sedgwick (2003) and others identify, human-animal encounters may assist us in non-dualistic pedagogical approaches. Different interspecies relations allow for different pedagogies and evoke different kinds of affects.

Equally, different animals (the lion, the peregrine and the horse to mention a few interesting examples) symbolize different forms of rulers, governing, governance and management, and thereby bring us different languages and words for interspecies pedagogies. Flying, thinking and feeling with a peregrine falcon may enable leaders to formulate questions and responses concerning leadership, governance or management in a certain manner, since the bird and predator embodies certain ways of existence, of moving about and relating. For example, the peregrine falcon emblematically embodies a view from the sky and an overview from above. When thinking about peregrines, we often move directly to the act of hunting. Perhaps we get an acute sense of attacking a prime prey, a starling maybe, with accelerated speed and precision. The affects that pop up here are high intensities of life and death, hunt, hunger, fear, attacking and killing.

Bracketing semiotics, the figure of the peregrine will allow us to feel the how of being entangled with and conditioned by the atmosphere. Flying, thinking and feeling with a peregrine allow us to challenge the 'anthro' in the Anthropocene (Massumi 2018) and to think in a more-than-human manner. We could close our eyes for a minute and allow ourselves to think of the air that envelops the peregrine and allows it to skydive and fall freely, to swirl and work with the turbulences of air: The atmosphere in the sky that facilitates the mode of flying and soaring, the way the particles in the air float through the wings and feathers. Perhaps on the hunt or perhaps in playful ways as when eagles like peregrines soar in the air to find new winds that may carry them up or permit them to stay still in the air. If we get the opportunity to skydive with peregrines, we may get access to an 'education of the senses' involving more than the eye, the hunt, the killing, the speed, more than absolute life and absolute death, perhaps joy and relationality.

Flying with a peregrine permits a shift in ordinary distributions of power and knowing positions. It is, however, extremely difficult and expensive to fly with peregrines. Similarly, new sorts of intra-actions with domesticated animals may help us deconstruct the god trick of not-situated knowledge (Haraway 1991). Simultaneously domesticated horses may be promising companions in this endeavour of entrainment (Game 2001; Patton 2003). Using a horse as a companion species (Haraway 2008) to feel and think with opens up affective and mental spaces that differ from peregrine-human spaces. This does not necessarily happen in the form of a total transfer to an unknown desolate wilderness but rather as a queering of the ordinary ways of dealing with the world (Staunæs and Raffnsøe 2018), a queering that allows us to question anthropo-, ego- and ethno-centric aspects of being, relating and leading in the Anthropocene.

Etymologically and culturally, there is a close connection between (self) management, leadership and horses. In all likelihood, the modern term 'management' is derived from the Italian word *maneggiare*, 'to handle and train horses' (Hammond 2016, p. 133), and influenced by the French *manège*, meaning 'horsemanship'. The primary signification of the English term 'manage' in the sixteenth century was to 'put (a horse) through the paces of the manège' (Concise Oxford English Dictionary 2009, p. 866). In turn, the French and Italian terms ultimately go further back to the Latin word *manus*, signifying 'hand' (Lewis 1999). Etymologically, the term 'management' thus indicates the art of training or directing a horse by holding its reins in the hand. Immediately, this points to the activity of supervising, controlling and disciplining the animal while one holds the reins in the manège; but similar activity may occur while one travels on horseback or by carriage.

Paintings and statues show us that horses, for centuries, have been among the chosen accessories for showing the imperial power of princes and kings. It is obviously not this kind of ruling force that equine-human sessions are interested in promoting. At the leadership learning laboratory, the horses are not carriers of kings or signs of absolute monarchy but presented as 'four-legged colleagues' and 'animal coaches' with their own pedagogical raison d'être. They are staged as 'new creatures of imagined possibilities' (Haraway 2008) and interactions with horses promise an alternative place for learning the art of leadership.

AMPLIFYING THE SENSORIUM AND OPENING THE BODY

When asked about which particular experiment with interspecies pedagogy that impressed some of the human participants who have attended the equine-human leadership laboratory, several of them point specifically to an exercise on attunement with the horse in the field. The impression lasting after the event is described as 'A deep, internal silence in the moment', 'The demand of being and staying present and in the moment', 'authenticity', 'a strong feeling of connection when listening and not letting oneself get disturbed by blurred outer impressions'. But before turning to this exercise, let us walk into a horse pen that amplifies the sensorium and open up the body in ways helpful for interspecies pedagogies:

> While interviewing one of the coaches at the ranch, we walked across the green grazing grounds and entered a horse circus ring, a round enclosure. Being the standard size for a horse circus ring with a diameter of 13 meters and a high wooden fence, the ring gave the horse the best conditions for using the centrifugal force in exercises. Besides conditioning the psychical presence of the horse and rider, the system was also a sort of echo chamber, amplifying and multiplying the sounds of human voices, horse neighs, moving bodies, sand, wind, and air: I was hit by the difference between the soundscapes of the field and the manège. In the field, my voice seemed to melt into the air. In the manège, by contrast, my voice was thrown back and forth with such intensity that I felt the echoing, doubling, tripling of sounds as a stab in my chest.
>
> It was mind-blowing. The sound waves started in one direction but multiplied and felt as if they were coming in their hundreds, from all directions and in increasingly new patterns of interference. I was overwhelmed and sensed the auditory intensity as a tonal penetration of space and being. I could close my eyes and shut out the visual sensations, but I did not have a mechanism for closing my ears. Only hands or perhaps earmuffs could help me cut the connection and protect me from being touched by the sound waves. This soundscape hit me deeply and altered my perception of my size and being. Fascinated, I lowered my voice. I raised it. I experienced how the spoken language and linguistic meanings were suspended while sounds and rhythms were exaggerated. When I left the ring and walked out into the grazing ground, I felt changed. I was beginning to experience and know the world differently.

The organizational soundboard is seldom the focus. The example with the amplification of sound makes us feel how sensations are deeply intertwined with the matter and milieu that organizations are made of. The entanglement of ring/manège, voices and bodies allowed an experience of multimodalities. The fold acted as an amplifier for old wisdom already known: Listening and sensing is a different kind of knowing. An intensity as a vibe. A shock. Through the chest. Through the gut or the disturbance of bodily balance. Not necessarily as a tone, but as a rhythm and vibrations made, the sounds of the ring arrangement allowed the researcher's body to enter into new openings and be capable of being affected. It became possible to listen not only through the ears but through the entire bodily and sensorial apparatus.

This capability to be affected by sound emerged in this experiment through a specific entanglement normally used to train a horse's ability to join the herd and move in circles at a fast pace, yet, here, it entered into an experiential choreography of voice hearing and voice use. The material environment of the circus ring mattered and invoked a refined sensational awareness that helped open the human body; but as the next experiment demonstrates, awareness in itself does not ensure a new way of wondering or connecting.

EMPHASIZING MUTUAL ENTANGLEMENT

If leadership then, as we defined it in the beginning of the chapter, is about setting a direction to make sure others are conducting their projects in the right way, successful interspecies pedagogy demands a responsive animal but also a human able to be responsive and take responsibility for the relationship:

> I attended a session with two human coaches and five horses. We went out to the grazing ground where one of the human coaches asked me to choose and contact a horse. Preferably, the human coach suggested, another one than the big, beautiful, white gelding we had worked with in the previous session. The coach did not define 'contact', but repeated from the last session that I was not allowed to enter the pen or to touch the chosen horse with my hands. I chose a black mare grazing peacefully close to the fence. Contact? I am good at getting in contact with people, I thought, but I have had only few experiences with horses. Standing outside the fence, I talked. I called out to the mare. I clapped. I jumped. I tried in any manner to draw attention to myself. The horse's ears stayed alert. They kept turning like small aerials following the sounds of my actions; however, I felt that nothing happened. No contact? Remembering the amplification of sensations in the horse ring, I changed track. Instead of voicing my existence and acting out, I tried to become smaller. I began looking at the horse. I glanced. I stared. I felt nothing happened. I did it for minutes. I did more of the same. For an hour. Still no reply. I could not motivate the horse to care about me. I was ready to jump over the fence and place myself on the horse's back! At the

end of the session, the mare lifted her tail and deposited horse droppings on the grazing ground. At a slow pace, she turned to her fellow horses and left me at the side. Contact? What a companion!

Next week, the patient human coach asked me to try again to establish what she termed 'an energetic relation' with the same mare. I tried through empathically hailing, staring, and just standing. No contact. The human coach asked me to "stay in the moment and think less". As she said: "Nobody is interested in someone who is not interested in them". What did she mean? I was furious. I was very interested in getting in contact with this horse! I tried again, and nothing happened. Eventually, the coach asked me to close my eyes and lie down flat in the grass. Twenty minutes passed before I sensed the earth tremble. Not as an earthquake, but as small stabs of the sound of grazing through my entire body. I was in contact with a horse interested in and doing its favourite thing: grazing.

What may this interspecies pedagogy teach the human participant about why she missed the contact in the first place? Success demands an intervention design allowing the horse to utter its interest. It is not just a matter of picking the right companion species. Additionally, it is to acknowledge the design of the research situation itself and how the 'animal-figure' is made of the situation.

By re-reading a range of experiments with rats, starlings and parrots, Vinciane Despret manages to show how animal experiments always imply interspecies pedagogies. Following up upon the issue of designing experiments concerning how rats (and lab directors) learn, Vinciane Despret (2016) makes an argument for what we call interspecies pedagogies when she asks, 'What would animals say if we asked the right questions?' Despret argues that experiments are often designed in a way that only allows the animal to answer in one way and prohibits other modes of responding. In order to be moved and respond the animal needs a relationship. What really motivates is not just a piece of cheese (as rats are often given), a peanut (as starlings are fed with) or a carrot (as horses are given). Discussing the classical experiments of behavioural conditioning devised by, for instance, B. F. Skinner and Ivan Pavlov, Despret writes that the entire device is carried out in such a way that it blocks the possibility that the animal could show how he takes a position with respect to what is asked of him. The funny thing, Despret writes, is that after a failed experiment, many animals succeed in what they were asked about in the experiment. After the experiment, mutual interest and non-purified ways of asking seem to evolve, and then the animal is able to answer in his own habits and through other registers. Getting the animal to answer is not a matter of a 'ruse' but a matter of caring for the mutual relationship and building a responsive design allowing the other to become interesting: of interest is the person who makes someone or something else capable of becoming interesting (Despret 2016). Interspecies learning experiments is then, Despret declares, not about revealing tricks or triggers but to think of the lab as real-world practice in which a pedagogical relation must be established and its shifting pulse, rhythms and intensities are cared for, fabricated, twisted, negotiated and followed—over time. 'Interest needs to be built' (Despret 2016, p. 95).

Quoting and rephrasing Iren Pepperberg's learning experiments with parrots, Despret writes:

> This makes the exercise all the more demanding, as it requires cunning and tact, cunning and care. The attunement between tutor and student will be all the more subtle, all the more fitting: slowing down when it gets difficult, speeding up to avoid boredom, intensifying the interaction to ensure ... that the effects of learning are as close as possible to what would happen in the real world, namely, the ability to obtain things and influence others. (Despret 2016, p. 96)

Interest implies a sincere relatedness, which is not to be forced and is not a one-way relation done 'my way' (Despret 2004). In the beginning of the second horse-leader experiment, the researcher did not actually query the horse; why should the horse then answer? The human participant, who was worried about not getting in contact (and thereby not performing well), stuck to already proven (human) notions of contact such as glancing and friendly chatting, the woman who was desperately seeking calmness in the grass grasped a vibe and followed a rhythm. Perhaps this triggered an energetic connection.

In the experiment, a shift suddenly took place from seeing to sensing. Perhaps the (forced) primate of vision made it difficult to be (or stay) in contact. In contrast to human eyes, the eyes of a horse are placed on each side of the head and have horizontally elongated pupils. While peregrine falcons are predators, horses are prey animals that watch the world panoramically with a minimum of blind spots. Without even moving its head, a horse has a sight radius of 360 degrees. Looking into its eye may cause it to fear or flee; in some cases, it may just freeze. Staring may not support a contact zone but rather a division zone. Letting go (even shortly) of the ocular-centric ways of making contact may open other ways of relating. Behaving attentively and training a capacity to let go of already established practices permitted a trans-corporeal energetic relation across species. Based on several studies we argue that horses are brilliant 'companion species' (Haraway 2008) at leadership development programmes (Kelly 2014; Maurstad et al. 2013), due to 'their effective reflection of people's energy levels, leadership, and communication capabilities but in particular, they have been found to be extraordinary at evaluating the legitimacy of a leader' (Pentecost 2017, p. 10).

The lesson for the researcher from this experiment might be to co-design a setting that makes one able to give a sensorial *response* rather than just produce a sensorial reaction (Despret 2004): 'learning to be carried along in the flow, learning to become in tune with or in the train of' (Game 2001, p. 3).

An Almost Cellular Experience

In the following weeks, I was expected to 'get in contact' with and 'create an energetic relation' with the mare again. And it actually happened but in a different sense than the grazing experiment. These moments of contact took place in a square pen of sand surrounded by a low fence. Before entering, we had practiced a guided meditation to get 'out of the head and into the body' as the human coach explained to me. While seeing purple and yellow colours behind my eyelids, I sensed cells and bubbles in frozen yet moving forms in my stomach. Something called upon me in my solar plexus. I was asked to bring this sensation with me into the horse pen and to the waiting mare, Romany. Walking into the pen, approaching Romany, with my eyes still closed, I sensed some tiny movements in my body. Touching the horse with my hands was now allowed, but it was suggested that eyes remained closed: I went into the pen followed by the two human coaches. I had closed my eyes, but the human coaches prevented me from standing or getting behind the horse and thereby at risk of being kicked. I had an experience of what the coach might term energetic relations. It was almost a cellular experience. It was the sensation of being relaxed, of loosening every tiny joint, every little bone, from my feet, knees, elbows, shoulders, back, neck, and hips. It felt like click, click, and click, piece by piece. I was standing in the same spot and in the same posture for what felt like an eternity. I was swaying, bending like a cornstalk with the wind. Almost falling. But I didn't, due to the supportive connection between us. As if there was a kind of air pressure preventing my collapse. I sensed the air stemming from the breath of the horse, and I joined the rhythm: Sucking in the air, expelling the air, sucking in the air, expelling it. We were breathing together.

Behind my eyelids, I saw images of cells, hair, bubbles; and in my entire body, I felt the images of horse skin, the thickness of hair from a mane, droplet-shaped cell membranes, fluids, lights, atoms. It was a weird sensation of gliding slowly in and between all those elements, of connectedness and infinity; and it made me invoke the atmosphere of everything's connectedness and infinity in the ending 'Jupiter and beyond infinity' of the science fiction film *2001: A Space Odyssey by Stanley* Kubrick from 1968. The horse danced around me, nudged my back and my neck and I—still with eyes closed—just surrendered to the situation. Trusting the animal and the two human coaches. The vibrations of the big animal massaged new sensations into my body, new thoughts into my mind. With its muzzle, the horse touched and pushed me in my lower back as if massaging my infiltrated psoas. I allowed myself to open up to what seemed really unfamiliar, uncanny, and weird—being touched by, rather than touching, the creature.

The human seismograph witnesses something about developing a capability of relating differently. What seems most striking is the experience of learning to not only touch but become touchable, to be able to be touched and feel the touch. To not only respond but to become able to respond and feel the response, to become response-able, as Karen Barad (2012) puts it. This term helps us understand how the successful interspecies pedagogy both demands and aims to contribute to an 'energetic relation' that constitutes 'response-able' students who allow themselves to be affected and not simply ruling nor being reactive.

This interspecies pedagogy allows the human to experience hitherto unknown affective zones, as she is gradually moved from prioritizing the faculty of seeing to being primarily affected by the auditory senses as well as the sense of balance, of being grounded. It was a situation of being attuned by the horse but also of becoming more aware of oneself, yet in a different manner. Through this attunement, the researcher moved in unpredictable directions, and it initiated a kind of embodied experience of being radically intertwined with another creature and at the same time changed.

In the grazing experiment, the relation between human and horse morphed from an encounter of separate corpuses to the feeling of an entangled vibrant creature. This animated her to hesitate and stay in the feeling of the situation without immediately acting on or manipulating the situation in ways that would permit her to distance herself and phase out.

Listening here is to become smaller, more sensational, to fall into the pulsation and rhythms of other bodies and of the landscape of the fold. Going with the sensation allowed the researcher to leave behind the horse and the human as separate beings and thereby to feel, think, wonder and ask from within—rather than from above or from outside.

LEARNED LESSONS

What may the interspecies pedagogy involving horses teach us? Several issues pop up if one takes a closer look at the informal feedback survey that the human coach received. Feedback e-mails stress: 'I am convinced that other tools than horses could be used, however, it works with exactly horses!'; 'The horse helped me brush out my leadership challenges'; 'The strength is the concrete experiences [with horses] because it demands other and not tried outsides of yourself'; 'The horse's response enlarged my own sensations. In this sense, the companionship with the horse is a physical manifestation of emotional parts of my personal leadership practices and priorities.'

When encountering and adjusting to a much larger not necessarily predictable animal in the horse pen, the human participants thus feel forced to open up different registers of sense and attention. While usually relying on remote senses, such as sight, they increasingly begin to return to senses where one is in close or direct contact and where it is difficult to cut connections such as touch, taste and smell.

In this way, they become aware that being constantly connected and feeling continuously affected is essential if one is to respond on par to a challenging situation in which one is placed with other beings. Concomitantly, however, they realize that the ability to sense in this manner is not a matter of course. It presupposes a capability and an active effort to tune into and accord attention to other beings and the ways they pay attention to the exchange that they share (Haraway 2003; Despret 2019). In the established intra-action with a not large and volatile but also very sensitive and attentive equine animal, this point becomes particularly accentuated.

In the horse pen where the necessity of listening attentively, sensing and becoming smaller in order to engage actively and adequately is evident, the idea and practice of a self-contained white, liberal, unbiased, enlightened subject possessing the prerogative of privileged agency becomes strikingly inadequate. Precisely by taking refuge to what seemed at first foreign to her, the researcher in unison with other participants consented to give up the privileged position of sovereignty and privileged agency and at first experienced a somewhat unpleasant loss of control. In the long run, however, she managed to go to places that she would not have been able to visit and to achieve something that she would not have been able to do on her own, had she not been prepared to confide in her equine companion and the prospects of the outcome of an exchange with other beings. She distanced herself from a traditional phallic conception of leadership as the capacity to bring about a particular result directly by a simple act of the will (Raffnsøe 2013, p. 254). Precisely by avoiding expressing herself in the form of direct potency, she managed to express and regain herself in indirect and mediated ways that she could not herself have foreseen.

Leadership labs of the kind described here can be crucially important for leaders. Whereas experiences in this setting permit them to develop stamina when faced with unpleasant loss of control and risk-taking, they concomitantly get the feel of the richly rewarding intra-actional processes. It may be of primary importance for leaders to be able to draw upon these kinds of experiences with taking leads in interspecies already when they return to and try to lead in traditional human organizational political contexts. Yet, in a contemporary Anthropocene setting where life and nature on Earth has increasingly begun to appear as a large, irritable and easily excitable physical and animated being that is susceptible, reacting and responding vehemently, such experiences with interspecies intra-action and leadership that respects dispersion of agency, such experiences with leadership in leadership learning labs may become even more crucial.

EXPERIENCES AND IMPLICATIONS

Let's finally make some theoretically informed speculations concerning the reflections from the participants as well as the auto-ethnographic snapshot to point out interesting key features that appear as leaders experiment with and experience interspecies pedagogies.

As indicated by Lisa Blackman (2012), attunement should not be conceived as the mere process of automatic imitation but rather as a process of moving with and through affectivity that involves 'the sending of rapid and automatic or involuntary forms of non-verbal communication' to others (Blackman 2012, p. 82). Attunement is a kind of energetic exchange; circulation and transmission among human as well as non-human bodies (recall the scene where the horse pushed the leader around). The researcher is not just attuning to the horse. The horse is not just attuning to the researcher. They are attuning to one another and becoming a me-and-horse in this process of what Brian Massumi (2015) calls 'differential attunement'. In addition, attunement involves a shift of modality. The perception of the grazing horse made clear that differential attunement involves selective imitation, making it possible to switch from one modality to a different modality (for instance, from observing action to not only hearing but feeling sound).

Secondly, the sensation from the horse-leader surprises the researcher, insofar as the differential or differing attunement results in a renewed self-awareness and possibility of touching oneself. This experience may be characterized as auto-affection. According to Jacques Derrida and Patricia Clough, auto-affection implies turning oneself towards oneself, but in an awareness of oneself as one affected by others and affected by being affected (Derrida 1976, p. 235; Clough 2000).

It involves sensing how one is being moved and how one succeeds in transforming oneself. In Barad's terminology, listening to, sensing and being touched by the other are also to 'intra-act' (2012). It is to be response-able, by designing a setting that makes one able to respond and to let responses received from others be felt (see also Despret 2004). The human participant in the experiment was not aware in advance that sensing the horse grazing could be an energetic relation or the contact required; however, the experiment cultivated a capability to dare to resist human exceptionalism in educational encounters (Hohti and MacLure 2021), care for the horse and her own presence in ways not expected.

INTERSPECIES ETHICS

When entering this kind of 'unexpected land', one continuously runs the risk of romanticizing the alternative places and conceiving them as protected, privileged areas or reservations in stark contrast to the places already known (Hvenegård-Lassen and Staunæs 2015). If not carefully conducted and conceived, sensing with horses and working with Indigenous American philosophy on natural horsemanship could become yet another instrumental device whereby the 'promising creature' is turned into a prosthesis for (White Western) human researchers with the purpose/effect of simply enlarging the scope of an assemblage centred around the human. The danger is that training affective capabilities may become a kind of inverse paternalism in the pater/manager, while

88 D. STAUNÆS AND S. RAFFNSØE

pretending to minimize himself, mutates and absorbs the other while still exercising 'power over' what is managed.

This interspecies pedagogy breaks open the traditional pedagogical relationship that though inviting in animal others in processes of becoming seems to privilege the human as the knower/educator and consequently focuses on guidance of the horse, attention and application (Hagström 2016).

In our case, given to other pressing issues, the pedagogical issue is to experience learning processes where the animal is the educator and that illuminate how and what humans may become. Consequently, new openings must be repeated and the experiments run repeatedly.

If the laboratory and the experiment, as suggested, are always entangled with the world and realities worked upon, affective pedagogies involving more-than-human encounters as a road to 'learning to be affected' call for an interspecies ethics of care that also involves the possibilities of *not* listening and *not* attuning. An ethics that also allows foreclosure for the human, non-human as well as the more-than-human. As one of the above experiments showed, the horse was capable of refusing to be available to uninterested and unworthy relations, and the pedagogical setting assisted precisely this refusal and the 'disruptive power of choosing not to care about what we are enjoined to' (Woolf 1996, cited by Maria Puig de la Bellacasa 2017, p. 5) or invited into. A laboratory employing aesthetics and affects that amplifies sensations, cultivates mutual entanglements and allows us to breath together must permit ongoing evaluation and decline experiments that may create harmful and poisonous worldmakings. Sensorial experiments involving animals as well as humans need an ethics of cutting connections: an ethics of not just becoming and transforming, but also of *not* connecting (like that), *not* becoming (like that), *not* transforming (like that). In other words, interspecies ethics must include what Fred Moten and Stefano Harney (2013) call 'the refusals of refusals', to refuse interpellation that does not fit, that does harm or/and hurts. This means that ethically sound interspecies pedagogies must design an intervention for leadership in planetary futures, which implies the possibility of refusing interpellations based on not knowing, not responding upon and not respecting one another (Moten and Harney 2013).

Acknowledgement Many thanks to the horses and humans (especially Romany, Lucas and associate professor Sølvi Degnegaard) for making possible experience with, observations and speculations of interspecies intra-action and learning.

REFERENCES

Barad, K. (2012). On touching: The Inhuman that therefore I am. *Differences: A Journal of Feminist Cultural Studies,* 23(3), 206–223.

Birke, L., & Hockenhull, J. (2015). Journeys together: Horses and humans in partnership. *Society & Animals,* 23, 81–100.

Birke, L., Hockenhull, J., & Creighton, E. (2010). The horse's tale: Narratives of caring for/about horses, *Society and Animals,* 18, 331–347.

Blackman, L. (2012). *Immaterial bodies: Affect, embodiment, mediation.* Sage.

Chakrabarty, D. (2021). *The climate of history in a planetary age.* University of Chicago Press.

Clough, P. (2000). *Autoaffection: Unconscious thought in the age of teletechnology.* University of Minnesota Press.

Concise Oxford English Dictionary. (2009). Luxury Edition. Oxford University Press

Dahl, Robert A. (1957). The concept of power. *Behavioral Science,* 2(3), 201–215.

Derrida, J. (1976). La voix et le phénomène. Introduction au problème du signe dans la phénoménologie de Husserl. Presses Universitaires de France.

Despret, V. (2004). The body we care for: Figures of anthropo-zoo-genesis. *Body & Society,* 10(2), 111–134.

Despret, V. (2016). *What would animals say if we asked the right questions.* University of Minnesota Press.

Despret, V. (2019). *Habiter en oiseau.* Actes sud.

Game, A. (2001). Riding: Embodying the centaur. *Body & Society,* 7(4), 1–12.

Hagström, E. (2016). A halter and a lead rope: Shifting pedagogical imaginaries of becoming within a human–horse relationship. *Gender and Education,* 28(2), 298–313.

Hamel, G. (2007). *The future of management.* Harvard Business School Press.

Hamel, G. & Zanini, M. (2020). *Humanocracy: Creating organizations as amazing as the people inside them.* Harvard Business Review Press.

Hammond, G. (2016). *The Language of Horse Racing.* Routledge.

Haraway, D. J. (1991). *Simians, cyborgs, and women: The reinvention of nature.* Free Associations Books.

Haraway, D. J. (2003). *The companion species manifesto: Dogs, people, and significant otherness.* University of Chicago Press.

Haraway, D. J. (2008). *When species meet.* University of Minnesota Press.

Haraway, D. J. (2016). *Staying with the trouble. Making Kin in the Chthulucene.* Duke University Press.

Hohti, R., & MacLure, M. (2021). Insect-thinking as resistance to education's human exceptionalism: Relationality and cut in more-than-human childhoods. *Qualitative Inquiry,* 1–11 (preprint).

Hvenegård-Lassen, K., & Staunæs, D. (2015). ". . . And then we do it in Norway": Learning leadership and Nordic Whiteness through affective contact zones. In R. Andreassen & K. Vitus (Eds.), *Affectivity and race: Studies from a Nordic context* (pp. 77–94). Ashgate.

Kelly, S. (2014). Horses for courses: Exploring the limits of leadership development through equine assisted learning. *Journal of Management Education*, 38(2), 216–233.

Knudsen, B. T., Stage, C., & Zandersen, M. (2019). Interspecies park life: Participatory experiments and micro-utopian landscaping to increase urban biodiverse entanglement. *Space and Culture*. https://doi.org/10.1177/1206331219863312

Kotter, J. P. (2012). *Leading Change*. Harvard Business Review Press.

Kramer, M. R., Pfitzer, M. W., & Mahne, H. (2020). How global leaders should think about solving our biggest problems. *Harvard Business Review*. https://hbr.org/2020/01/how-global-leaders-should-think-about-solving-our-biggest-problems

Lewin, K. (1948). *Resolving social conflicts*. Harper and Row.

Lewis, C. T. (1999). *Elementary Latin Dictionary*. Oxford University Press.

Marres, N. (2012). Experiment: The experiment in living. In C. Lury & N. Wakeford (Eds.), *Inventive methods: The happening of the social* (pp. 76-95). Routledge.

Massumi, B. (2015). *Politics of Affect*. Polity.

Massumi, B. (2018). Becoming-animal in the literary field. In B. Boehrer, M. Hand, & B. Massumi (Eds.), *Animals, animality, and literature* (pp. 265-283). Cambridge University Press.

Maurstad, A., Davies, D., & Cowles, S. (2013). Co-being and intra-action in horse–human relationships: A multi-species ethnography of be(com)ing human and be(com)ing horse. *Social Anthropology*, 21(3), 322–335.

McGregor, D. (2006). *The human side of enterprise*. McGraw Hill.

Mignolo, W. (2015). Sylvia Wynter: What does it Mean to Be Human? In McKittrick, K. (Ed.). Sylvia Wynter. *On being Human as Praxis*. Duke University Press.

Morriss, P. (1987/2002). *Power: A philosophical analysis*. Manchester University Press.

Moten, F., & Harney, S. (2013). *The undercommons: Fugitive planning and black study*. Duke University Press.

Patton, P. (2003). Language, power, and the training of horses. In C. Wolfe (Ed.), *Zoontologies: The question of the animal* (pp. 83-100). University of Minnesota Press.

Pentecost, A. L. (2017). The effects of equine assisted leadership programs on perceived professional development outcomes. Liberty University A Dissertation Presented in Partial Fulfillment Of the Requirements for the Degree Doctor of Education Liberty University September 20, 2017.

Puig de la Bellacasa, M. (2017). *Matters of care: Speculatives ethics in more than human worlds*. University of Minnesota Press.

Raffnsøe, S. (2013). Beyond rule: Trust and power as capacities. *Journal of Political Power*, 6(2), 241–260.

Raffnsøe, S. (2015). *Philosophy of the Anthropocene: The human turn*. Palgrave.

Raffnsøe, S., Mennicken, A., & Miller, P. (2019). The Foucault effect in organization studies. *Organization Studies*, 40(2), 155–182.

Raffnsøe S. (2022). *The Anthropocene: An All-Decisive Threshold in the History of the Earth*. Bloomsbury.

Raffnsøe, S., & Staunæs, D. (2014). Learning to stay ahead of time: Moving leadership experiences experimentally. *Management and Organizational History*, 9(2), 184–201.

Schön, D. (1991). *The reflective Practitioner. How Professionals Think in Action*. Ashgate Publishing Group.

Sedgwick, E. K. (2003). Pedagogy Buddhism. In E. K. Sedgwick (Ed.), *Touching feeling: Affect, pedagogy, performativity* (pp. 153-182). Duke University Press.

Staunæs, D., & Raffnsøe, S. (2018). Affective pedagogies, equine-assisted experiments and posthuman leadership. *Body & Society*, 25(1), 57–89.

Wynter, S. (2001). Towards the Sociogenic Principle: Fanon, Identity, the Puzzle of Experience. Duran-Cogan, M.F. and Gomez-Moriana, A. (Eds.). *National Identities and Socio-political Changes in Latin America*. Routledge.

Wynter, S. (2003). Unsettling the coloniality of being/power/truth/freedom: Towards the human, after man, its overrepresentation—An argument. *CR: The New Centennial Review*, 3(3), 257–337.

CHAPTER 5

Engines of Affect: Experimenting with Auditory Intensities in the Jamaican Sound System Session

Julian Henriques

Affect has been enjoying considerable research interest and enthusiasm in recent years. This might be because in an age of contagions memes, social media trending and "going viral," we have become more interested in connections, energies and relationalities that defy conventional epistemological classification as "objects" and thereby disciplinary boundaries. Affect calls for experimental methodologies. This chapter explores several types of experiment in the context of the Jamaican dancehall sound system scene. To do this requires leaving the academy and the controlled environment of its laboratories for the somewhat chaotic streets of Kingston—a valuable experimental setting in which new knowledge can be unearthed.[1]

---

[1] Rather than on the workbench of a university or corporate laboratory as has been investigated. See Bruno Latour and Steve Woolgar (1979).

J. Henriques (✉)
Goldsmiths, University of London, London, UK
e-mail: J.Henriques@gold.ac.uk

Firstly, the chapter adopts an experimental *practice-as-research* methodology to reveal the techniques, practices and embodied *ways-of-knowing* of the Jamaican sound system audio engineers themselves (D'Aquino et al. 2017). Their expertise covers not only matters of electronics but also affect, as they modulate auditory vibrations impacting on the bodies of the crowd (audience). This is called "building the vibes."

In the second place, amidst the popular culture of Jamaica, the open-air sound system dancehall sessions on the city streets can be considered an experimental apparatus for generating affective intensities for the crowd. Such vibrational propagation of positive affect is necessary because to survive in the ruthlessly competitive street economy of the ghetto, each sound system is obliged to attract the biggest crowd possible in the communities suffering extreme poverty and quite often violence. Central to the engineers' *ways-of-doing* is modulation of the *sounding* of their system, such as the heaviness of their bass, for instance. This testifies to the social, cultural and economic needs for which sound system dancehall sessions provide some satisfaction and respite. Building and maintaining a sound system's following often involves a different location each night "experimenting" with the tuning of the equipment according to the architecture of the outdoor venue (walls, parked vehicles etc.). The engineer also has to pay attention to the varying number of absorptive bodies making up the crowd at any one point in the night. In short, the sound system set of equipment is claimed here to be an *engine of affect*.

This leads to the third type of theoretical experimentation which is described as *thinking-through-vibrations*.[2] This can be described as the researchers' version of the engineer's *ways-of-knowing* and *ways-of-doing* insofar as each aim to capture the nature of relationships, resonances, intensities and dynamic energies of auditory propagation. Thinking-through-vibrations is cast in terms of the nomenclature of standard wave mechanics, such as the peaks and troughs of the pulsations of sound waves. This chapter argues that thinking-through-vibrations is a particularly useful way of approaching affect. The central claim is that the propagation of auditory vibrations and the transmission of affect are each best understood in terms of the standard model of wave mechanics. This says nothing new about sounding, but hopefully contributes to our understanding of affect.

---

[2] This is an approach I have developed over several years, see Julian Henriques (2010, 2014). Also, this approach has been adopted for researching other areas, see, for example, Malou Juelskjær and Dorthe Staunæs (2016).

The hypothesis is not that sounds trigger feelings—they evidently do—but that sounding and feeling are both vibratory events.

One of the attractions of the "turn to affect" has been as a turn away from the rationalistic confines of linguistic, discursive and data analytical methods. Instead, affect offers a recognition of the theoretical and methodological value of precisely the kind of flows and transient events that sounding expresses.[3] The association of music and sounding with affect has given rise to fear of each that is as ancient as civilisation itself. Plato famously banned poets and musicians from his Republic. Today understanding affect and communication has never been more urgent. Fake news, "alternative facts," QAnon paranoia and conspiracy theories trending across social media threaten to undermine the shared reality on which every society has to be based. This makes it both the best and worst moment to use affect theory to question the ideas of "knowledge" and "facts" constituted by dominant Western epistemological and ontological paradigms founded on the Enlightenment ideal of the rational individual.[4] To our great cost, neither rationalism nor individualism is at all well-equipped to address the avowedly non-rational appeal of Trumpism, for instance. Facts and information may be able to change minds, but for those who feel alienated and ignored by mainstream society the organ of change is that of affect—most definitely the heart.[5]

WORKSHOPS OF AFFECT

The small-scale workshop is where the audio engineers design, build, test and maintain their engines of affect (Fig. 5.1). This cottage industry is little less than an experimental laboratory for sounding, making it a good place to start investigating the practical nature of sounding as affect. A sound system is an assemblage of component parts, often repurposed and reconfigured in ways never envisaged by the manufacturers. This is typical of the kind of diasporic African experimental irreverence for the designed purpose of a technology; it gave us hip-hop turntablism and in Jamaica

[3] For a useful collection of essays on affect and music, see Marie Thompson and Ian Biddle (2013).

[4] The critique of the rational individual and its cleavage from the social has been a long-standing interest of mine. See Henriques (1984, 1998).

[5] Examples of current research on the limitations of a rationalistic approach would include Daniel Williams (2020) and Dan Kahan (2017).

Fig. 5.1   Jam One HQ workshop yard, Kingston, Jamaica

deejaying and reggae dub music. The workshop practices provide a valuable point of access to the engineers' *way-of-making* and *way-of-knowing* (Henriques forthcoming). The kind of craft workshop, for which Anthony Myers's Jam One HQ provides an example, has long been recognised as the site for where situated, tacit and embodied knowledge abounds.[6] It is argued here that this is precisely the kind of knowledge required to understand affect. Indeed, modulating sounding and modulating affecting, to the engineers' hands and ears, are one and the same thing, as explored in the sections that follow whereby the sound system is considered a vibratory means of affective production.

Anthony Myers, owner of Jam One sound system, cannot be described other than as a master craftsman (Sennett 2008). Since the 1980s, he has been designing and constructing sound systems, and he is now recognised as one of the leading sound men on the island, as indicated by his position as designer and builder for the internationally renowned King Jammy sound system and recording studio. The Jam One HQ yard includes a component repair workshop, a wood workshop for building the speaker boxes, a testing area for the assembled sound and a bar (detailed in Henriques forthcoming). Myers has several engineers and apprentices in his workshop providing them with the classic workshop learning environment originally established with the craft guilds in Medieval Europe and Asia (Lave and Wenger 1991). Each sound system set of equipment is more or less unique, according to the personal style and taste of the owner who commissioned it.

Not surprisingly the engineers' *ways-of-knowing* required for sounding and affecting fall outside—or, more to the point, have been pushed beneath—dominant regimes of scientific rationality. They have, however, received a certain amount of recognition for example with Michel Foucault's concept of subjugated knowledges, Gilles Deleuze and Félix Guattari's of nomad science and Boaventura de Sousa Santos's of epistemologies of the south. Their aim, Santos states, "is to identify and valorise that which often does not even appear as knowledge in the light of the dominant epistemologies, that which emerges instead as part of the

[6] It is important for me to acknowledge that my understanding of sound system engineering has been derived directly from the audio engineers with whom I have been in conversation over many years. Besides Anthony Myers, I should name Winston "WeePow" Powell, Denton Henry and the late Horace McNeal, each of whom I thank for their generosity of time and knowledge.

struggles of resistance against oppression and against the knowledge that legitimates such oppression" (Santos 2018, p. 2). This "provincializing," to use Dipesh Chakrabarty's term, of white, male metropolitan knowledge systems, provides a framework for a conceptual alliance between sounding and affecting at the core of the present vibrational analysis (Chakrabarty 2000).

Sound system audio engineering involves an experimental attitude, as it is the root source of so much innovation. As the saying goes "every spoil is a style," in other words, mishaps are creative. Designs have been refined over many decades on the basis of an aesthetic dictated by the necessities of local conditions and availabilities. It is in this manner that Jamaican recording studios were assembled in the 1970s, such as, most famously, the late Lee "Scratch" Perry's Black Ark studio. In both instances such practical limitations inspired considerable creativity—sufficient to invent the hugely influential reggae genre of dub—which is in fact precisely the music sound systems were specifically designed to play. Sound system engineering techniques include a methodology of experimental trial and error and "tinkering" as Headley Jones, the inventor of the sound system (2010, p. 122), describes it. This affords the opportunity for Myers to "buck up a specs," as he would say, that is, bump into a specification (for a speaker box design).[7] Engineers like Myers work from what they can hear, rather than component manuals or what they might have learnt from electronic engineering textbooks. They are truly connoisseurs of sound, and I would add, affect.

SOUND AFFECTS AND SOUND FX

The relationship between auditory vibrations and those of affect is well-recognised in the engineers' working practices to the extent that it can be said they modulate the sounding of the set to modulate the affective mood of the crowd. The engineers would not think in terms of the concept of affect, but rather of the term "vibes" commonly used to describe the feeling of an atmosphere. Further to this, besides their knowledge of the standard science of wave mechanics and textbook electronic engineering, the sound system men and women often have an appreciation of what is called "scyence." This is a subtle science akin to Voodoo or as it is called in

---

[7] Interview with Anthony Myers, One Jam HQ, 13 Minott Terrace, Kingston, Monday, 29 May 2017, see Henriques (forthcoming).

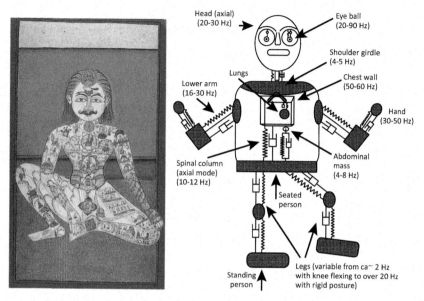

Fig. 5.2 (Left) The Subtle Body: Sapta Chakra, from a Yoga manuscript in Braj Bhasa language, 1899, British Museum, Wikimedia Commons. Note the chakras, or vibrational energy centres, descending from the crown of the head to the genitals; (right) The Gross Body: Adapted from Nina Eidsheim's *Sensing Sound: Singing and Listening as Vibrational Practice*. Durham: Duke University Press, 2015, page 173

Jamaica, Obeah (see O'Neal 2020; Paton 2017). In a global context, it can be compared with alchemy or the Eastern spiritual traditions in which the human body is conceived as a series of chakras, each with their own particular frequency of vibration (Fig. 5.2). Such traditions give a better handle on the nature and transmission of affect than that offered by Western scientific paradigms. The engineers certainly consider themselves scientists, professors and the like and calling themselves such, as with the dub producers Mad Professor or Scientist or the Birmingham-based Scientist sound system (see Jones and Pinnock 2018). The idea of vibration can thus be identified as the common denominator between standard mode, subtle scyence and affect. Sound effects (SFx), such as sirens, gunshots and reverb—providing the sonic signature of a sounds system—equate with the affects of sounding.

Sound wave mechanics are considered here to be serving as an analogue for those of mood, feeling, emotion and affect. Sounding and affecting have three common denominators. One is *intensity*, that is, their energy, weight or amplitude. With sounding, this is the pressure of pulsations through the propagating medium, intensities of affect are the pressure of feeling the lived experience of the moment. Sound waves and feelings are both forces of excitation, that is, dynamic events. Sound waves are measured in atmospheric pressure (decibels, dB) on the eardrum, for example. The excitation of affect would be the audience's engagement with an event, less easy to measure, but where the length or level of applause might serve as a proxy. Both sound and affect subscribe to a Heraclitan world view where the flux of motion is the ultimate reality, stasis the illusion. Sounds and feelings are not stable objects, or things that are consistent in space or time, but only exist in and as dynamic events. Both are sustained only as long as they have a means of production, as it were, a means of propagation, for which the dancehall sound system provides a large-scale example (Henriques 2011). As Ben Anderson puts it, "affect as a synonym for life's exuberant generativity" (Anderson 2014, p. 90). Moving is feeling moved, as with the dancers' "moves" in the session; affect can be choreographed.

With sound waves, the intensities are the wave peaks of the compression (concentration) that follow the troughs of rarefaction (expansion, relaxation) of the elastic medium of the gaseous air (Fig. 5.3). This dynamic of concentration and relaxation is central to the German phenomenologist Hermann Schmitz's understanding of affect. Schmitz identifies the central dynamic of the felt body as "the intertwined tendencies of contraction and expansion" (Schmitz 2019, p. 65) that correspond exactly to the compression and rarefication that describe sound waves. Each pulsation is a unique performed event and if not exactly an experiment, always—literally—a work in progress. Schmitz's key concept of the *felt body* is critical as it conceives of embodiment as affectively constituted, rather than it being eviscerated by the mind. As he puts it, "*The felt body (Leib*) that is neither body nor soul, but an entity which is spatially extended in a way similar to sound" (Schmitz 2002, p. 492). This approach is diametrically opposed to the standard ocularcentric privilege of the single fixed point of view. Sounding and affecting, by contrast, take place as periodic events across the three-dimensional volume of a propagational field.

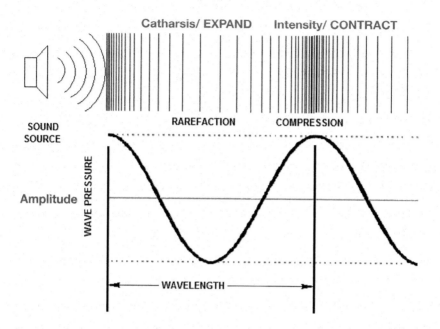

Fig. 5.3 Wave mechanics: the expansion and contraction of the medium

Defined by the energy of their motion, both sounding and affecting are invisible forces. They are evident only by their effects on what is being moved, as with an eardrum for sounding, or a person for affect. With standard wave mechanics, this is the flow of energetic pulsations that touch ear and body surface. With affect, this is the MC's extemporising flow on the mic or the dance crew in the flow of their moves, in each case often "in a zone" entirely by-passing cognitive reflection to rely on embodied techniques and practices.[8] It is important to remember it is dynamic energies that are flowing rather than the physical transport of a substantial matter as with the water of a river or wind as the blowing of gaseous air (see Henriques 2008). Moreover, the vibrational communication of affect is to be contrasted with chemical transmission and the pheromones that have been identified as affecting feelings.

---

[8] Such "flow states" have become a research topic, see Mihály Csíkszentmihályi (2008).

Amplitudes are required for the transmission, that is, propagation, of both sounding and affecting. Dynamic energies cannot stand still in one place; they have to move and spread. Sound waves propagate out in every direction from their source. Similarly, the transmission of affect is long established as a key issue. One reason for this is the notion of the free flow of feelings undermines the sanctity of the rational individual defined, at least since Descartes, as the autonomous mind. Hence the fear of the collective, the mob or the crowd that Gustave Le Bon famously articulated at the beginning of the twentieth century (Le Bon 1990). Both sounding and affect are social and have to be shared; they appear to break the laws of classical Newtonian physics that stipulate there can be no action at a distance. Of course, there are no empty spaces that sound and feeling are required to jump across, but rather the fullness of a propagating medium, as discussed below. The unsettling feature of sound and affect is their lack of boundaries; they are promiscuous, so readily transgressive.

The second common denominator between sounding and affecting is *frequency* as these intensities are never continuous, but rather periodic, running in repeating cycles, circuits, oscillations and recursions (see Henriques 2014, p. 84). The periodic motion of such varying or alternating patterns is measured as Hertz (Hz), that is, events per second, where a raising of pitch can increase intensity, or RPM (revolutions per minute), where an increase in tempo can have the same energising effect, for example. Similarly, affect is discontinuous. Feelings are described as coming in waves, surges, rushes and flushes such that we can be "overcome" and "overwhelmed" by them. There are mood swings between highs and lows, at their most extreme described as the bi-polar disorder switching between elation and depression. A continuous repetitive cycle can also increase intensities, especially when this is at low frequency and high volume, as with a heavy bassline.

The third common feature that sounding and affecting share is that neither subscribe to the idea that communication has to be about representation.[9] Brian Massumi has emphasised the pre-discursive, pre-individual nature of affect (Massumi 2002). Both sounding and affecting are highly communicative, contagious even, but neither rely on signifying systems, code or other such conventions. This undermines the privilege Aristotle accorded the visual faculty as being the purest and thereby the

[9] Shelley Trower's *Senses of Vibration* (2012) gives an excellent historical account of the concept of vibration.

most suitable basis for philosophical knowledge. Later, with the Renaissance, the single point of view of perspective provides the perfect metaphor for our visual identity (Rotman 1987). Ocularcentrism removes us from the world, in contrast to the proximate contact necessary for all the other senses. Vibrations literally shake up and even disintegrate the unitary subject.

Both sounding and affecting are directly expressive in and of themselves; they are gestural and performative, rather than denotive and conative, actual and immediate rather than mediated. Sounding and affect both make sense via the volumes of analogue variation, rather the binary differences as constructed by formal systems. Henri Lefebvre's rhythm analysis can be taken as another important example of a meaning outside of representation. Prosody is paradigmatic for both sounding and feeling. A person's speaking voice gives expression to each of us as a particular unique individual; our tone of voice communicates our feelings as the meaning of what we are saying.[10] Feelings are literally vibratory. Indeed, Gary Tomlinson in his seminal *A Million Years of Music* takes the association of feeling with pre-musical pre-linguistic sounding as the foundation of human language (Tomlinson 2015).

The propagation of vibrations of both sounding and affect is antithetical to the dominant Western philosophical tradition in terms of epistemology. Their energetic constitution undermines the primacy of knowledge being of self-identical objects for which movement is only ever an exterior force. This has been described as reification, whereby process is crystallised as product. Raymond Williams puts this succinctly: "The strongest barrier to the recognition of human cultural activity in this immediate and regular *conversion of experience into finished products* ... [this is conversion] into formed wholes rather than formative processes" (R. Williams 1977, p. 128, emphasis added). This is especially relevant for thinking-through-vibrations as expressed with the verb *sounding*, rather than the object *sound*, or as Christopher Small coined the term, *musicking*, as the entire set of activities required to stage any music event, contrasting with the conventional ideas of music as an object, such as a score or recording (Small 1998). In this vein, the verb *affecting* is more appropriate than the noun, as would be consistent with Alfred North Whitehead's process philosophy ([1929] 1969).

---

[10] Currently voice recognition software is being rolled out by banks and others as a method of confirming identity.

Furthermore, the dynamic, vibrational ontology is a marked contrast to the ontology of the dominant Western philosophical tradition founded by the isolated (rational) individual whose best weapon for achieving certainty is (Cartesian) doubt. With consciousness bottled up in the skull, its task is to reconnect with the outside world via its representation of it.[11] The senses are imagined as conduits between the outside (*res extensa*) and the inside (*res cogitans*) worlds. With vibrations, starting from the assumption of connections, relationalities and permeabilities, rather than divisions, the task then is to understand how such dichotomies are constituted. Vibrations offer one way to understand these relationalities with concepts such as feeling, emotion, impulse and affect.

Schmitz is quite specific about what is going on with such traditional divisions, calling them "*psychologistic–reductionist–introjectionist* objectification," where

> [t]he realm of experience is dissected by ascribing to each conscious subject a private inner sphere containing their entire experience. This is done, at first, under the name "soul." The external realm remaining between the souls is ground down to features of a few kinds that are ideally suited for statistics and experiments due to their intermomentary and intersubjective identifiability, measurability and selective variability. (Schmitz et al. 2011, p. 247, emphasis in original)

This is to describe the diminished, impoverished version of the body-environment relationship that to a very large extent is considered the basis of common sense, as well as philosophical and scientific understanding.

PHONOMORPHIC TECHNIQUES

The engineers' *ways-of-knowing* and *ways-of-making* are evident in the building of the means of production of vibrations, that is, the sound system set of equipment. They are also evident in the techniques engineers have developed of modulating the sounding of the music it plays. This comes down to the experimental manipulation the frequencies and amplitudes of the audio signal in such a manner as to maximise the affective intensities for the crowd. I call these phonomorphic (sound-shaping)

---

[11] Historically this has not always been the case, see Julian Jaynes (1976); Iain McGilchrist (2009).

techniques to distinguish them from the phonographic (sound-writing) instrument of the sound system itself. As a phonographic instrument, the engineers are only ever "reprocessing a product that's been processed already" as one engineer put it to me.[12] As with the reggae dub studio engineer such limitations have proved to be a major creative stimulant. Another engineer's telling comment: "We abuse equipments [*sic*], what the man makes the things to do, we ahead of it" (Henriques 2011, p. 75). This is to say, the engineers freely modify and repurpose components to suit their needs. These remarks are indicative of the experimental *ways-of-knowing* and *ways-of-making* prevailing in the Jamaican street technology. The "knowledge" that results is always provisional, rather than orthodox. It is perhaps best described in ecological terms, as with James Gibson's ecological psychology, where he talks about the "information pick-up" that an organism derives from its active exploration of the surfaces of its environment (see Gibson 1986). Knowing in this way is principally a matter of the senses and sensation, rather than signification. Such *ways-of-knowing* are equally appropriate to sounding and affecting.

In the sound system context, the engineering of sound and affect is achieved by means of three phonomorphic techniques. The first is the manipulation of volumes, not so much overall volumes levels, discussed in terms of intensities above, but the shape of the volume of an audio signal over its duration. The attack envelope of a signal, as it is known, describes the speed at which a signal reaches its peak volume and the time it takes to fade away (Fig. 5.4). This is very important for the quality of the sounding of the set as the quicker or more sudden the onset of a sound the more

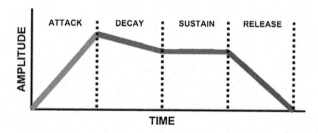

Fig. 5.4 The attack envelope of an audio signal

[12] Interview with Stone Love audio engineer Horace McNeal, at his workshop, Torrington Avenue, Kingston, 18 September 2003, quoted in Henriques (2011, p. 47).

auditory and affective impact it has (Henriques forthcoming). Suffice it to say here simply that a slow build-up of volume leading to a crescendo provides a completely different musical experience to a sudden onset crash of sound. This sharp attack is particularly important for the reproduction of the sound of percussion instruments as the engineers are well aware, aiming always to maximise the affective engagement of the crowd.

The second set of phonomorphic techniques address the *frequencies* of the audio signal, rather than its volume. The idea of filtering frequencies makes a direct correlation between sound engineering and affect engineering, such that filtering frequencies become filtering *feelings*. This is not to say that there is a direct causal relationship between a wave of sound and a wave of affect. Rather, the equation of sounding and engineering calls for the engineers' *ways-of-knowing* to be included as a key element in the circuit. This is to say, the engineers' *evaluative judgement* is required to decide which frequencies to increase and which to attenuate—this is what makes the connection between sounding and affecting. These evaluations are embodied in their skills, experience and the entire living tradition of the dancehall street culture. Without this deep tacit understanding between listener and listened there is little sense or feeling to the kind of vibrations under discussion here (as distinct from the physically violent kind, such as an earthquake).

The sound system set is designed for the engineers to have control over the frequency distribution of the audio signal by means of two key components. One way of filtering frequencies is with the EQ (graphic equaliser) that operates on the signal as a whole, boosting some frequencies and supressing others. This component is common to all PA (public address) systems, such as those used for gigs and concerts. The other is the way the engineers filter frequencies with a crossover component; this is in effect a filter gate that selects a certain frequency band for separate processing. This device is used to allow each frequency band to be amplified by its own specialist amplifiers, which can thereby work at their most efficient. This is a huge benefit for the quality and clarity of the sounding, such that each frequency has its own "space" unmuddied by others. The eight octaves of human hearing are usually split into four or five frequency bands on Jamaican systems. A PA system, on the other hand, uses only a three-way frequency split, while standard domestic systems amplify frequencies together without any separation—resulting in considerable loss of quality.[13] As the engineers are at pains to perfect, it is the qualities of the sounding that have a major positive influence on affective engagement of the crowd.

The final phonographic technique is the art of the mix, that is to say, balancing amplitude and frequency values across the auditory spectrum of the output of the set of equipment (as distinct from that of the recording studio mixing desk). This is the technique by which the engineer tunes the set, as a musical instrument has to be tuned. Each sound system has its own tone and *timbre* (sound colour) that is recognised by its hard core "followers" and easily distinguished from other sound systems.[14] Similarly, a particular saxophone or piano has its own unique auditory character, much like our own speaking makes each of us distinct. Indeed, the tuning of a sound system is often a matter of personal taste. Timbre describes the overtones and undertones of sounding, resonating with the associations and memories of affective intensities. The engineers' tuning of a set calls upon their connoisseurship to achieve; the engineers are altering what Raymond Williams would call a "structure of feeling" by means of auditory vibrations (see 1977, pp. 129–135). In short, both sounding and affecting are concerned with *qualities* of lived experience, as distinct from either their material quantities or any formal structures, either musical or linguistic for which these furnish a medium.

While the engineers' phonomorphic techniques make a vital contribution to the vibes of the session, it is also important to point out that other crew members are equally devoted to this end with their performance techniques.[15] By contrast with the vibrational work of the engineers, the crew's performance techniques are expressed discursively. These include call and response (antiphony, refrain) between crowd and MC (DJ), or the crowd's demand for a "rewind" or "wheel and come again" (for the selector playing the track over again) or the "hyping up" the crowd with their chat. In addition to the classic DJing techniques of the "bass drop" and the choice of speed tempos, sound system engineers have made their sound Fx, mentioned above. The live improvised performance of the session makes each one an experimental event: without score or script no two sessions are the same. All this together with attunement of dancers with

---

[13] Currently audiophile domestic sound equipment also deploys these "active" crossovers, pioneered by Jamaican engineers.

[14] See Isabella van Elferen (2020) for an excellent account of the complexities of timbre.

[15] Henriques (2011) deals with performance techniques in some detail.

the music and their entrainment with each other make the dancehall session an intensely affecting milieu, or as it is described below, *atmosphere*.

THE AFFECTIVE SPACE OF THE SESSION

The sound system dancehall sessions on the Kingston streets are the experimental test bed for each tuning or sound system design modification and each and every innovation in style, fashion or dance move. The success of any modification is judged by the crowd's approval, expressed in various ways, most strikingly in the sound system "clash" where sounds compete for the approbation of the crowd. Their verdict is earned not only on the basis of their selection of music but importantly on the quality of the sounding of the music played on each of the competing sets of equipment (Henriques 2011, pp. 182–186). Thus, sounding is continually being purposed for affective intensity.

The key feature of the crowd's experience of the dancehall session is *sonic dominance* (Henriques 2003). It is claimed here that the amplified volumes or pressure (dB) of the sounding of sonic dominance are directly proportional to affective intensity. This is the overwhelming experience of sounding in situated, embodied and shared space of the sound system dancehall session. This has a visceral full-body, intensity, immediacy and intimacy that is literally indescribable. You just have to be there to experience the haecceity (thisness) of it, what Hermann Schmitz identifies in his New Phenomenology as "here-now-being-this-I" (Schmitz 1990, p. 280, quoted in Griffero 2016, p. 45). Concerning sounding and affecting the most important aspect of sonic dominance is how the liminal threshold overload of sounding undermines the normally privileged individual cognitive processes; sounding at this level falls under the radar of rationality, opening the floodgates of affect, it can be said. The entire apparatus of the dancehall session, in effect, provides a laboratory to explore the transmission of affect freed from the prison house of language, to use Frederick Jameson's phrase, escaping the strictures of visual dominance and our everyday habits of thinking (Jameson 1975).

It is comparatively easy to appreciate how suitable experimental conditions are achieved. The night-time darkness, the movement of the dance, the intimate tight shared social space of the open-air dance floor and, of course, the extremely powerful amplified sounding of the music. Most important for engineering such immersive effects is the configuration of the speaker stacks, as they are called. To achieve the best possible results, the engineer's first task upon arriving at any venue is to decide where to position his two, three or four stacks of speakers in relation to the architecture of walls, roofs and maybe parked vehicles.

There are two spatial dimensions to the configuration of the sounding of the set in the dancehall. One is the vertical height of the speaker stacks of about 3–5 metres, with the bass bins (boxes) on the ground and the (treble) tweeters on top. The other is their horizontal configuration directed inwards onto the crowd in the middle (Fig. 5.5). This contrast with standard PA system at a live concert where two columns of speakers either side focus attention on the stage. A sound system is a phonographic instrument, playing recorded music, so attention is not distracted by a live performer—there is only the sounding of the music itself that the crowd centre stage performs with their dance moves. The crowd places themselves inside the sounding as a contrast with headphone listening where the listener places the sounding inside himself or herself.

Thinking-through-sounding is particularly important for describing the affective space of the dancehall session. This is because the very idea of space itself has been almost entirely colonised by the rationalist philosophy that it is empty, homogenous and continuous, that is to say, space as an "empty" geometrical abstraction. While this is extraordinarily useful in practical terms, it is a complete travesty of our embodied lived experience. Far from being a pre-existing empty container of things, unless it is a vacuum, what we call "space" is in fact always full—it is a medium. This is another of the vital contributions that James Gibson makes with his ecological psychology when he says: "We live in an environment consisting of

Fig. 5.5 The vertical and horizontal configuration of sound system speaker stacks

substances that are more or less substantial; of a medium, the gaseous atmosphere; and of the surfaces that separate the substances from the medium. *We do not live in 'space'"* (Gibson 1986, p. 32). Gibson goes on to describe a medium as able to function as such by being without transitions or partitions, as with an electromagnetic field, for instance. Gibson used the example of the water as the medium that "affords" fishes the ability to swim, for example (see Gibson 1986). So when the "space" of the dancehall is recognised instead as full of the vibratory medium of the gaseous air, it is comparatively easy to conceive of this medium as propagating affect as it does sound waves.

If the compression of air molecules affords auditory propagation, what then is the medium of affect? The claim here is that an affective medium can best be understood as an *atmosphere*. This is the intangible array of feelings to which we are supremely sensitive evoked by rooms, spaces and places that Tonino Griffero (2016) has taken as a subject of investigation. An atmosphere is a textured, vibrational field, a milieu, it has fullness, a thickness and a body to it; it has a stride, a rhythm and a groove, boundless yet entirely present here and now. With the concept of atmosphere, we can supplement ideas from wave mechanics with those from the "mechanics" of the lived experience of our social and cultural world. A dancehall session is nothing if not an affective atmosphere.

What makes the idea of atmosphere attractive for understanding affective environments is that they are multisensory and multimedia affairs requiring the corporeality of the lived body. The concept of atmosphere was rather neglected until recently, but Tonino Griffero, drawing on the phenomenological philosophy of Hermann Schmitz, has the ambition to bring it to the forefront, not least for understanding affect. Griffero defines an atmosphere as "a sensorial and affective quality widespread in space. It is the particular tone that determines the way one experiences her surroundings. ... Studying atmospheres means ... to analyse (above all) the range of unintentional or involuntary experiences and, in particular those experiences which emotional 'tonalise' our everyday life" (Griffero 2019, n.p.). Atmospheres, then, are by definition situated, embodied and spatialised. Griffero's work provides a most valuable resource for the present vibrational investigation (see, e.g., Anderson 2009; Peters 2015, 2000). What is particularly important for understanding the sounding and affecting is the nature of the spaces it occupies or more accurately the spaces it *generates*—as a charged energetic dimension.

Schmitz describes an embodied pre-dimensional, non-geometrical "surfaceless space" in which affect operates. The way the term "surfaceless space" appears quite counter-intuitive is evidence of its provocation for our visual-spatial conventions and habits. Schmitz gives several examples of the way surfaceless space extends without measure, including the underwater swimmer's experience of the water around them. According to Schmitz, it is ethereal, transcendent, immaterial and subjective, and is the complement to the material objective aspect of its wave mechanics of concern so far.

The field of affecting and sounding is also rather different from Marshall McLuhan's idea of *acoustic space* or Pierre Schaeffer's of the *soundscape*. This, while stimulating the growth of the entire field of sound studies, essentially conceive of sound as an auditory layer on top of conventional topographic and geometric space (Ingold 2007). This bypasses our inescapable corporeal commitment to what Schmitz identifies the *felt body* (*Leib*) and with this the entire sociocultural milieu that allows the engineers to form their evaluative judgements. For Schmitz, surfaceless space is invariably infused with feelings: "Emotions are atmospheres poured out spatially. An atmosphere in the sense intended here is the complete occupation of a *surfaceless space* in the region of experienced presence. This surfaceless space, apart from emotions, can also be occupied by the weather experienced as enveloping you or by (e.g. festive, pregnant or calm) silence" (Schmitz et al. 2011, p. 255, emphasis added).[16] Such boundless surfaceless space is the foundational energetic field of human consciousness before the superimposition of our rational faculties that divides mind from body and world. The dancehall session is an example of a place where sounding and affecting are *making* space, reversing the conventional wisdom that space makes sounding and affecting. This is the generative power of vibrations.

As a counter example to this specifically modern divisive approach to embodiment and environment, Schmitz returns to ancient Greece, where he pinpoints the seismic shift that birthed our current worldview. This pivot he locates in Homer's writing down of previously oral narratives—specifically in the difference between, on the one hand, Hector, Achilles and the characters of the *Iliad* and, on the other hand, Odysseus as the

---

[16] See also Hermann Schmitz (2019).

hero of the *Odyssey*.[17] Odysseus can be considered a modern person in the sense that he has his own will, desires and fate. The heroes of the *Iliad*, by contrast, are subject to the will and whims of the gods. They do not understand themselves as separate from the forces of their environment—what we would dub *affect*, as the engineers do quite literally. This limitless world is the *Apeiron*; for Julia Kristeva (1998) drawing on Jacques Derrida's reading of Plato, this is the *chora*, defined as the indescribable source of being. When the medium of the space of the world is limitless then there are no partitions or limitations to the spread of affect. From my own research, another example of surfaceless space would be the sensory experience of the foetus in the womb where there is a complete continuity between itself, the intrauterine environment and the world—as sensed entirely through auditory faculty (Gelat et al. 2019).

Conclusion: Bodies of Affect

To conclude we can ask what the particular specific phenomenon of the sounding and affecting of the dancehall session can tell us about the more general issues of the nature of embodiment and environment. Once bodies are conceived energetically, then the dichotomy between individual and society, or mind and body, rapidly dissolves. By contrast, the orthodox reification of bodies as machines necessarily separates them from their environment. Both sounding and affecting depend on relationship, between listener and listened (i.e., listened-to), or between affecter and affected. The more powerful this vibrational relationship the more easily the two merge and mingle into onto one. This is very exciting.[18]

Theorising affect as vibrational intensities not only yields a more adequate understanding of their propagation but also holds the promise of a novel "experimental" reconfiguration of the world. This is one where the subjective and the objective are not forever banished from each other and the rationalist individual dissolves, as with Karl Marx and Frederick Engels's famous phrase "all that's solid melts into the air" (1967, p. 83). This involves recognising those who already demonstrate experience in

---

[17] Schmitz is not alone in making this conjecture, see Albert Lord ([1960] 2000); F. Edward Cranz (2006); Julian Jaynes (1976); Iain McGilchrist (2009).

[18] It introduces a concept of a distributed field of consciousness, as is consistent with Edwin Hutchins's concept of cognition in the wild, or Andy Clarke's of the extended mind, rather than this most valuable of human faculties being trapped in the brain entombed in the skull, see Edwin Hutchins (1995); Andy Clark and David Chalmers (1998).

auditory and affective vibrational fields—namely the Jamaican sound system engineers—and especially what we can learn from their non-epistemic *ways-of-knowing*. In practical and political terms, it is these knowledge systems that have for decades been grappling with the ecological disasters brought about by climate change to which the Global North is belatedly waking up.[19] With vibrations of sound and affect, we enter the live dynamic energetic world-in-process with its forces, fluxes and flows; this leaves behind the reified one of fixed impenetrable objects. With vibrations the lodestar is experiment, rather than certainty.

REFERENCES

Anderson, B. (2009). Affective atmospheres. *Emotion, Space and Society*, 2, 77–81.
Anderson, B. (2014). *Encountering affect: Capacities, apparatuses, conditions*. Ashgate.
Chakrabarty, D. (2000). *Provincializing Europe: Postcolonial thought and historical difference*. Princeton University Press.
Clark, A., & Chalmers, D. (1998). The extended mind. *Analysis*, 58, 7–19.
Cranz, F. E. (2006). *Reorientations of Western thought from Antiquity to the Renaissance*, N. S. Struever (Ed. and Intro.). Routledge.
Csíkszentmihályi, M. (2008). *Flow: The optimal psychological state*. Ingram International.
D'Aquino, B., Henriques, J., & Vidigal, L. (2017). A popular culture research methodology: Sound system outernational. *Volume!*, 13(2): 163–175. Retrieved October 24, 2017, from http://revues.org/5249; http://www.cairn.info/revue-volume-2017-1.htm
Eidsheim, N. S. (2015). *Sensing sound: Singing and listening as vibrational practice*. Duke University Press.
Elferen, I. v. (2020). *Timbre: Paradox, materialism, vibrational aesthetics*. Bloomsbury Academic USA.
Gelat, P., David, A. L., Haqgenas, S. R., Henriques, J., Thibault de Maisieres, A., White, T., and Jauniaux, E. (2019). Evaluation of fetal exposure to external loud noise using a sheep model: quantification of in utero acoustic transmission across the human audio range. *American Journal of Obstetrics and Gynecology*, 221(4), pp. P343.E1–343.E11.
Gibson, J. J. (1986). *The ecological approach to visual perception*. Lawrence Erlbaum Associates.

---

[19] See my ERC-funded research project Sonic Street Technologies, http://sonic-street-technologies.com/

114   J. HENRIQUES

Griffero, T. (2019). Editorial statement for Mimesis International Atmospheric spaces series, for Schmitz, H. *New phenomenology: A brief introduction* (n.p.). Mimesis International.

Griffero, T. (2016). *Atmospheres: Aesthetics of emotional spaces.* Routledge.

Henriques, J. (1998). Social psychology and the politics of racism. In J. Henriques, W. Hollway, C. Urwin, C. Venn, & V. Walkerdine, *Changing the subject: Psychology, social regulation and subjectivity* (pp. 58–87). Routledge. (Original work published 1984).

Henriques, J. (2003). Sonic dominance and the reggae sound system. In M. Bull & L. Back (Eds.), *Auditory culture reader* (pp. 451–480). Berg.

Henriques, J. (2008). Sonic diaspora, vibrations and rhythm: Thinking through the sounding of the Jamaican dancehall session. *African and Black Diaspora*, 1(2), pp. 215–236.

Henriques, J. (2010). The vibrations of affect and their propagation on a night out on Kingston's Dancehall scene, *Body & Society*, 16(1), pp. 57–89.

Henriques, J. (2011). *Sonic bodies: Reggae sound systems, performance techniques and ways of knowing.* Continuum.

Henriques, J. (2014). Rhythmic bodies: Amplification, inflection and transduction in the dance performance techniques of the "bashment gal." *Body & Society*, 20, 79–112.

Henriques, J. (forthcoming). *Sonic Media.*

Hutchins, E. (1995). *Cognition in the wild.* MIT Press.

Ingold, T. (2007). Against soundscape. In A. Carlyle (Ed.), *Autumn leaves: Sound and the environment in artistic practice* (pp. 10–13). Vibro Double Entendre.

Jameson, F. (1975). *The prison-house of language: A critical account of structuralism and Russian formalism.* Princeton University Press.

Jaynes, J. (1976). *The origin of consciousness in the breakdown of the bicameral mind.* Houghton Mifflin.

Jones, H. (2010). The Jones high fidelity amplifier of 1947. *Caribbean Quarterly*, 56(4), pp. 97–107.

Jones, S., & Pinnock, P. (2018). *Scientists of sound: Portraits of a UK reggae sound system.* Bassline Books.

Juelskjær, M., & Staunæs, D. (2016). Orchestrating intensities and rhythms: How post-psychologies are assisting new educational standards and reforming subjectivities. *Theory & Psychology*, 26(2), pp. 182–201.

Kahan, D. M. (2017). Misconceptions, misinformation, and the logic of identity-protective cognition. Cultural Cognition Project Working Paper Series No. 164.

Kristeva, J. (1998). The subject in process. In R.-F. French & P. Lack (Eds.), *The Tel Quel Reader*, Routledge, pp. 133–178.

Latour, B. & Woolgar, S. (1979). *Laboratory life: The social construction of scientific facts.* Princeton University Press.

Lave, J. & Wenger, E. (1991). *Situated learning: Legitimate peripheral participation.* Cambridge University Press.

Le Bon, G. (1990). *The crowd: A study of the popular mind*. T. Fisher Unwin.
Lord, A. B. (2000). *The singer of tales*. Cambridge University Press. (Original work published 1960).
Marx, K. & Engels, F. (1967). *The communist manifesto*. Penguin.
Massumi, B. (2002). *Parables of the virtual: Movement, affect, sensation*. Duke University Press.
McGilchrist, I. (2009). *The master and his emissary: The divided brain and the making of the Western world*. Yale University Press.
O'Neal, E. (2020). *Obeah, race and racism: Caribbean witchcraft in the English*. The University of the West Indies Press.
Paton, D. (2017). *The cultural politics of Obeah: Religion, colonialism and modernity in the Caribbean world*. Cambridge University Press.
Peters, J. D. (2000). *Speaking into the air: A history of the idea of communication*. University of Chicago Press.
Peters, J. D. (2015). *The marvellous clouds: Towards a philosophy of elemental media*. University of Chicago Press.
Rotman, B. (1987). *Signifying nothing: The semiotics of zero*. Macmillan.
Santos, B. de S. (2018). *The end of the cognitive empire: The coming of age of epistemologies of the south*. Duke University Press.
Schmitz, H. (2002). Hermann Schmitz, the "New Phenomenology". In: A.-T. Tymieniecka (Ed.) Phenomenology World-Wide. Analecta Husserliana (The Yearbook of Phenomenological Research), vol 80 (pp. 491–494, 942). Springer.
Schmitz, H., Müllan, R. O., & Slaby, J. (2011). Emotions outside the box: The new phenomenology of feeling and corporeality. *Phenomenology and the Cognitive Sciences*, 10(2), 241–259.
Schmitz, H. (1990). *Der unerschöpfliche Gegenstand*, Bouvier.
Schmitz, H. (2019). *New phenomenology: A brief introduction*. Mimesis International.
Sennett, R. (2008). *The craftsman*. Allen Lane.
Small, C. (1998). *Musicking: The meaning of performing and listening*. Wesleyan University Press.
Thompson, M., & Biddle, I. (Eds.). (2013). *Sound, music, affect: Theorizing sonic experience*. Bloomsbury.
Tomlinson, G. (2015). *A million years of music: The emergence of human modernity*. Zone Books.
Trower, S. (2012). *Senses of vibration*. Bloomsbury.
Whitehead, A. N. (1969). *Process and reality*. The Free Press. (Original work published 1929).
Williams, D. (2020). *Motivated ignorance, rationality, and democratic politics*. Synthese.
Williams, R. (1977). *Marxism and literature*. Oxford University Press.

CHAPTER 6

Experimentation in and with the Stream: Music, Mood Management and Affect

Mads Krogh

Moodagent is the name of a small, Danish-owned music-streaming service. It offers users the opportunity to generate playlists based on a chosen piece of music and to adjust these via five "mood and tempo sliders" (labelled Sensual, Tender, Happy, Angry and Tempo). You can "[c]hoose your moods", as the company website has it. "You're in control", as "Moodagent blends patented AI technology with your moods and taste to create a uniquely personalized music streaming experience" (Moodagent 2019). This promise speaks to music's well-known capacity to move, energize, create atmosphere, afford emotions or, in a word, affect (Thompson and Biddle 2013). Indeed, this is a seminal reason why music matters to many people as part of everyday life or public events (DeNora 2000; Hesmondhalgh 2013). It also speaks to the personal but highly dynamic condition of musical engagements. For example, taste in music is an intimate phenomenon, often linked to self-remembrance and self-narration (Ruud 2013), but it is also outward-oriented and flexible, that is,

M. Krogh (✉)
School of Communication and Culture, Aarhus University, Aarhus, Denmark
e-mail: musmk@cc.au.dk

B. Timm Knudsen et al. (eds.), *Methodologies of Affective
Experimentation,* https://doi.org/10.1007/978-3-030-96272-2_6

117

continually assembled according to context and practical circumstances (Nowak 2016a). Taken together, these points make music a potent means of "world building" (DeNora 2000, p. 44). But, as revealed by Moodagent's description of itself, the agency involved in such world-making is dispersed. In fact, if interactive playlists are themselves, in the company's parlance, mood*agents*, they are so in a distributed, personal-algorithmic, techno-embodied, socio-material sense.[1]

In this chapter, I discuss the relationship between music streaming, mood management and affect. Moodagent illustrates the complexity of this relationship, whose importance is, however, in no way restricted to this particular service. A host of competitors such as Stereomood, Songza, Musicovery and pre-internet pioneers such as Muzak and Yesco (Anderson 2015; Baade 2018) helped pave the way for musical mood management as a market that now includes giants of the streaming industry such as Spotify and Apple Music. I discuss the aforementioned relationship in the perspective of this broader field, first, by examining how the concept of affect is used and understood by music-media scholars. This allows me to elaborate some of the implications of music's capacity for mood management or, indeed, world-making. Secondly, I add to the existing research field by considering how streaming, and in particular activities of digitized musical mood management, might entail a sense of affective experimentation. I develop this notion, balancing a loose everyday idea of experimentation with a rigorous techno-scientific meaning of the term. Moreover, I trace a sense of both stability and openness in understandings of affect and experimentation—a sense that while patterns of musical mood management are systematized and abstracted to afford reproduction, such systematization also retains a margin of indeterminacy. To develop this point, I regard streaming (or the stream) as a distributed phenomenon—an affective arrangement in which socio-technological, musico-cultural, auditive, emotive and bodily states co-produce both listener experience and platform affordances. This resonates with the hybrid idea of agency noted in connection with Moodagent. The concept of affective arrangement is borrowed from Jan Slaby (2019), who emphasizes the reproduction of affective dynamics (see also Schütze et al. this volume). Still, it provides, I argue, a starting point for considering the mentioned sense of openness, as well. Finally, to supplement the discussion of affective experimentation, I introduce and briefly analyse a methodological experiment of engaging

---

[1] By April 2022, Moodagent seized its operation as a standalone streaming service.

with the stream. Namely, a series of workshops which were arranged in the Department of Dramaturgy and Musicology at Aarhus University from December 2018 to November 2020, with the aim of affording dialogue and (creative) reflection on the workings of the affective arrangement of digitized musical mood management. These workshops demonstrate the affective charge of abstractions of music categories and listener profiles, which I suggest manifests the above-mentioned ambivalence of stability and openness as conceived from a user perspective. As with the notion of affective experimentation, this adds to earlier music-and-media studies in terms of how to approach the relationship between music streaming, mood management and affect.

WHAT IS AFFECTIVE ABOUT MUSIC STREAMING?

In his 2015 article "Neo-Muzak and the Business of Mood", Paul Allen Anderson details recent historical connections of music, media, mood management and affect. This makes the article an appropriate starting point for my discussion. Anderson traces a "practice of virtual vicarity", whereby "emotional activity otherwise branded as personal" has been partially exteriorized and "mechanized" via musical soundtracks (2015, p. 813). He terms this the Muzak effect after the Muzak Corporation, which from 1934 supplied music on a subscription-radio model to homes, restaurants, hotels and, from the 1940s, increasingly industrial settings. Music was marketed as "an affective stimulant for the industrial workplace" (2015, p. 815), and in time "entire workdays could be mapped according to finely tuned circuits of escalating stimulation and alertness and intermittent de-escalation" (2015, p. 822). In other words, circuits in the form of playlists curated according to scientific (music-analytical and psychological) principles: "Different ... sequences started from and reached different levels of affective stimulation and mood enhancement" (2015, p. 822) as an arrangement for optimizing worker and consumer engagement. With the advent of personalized digital media (e.g., music-streaming services) and mobile, individualized listening (via laptops, smartphones and earbuds), the task of sonic mood management increasingly fell to the individual—although still within a setting of scientific curation (e.g., of playlists sorted by mood or activity, or context-sensitive recommendations like those provided by Moodagent; I return to this below). Moreover, as Anderson remarks, "[t]here is an implicitly pedagogical aspect at work here; listeners are being encouraged and trained to classify, publicize (share), and manage their moods according to the generic assignations and templates of emotional life provided by neo-Muzak playlists and algorithms" (2015, p. 828).

Anderson's errand is critical. He demonstrates a reification and standardization of affect and, by extension, the lives of contemporary affective labourers. He confirms a point widely accepted today: affect and rationality (or rationalization) should not be regarded as irreconcilable (Kahl 2019, p. 4). Moreover, he critiques some strands of affect theory for being inattentive to the business of mood (Anderson 2015, p. 818)—the "public and private life of affect at ground level" (2015, pp. 812–813)—while inadvertently underpinning the subjectively decentred affective engineering attempted by the culture industries (2015, p. 838). Conversely, in Anderson's account, the concept of affect and its link to, for example, mood and atmosphere are considered less from the point of view of high theory and more as something that occurs within a broad historical and disciplinary field.

Anderson's critical stance resonates with that of Rasmus Fleischer, who argues for the emergence of a post-digital sensibility in following the musical abundance provided by digital platforms and an accompanying waning of affect. In his take on affect, Fleischer is explicitly Spinozist-Deleuzian. Thus, what is at stake in digitized music consumption is "the capacity of the body to be affected by music" (Fleischer 2015, p. 255). However, what happens, Fleischer asks, "when we are confronted with so much music … that it exceeds our capacity for being affected by all of it?" (2015, p. 257). This forces the listener to rely on categories and recommendations, which in Spinozist-Deleuzian terminology may be conceived of as abstract ideas as opposed to common notions. The former may be "all kinds of classes, species and kinds [e.g., standardized mood categories] as well as quantifications in general" (2015, p. 257). However, with abstract ideas, we only imagine (the meaning of music) instead of entering into an actual affective relationship: we "retain an extrinsic *sign*, a variable perceptible characteristic that strikes our imagination, and that we set up as an essential trait" (Deleuze 1988, p. 45). By contrast, common notions manifest "the idea of something in common between two or more bodies that agree with each other, i.e., that … affect one another in keeping with this intrinsic agreement. … Thus a common notion expresses our capacity for being affected" (Deleuze 1988, pp. 44–45).

While music would always have the potential to move listeners, Fleischer's point in introducing these Spinozist-Deleuzian terms is to distinguish whether it does so in a way that "produce[s] common notions that unite the affected bodies" and, thus, "increase[s] their ability to act" (2015, p. 257). In turn, this has to do with the affordance of passions and/or actions, the two types of affect recognized by Spinoza. While the former may either increase or decrease the body's power of acting, the latter "immediately express[es] the affecting body" (Fleischer 2015, p. 258). Not surprisingly, in this perspective, streaming-based mood listening seems inferior to more actively engaging types of musical experience, for example, the bodily felt (as opposed to merely heard) bass materialism of dance-music sessions.[2] While the advance of streaming services has, thus, according to Fleischer, caused a waning of affect, it also highlights the importance of such corporal and collective musical activities or, more broadly, an emergent post-digital sensibility.

As with Anderson's account of neo-Muzak, and disregarding the analytical and reflective depth provided by both authors, there is something totalizing about Fleischer's diagnosis, which sits uneasily with more empirically driven research into the practices of actual listeners. In this respect, prominent contributions have been made by Raphael Nowak and Anja Nylund Hagen[3] utilizing a range of empirical methods—for example, interviews, diaries, focus groups and online ethnography—to monitor and analytically distinguish informants' use of music for mood management (and other purposes), and how this affects their everyday lives. Interestingly, considering Fleischer's point about the waning of affect, one common insight is that practices of music streaming are diverse and not (necessarily) passive. As Hagen notes, "music-streaming services invite multiple approaches to and uses of digital music" (2015, p. 639). Platform affordances may be variously engaged. Provided categories, curated playlists, autogenerated recommendations and so forth may be supplemented, manipulated or 'misused' (e.g., ironically). Listening may oscillate between "careful planning and serendipitous encounters" (Hagen 2016, p. 242). User choices, habits or profiles may be tweaked to suit public exposure (e.g., followers) or personal agendas (e.g., of habit change; Hagen and Lüders 2016). In sum, "streaming services ... afford diverse *modes of*

---

[2] On this line of music-affect research, see Goodman (2010); Henriques (2010); Jasen (2016).

[3] Nowak (2016a, b, and with Bennett 2014) and Hagen (2015, 2016, and with Lüders 2016). See also Skånland (2013), Johansson et al. (2017), Nag (2017), Tronvoll (2019), Siles et al. (2019).

experience that relate to listening and encountering music, as well as dealing with the technology" (Hagen 2016, p. 242; emphasis in original).

In Nowak's work, the complexity of everyday listening to digital music is emphasized in the description of "[h]eterogenous modes of consumption [that] intertwine the materiality of technologies with individuals' repertoires of musical preferences" (2016a, p. 25). Thus, listeners engage in acts of "emotional reflexivity" (2016a, p. 66), where affects produced by music but afforded by technologies and "the structures of everyday context" (2016a, p. 68) are felt and reacted to. In turn, this leads to the development of "role-normative modes" attuned to various sites and situations in everyday life: "In regard to the emergence of musical affects, I argue that music is assigned particular roles by individuals in terms of how it can accompany them in everyday contexts. ... Individuals attempt to reproduce occurrences of adequate music by developing patterns of consumption that I call 'role-normative modes of listening'" (Nowak 2016a, p. 79). Beyond the issue of complexity, Nowak's concepts of heterogeneous modes of consumption and role-normative modes of listening resonate with the idea of affective arrangements that I noted by way of introduction. That is, a state where agencies and affects are distributed across various elements of the listening situation, moulded and stabilized in a state of co-functioning (I return to this below). Nowak also explores the issues of control or agency and attention or reflectivity, which were central to Anderson and Fleischer. Indeed, his concern with adequacy may, I think, supplement the Spinozist-Deleuzian perspective wielded by Fleischer. In Nowak's account, "adequateness is reached when music corresponds to a suitable accompaniment to an everyday context" and "[t]he interpretation of whether the musical accompaniment to a context is adequate or not lies in individuals' emotional reflexivity" (2016a, p. 81). Thus, adequacy concerns the successful implication of music in the affective arrangement of everyday activities, as felt or emotionally experienced by listeners. This comes close to the Spinozist-Deleuzian idea of joy and sadness as corresponding to affections (e.g., by music), which respectively increase or decrease our ability to act. As Deleuze notes, feelings relate to how affections are experienced, that is, to ideas that may be inadequate insofar as they only represent an external cause (1988, p. 73). However, in the case of common notions, where an affection agrees with the constitution of the affected, the cause is not external but shared, and, thus, "common notions are necessarily adequate ideas" (1988, p. 55).

I will return to these considerations of music and affect inspired by Deleuzian thinking. However, it should be noted that, generally, such theoretical perspectives are scarce in the empirically driven research referenced here. The concept of affect is used to signify moods, emotions, atmosphere, being moved and so on. That is, it is used in accordance with the broad notion of affectivity suggested by Slaby and Mühlhoff (2019, p. 30), but without much philosophical scrutiny. For example, Nowak acknowledges that "[t]he challenges presented by an analysis of music's affects lie in the definition of what an 'affect' is, in the conditions of its emergence, and in how it is grasped upon and interpreted" (2016a, p. 69). In fact, he contends that focusing on the conditions of affects' emergence (i.e., what may be described in terms of heterogeneous modes of consumption) offers a way out of the non-representational challenge posed by a Deleuzian understanding of affect (2016a, p. 70). However, simultaneously, this bypasses what could have been learned from engaging Deleuze or other philosophical pioneers of affect theory. This example, and in a wider sense the juxtaposition in this section of various theoretical positions and empirical sensibilities, speaks, I think, to the role of affect as what Slaby and von Scheve describe as a working concept. While they consider affect "primarily" a matter of "dynamic processes *between* actors and *in* collectives" (2019, p. 14; italics in original), they contend that "concepts [including that of affect] function as connectors between fields and as rallying points for the convergence of perspectives". In case of disputes, concepts "help 'contain' disagreement by providing a common—if tentative and shifting—frame of reference for diverging perspectives" (2019, p. 10), which in turn affords conceptual development. The contributions summarized here develop various—partly coinciding, partly diverging—perspectives on the relational dynamics of digitized musical mood management. In the following, I seek to contribute a perspective of affective experimentation.

Affective Experimentation

In both the loose everyday sense of "a tentative procedure" and according to a stronger, scientific notion of rigorously testing or putting something "to a proof" (Oxford English Dictionary, Sept. 2020), there is certainly something experimental about music streaming. Users try out platform features. In fact, services afford such "trying out", as comprehensive instructions are usually relegated to website help sections. The variety of usage documented by research on streaming habits testifies to this every-day experimentation, and the formation of role-normative modes of listening illustrates a systematic dimension in how this experimentation gradually turns trial and error into proven ways of mood management, for instance. On the side of platforms, vast and thoroughly rationalized systems of music information retrieval (MIR) and user-data analysis combine to generate playlists and other sorts of recommendations, to match ads with target users, to drive the organization and development of platform features and so on (Drott 2018a; Goldschmitt and Seaver 2019; Prey 2016). An array of scientific disciplines inform this algorithmic "background structure" (Reckwitz 2020)—for example, computer, information and neuro science; library studies; psychology; sociology and musicology (Inskip 2011; Knees and Schedl 2016). Some of these have strong traditions for experimental work and, moreover, the systematic correlation of music recommendations and efforts to monitor user behaviour by platforms resembles a procedure of systematic testing. Indeed, the procedures of datafied music recommendation may be mapped to a large extent onto the definition of experiments suggested by Wolfgang Krohn and Johannes Weyer (1994, p. 175). Thus, they entail

1. "the drawing up of a theoretical design [e.g., in terms of recommendation algorithms based on MIR and psychographic descriptions of users] and the formulation of hypotheses concerning the occurrence of (future) events [e.g., in terms of user behaviour]". For example, predictive claims are implied in promises about the effects and efficiency of platform advertising (see Spotify Ad Studio 2020).

2. "the setting up of an experimental situation [e.g., the arrangement of interface, music recommendations and ads offered to particular users] that can serve as a means of testing theoretical assumptions [in terms of hypothesized effects]; this includes knowledge of the relevant boundary conditions [e.g., as regards user context], the controlled variation of parameters [i.e., features of the arrangement] as well as the making of arrangements for the observation of effects [via surveillance and datamining]". Naturally, knowledge of boundary conditions and controlling parameters in the experimental situation present a challenge for streaming platforms—particularly, considering the active part of users. However, in recent years, significant efforts have gone into developing means of knowing and describing user context on a par with descriptive, parameter-based

mappings of music.[4] Indeed, the orientation towards mood- and activity-based music recommendations by Moodagent and other services illustrates what is sometimes referred to as the "contextual turn" in streaming (Prey 2018). This turn underlines that platforms do in fact attempt to know the experimental situation and the significance or effects of particular parameters (e.g., musical or contextual), which can be varied in the provision of recommendations.

3. "the establishment of an organised research process embedded in a network of scientific institutions". Platform research departments are well integrated in the scientific community around MIR and related strands of computational research. Moreover, institutionalization as noted by Krohn and Weyer may entail the development of standards (Gooding et al. 1989, p. 3) such as the descriptive parameters mentioned or procedures and metrics for specifying user context, behaviour or other effects of recommendations. In fact, this illustrates how the standardization of affect noted by Anderson might be taken quite literally, albeit not entirely on the part of users.

Krohn and Weyer present their definition in a discussion of real-life experiments. That is, "the testing of risk-involving technologies" (1994, p. 173) in a real-life context, beyond the secluded space of the laboratory. Naturally, the affordance and effects of musical mood management cannot be tried out or fully determined before involving actual users because of the experimentation performed by these users, but also because of the individualized or, in Reckwitz's terms, singularized character of the service provided by platforms (2020, p. 4). The monitoring of listeners aims to afford a "uniquely personalized experience", to return to Moodagent's presentation of itself. In fact, users are profiled at a sub-personal level (Prey 2018), according to, for example, location or time of day, just as the contextual turn in music recommendation promises to cater for "any given moment" as people turn to streaming "to discover ways to enhance their lives" (Spotify Advertising 2017). Catering for any given moment or, in other words, for an infinite line of potentially different situations would

---

[4] MIR parameters range from textual (e.g., tempo, rhythm, key) to purely contextual (e.g., user age, location, device) with some in between (e.g., mood, energy, popularity, valence). The listed parameters are derived from Spotify's Application Development Interface (Spotify for Developers 2020). The latter are listed as track features, but obviously emulate music as it is experienced by users.

seem to require a service with an infinite adaptability. That is a service whose use potential or affordances cannot be fully predetermined, contrary to the traditional scientific idea of generalized principles discovered in the laboratory and subsequently used to predict real-life events. According to Reckwitz, the pursuit of this type of service—valued because of its singular, individualized and irreducible uniqueness—is a mark of current times or what he terms "the society of singularities" (2020). Whereas some goods might (still) be valued because they fulfil general standards (e.g., medicine), this is only indirectly the case for music recommendations, where the scientific, rationalized, abstract apparatus of music-and-user intel is blackboxed or relegated to a role as, again, a background structure (Krogh 2020).[5]

In his 2011 article on the rise of the "security-entertainment complex", which would certainly include the digitized music industries, Nigel Thrift makes a related point about the role of experimentation on an epochal level. Noting a range of socio-technological changes, based on digitization and giving privilege to movement, feedback and interactivity, he contends that the "descriptive regime" of the world is shifting: "[T]here is ... a 'general modification of event-ization' based upon the back and forth of moving fields of data which are able to track and trace human 'motivations' by reworking them in much richer ways than were possible in the era of writing" (2011, p. 8; quoting Stiegler). This constant reworking is accompanied by a "state of provisionality, a world always almost there, and thus always elastic in the way it leans into the moment, a world of infinite mobilisation" (2011, p. 8), which in turn calls for an experimentalist stance:

> The security-entertainment complex ... produces a stance towards the world which is naturally experimental and which is able ... to employ technology to make this experimental stance "irresistible". This "irresistible" experimental stance aspires to be all-encompassing, but it must perforce retain an

---

[5] This apparatus is evident to users in, for example, generalized categories featured in platform interfaces (of genre, activity, mood etc.) or the possibility of accessing one's user history. Similarly, the monitoring of user activities by platforms is explicated in privacy policies. But while this is a prerequisite for platform services, it is not something users necessarily like being reminded of, as illustrated by the public outcry when, in 2015, Spotify attempted to expand the range of information collected to include, for example, GPS data and voice commands (Drott 2018a, p. 233). See also the reaction of workshop participants considered below.

open-endedness if it is to be effective, and this open-endedness provides all manner of opportunities to experiment in ways which allow for its interrogation and recomposition. (2011, p. 7)

Thrift discusses this experimentalist stance not only as a consequence of socio-technological changes but also as something to be developed in social research (see Coleman this volume). The experimental open-endedness refers to the uncertainty of outcomes, which has to be part of even the most rigorous experimental procedures, if the experiment is to show anything. However, Thrift extends this uncertainty to include the construction of experimental settings, data and results, which makes for a more fundamental idea of open-ended procedures. The challenge of research is no longer (in the context of the security-entertainment complex) to generate data (which is already abundant), but to navigate constantly moving datasets and to form new associations.[6] Thus, Thrift advocates experimentation in social science (and beyond) as a "production without guarantees, based on … an explicit return to a kind of nomadism which no longer privileges fixed territory [see the fixed boundaries of the laboratory] as necessary to produce effects but which does not therefore think that the attachments of territory are somehow unimportant" (2011, p. 18). In a sense, this evens out what I noted above as the difference between a loose and a stronger sense of experimentation, and, moreover, the perspective raised by Thrift cuts across the division which has structured my discussion of commercial techno-scientific infrastructure and everyday musical life. The descriptive regime and "experimental economy" that accompany the security-entertainment complex affect the world as it is perceived, as well as in its continued (re)creation. It is a regime of world-making affecting "the ontological horizons of human societies" (Thrift 2011, p. 7) .

In keeping with this perspective, I regard music streaming as a distributed phenomenon. To navigate the stream as an everyday user is to engage in an environment of social roles, everyday spaces and situations, musical repertoires, technological affordances, platform interfaces and the commercial techno-scientific background structure of datamining, music intel, psychographic analysis and context-sensitive recommender algorithms.

---

[6] It should be noted that Thrift bypasses the obvious issues that researchers experience with accessing the abundant data produced, for example, by music-streaming platforms (Prior 2018, p. 47).

Multiple relations of feedback, mediation and co-operation mark this environment, thereby dispersing "the efficiency or effectivity", to which the notion of agency usually refers, "across an ontologically heterogenous field" (Bennett 2010, p. 23). Being a user or experiencing oneself as such is an emergent feature of this environment—emerging in-between or in "the milieu" of the various factors mentioned (Massumi in Deleuze and Guattari 1987, p. xvii). Indeed, both the affective training discussed by Anderson and the emotional reflexivity described by Nowak play out (co-operatively) in this milieu (of standardized mood playlists and practices of mood listening, for instance).

As noted, Slaby uses the notion of affective arrangement to signify this distributed state of factors co-operating in the creation of a "situated affectivity" (2018). Specifically, he defines affective arrangements as "material-discursive formation[s] as part of which affect is patterned, channeled, and modulated in recurrent and repeatable ways" (Slaby et al. 2017, p. 5). The notion of arrangement is derived from the French, Deleuze-Guattarian notion of *agencement* (Slaby 2019, p. 111), which is otherwise often translated as assemblage, and in keeping with assemblage theory (e.g., DeLanda 2016) affective arrangements should be regarded as contingent or, in Slaby's words, "performatively open-ended" (Slaby et al. 2017, p. 5). Still, there is, as noted, an emphasis in the conception of affective arrangements on the creation of "recurrent and repeatable" affects or, to put this differently, "[o]ne might speak of affective arrangements as *affective affordances* as they present 'prepared occasions' for getting affectively involved or immersed in specific ways" (Slaby et al. 2017, p. 5; emphasis in original).

I contend that, in the milieu of music streaming, affective experimentation produces teleologies: a sense of predictable effects connected to particular listening strategies (role-normative modes), technological features, interfaces, personalized and context-specific recommender services, and more. Indeed, the emotional reflexivity connected to mundane processes of trial and error and the techno-scientific systems of datamining and analysis that I have commented on above aim at singling out specific associations of music and affect from the mesh of the milieu as distinct and reproducible. This fixation or capture of particular affects from within the intensive flow of everyday listening performs a decontextualization, evident, for example, in the formation and labelling of playlists by reference to moods or emotions that may literally be replayed on later occasions. Naturally, there is no guarantee that affects will reoccur. In fact, the experimental capture of musical affects might be regarded as the translation of common notions into abstract ideas (recall the Spinozist-Deleuzian concepts invoked by Fleischer), which might diminish affective flows. But still, it produces a sense of teleology in the use of streaming platforms in accordance with the notion of affective arrangements as used by Slaby.

Moreover, the experimental openness noted by Thrift correlates with the irreducible singularity of the product offered by, for example, Moodagent or Spotify (to enhance "any given moment") and more basically with the fundamentally processual condition of the stream—always unfolding like sound in time and space, and always on its way towards the next song (Drott 2018b). If affective experimentation provides a sense of teleology—that is, a sense that appropriate affects will be engendered by the arrangement—then, at least in part, it does so in an open-ended manner, that is, without reservations, come what may. Perhaps this makes even better sense if we consider the experimental capture of musical affects not only along the lines of the Spinozist-Deleuzian concept of abstract ideas but by implication of Deleuze's idea of abstraction as explained by Brent Adkins (2016). That is, as signifying the "intensive rather than extensive, concrete rather than discrete" (p. 357). The experimental abstraction of musical affects, for example, in the form of mood labels, entails the formation of discrete, extensive categories. But such categories, decontextualized as they are, always hold the potential for concretion or recontextualization. They are abstract in the sense of offering a "virtual" basis (p. 359) for discrete enactments of, for example, music recommendations or actual listening experiences. In this way, affective experimentation evokes a sense of affectivity less aligned with recurrent moods or the repeatable dimension of affective arrangements and more akin to a Massumian understanding of affect as "indeterminate potential" (Kahl 2019, p. 4; see Massumi 2002, 2015). However, as noted, this sense of openness ties in with the expectation that services will accommodate "any given moment".

EXPERIMENTATION IN AND WITH THE STREAM

Despite the valuable efforts of Nowak, Hagen and others, not a lot has been done empirically regarding the particular issue of music streaming and affective experimentation. Moreover, to embrace the sense of simultaneous stability and openness, teleology and indeterminacy, which I have argued is entailed in affective experimentation, would perhaps require methodological steps beyond those typically employed in social and cultural research. At least, this was the idea behind the above-mentioned series of workshops arranged at the Department of Dramaturgy and Musicology at Aarhus University. In the context of critical-pedagogical engagement with digitized music culture, these workshops involved groups of students in activities aimed at affording dialogue and reflection on the participants' experiences as users of music-streaming services and, particularly, the impact of categorization in this context. The activities involved interviews and dialogue regarding streaming habits, the use of platform features and experiences of user profiling (utilizing a rudimentary interview guide), the examination of apps displaying music-and-user intel (particularly Spotify.me and Organize Your Music[7]) and manual attempts at drawing maps of music categories compared with platform recommendations. However, an ethos of open-ended experimentation (recall Thrift[8]) was attempted both in the design of activities—for example, in the use of loosely formulated questions and tasks inviting participants' elaboration—and in the way activities were adjusted from one workshop to the next based (in part) on discussion with participants. Generally, activities were carried out in groups of two or three persons. Some workshops were stand-alone events for which participants had volunteered. Others were offered as part of courses on a par with other learning activities but with no assessment involved. Some workshops were recorded consentingly in sound or video, while others merely resulted in notes and, in some cases, products such as the above-mentioned genre maps. Eighteen students participated in five stand-alone workshops, while another five workshops were implemented in as many courses. Each lasted one to two hours.[9]

---

[7] Spotify.me was offered as a feature of Spotify for Brands from 2017 to 2020, while Organize Your Music is available at http://organizeyourmusic.playlistmachinery.com. Other apps included in workshops were Musictaste.space (https://musictaste.space), Discover Quickly (https://discoverquickly.com), Musicmap (https://musicmap.info), Obscurify (https://obscurifymusic.com/login) and Every Noise at Once (http://everynoise.com). Workshop participants accessed these apps individually, voluntarily and with a guide for how to unsubscribe.

[8] See also Markham and Pereira (2019), whose notion of experimentalism aided workshop development.

[9] I would like to thank all workshop participants for their enthusiastic engagement, making this chapter possible.

Engaging workshop participants to reflect on streaming habits, music categorization and related issues involves engaging the affective arrangement of musical mood management discussed above in a way that may direct attention to its workings. This was achieved in the decontextualized space of the workshop (in parallel with the laboratory) and by the introduction of activities and props (e.g., apps and maps). We might regard these methodological steps as relaying or (re)mediating the affective arrangement as a "method assemblage" (Law 2004). Specifically, discussing apps such as Spotify.me or Organize Your Music, which demonstrate, respectively, the personal profiling and MIR-based categorization performed by Spotify, might be regarded as the introduction of devices into the arrangement, which affords "defamiliarization", thereby allowing a perspective of research to emerge (Markham and Pereira 2019, p. 6). This resonates with the methodological devising discussed by Celia Lury and Nina Wakeford. They note how methods are often bound up with instruments aimed at capturing something while, simultaneously, contributing to what is captured, which means they "draw attention to the uncertain but not unorganized relation between the action of a method and its effects" (2012, p. 10). In the present context, this goes both for the methods of the affective arrangement (i.e., listening habits etc., reflected on by workshop participants) and the workshop methodology (e.g., the choice of activities and apps) aimed at investigating affective experimentation.

In keeping with the above-mentioned aim, manifestations of categorization (of music, moods, users etc.) in music streaming were central to the devising of workshop activities. As abstractions, categories manifest a capture or fixation of particular affects within the intensive flow of the arrangement of digitized musical mood management, a capture that may, again, afford defamiliarization—particularly when encountered as a data-generated user profile (as in Spotify.me) or a system of genres and moods (as in Organize Your Music). This was expressed by workshop participants commenting on the "confusing", "mind-boggling", "troubling" or, even, "scary" experience of realizing the scope of the platforms' background structure. In the words of one participant, Spotify's ways of generalizing felt "offensive", while another felt that music should be a "free space" and that Spotify could never really know, for example, the social implications or sense of "safety" implied in some listening—such associations were lost in the platform's attempt at "simplifying something that is [always] more complicated".[10] Perhaps one might regard abstractions, such as the categories encountered by workshop participants, as impacting the intensive flows of the affective arrangement like a mesh or grid creating repercussions, interference or diffraction in the stream affording dialogue and reflection to move beyond the mentalist, rational and representational implications of this term. That is, to move in the direction of diffraction as an affectively productive method entangling "matter and meaning" (participants *feeling* troubled, offended etc.) to afford "more creative insights" (Bozalek and Zembylas 2017, p. 115).[11] Again, this resonates with the ethos of open-ended experimentation (see Blackman 2015). However, it should be noted that caution was far from the only emotion or attitude accompanying the reflection and dialogue facilitated by the workshops. Surprise, enthusiasm and laughter were other prominent reactions illustrating the intensity of engaging the system of abstracted music-and-user intel and, by extension, the affective charge of the arrangement of digitized musical mood management.

The teleological implication of experimentation discussed above was manifest in the workshops in what might be regarded as an ambivalent affirmation of abstractions. Thus, while several participants expressed doubts about categorizations of music or listening habits, such reservations were simultaneously dismissed by a tentative adhering to the authority of the techno-scientific background structure. For example, one participant's reaction to Spotify.me's listing of her top artists was "what the fuck … but fair enough", suggesting that even though she could not recognize the listing, it had to be true. Similarly, another participant reasoned that "I am somewhat surprised that this is what I have heard most of all, but perhaps. … It might be right; it just wasn't what I thought." Such statements were accompanied by explanations of and collective reasoning in elaborating stats. For example, listings of 'odd' top artists and top tracks were explained by recent activities (such as exam work, parties, a family visit etc.), and there was some speculation about what might be

[10] There is an obvious correspondence in these reactions to those encountered by Bucher in a broader study of everyday users' affective encounters with algorithms in social media, search engines and recommender services (2018).

[11] The idea of "diffraction as method" has been developed by Barad (2007), drawing on Haraway (1992). In line with Bozalek and Zembylas (2017), I do not think reflection and diffraction should be regarded as irreconcilable ways of thinking or doing research. For example, the idea of "emotional reflexivity" used by Nowak might be regarded as sensitive to the diffractive entangling of matter and meaning.

entailed in unfamiliar genre categories (e.g., neo-mellow, indietronica, post-teen pop), moods (chill, amped, happy) or psychographic labels (such as "You are high energy", again from Spotify.me). Dialogue between the participants might be conceived as adding meaning to or interpretively fleshing out the abstractions performed by platforms and presented by the apps—as a collective act of (re)aligning with the affective arrangement of everyday listening. Moreover, rather than simply reflecting preestablished facts (as with a representational understanding of reflexivity), explanations were set forth, tried out, backed or revised within the collective space of the workshop—in the in-between of techno-scientific metrics, personal experience and social dynamics, discursive elaboration and affective attunement. The intertwinement of the latter was directly sought, for example, by some participants 'testing' interface explanations of genre categories against concrete examples to hear if they 'made sense', thus investing their own bodily experience in situ. However, more generally, the above-mentioned intensity of workshop activities—for example, surprise or embarrassment over 'revelations' in terms of listening patterns or 'guilty pleasures'—might be regarded as a driver of the explanations and elaborations that were provided. In a sense, the combination of 'odd' stats and the authority of the techno-scientific background structure seemed to catalyse a widespread feeling that participants had to explain themselves or that stats had to be elaborated to make sense. In turn, this means that the affirmation of abstractions and the authority of the techno-scientific background structure were also collectively performed, and just as the teleology of the affective arrangement relies on experimental procedures (techno-scientifically and in everyday life, as discussed above), so it was experimentally (re)produced within the setting of the workshops.

The affirmation of abstractions and the implied teleology could be linked to the discomfort experienced by some workshop participants when realizing the scope of the platforms' background structure—that is, to a sense of being reduced to predictable patterns in accordance with the caution against standardization expressed by Anderson. However, even among the most critical participants, a fairly pragmatic attitude accompanied the engagement with music-and-user intel in the form of the aforementioned apps. Both Spotify.me and Organize Your Music offer a playlist-formation option. In other words, stats can be translated into personalized or parametrically specified (e.g., genre- and mood-based) playlists, and it was remarkable that even after criticizing the system of abstraction, several participants chose to add the playlists that they were offered to their Spotify profile—some enthusiastically noting that this was a "fun" possibility—while others expressed their intention to return to the apps. Indeed, as this indicates, the workshop participants seemed generally to embrace the experimental ethos of the workshops also in a future sense, as accordant with their real-life musical engagements. This might be read as the prospective infolding of apps and other means of workshop devising in the affective arrangement of everyday listening in a pragmatic enaction of teleologies, not as predeterminations but rather as abstract lines of projecting relations of, for example, musical mood management or, in a wider sense, musical affects into future scenarios and situations. This resembles the notion of affect as indeterminate potential, although again, tied in to the arrangement of music mood management.

In Conclusion

In terms of the overall discussion in this chapter of the relationship between music streaming, mood management and affect and what may, in this context, be entailed by the notion of affective experimentation, the experimental workshops demonstrate the affective charge of categories diffracting the experience of music streaming according to workshop participants, that is, from a user perspective. This charge was revealed in the emotional engagement and, more basically, the drive of participants to collectively navigate the ambivalent sense of teleologies and indeterminacy, stability and openness in the affective arrangement of digitized musical mood management. Methodologically, the workshops relayed this arrangement into a state of defamiliarization devised via activities and props drawing attention to its workings. In other words, if affective experimentation occurs in the stream as an aspect of everyday musical mood management, it is highlighted by engaging with the stream in the reflections and engagement produced by the workshops. This offers an empirical grounding for the discussion of affective experimentation sensitive to the distributed and dynamic character of the affective arrangement and, indeed, the inherent ambivalence of stability and openness. The emergent, tentative and mutable meanings ascribed to streaming habits, platform features and music-and-user intel illustrate this sensitivity. Meanings emerged not merely in the dialogue of workshop participants, but within the defamiliarized setting, in the interplay of techno-scientific metrics, personal experience and social dynamics, discursive elaboration and affective attunement. Similarly, it is remarkable how the production of teleologies that characterizes streaming services and everyday listening was pragmatically (re)enacted in the workshop setting—in the collective interpretation of abstract categories and personal streaming habits. Again, this speaks to the emergent character of the affective arrangement and the sensitivity of the methodological approach.

Compared to earlier studies of digitized musical mood management and affect, the focus in this chapter on affective experimentation indicates a somewhat understudied topic. This is indicated by the first section, which also mapped out a multivalent understanding of affect. I have combined this with an equally diverse—loose and rigorous, teleological and open—notion of experimentation, and I propose the experimental workshops as a methodological bid at how to enable an appropriate empirical sensitivity. It is certainly the case that previous studies in this area have involved users, but not with the experimental, diffractive intention pursued here. Hopefully, these conceptual and methodological steps may incite further excursions into the vastly important but equally complex relationship between music, mood management and affect—into the in-between, that is, of datafied techno-scientific experiments by commercial agents such as Moodagent or Spotify and intimate user practices of trying and testing, feeling one's way through everyday musical life.

References

Adkins, B. (2016). Who thinks abstractly? Deleuze on abstraction. *The Journal of Speculative Philosophy*, 30(3), 352–360. https://doi.org/10.5325/jspecphil.30.3.0352

Anderson, P. A. (2015). Neo-Muzak and the business of mood. *Critical Inquiry*, 41(4), 811–840. https://doi.org/10.1086/681787

Baade, C. (2018). Lean back: Songza, Ubiquitous listening and internet music radio for the masses. *Radio Journal: International Studies in Broadcast & Audio Media*, 16(1), 9–27. https://doi.org/10.1386/rjao.16.1.9_1

Barad, K. M. (2007). *Meeting the universe halfway: Quantum physics and the entanglement of matter and meaning*. Duke University Press.

Bennett, J. (2010). *Vibrant matter: A political ecology of things*. Duke University Press.

Blackman, L. (2015). Researching affect and embodied hauntologies: Exploring an analytics of experimentation. In B. T. Knudsen & C. Stage (Eds.), *Affective Methodologies* (pp. 25–44). Palgrave Macmillan.

Bozalek, V., & Zembylas, M. (2017). Diffraction or reflection? Sketching the contours of two methodologies in educational research. *International Journal of*

Qualitative Studies in Education, 30(2), 111–127. https://doi.org/10.108
0/09518398.2016.1201166

Bucher, T. (2018). *If...then: Algorithmic power and politics.* Oxford University Press.

DeLanda, M. (2016). *Assemblage theory.* Edinburgh University Press.

Deleuze, G. (1988). *Spinoza: Practical philosophy.* City Lights Books.

Deleuze, G., & Guattari, F. (1987). *A thousand plateaus: Capitalism and schizophrenia* (B. Massumi, Trans.). University of Minnesota Press.

DeNora, T. (2000). *Music in everyday life.* Cambridge University Press.

Drott, E. (2018a). Music as a technology of surveillance. *Journal of the Society for American Music,* 12(3), 233–267. https://doi.org/10.1017/S1752196318000196

Drott, E. (2018b). Why the next song matters: Streaming, recommendation, scarcity. *Twentieth-Century Music,* 15(3), 325–357. https://doi.org/10.1017/S1478572218000245

Fleischer, R. (2015). Towards a postdigital sensibility: How to get moved by too much music. *Culture Unbound: Journal of Current Cultural Research,* 7(2), 255–269. https://doi.org/10.3384/cu.2000.1525.1572255

Goldschmitt, K. E., & Seaver, N. (2019). Shaping the stream: Techniques and troubles of algorithmic recommendation. In D. Trippett, M. M. Ingalls, & N. Cook (Eds.), *The Cambridge Companion to Music in Digital Culture* (pp. 63–81). Cambridge University Press.

Gooding, D., Pinch, T., & Schaffer, S. (Eds.) (1989). *The uses of experiment: Studies in the natural sciences.* Cambridge University Press.

Goodman, S. (2010). *Sonic warfare: Sound, affect, and the ecology of fear.* MIT Press.

Hagen, A. N. (2015). The playlist experience: Personal playlists in music streaming services. *Popular Music and Society,* 38(5), 625–645. https://doi.org/1 0.1080/03007766.2015.1021174

Hagen, A. N. (2016). Music streaming the everyday life. In R. Nowak & A. Whelan (Eds.), *Networked music cultures: Contemporary approaches, emerging issues* (pp. 227–245). Springer.

Hagen, A. N., & Lüders, M. (2016). Social streaming? Navigating music as personal and social. *Convergence: The International Journal of Research into New Media Technologies,* 23(6), 643–659. https://doi.org/10.1177/1354856516673298

Haraway, D. (1992). The promises of monsters: A regenerative politics for inappropriate/d others. In L. Grossberg, C. Nelson, & P. A. Treichler (Eds.), *Cultural Studies* (pp. 295–337). Routledge.

Henriques, J. (2010). The vibrations of affect and their propagation on a night out on Kingston's dancehall scene. *Body & Society,* 16(1), 57–89. https://doi.org/10.1177/1357034X09354768

Hesmondhalgh, D. (2013). *Why music matters.* Wiley Blackwell.

Inskip, C. (2011). Music information retrieval research. In A. Foster & P. Rafferty (Eds.), *Innovations in Information Retrieval: Perspectives for Theory and Practice* (pp. 69–84). Facet Publishing.

Jasen, P. C. (2016). *Low end theory: Bass, bodies and the materiality of sonic experience.* Bloomsbury.

Johansson, S., Werner, A., Åker, P., & Goldenzwaig, G. (2017). *Streaming music: Practices, media, cultures.* Routledge.

Kahl, A. (2019). Introduction: Analyzing affective societies. In A. Kahl (Ed.), *Analyzing affective societies* (pp. 1–26). Routledge.

Knees, P., & Schedl, M. (2016). *Music similarity and retrieval: An introduction to audio-and web-based strategies* (vol. 36). Springer.

Krogh, M. (2020). Context is the new genre: Abstraktion og singularisering i digital musikformidling. *Norsk medietidsskrift,* 27(3), 1–15. https://doi.org/10.18261/ISSN.0805-9535-2020-03-05 ER.

Krohn, W., & Weyer, J. (1994). Society as a laboratory: The social risks of experimental research. *Science and Public Policy,* 21(3), 137–183. https://doi.org/10.1093/spp/21.3.173

Law, J. (2004). *After method: Mess in social science research.* Routledge.

Lury, C., & Wakeford, N. (2012). *Inventive methods: The happening of the social.* Routledge.

Markham, A. N., & Pereira, G. (2019). Analyzing public interventions through the lens of experimentalism: The case of the museum of random memory. *Digital Creativity,* 30(4), 235–256. https://doi.org/10.1080/14626268.2019.1688838

Massumi, B. (2002). *Parables for the virtual: Movement, affect, sensation.* Duke University Press.

Massumi, B. (2015). *Politics of affect.* Polity.

Moodagent. (2019). Music streaming redefined. Retrieved August 21, 2020, from https://moodagent.com

Nag, W. (2017). Music streams, smartphones, and the self. *Mobile Media & Communication,* 6(1), 19–36. https://doi.org/10.1177/2050157917719922

Nowak, R. (2016a). *Consuming music in the digital age: Technologies, roles and everyday life.* Palgrave Macmillan.

Nowak, R. (2016b). When is a discovery? The affective dimensions of discovery in music consumption. *Popular Communication,* 14(3), 137–145. https://doi.org/10.1080/15405702.2016.1193182

Nowak, R., & Bennett, A. (2014). Analysing everyday sound environments: The space, time and corporality of musical listening. *Cultural Sociology,* 8(4), 426–442. https://doi.org/10.1177/1749975514532262

Oxford English Dictionary. (Sept. 2020). "experiment, n.". Oxford University Press.

Prey, R. (2016). Musica analytica: The datafication of listening. In R. Nowak & A. Whelan (Eds.), *Networked music cultures* (pp. 31–48). Palgrave Macmillan.

138   M. KROGH

Prey, R. (2018). Nothing personal: Algorithmic individuation on music streaming platforms. *Media, Culture & Society,* 40(7), 1086–1100. https://doi.org/10.1177/0163443717745147

Prior, N. (2018). *Popular music, digital technology and society.* Sage.

Reckwitz, A. (2020). *The society of singularities* (V. A. Pakis, Trans.). Polity Press.

Ruud, E. (2013). *Musikk og identitet.* Universitetsforlaget.

Siles, I., Segura-Castillo, A., Sancho, M., & Solís-Quesada, R. (2019). Genres as social affect: Cultivating moods and emotions through playlists on spotify. *Social Media+ Society,* 5(2), 1–11. https://doi.org/10.1177/2056305119847514

Skånland, M. S. (2013). Everyday music listening and affect regulation: The role of MP3 players. *International Journal of Qualitative Studies on Health and Well-being,* 8, 20595. https://doi.org/10.3402/qhw.v8i0.20595

Slaby, J. (2018). Affective arrangements and disclosive postures: Towards a post-phenomenology of situated affectivity. *Phänomenologische Forschungen,* 2018, 197–216. https://doi.org/10.28937/1000108209

Slaby, J. (2019). Affective arrangement. In J. Slaby & C. v. Scheve (Eds.), *Affective societies: Key concepts* (vol. 1, pp. 109–118). Routledge.

Slaby, J., & Mühlhoff, R. (2019). Affect. In J. Slaby & C. v. Scheve (Eds.), *Affective societies: Key concepts* (vol. 1, pp. 27–41). Routledge.

Slaby, J., Mühlhoff, R., & Wüschner, P. (2017). Affective arrangements. *Emotion review,* 11(1), 3–12. https://doi.org/10.1177/1754073917722214

Slaby, J., & von Scheve, C. (2019). Introduction: Affective societies – Key concepts. In J. Slaby & C. v. Scheve (Eds.), *Affective societies: Key concepts* (vol. 1, pp. 1–24). Routledge.

Spotify Ad Studio. (2020). Turn up your music marketing. Retrieved January 16, 2020, from https://adstudio.spotify.com/turn-up-your-music-marketing

Spotify Advertising. (2017). I feel you, and your ads. Retrieved September 17, 2020, from https://ads.spotify.com/en-US/news-and-insights/i-feel-you-and-your-ads/

Spotify for Developers. (2020). Get audio features for a track. Retrieved January 10, 2020, from https://developer.spotify.com/documentation/web-api/reference/tracks/get-audio-features/

Thompson, M., & Biddle, I. D. (Eds.) (2013). *Sound, music, affect: Theorizing sonic experience.* Bloomsbury Academic.

Thrift, N. (2011). Lifeworld Inc.: And what to do about it. *Environment and Planning D: Society and Space,* 29(1), 5–26.

Tronvoll, B. (2019). Digital enabled experience: The listening experience in music streaming. *International Journal of Music Business Research,* 8, 6–38.

CHAPTER 7

Experimentations in Pandemic Boredom

Susanna Paasonen

The quarantines, lockdowns and practices of social distancing during the global COVID-19 pandemic have been identified as a "boom time for boredom" (e.g., Rosenwald 2020; Hunt 2020). With the calls to stay at home, travels aborted and cities going in lockdown, life-spheres were quickly and violently reorganised and shrunk across continents. Days could seem to follow one another without much change to their rhythm and scenery in an undifferentiated temporality akin to something like a perpetual Tuesday so that "three out of every four Americans have reported being bored stiff" (Blades 2021). The diagnoses of epidemic boredom within the COVID-19 pandemic have owed to the lack of physical mobility or sociability extending beyond networked, screen-based encounters, these themselves turning dull especially for those whose work tasks require them, day in and day out. Not being able to go out and get about is, simply, boring.

On a meta-level, the coronavirus pandemic has been identified as something of a "natural experiment" in both experiencing boredom and studying it (Talbot 2020).

S. Paasonen (✉)
University of Turku, Turku, Finland
e-mail: suspaa@utu.fi

© The Author(s), under exclusive license to Springer Nature
Switzerland AG 2022
B. Timm Knudsen et al. (eds.), *Methodologies of Affective
Experimentation*, https://doi.org/10.1007/978-3-030-96272-2_7

If you wanted to design an experiment to bring about boredom, you couldn't do better than the pandemic. Cooped up in our homes and apartments, we've been stripped of our everyday routine and structure. And without distractions, we are left feeling understimulated. It is this state of restless desire to do something—anything!—without a way of achieving our goal (if we even know what it is) that is the essence of boredom. (Friedman 2020)

Boredom is basically a matter of affective flatness—not an affect as such. If considered an affective experiment, the pandemic then focuses attention on a blandness of experience where intensities of feeling come across as lacking even as these are keenly desired (Anderson 2021, p. 198).

While it is banal to claim that, during the time of this writing late in the year 2020, we are living in historic times (since this is technically always the case), there is little doubt as to the specificity of this moment of crisis and uncertainty. The degree to which this moment was particular in the degrees of boredom it evoked is, however, a different matter, given that cultural diagnoses have foregrounded boredom as a key cultural zeitgeist characteristic, dynamic, symptom and symbol well before the year 2020. Concerns with affective flatness, or even nothingness, as being characteristic to the socio-cultural moment are both tenacious and long-standing; melancholy, ennui and boredom were all seen to comprise a nineteenth-century *mal du siècle* (Anderson 2004; Goodstein 2005; Toohey 1988).

This chapter argues that the specific circumstances of the pandemic moment offer avenues for thinking through the continuities, discontinuities and paradoxes involved in zeitgeist diagnoses of boredom in cultural inquiry, and asks what considerations of ambiguity may add to our understanding of its shape and impact. In doing so, it makes use of analyses of boredom brought forth by lockdowns to experiment with ways of differently understanding cultural diagnoses of boredom as they connect to networked media in particular. A moment in which the shortage of distractions, not their ample supply, and the lack of routines, not their grinding repetition, are seen to result in boredom involves a discursive reversal of causes, effects and cures. This, I argue, offers productive avenues to think about how the affective flatness of boredom comes about and how people live with it.

Starting with the figure of stalled time and fixed place within the pandemic, this chapter examines the ambiguities of boredom in a broader temporal perspective. It addresses the argued specificity of boredom as a modern mood and form experience, asking what methodological choices have contributed to broad consensus on the issue. Shifting focus to psychological and sociological inquiry, it then attends to the different, often mixed accounts of boredom where media is seen as both its cause and cure. Moving from cultural theory to contextual circumstance and back again, the chapter asks what kinds of worlds boredom is seen to build as it is presented as a problem, a solution and a more ambiguously positioned rhythm of experience. Finally, by addressing ambiguity in studies of affect, it argues against dualistic divides drawn between that which paralyses (boredom) and animates (excitement) bodies, tending towards seemingly irreconcilable yet coexisting dynamics of feeling instead.

FLATTENED OUT

Across disciplinary divides, scholars generally define boredom as an issue of diminished potentiality, interest and liveliness that eats away at enjoyment taken in life, so that things no longer hold interest or seem to matter (Anderson 2004, p. 740). As interest gets sucked away, time itself seems to be grinding to a halt and one's capacity to act in the world becomes atrophied: "Nothing seems to happen and thus time seems to stand still" (Slaby 2010, p. 101; Mann and Robinson 2009, p. 243). This may be an issue of circumstance: "A sense of boredom or simple tedium may be the result of, say, being shut up too long" (Toohey 1988, p. 151)—as with COVID-19 lockdowns and quarantines where affective blandness has been primarily identified as an issue of circumstance. Within these, the "shrunk space and time also feels too spacey and too long, a time of boredom that feels insignificant to and incompatible with the time of the crisis" (Xin 2020, p. 35); the present moment "seems to be dragging itself along unbearably, it is as if nothing leads up to it and nothing will come of it" (Johnsen 2011, p. 485). As an "experience without qualities", boredom then opens up something of an existential crisis, spanning from disaffection felt towards one's conditions of life to a felt sense of meaninglessness (Goodstein 2005, p. 406).

Boredom within cultural theory has been largely defined as a modern phenomenon connected to overload of external stimuli that distracts people to boredom. More specifically, this overload has been associated with the speeds of modernity, capitalism and their mechanised systems of production, transport and mediation. For Walter Benjamin (2002, pp. 108–109), the mass phenomenon of boredom "began to be experienced in epidemic proportions in the 1840s" as "weariness with life, deep depressions, boredom" resonant with the rhythms of industrial labour. In what is something of a founding argument in studies of boredom and modernity, the titillations of urban cities and the accelerating speeds of entertainment rendered focus impossible and gave rise to a blasé outlook of bored indifference: given the plethora of things to choose from, it became hard to choose, focus or care at all (Simmel 2002). This development accelerated with the emergence of modern media culture, from the cinema to the radio, and beyond, that bombarded the senses with audiovisual stimuli (Benjamin [1968] 2007; Kracauer [1963] 1995; Duttlinger 2007). The rhythms of modernity have been seen as simply incompatible with human cognition and sensation, and as feeding nervousness, unease, distraction and boredom. With industrialisation, both the production and consumption of culture, it is argued, sped up the rhythms of experience so that people just could not—and still cannot—keep up (Crary 1999; Anderson 2021, pp. 201–202).

Boredom has, in sum, been conceptualised as an outcome of modern capitalism and its multiple logics of monetisation where the rhythms of labour are relentless, where people are extensions to the machine and where premodern communities have been replaced with urban alienation. In connection to this, boredom has been identified as an outcome of leisure-time as it became differentiated in the course of industrialisation. Ennui, as historically identified with the idleness of the social elite (aka "the leisure class"), gave way to a dominant cultural mood of boredom across social strata (Leslie 2009), one "completely lacking and without profound resonance" (Haladyn and Gardiner 2017, p. 5). Following this line of argumentation, ennui was once the plague of the powerful with ample time on their hands while members of the lower social classes, tied to the grind of physical labour, were excluded from its grasp. With modernisation, consumer culture and mediated forms of entertainment came an affective flattening wherein idleness no longer yielded meaning (Thiele 1997, p. 492).

For Henri Lefebvre ([1958] 1991, p. 228), the boredom and greyness of everyday life, "its repetition of the same actions", are products of modernity where communal ties have been broken: "the all-too well known problem of saturation, of boredom, of lightning transitions from interest to tedium, produce techniques aimed at overcoming those very reactions" (Lefebvre 1995, p. 166). Yet others argue that the boring distractions of modernity render deep or profound boredom impossible, hence stopping people from reflecting on the nothingness—or, depending on perspective, the richness—of their being (e.g., Heidegger 1995; Kracauer [1963] 1995). Consequently, people never manage to be bored enough so that their experiences remain diminished. Boredom then meanders through a broad, heterogeneous range of cultural theory as something that results both from too much stimuli and from the stimuli being too flat and commodified; from there being either too much or too little to sense and to make sense of; and from lives growing empty, not being empty enough or not being empty in the right way.

BOREDOM AND HISTORICAL CONTEXT

Despite the range and diversity of academic work currently conducted under the interdisciplinary umbrella of "boredom studies", it is premised on boredom being coupled to modernity to the degree that understanding one necessitates accounting for the other. This premise is often backed up through etymology: although similar words have existed in other languages well before the nineteenth century, the argument goes, it is the introduction of the English term of boredom to popular discourse that encapsulates novel forms of experience so that modernity and boredom grow strictly interconnected (Pezze and Salzani 2009, p. 5).

To map out boredom as both "a reflective moment on the nature of subjective experience" and a "conceptual framework for sociocultural critique" (Haladyn and Gardiner 2017, p. 4), scholars often ground their arguments on analysis of literary texts so that, following Raymond Williams (1977), boredom is seen as a modern structure of feeling. Methodologically, the centrality of literary analysis raises the question of cultural forms and historical context, given that the modern novel, like the English word for boredom, was a product of the eighteenth century that gained dominance during the 1800s (Watt 1957). As a cultural form, the novel expanded possibilities for reflecting on both social contexts and individual lifeworlds, experiences and feelings, which concomitantly became the foci of academic inquiry in the emergent fields of psychology and sociology.

How writerly focus on people's experiential horizons in literary realism and in the Victorian novel connects to the emergence of the vocabulary on boredom is, however, far from self-evident. Rather than identifying accounts of boredom in nineteenth-century literature as speaking of something distinctly novel and unique to the moment, it can also be the case that the language around the shapes and nuances of experience expanded in fiction and social sciences alike during this period and that the centrality of boredom in accounts of modernity owes to such expansions. The emergence of literary accounts does not prove that the experiences described were unequivocally new as such.

Concepts such as *taedium vitae* (profound ennui) and *acedia* (lethargy or listlessness) descriptive of affective flatness were in use in classical Antiquity and early Christian texts, even as boredom scholars are firm in the argument that the "modern form of boredom … has no direct analogue in earlier types of subjective malaise" (Haladyn and Gardiner 2017, p. 5). Meanwhile, classics and religion scholars examining the uses of the notion of *acadia* from Hippocrates to medieval times position boredom much more freely as its cause or synonym (Benvenuto 2018; Wenzel 2017). Peter Toohey (1988, p. 151), for example, opens his discussion of ancient notions of boredom by stating that

> through fifteen hundred years of Western culture the notion of boredom has been a vital one. Ranging from dark age and medieval monastic acedia, from the 'English disease' of the seventeenth, eighteenth centuries and the French Enlightenment, from the *mal de* [*sic*] *siècle* of nineteenth-century Europe, to the 'nausea' and alienation of twentieth-century existentialists and Marxists, the concept has had a long and powerful history.

For Toohey, the phenomenological experience of boredom has simply been described with a different vocabulary across centuries.

Within sociology, modernity has been mapped out against the enchantments of premodernity characterised by communal belonging, even magic, so that the routine-bound and socially stratified lives of farmers and servants—somewhat paradoxically—come to stand in for lost fullness of experience (see Bennett 2001; Paasonen 2020; on historical imagination and premodernity, see also D'Arcens and Lynch 2018). According to this line of argumentation, running through the work of Karl Marx to Max Weber, Georg Simmel and Émile Durkheim, modern capitalism destroyed the enchantments, belongings and sociabilities of previous forms of life, breeding alienation and estrangement instead. Premodernity is the necessary comparator against which modernity and its structures of feelings have been outlined (Schnell 2020, p. 9), yet as disagreements between those studying premodern and modern boredoms show, neat periodisations are not easily achieved when addressing forms of experience in a historical context.

Attempts to demonstrate the specificity of boredom as a modern experience—of which there is no easy consensus across disciplines—through historical sources are met with methodological challenges in that such documentation does not extend to people's everyday experiences and especially not to those with lower social status. We simply have limited access to how premodern life was experienced beyond those who could write and whose records have been preserved, namely members of the clergy and the social elite. The speeds and boredoms of conveyor belt labour differ in obvious ways from the repetitive rhythms and chores of premodern manual labour. However, given the degree to which studies of everyday life have identified mundane repetitive routines, habits and rhythms as not merely that which structure the quotidian but also as that which fundamentally bores (Highmore 2004), it can be asked how we can know that premodern lives—unaffected by media technologies, urban thrills and the rhythms of capitalism—were free of boredom.

As historical imagination does not necessarily meet historical evidence, there are few means of knowing how rich or flat, magical or dull, meaningful or boring premodern lives may have felt. And if this is something we cannot know for the lack of historical documentation, the argument for boredom as a uniquely modern phenomenon is less solid than it may appear within its reiterations. This also means that the causal logic that sees the media as an apparatus for boredom is open to questioning.

RESCUES FROM BOREDOM

Twentieth-century cultural diagnoses saw boredom as the general flattening of experience, spreading horizontally across Western societies as an affective pandemic of sorts with the aid of film, radio and television. More recently, networked media, and social media in particular, have been identified as machines of boredom in their habitual rhythms capturing users in numbed blandness of "digital disaffect" (Lorenz 2018; Petit 2015). There is considerable continuity to these diagnoses, even as the contexts and examples they address, from 1930s cinema to 2020s Instagram cultures, differ drastically. For Michael Hand (2017, p. 116), contemporary life, of which social media forms a ubiquitous part, marks an intensification of modern boredom in its "fragmentation, repetitiveness, standardisation and commodification" where the speeding up of life results in uniformity of experience and where people passively engage with trivia to distract themselves. Social media then become the terrain of "'digital boredom' which characterises contemporary life as technologically mediated, repetitive, rushed and denying solitude and in which multiple practices of presencing, tracking and connecting are at once efforts to alleviate boredom, contributing to experiences of boredom, and occluding the possibility of a more profound boredom" (Hand 2017, p. 115).

As much of everyday life—from schooling to work tasks, shopping and social interaction—shifted online with COVID-19, networked media, addressed as a tool for boredom in many an academic and journalistic account, became reframed as an instrument for managing it. Social media has been identified as a coping mechanism among adolescents dealing with COVID-19 anxiety (Cauberghe et al. 2020) and the networked excitements on offer—"a new dance on TikTok"; "a virtual vacation, … book club, cooking club, or a club that studies medieval art" (Westgate 2020; Sreenivasan and Weinberger 2020)—have been recommended as cures for COVID-19 boredom (e.g., Chao et al. 2020). No longer a figure of rush or solitude denied, social media have been reframed as the means to set in motion time that feels to be standing still and for breaking away from social isolation. As face-to-face communication, which critics of networked exchanges routinely position as more authentic, real, meaningful and threatened by ubiquitous social media use (e.g., Turkle 2014), has posed the risk of infection with potentially lethal consequences, familiar lines of argumentation have been at least temporarily reorganised.

Psychological literature differentiates between circumstantial state boredom as "both the (objective) neurological state of low arousal and the (subjective) psychological state of dissatisfaction, frustration, or disinterest in response to the low arousal" and trait boredom as an individual propensity to experience boredom (Vogel-Walcutt et al. 2012, p. 102). In this framing, situations can be boring, and some people are more easily bored than others. Bringing understimulation together with sensations of frustration, anxiety and stuckness in situations beyond one's control, the pandemic has been seen to result in broad state boredom that people find hard to cope with (Martarelli and Wolff 2020). It has been especially seen to threaten those susceptible to boredom by trait so that they may resort to "excessive drinking, abusing drugs (for example, stimulants), overeating, or even compulsive use of social media" (Sreenivasan and Weinberger 2020).

To amend this and to help people out of boredom during lockdowns, psychologists Shoba Sreenivasan and Linda E. Weinberger (2020) provide a series of tips, from adding fun to one's routines to connecting with others, exercising, cultivating one's curiosity, treating oneself (within the confines of moderation), trying to veer away from doomscrolling news updates and practicing gratitude and kindness in accordance with the tenets of positive psychology. Social psychologist Erin C. Westgate (2020) chimes in with suggestions of reminding oneself of the meaning and purpose of social distancing, finding rhythm and structure to one's daily routines, embracing novelty, making room for guilty pleasures and connecting with others. Here, both networked media and habitual routines, largely identified as causes for contemporary boredom, shift discursively to act as cures instead. It is such shifting of causes, effects and cures, I argue, that renders the pandemic moment productive as an experiment in boredom in both experiential and analytical sense.

Originally writing in the mid-1970s, Stan Cohen and Laurie Taylor (1992, p. 45) saw routines giving rise to "boredom, monotony, tedium, despair" that people try to momentarily escape through casual distractions. This line of thinking, where the stuckness and repetition of habitual routines yields boredom, bears resemblance to Mihály Csíkszentmihályi's (2000, p. 141) contemporaneous discussion on the ubiquity and pervasiveness of boredom and anxiety in everyday life that are countered with attempts at managing, avoiding and alleviating tedium—for example, by daydreaming, reading or watching television. Csíkszentmihályi (2000, p. 3) associates boredom especially with work in contrast to leisure catering different kinds of pleasures: "the former is what we have to do most of the time against our desire; the latter is what we like to do, although it is useless". While Csíkszentmihályi goes on to challenge this dichotomous view of work and play, he basically considers boredom as an issue of motivation and pleasure connected to circumstance. It then follows that boredom, shifts and lifts, and ranges in its pervasiveness without qualifying as a general crisis of meaning, and certainly without being an outcome of leisure as such.

A similar notion of boredom management emerged in students accounts of mundane media and communication technology use that I collected for my class on media and networks from 2012 to 2018. It described browsing social media during boring lectures and other tedious circumstances—bus rides, solitary lunches—where the surrounding world held little interest. Some students described their personal networked devices as primary foci of entertainment so that if a mobile phone or laptop broke down or the network connection failed to work boredom grew imminent: "Often, when things are frustratingly boring, I open the computer as last resort in order to have the Net entertain me. If the Net doesn't work, I'm doomed to boredom." This account echoes promises attached to social media in corporate rhetoric as the loci of virtually endless novelty, entertainment and distraction—catered, for example, by clickbait such as Bored Panda, Boreburn and Boredom Therapy promising to battle the impending boredoms of everyday life (Kendall 2018).

The call for users to engage with social media as a means of escaping boredom is, of course, diametrically opposed to critiques according to which social media itself bores. The case is nevertheless less clear-cut than it may appear, given how it becomes the task of individual users to manage the flows of available data in order to be un-bored, even as how these flows are algorithmically curated according to the principle of homophily, love of the same, where similarity is seen to attract and breed similarity (Chun 2018). The already seen and the novel, the boring and the interesting intermesh in rhythms where one can be alternatively "bored, not bored, bored, not bored, bored" (Petit 2015, p. 180).

As social media is figured to be a solution to boredom, the challenge is to find sufficiently novel and interesting content as a curatorial quest of sorts. Tina Kendall (2018, p. 81) identifies social media users as "above all as boredom managers—agents who are responsible for, and capable of coordinating, the affective texture of their own experience as it unfolds in real time". The affective texture of experience simply takes work, even when the activities involved are those of leisure or ones aiming to lift the boredom of work tasks. As in Csíkszentmihályi's discussion of boredom and pleasure, a binary division between work and play then fails to hold—not least given the degree to which the spaces and times of work and leisure intermesh. In what Melissa Gregg (2011) addresses as "presence bleed", smart devices and mobile technologies move work into the personal realm so that labour extends well beyond formal workplaces and working hours. This bleed is further accelerated within the pandemic for those who have worked remotely from home using the same devices for occupational tasks as for the purposes of entertainment and reorganising their work hours around private and domestic commitments.

Following the diagnostic frame of modernity and boredom, all this would speak of the tedium of life in industrialised capitalism that offers mediated distractions as placebos of kinds to the ills that it itself causes, adding to further shallowness and unhappiness. My interests lie in less definite and causal accounts of the experiential horizons of networked media that leave room for affective ambiguity—the ambiguities of boredom included. I find it necessary to move to more contextually grounded forms of inquiry that are open to the complexities of everyday life and the diverse affective ranges within which it is experienced. This calls for more flexible and expansive ways of understanding how affective flatness oscillates with interest, excitement, pleasure and surprise in both quotidian rhythms and patterns of social media use. Since a discussion of my empirical work on affective ambiguity and networked media is not possible here due to limitations of space (see Paasonen 2021), I offer something of an exemplary anecdote instead.

Networked Frivolity

During the first wave of COVID-19 lockdowns in the spring of 2020, it became an international trend for people to recreate famous artworks at home with the domestic materials at hand and to share the outcome on social media, tagged as #quarantinart, #isolationart, #covidclassics and things beyond. People recreated art historical classics as live tableaus in mundane spaces, documenting them and posting the remakes and originals side by side for others to witness, compare and hopefully enjoy. The shots foregrounded circumstantial creativity where the human and inhuman bodies of classical paintings were replaced with something completely different: collar lace with hoarded toilet paper; animal models with human ones, and vice versa; helmets with tinfoil hats; swords with toilet brushes; and gallant horses with wheelchairs, perplexed dogs, annoyed cats and fluffy toy unicorns.

Calls for re-enactments were shared by art museums that were forced to close their doors and extend audience outreach to digital platforms. The efforts of some social media groups, such as the Russian Izoizolyacia, grew viral. In a thread that I myself found particularly gratifying, a Facebook group dedicated to photos of bad art found in second-hand shops around the world was temporarily reimagined as these shops were no longer open. People then turned to recreating images of previously posted, often markedly bizarre and maladroit pieces of visual art, some of which had gained hundreds, if not thousands of likes, wows, hahas and snarky comments, effectively forming a contingent and contextually bound canon of amazingly terrible art. With great care and attention to detail, people crawled around in their backyards, refashioned their living rooms, painted their bodies and repurposed domestic objects, family members and companion species as more or less willing props in order to approximate such lowbrow objects of art.

Such networked silliness is hardly novel in social media that thrives on the sharing of memes and cat videos, nor was recreational creativity a zeitgeist phenomenon specific to the year 2020. I suggest that this particular strand of frivolity, combined with the degrees of care and attention that people put into their recreations for the sheer purpose of merriment, pushes analysis beyond easy juxtaposition between the silly and the serious, things that distract and those that matter. These shared, often laborious recreations speak of finding interesting things to do under conditions that threaten to flatten one's sense of liveliness—and, no less crucially, of the pleasures gained from participating in networked social theatre unfolding in posts, comments and reactions. Since new pictures of bad art could not be shared, previously bad art became the focus of creative making in a collective effort of and experiment in affective management. Some motivated their efforts through attempts of fighting boredom; some just felt otherwise compelled.

Whatever was being done here in terms of boredom, broad diagnoses of ubiquitously bland, flat and meaningless modernity (and late modernity), as repeatedly evoked in cultural theory, fail to do the critical work required for analysing it. In order to explain at least some of this, it is necessary to consider mundane fascinations and boredoms in more expansive and ambivalent terms—be it in the pandemic context or beyond. Conceptualised as a "natural experiment", lockdowns can be productively used for critically revisiting the master narrative of boredom so that contextual nuance and ambiguity become central concerns and analytical foci. Within the pandemic, boredom has been diagnosed to emerge from the lack of external stimulus rather than from its excessive supply while both networked media and quotidian routines are seen to afford releases from the heaviness of boredom, rather than function as their cause. All this sets established conceptualisations of boredom in motion and helps to foreground discontinuities and ambiguities that cut across them. What may come across as a uniform telling of affective flatness is, on closer inspection, rife with paradox and discontinuity, from the limits of methodological choices to disagreements over historical periodisation or the causes of and the cures for boredom.

Following Csíkszentmihályi, Cohen and Taylor alike, boredom remains perpetually present and is therefore ultimately impossible to escape: it is less a spectral threat looming on the horizon than a quotidian backdrop or base note for the rhythms of everyday life. Minor and major instances of interest, excitement and desire cutting into and playing with boredom entail shifts in rhythm and intensity that move bodies from one state to another (also Paasonen 2018, p. 227). In different ways, sociological and psychological queries have framed the affective flatness of boredom as oscillating with affective intensities that make things matter and increase the pleasure taken in life. As boredom is set in an active dynamic with interest, joy, anger and a range of affectations beyond, experience itself entails their fundamental inseparability. Rather than understanding boredom as the opposite of enchantment or excitement, the issue can then be conceptualised as one of shifting intensities and qualities of experience—as in the cycles of "bored, not bored, bored, not bored, bored".

Writing on the affordances of hyper-casual gaming in the context of COVID-19 lockdowns, Liu Xin (2020) points out that the repetitive rhythms of networked media do not just bore and dull: they can equally function as techniques of self-care that maintain and possibly add to the liveliness of bodies. This means that routine and repetitive things (such as the rhythms of a casual game or the newsfeed of a social media platform) can be enchanting and comforting precisely due to their dullness so that predictability and routine intermesh in ways irreducible to the specific circumstance within which they are experienced. Repetitive routines oscillate in sharper and duller registers of attention and feeling so that it is not possible to mark them as being either causes of or cures for boredom.

Ambiguities of Boredom

As a "boom time for boredom", the COVID-19 pandemic is argued to be historically specific. Meanwhile, broad diagnoses of boredom and modernity have remained relatively unaffected by twentieth-century crises and times of rupture, such as the "Spanish" flu pandemic (1918–1920), the Great Depression (c. 1929–1939) or the First and Second World Wars (1914–1918; 1939–1945) all of which, in different ways, undid the conditions and rhythms of life, and life itself, on expansive and radical scales. The predominance of boredom in cultural analysis amounts to something of a master narrative recounted in different variations without sufficiently attending to contextual specificities and multiplicities of experience, as these are bound to play out under different regional, economic, legal and political circumstances among people of varying ages, genders, ethnicities, classes, religions, abilities or citizenship statuses. As Hand (2017, p. 124) notes, the narrative of digital boredom that he sets forth comprises "a largely melancholic, romantic and often pejorative critique of everyday life" that does not aid explorations in the ambiguity of networked exchanges. The same applies to many other retellings of modernity, media and boredom.

There is persistent ambiguity to boredom, despite the seemingly unequivocal qualities of affective flatness that define it. For Alison Pease (2012, p. 4), "boredom is experienced as an irritating emptiness, a desire for something unknown to relieve the claustrophobic, enervating sense of time passing slowly". In this sense, it entails agitation—"a corporeal irritation or restlessness, an agitated inertia in response to a current situation that holds no interest, both temporally and spatially" (Hjorth and Richardson 2009, p. 32). In a literary framework, Sianne Ngai discusses the seemingly paradoxical aesthetic category of "stuplimity" where boredom meets astonishment in simultaneous excitation and fatigue. For Ngai (2000), stuplimity builds on repetition and is at once dulling, irritating and agitating.

Ngai (2012) further positions the interesting and the boring in a dynamic relation where the one feeds the other—much less as polar opposites than as intermeshing intensities. Moving Ngai's conceptualisation from literary analysis to the context of networked media and everyday life, it helps to map out experiences thereof as ambiguous amalgamations of excitement and boredom in constant motion. For psychologist Silvan S. Tomkins (2008), interest is one of basic positive affects that, when growing in intensity, turns to excitement. Excitement is elusive in that it grows thinner with repetition and familiarity, yet it also invests life with a sense of magic, to the degree of being the stuff that makes the self (Tomkins 2008, p. 193). Bringing Tomkins' discussion of excitement together with Ngai's examination of ambiguity helps to see how the affective flatness of boredom comes speckled with minor and major fascinations so that our life-forces can be simultaneously amplified and atrophied as we are made and unmade in our encounters with the world.

Reframing boredom as a herald rather than a symptom, Ben Anderson (2021, p. 205) arrives similarly at affective ambiguity and identifies boredom as "the inarticulate expression of a desire for more to life". To approach boredom on such terms, he further proposes, makes it possible to "encounter boredom for its potentiality, for its restlessness, for how it moves subjects into new relations and attachments" so that scholars can "suspend judgement and follow what opens up in the wake of the detachment that is boredom, staying close to and valorising escape attempts, from daydreaming to world historical revolutions" (Anderson 2021, p. 205). Indeed, within all kinds of quotidian practices, interest cuts through and intermeshes with boredom and gives rise to instances of everyday marvel (Bennett 2001), the fascinations of which are in dynamic tension with the flatter notes of feeling of which much everyday life is composed. Understanding boredom as attached to fascination, enchantment, interest and excitement does not mean subscribing to an understanding of affective spectrums oscillating between positive and negative intensities in a binary manner, or as shifting from richness of sensation to the flatness of ennui and back again (although this is also possible). To conceptualise such intensities as intermeshed is a means to foreground ambiguity in both experiences of everyday life and cultural analysis, so as to account for the unstable ripples of affect that cut through and fuel individual, social and collective lives, both within pandemic times and beyond.

Conclusion: Thinking with Ambiguity

Working with and through ambiguity in the context of boredom means (at least) two things: acknowledging the intermeshing and unpredictability of different intensities of feeling and trying to hold on to seemingly irreconcilable tensions without attempting to resolve them. Ambiguous things are not the one or the other, this or that, but *both and* (see Coleman 2016). Boredom is both a modern experience, and not; the same things that bore excite and give joy. As indeterminacy of meaning, ambiguity is by necessity messy, as are the diffuse phenomena that make culture, society and the world beyond. In this sense, academic embrace of ambiguity means following John Law's (2004, pp. 2, 3) call for analytical approaches capable of dealing with "mess, confusion and relative disorder ... things that slip and slide, or appear and disappear, change shape or don't have much form at all" and finding "ways of knowing the indistinct and the slippery without trying to grasp and hold them tight".

My suggestion is that approaches open to and respectful of ambiguity, affective and other offer means of countering cultural critiques casting networked media, and social media in particular, as machines of distraction, boredom and unhappiness in unequivocal terms (e.g., Lovink 2019; Pettman 2016). I also suggest that, by violently shifting our concrete conditions of life, the extended pandemic time of exception has opened up experimentational spaces for coining more granular and situated understandings of the worlds we make in our cohabitations with physical spaces, devices, media streams and bodies of people. Being stuck in place, and time feeling stuck, has allowed for rethinking causalities in how boredom comes about, what it allows for and generates and what roles networked media play in this. Carrying such experimentational lessons over to post-pandemic times involves the promise of productively ambiguous forms of critical thought.

REFERENCES

Anderson, B. (2004). Time-stilled space-slowed: How boredom matters. *Geoforum, 35*, 739–754.
Anderson, B. (2021). Affect and critique: A politics of boredom. *Society and Space,* 39(2), 197–217.
Benjamin, W. (2002). *The arcades project* (H. Eiland & K. McLaughlin, Trans.). Harvard University Press.
Benjamin, W. (2007). *Illuminations* (H. Arendt, Ed. & H. Zohn, Trans.). Schocken Books. (Original work published 1968).
Bennett, J. (2001). *The enchantment of modern life: Attachments, crossings, and ethics.* Princeton University Press.
Benvenuto, S. (2018). The silent fog. *American imago, 75*(1), 1–23.
Blades, R. (2021, March 21). The endless "existential crisis": Finding meaning in the midst of COVID boredom. *Healthy Debate.* Retrieved December 17, 2021, from https://healthydebate.ca/2021/03/topic/covid-boredom/
Cauberghe, V., Wesenbeeck, I. Van, Jans, S. De, Hudders, L. & Ponnet, K. (2020). How adolescents use social media to cope with feelings of loneliness and anxiety during COVID-19 lockdown. *Cyberpsychology, Behavior, and Social Networking.* Preprint retrieved from https://www.liebertpub.com/doi/full/10.1089/cyber.2020.0478
Chao, M., Chen, X., Liu, T., Yang, H. & Hall, B. J. (2020). Psychological distress and state boredom during the COVID-19 outbreak in China: The role of meaning in life and media use. *European Journal of Psychotraumatology, 11* (1). https://doi.org/10.1080/20008198.2020.1769379
Chun, W. H. K. (2018) Queering homophily. In C. Apprich, W. Hui Kyong Chun, F. Cramer & H. Steyerl, *Pattern discrimination* (pp. 59–97). Minnesota University Press/Meson Press.
Cohen, S, & Taylor, L. (1992). *Escape attempts: The theory and practice of resistance to everyday life* (2nd ed.). Routledge.
Coleman, R. (2016). Austerity futures: Debt, temporality and (hopeful) pessimism as an austerity mood. *New formations, 87*, 83–101.

Crary, J. 1999. *Suspensions of perception: Attention, spectacle, and modern culture.* MIT Press.

Csíkszentmihályi, M. (2000). *Beyond boredom and anxiety: Experiencing flow in work and play. 25th anniversary edition.* Jossey-Bass Publishers.

D'Arcens, L. & Lynch, A. (2018). Feeling for the premodern. *Exemplaria: Medieval, Early Modern, Theory,* 30(3), 183–190.

Duttlinger, C. (2007). Between contemplation and distraction: Configurations of attention in Walter Benjamin. *German Studies Review,* 30(1), 33–54.

Friedman, R. A. (2020, August 21). Is the lockdown making you depressed, or are you just bored? *The New York Times.* Retrieved December 17, 2021, from https://www.nytimes.com/2020/08/21/opinion/sunday/covid-depression-boredom.html

Goodstein, E. S. (2005). *Experience without qualities: Boredom and modernity.* Stanford University Press.

Gregg, M. (2011). *Work's intimacy.* Polity Press.

Haladyn, J. J., & Gardiner, M. E. (2017). Monotonous splendour: An introduction to boredom studies. In M. E. Gardiner & J. J. Haladyn (Eds.), *Boredom studies reader: Frameworks and perspectives* (pp. 3–18). Routledge.

Hand, M. (2017). #boredom: Technology, acceleration, and connected presence in the social media age. In M. E. Gardiner & J. J. Haladyn (Eds.), *Boredom studies reader: Frameworks and perspectives* (pp. 115–129). Routledge.

Heidegger, M. (1995). *The fundamental concepts of metaphysics: World, finitude, solitude* (W. McNeill & N. Walker, Trans.). Indiana University Press.

Highmore, B. (2004). Homework: Routine, social aesthetics and the ambiguity of everyday life. *Cultural Studies,* 18 (2–3), 306–327.

Hjorth, L. & Richardson, I. (2009). The waiting game: Complicating notions of (tele) presence and gendered distraction in casual mobile gaming. *Australian Journal of Communication,* 36(1), 23–35.

Hunt, E. (2020, May 3). Why it's good to be bored. *The Guardian.* Retrieved December 17, 2021, from https://www.theguardian.com/global/2020/may/03/why-its-good-to-be-bored

Johnsen, R. (2011). On boredom. *Ephemera,* 11(4), 482–489.

Kendall, T. (2018). "# BOREDWITHMEG": Gendered boredom and networked media. *New Formations,* 93, 80–100.

Kracauer, S. (1995). *The mass ornament: Weimar essays* (T. Y. Levin, Trans. & Ed.). Harvard University Press. (Original work published 1963).

Law, J. (2004). *After method: Mess in social science research.* Routledge.

Lefebvre, H. (1991). *Critique of everyday life,* vol. 1 (J. Moore, Trans.). Verso. (Original work published 1958).

Lefebvre, H. (1995). *Introduction to modernity: Twelve preludes September 1959– May 1961* (J. Moore, Trans.). Verso.

Leslie, I. (2009). From idleness to boredom: on the historical development of modern boredom. In B. Dalle Pezze & C. Salzani (Eds.), *Essays on boredom and modernity* (pp. 35–59). Rodopi.

Lorenz, T. (2018, April 3). Generation Z is already bored by the internet. *The Daily Beast*. Retrieved December 17, 2021, from https://www.thedailybeast.com/generation-z-is-already-bored-by-the-internet

Lovink, G. (2019). *Sad by design: On platform nihilism*. Pluto Press.

Mann, S. & Robinson, A. (2009). Boredom in the lecture theatre: An investigation into the contributors, moderators and outcomes of boredom amongst university students. *British educational research journal*, 35(2), 243–258.

Martarelli, C. & Wolff, W. (2020). Too bored to bother? Boredom as a potential threat to the efficacy of pandemic containment measures. *Humanities and Social Sciences in Communications*, 7. https://doi.org/10.1057/s41599-020-0512-6

Ngai, S. (2000). Stuplimity: Shock and boredom in twentieth-century aesthetics. *Postmodern culture*, 10(2): 1–20.

Ngai, S. (2012). *Our aesthetic categories: Zany, cute, interesting*. Harvard University Press.

Paasonen, S. (2018). Affect, data, manipulation and price in social media. *Distinktion: Journal of Social Theory*, 19(2): 214–229.

Paasonen, S. (2020). Distracted present, golden past? *Media theory*, 4(2): 11–32.

Paasonen, S. (2021). *Dependent, distracted, bored: Affective formations in networked media*. MIT Press.

Pease, A. (2012). *Modernism, feminism and the culture of boredom*. Cambridge University Press.

Petit, M. (2015). Digital disaffect: Teaching through screens. In K. Hillis, S. Paasonen & M. Petit (Eds.), *Networked affect* (pp. 169–183). MIT Press.

Pettman, D. (2016). *Infinite distraction*. Polity.

Pezze, B. Dalle & Salzani, C. (2009). The delicate monster: Modernity and boredom. In B. Dalle Pezze & C. Salzani (Eds.), *Essays on boredom and modernity* (pp. 5–33). Rodopi.

Rosenwald, M. S. (2020, March 28). These are boom times for boredom and the researchers who study it. *The Washington Post*. Retrieved December 17, 2021, from https://www.washingtonpost.com/local/these-are-boom-times-for-boredom-and-the-researchers-who-study-it/2020/03/27/0e62983a-706f-11ea-b148-e4ce3fbd85b5_story.html

Schnell, R. (2020). *Histories of emotion: Modern–premodern*. Walter de Gruyter.

Simmel, G. (2002). The metropolis and mental life (1903). In G. Bridge & S. Watson (Eds.), *The Blackwell city reader* (pp. 103–110). Wiley-Blackwell.

Slaby, J. (2010). The other side of existence: Heidegger on boredom. In D. Marguelies Flach & J. Söffner (Eds.), *Habitus in habitat II: Other sides of cognition* (pp. 101–120). Peter Lang.

Sreenivasan, S. & Weinberger, L. E. (2020, October 6). I'm so bored: An over-looked effect of the COVID-19 pandemic lockdowns. *Psychology Today.* Retrieved December 17, 2021, from https://www.psychologytoday.com/us/blog/emotional-nourishment/202010/i-m-so-bored

Talbot, M. (2020, August 20). What does boredom do to us – and for us? *The New Yorker.* Retrieved December 17, 2021, from https://www.newyorker.com/culture/annals-of-inquiry/what-does-boredom-do-to-us-and-for-us

Thiele, L. P. (1997). Postmodernity and the routinization of novelty: Heidegger on boredom and technology. *Polity, 29*(4), 489–517.

Tomkins, S. S. (2008). *Affect imaginary consciousness: The complete edition.* Springer.

Toohey, P. (1988). Some ancient notions of boredom. *Illinois Classical Studies,* 13(1), 151–164.

Turkle, S. (2014). *Alone together: Why we expect more from technology and less from each other.* Basic Books.

Vogel-Walcutt, J. J., Fiorella, L., Carper, T. & Schatz, S. (2012). The definition, assessment, and mitigation of state boredom within educational settings: A comprehensive review. *Educational Psychology Review,* 24(1): 89–111.

Watt, I. (1957). *The rise of the novel: Studies in Defoe, Richardson, and Fielding.* University of California Press.

Wenzel, S. (2017). *The sin of sloth: Acedia in medieval thought and literature.* University of North Carolina Press.

Westgate, E. C. (2020, March 27). 6 things you can do to cope with boredom at a time of social distancing. *The Conversation.* Retrieved December 17, 2021, from https://theconversation.com/6-things-you-can-do-to-cope-with-boredom-at-a-time-of-social-distancing-134734

Williams, R. (1977). *Marxism and literature.* Oxford University Press.

Xin, L. (2020). Im/possible boredom: Rethinking the present of the gamer subject. *Media Theory,* 4 (2), 33–54.

PART II

Understanding Affective Experimentation as a Research Method

CHAPTER 8

Worlding with Glitter: Vibrancy, Enchantment and Wonder

Rebecca Coleman

If you can, find something that is glittery. Perhaps you have a tub of the sparkly particles in a craft box, or there is a children's toy covered in glitter lying around. There could be glitter on the page of a magazine or book. You might have a pot of glitter nail varnish or an eye shadow or some other twinkly cosmetics in a drawer. Maybe your kitchen counter or a light shade contains pieces of glitter, or there is a shimmering thread in a curtain or cushion. Perhaps you'll need to look further afield and work with a more expansive understanding of glitter: the glistening of water on a surface, the slime of a snail's trail, or the sheen of some spilled oil on the road. Maybe the window of a neighbour's home or the reflective tape on a vehicle catches the light and shines.

Once you have found your something glittery, spend some time contemplating it. Consider in particular the following questions, but also be aware of other questions or thoughts that emerge for you (this list is not exhaustive).

– *What is your glittery thing?*
– *How have you understood or interpreted what is glitter in order to find and settle on your thing?*

R. Coleman (✉)
University of Bristol, Bristol, UK
e-mail: rebecca.coleman@bristol.ac.uk

© The Author(s), under exclusive license to Springer Nature
Switzerland AG 2022
B. Timm Knudsen et al. (eds.), *Methodologies of Affective
Experimentation,* https://doi.org/10.1007/978-3-030-96272-2_8

- *What is glittery about your thing?*
- *What does the glitter do?*
- *How does the glitter make you feel?*
- *Does your glittery thing remind you of other glittery things? If so, ask the same questions of those things.*

We will return to these questions and others, and your reflections and responses to them.

Until a few years ago, I would describe my relationship to glitter as ambivalent. I did not have strong feelings about it—I did not gravitate towards glittery things, but neither did I avoid them. It surprised me, then, when I found myself writing a book that took glitter as its focus (Coleman 2020). A book about glitter emerged following two art-making workshops that I arranged with teenage girls in their school where they collaged imaginations of their futures. I had bought tubes of glitter alongside a range of other materials including paper, pens, stickers, pipe cleaners, stamps and magazines. I had not anticipated glitter becoming the focus of my attention. However, the tubs of glitter proved very popular with the collagers as they passed them around and across the table. The glitter moved from the collages themselves to human bodies and the classroom, as we and the classroom became covered in it. Most of this was accidental. One participant spent around 15 minutes at the art-room sink trying to wipe off the glitter that covered her school blazer before she went to the next class. It was also sometimes deliberate. One participant spread glue on a fingernail and shook the pot of purple glitter over it so she was wearing glittery nail polish. At the end of the workshops, the art-room table was smeared with glitter. The floor was also covered. Glitter clung to my clothes, bags and notebook long after the workshops had finished.

Glitter seemed to demand that I notice it, attend to it and consider its movement (how it sticks and scatters) as one of its central qualities. It seemed to me that the ways in which glitter moves can be understood in terms of an orientation to the future. For the teenage girls who participated in the collaging workshops, glitter became a significant material through which they could imagine their futures and visualise these imaginations. At the same time, much is currently being written about the future effects of glitter on the natural environment. These examples clearly indicate different futures; and they also indicate how glitter moves across different worlds—from crafting to imagined futures, from artificial material to environmental hazard. And, more importantly, how in this movement, glitter makes, or 'worlds', different worlds. The movement of glitter in and across different worlds is transformational and future-oriented. As it moves, glitter brings these worlds to life.

In this chapter, I focus on the two workshops I ran with teenage girls, where glitter emerged as especially significant. The workshops were held in a girls' secondary school (ages 11–18) in south east London. According to the latest report by the Office for Standards in Education, Children's Services and Skills (Ofsted), the school "serves a disadvantaged area and the proportion of students known to be eligible for free school meals is more than twice the national average. Around 85% of students are from minority-ethnic groups, with the largest groups having Black Caribbean or Black African heritages" (2012, 3).[1] Twelve girls in year 9 (aged 13–14 years old) who came from a range of racial and ethnic groups self-selected in the collaging workshops. I worked closely with the arts teacher in the school, and we arranged for them to take place over two consecutive days. She briefed the arts classes on the research and this became the basis for participants opting into it. The workshops were held during the usual, timetabled arts lessons in the arts classroom. The workshops were approved by the head teacher at the school and by my institutional research ethics committee. Informed consent forms were signed by both the girls and their parents/carers. The workshops were audio-recorded, and I also took photographs and recorded some video during them.

The chapter discusses the workshops as a contribution to affective and new materialist experimentation with methods and more specifically contextualises them within some recent work on worlding. In particular, it considers worlding in relation to methods, arguing that methods are one way in which worlds are, and might be, made. It highlights the future-orientation of worlding, arguing that this requires us, as researchers, to consider the politics and ethics of worlding. I draw out the significance of these ways of understanding worlding by detailing what glitter does, both to me and to the participants, in the workshops. I suggest that glitter functions to open up the possibilities of the future through how it cultivates capacities for enchantment and wonder for the participants. It concludes

---

[1] Ofsted carry out regular inspections of schools, and their judgements and reports form the basis of school league tables. I cannot cite the Ofsted report here as my institutional ethical approval requires the school to remain anonymous.

by drawing out from the specificities of glitter and these workshops to tentatively propose what a wider engagement with an experimentation with worlding might involve. Throughout, I pose questions for you to consider in relation to your own research methods and practices; you are, of course, free to engage with these or not, and to augment them with your own, further questions.

METHODS AS WORLDING

A good deal of recent work has examined the performativity (Law et al. 2011), enactment (Law and Urry 2004) or inventiveness (Lury and Wakeford 2012) of methods. While having different inflexions, what these various understandings propose is that methods are, and always have been, actively involved in the creation of the social worlds they study. In explaining their version of the double social life of methods, for example, John Law, Mike Savage and Evelyn Ruppert argue that methods are necessarily located in and constituted by the social world and "are in turn implicated in the social world. They are thus also of the social in the sense that they constitute and organise it. Or, to use the jargon, that they don't just represent reality out there but that they are also performative of the social" (2011, 8). Celia Lury and Nina Wakeford see methods as inventive, which refers both to the ways in which methods are not neutral or external tools but rather need to be specific to the problem that they address and change in the process of addressing it. Such a process of changing the problem might be understood in terms of the (re)invention of the social; as a method addresses a 'social problem', it changes it and makes a difference. For Law and John Urry, methods "do not simply describe the world as it is, but also enact it" (2004, 391). Given this activity of methods, they pose the conundrum of 'ontological politics':

> If methods help to make the realities they describe, then we are faced with the question: which realities might we try to enact? Neo-classical ones? Ameliorist agendas? Revolutionary realities? Anti-patriarchal or post-colonial worlds? Realities composed of post-structuralist partialities and shifting identities? Cyborg-like and materially heterogeneous worlds? These are just a few of the possibilities. And the issue of ontological politics, about what is or could be made more real, is all the more pointed since every time we make reality claims in social science we are helping to make some social reality or other more or less real. In a world where everything is performative,

everything has consequences, there is, as Donna Haraway indicates, no innocence. (2004, 396)

Law and Urry's reference to Haraway's work here flags the significance of there being no neutral or politically and ethically innocent method, an argument that Haraway has long been making (1988). One instantiation of this argument is in relation to worlding—the attention given to how worlds are shaped and take form. Haraway does not explicitly frame her understanding of worlding in methodological terms; however, in the sense that it is concerned with the active making of worlds, it is productive to consider what it might offer to doing affective and new materialist research. Of particular note is Haraway's comment that "it matters what matters we use to think other matters with; it matters what stories we tell to tell other stories with; it matters what knots knot knots, what thoughts think thoughts, what descriptions describe descriptions, what ties tie ties. It matters what stories make worlds, what worlds make stories" (2016, 12). Haraway's argument about the politics and ethics of worlding is made through the attention she gives to the specific matter through which worlds are worlded. This matter is both specific and diverse—knots, thoughts, descriptions, ties and stories. The implication of Haraway's point here is that that worlding potentially occurs through many different materials and that different materials materialise the world differently. It matters whether and how a world is worlded through knots and/or thoughts and/or descriptions and/or ties and/or stories. As Vicky Hunter and Helen Palmer (2018) put it, Haraway's work "calls into question the nature of matter itself, what we perceive and consider as human and non-human matter, what counts and what matters and, through doing so, enables the fostering of new ontological dispositions towards the world and worlds at large".

The ontological dispositions fostered by Haraway's understanding of worlding require us to consider what materials are involved in the making of worlds. It is noteworthy that these materials encompass non-human things as well as humans, and highlight the entanglements between them. Indeed, Hunter and Palmer suggest that "[w]orlding is a particular blending of the material and the semiotic that removes the boundaries between subject and environment, or perhaps between persona and topos" (2018). Working with Haraway's understanding of worlding therefore requires a three-fold thinking through of what materials are already involved in worlding, what materials might also or instead be involved in worlding (to draw through Law and Urry's argument) and the ways in which humans and non-humans, the material and semiotic, the subject and environment, the persona and topoi are distributed, mixed up and merged. Haraway's argument pushes us to examine what the materials through which worlds are worlded do, whether we consider them to be sufficient or whether other materials might make other worlds possible or stronger.

Did you find something glittery?
How easy or hard was it to find this thing?
What worlds are this glittery thing involved in (domestic, natural, children's, feminine ...)?
How is this glittery thing involved in making this world/these worlds?
Might it world differently/world a different world?

The ways materials world worlds can be thought through methodologically in terms of what we give attention to in our research and how. As discussed above, I did not anticipate that glitter would demand my attention, and that I would need to notice and consider how glitter was involved in the worlds of collaging and in imagining futures for the young women participating in the workshops. However, once I had noticed glitter, I could not stop noticing it and thinking about its ubiquity. I began to understand glitter as what Jane Bennett (2010) terms "vibrant matter". This conception of matter seeks to account for the life/liveliness of things, where things have the capacity to "act as quasi agents or forces with trajectories, propensities, or tendencies of their own" (2010, viii).

Bennett's term for capturing the vibrancy and affectivity of matter is 'thing-power', which "gestures toward the strange ability of ordinary, man-made items to exceed their status as objects and to manifest traces of independence or aliveness" (2010, xvi). For Bennett, then, things have an agency of their own. While they may be man-made, and hence are in relations with humans, they also have the capacity for autonomy—a life/liveliness that exceeds humans. They are not (only) brought to life by humans but have the potential to act or have a life outside of or in excess of what humans may do with them. For example, introducing her conception of vital materials, Bennett discusses how a range of items lying in a gutter—glove, pollen, rat, cap and stick—"commanded attention in its own right, as existents in excess of their association with human meanings, habits, or projects" (2010, 4). As she goes on to explain, being 'struck' by these items facilitated an understanding of their 'thing-power': "At the very least, it provoked affects in me" (2010, 4).

Bennett's argument connects matter and affect. Thing-power refers both to the capacity of things to act and for them to 'provoke affects'. Indeed, for Bennett, the capacity of a thing to act, to have agency, is at once an affective capacity. Thus, in addition to the examination of the materials that are or might be involved in worlding that Haraway's argument encourages, it is also productive to consider the affects provoked by such materials.

What does your glittery thing do?
How does the glitter make you feel?

In a first step, as these questions indicate, we might inquire into the affects elicited, surfaced or taking shape in us through our relations with specific materials. What things are we struck by? In what ways and with what affects/effects do they strike us? This involves the development of a noticing and an attentiveness to materials and to how agency is distributed across a wide range of matter and materials, both human and non-human. Such an understanding of the life/liveliness of non-human things requires a methodology capable of grasping such vibrancy and movement. If things are affective and have an autonomy that is bound up with humans but not always determined by them, Bennett asks:

> What method could possibly be appropriate for the task of speaking a word for vibrant matter? How to describe without thereby erasing the independence of things? How to acknowledge the obscure but ubiquitous intensity of impersonal affect? What seems to be needed is a certain willingness to appear naïve or foolish, to affirm what Adorno called his 'clownish traits'. (2010, xiii)

When I asked you to find and spend time contemplating something glittery, how did you feel?

The "willingness to appear naïve or foolish" that Bennett introduces here is part of what she describes as "a cultivated, patient, sensory attentiveness to nonhuman forces operating outside and inside the human body", which she explains as "learn[ing] how to induce an attentiveness to things and their affects" (2010, xiv, see also Stewart 2007; Coleman and Ringrose

2013).[2] In practical terms, this involves the attempt to "try to linger in those moments during which [vital materialists] find themselves fascinated by objects, taking them as clues to the material vitality that they share with them" (Bennett 2010).

Are you fascinated with the glittery thing you've found?
Are you able to cultivate a sensory attentiveness to what it does, its affects?

WORLDING FUTURES

The workshops with the teenage school students in which glitter became apparent as a vibrant material of worlding was organised around a methodology for imagining futures. Glitter, then, became apparent as a specific vibrant material through a specific exercise in which the participants imagined their futures. It is necessary, then, to consider further the significance of futures to worlding and taking up and developing Haraway's insistence that it matters what matter worlds worlds and Bennett's attentiveness to the affectivity of materials, the associations between materiality, affect, worlding and futures.

In their discussion of worlding, Hunter and Palmer ask, "What is a worlding? What is an -ing? Does the addition of a suffix -ing denoting the verbal noun phrase shift the world from a being to a doing; to a gerundive and generative process?"[3] Their response is that "[t]he performativity of the noun that repeats itself as a verb or gerund; the world's worlding, is the setting up of the world" (2018). In posing the question and responding as such, Hunter and Palmer draw attention to how worlding suggests a particular understanding of what the world 'is'—an ontology of becoming (rather than being) where 'what is' is in process. Worlding is the 'setting up of the world'. A key way the ontology of becoming is theorised in terms of its future-orientation. Elizabeth Grosz's work has explored becoming in terms of "a movement of becoming-more and becoming other, which involves the orientation to the creation of the new, to an unknown future" (2010, 49; see also Grosz 1999; Coleman 2009). More specifically for the concerns of this chapter, the future-orientation of materiality and materialisation has also been widely commented on. Understood as active in its own materialisation, matter is capable of change and trans-

---

[2] On glitter, naivety and foolishness, see also Coleman and Osgood (2019).
[3] For more on the significance of '-ings' to methods, see Lury (2018) and Jungnickel (2020).

formation (Coole and Frost 2010) and as such, for Karen Barad, "the future is radically open at every turn" (2007, 178). One way Haraway defines worlding is in relation to Sf. She argues,

> Sf is that potent material semiotic sign for the riches of speculative fabulation, speculative feminism, science fiction, science fact, science fantasy— and, I suggest, string figures. In looping threads and relays of patterning, this sf practice is a model for worlding. Sf must also mean 'so far', opening up what is yet-to-come in protean times pasts, presents and futures. (Haraway 2013)

She also defines Sf as "story-telling and fact telling; it is the patterning of possible worlds and possible times, material-semiotics worlds, gone, here and yet to come" (2016, 31). In both of these accounts, worlding through Sf is an "opening up what is yet-to-come" so that pasts, presents and futures loop and may be patterned differently. This is a non-chronological temporality, then, that as Tavia Nyong'o (2019) argues, "'anarranges' the development and linear timeline of history" (2019, 26). Explaining his concept of Afro-fabulation, Nyong'o argues that such a temporality draws attention to the politics and ethics of futurity: "The proposition here, against all liberal universalisms and scientific positivities, is to insist that we do not yet know what a human outside an anti-black world could be, do, or look like" (2019, 26). Worlding, then, creates the possibilities for re-imagining the relations between humans and environments, including a re-formulation and rejection of violent and exclusionary categories.

What futures would you like to open up?
How might you understand these futures in terms of worlding?

The workshops were organised so as to ask participants to imagine their futures. They were developed in the context of contributing to how affect and new materialist studies might focus attention on the materials and affects involved in worldings (see, e.g., Barrett and Bolt 2012; Coleman and Ringrose 2013; Knudsen and Stage 2015; Hickey-Moody and Page 2015; Coleman et al. 2019; Coleman 2020). While I did not anticipate glitter to emerge as a material that would demand my attention, the workshops were designed to be practice-based and to include a wide range of materials via which the future might be imagined and visualised.[4] I was interested in how working with materials as well as with words might open specific and perhaps novel ways for the participants to imagine their futures. That is, rather than interviewing the participants about their imagined futures, I saw the art materials as a way for them to explore and make their futures (see also Lyon and Carabelli 2016; Coleman 2017). Holding the workshops in one of the school's art rooms during a session in the school timetable dedicated to art clearly aided this aim; the young women were predisposed to working with materials and to make art, in terms of their expectations of what should happen in this class and what the space of the classroom provided (large tables, sinks) and afforded (the possibility of making a mess).

I understood the workshops to be in the spirit of a new materialist practice, where Anna Hickey-Moody and Tara Page explain, "[p]ractices, teaching and art production practices are modes of thought already in the act. Contemporary arts practices call us to think anew, through remaking the world materially and relationally" (2015, 1). For Hickey-Moody and Page, working with contemporary arts practices is a pedagogy, where learning and making are entwined and through which worlding takes place. E. J. Renold and Jessica Ringrose (2019) draw on the work of Erin Manning to argue that art "helps us glimpse 'a feeling forth of new potential'" (Manning 2016, 47). This understanding of art as engendering 'new potential' is a form of worlding, where what is at stake are the processes via which new possibilities might be made. They discuss their own feminist new materialist, arts-based, participatory methodologies developed with young people to understand and 're-animate' the potentiality of gender and sexuality in young people's lives, including how gender and sexuality might be done differently. In ways that resonate with Bennett's proposal to develop "a cultivated, patient, sensory attentiveness" (2010, xiv) to the affectivity of non-human things, Renold and Ringrose note that in order to grasp such processes of worlding "We have learned how this requires careful attention to the proto-possibilities of ideas as they roll, flow and are transformed through artefacts and events" (2019). Similarly, Kim Donaldson and Katve-Kaisa Kontturi (2019) discuss their practice and methodology of Feminist Colour-IN, where people colour in black and white designs while in a lecture or teaching situation, as "enabling the

---

[4]For further discussions of materials, collaging and methods, see Coleman (2009 and 2020) and Coleman and Osgood (2019).

agencies of the more-than-linguistic [to be] embraced, and the movements of the world are *followed* with great care and to create new understandings not only of the world but *with* it (Kontturi 2018)—with sounds, images, gestures, colours". They see the Feminist Colour-IN as the co-creation of new feminist knowledge "by making sense of genders, sexualities and art *through sensations*" (Donaldson and Kontturi 2019).

Does your research create art? Might it?

What such work highlights are the ways feminist new materialist methodologies and practices are framed in terms of a worlding that takes place through an attention to materials and sensations as they are in process. They also focus on various ways on 'art', which is understood in a specific way, through sense and sensation. Discussing this particular view of art, Hickey-Moody argues that "projects can only be seen to have made 'art' if they create a set of sensations" (2013, 125). Thus, a "product does not stand as art because it is created by an artist as 'art': it is only art when and if it makes a new aesthetic sensibility" (2013, 125). For Hickey-Moody (2013), such worlding practices through arts are especially important for young people as they "offer ... new qualitative senses through which people, things, or issues might be known, and through calling into being possible future trajectories associated with the specific qualitative states produced through arts" (2013, 124). Understood through this new materialist perspective, art generates the capacity of "calling into being possible future trajectories" through the creation of new sensations and sensibilities. Working with young people to make art, Hickey-Moody argues, has the possibility of producing such sensations and thus making new futures, new worlds. Art can generate a new sensibility towards the possibilities of young people. Art in this sense worlds.

What sensations and sensibilities does your research produce?
How are or might these be involved in worlding?

WORLDING WITH GLITTER

I felt and still feel silly and a bit embarrassed to be researching glitter.[5] I feel the need to claim glitter as worthy of serious study. This is despite me being invested in and having ways to frame researching everyday life and the potential for it to become different through a feminist perspective informed by theories of affect and new materialisms. One of the ways I have attempted to claim the seriousness and significance of researching glitter is through a focus on the affects that it generates in bodies other than mine. That is, as well as considering and reflecting on the affects provoked in me by glitter—as Bennett's work suggests—I also attempt to consider how the material seemed to occupy the young women participants in the workshops as it was passed around the art-room table, shaken and stuck on to paper, canvas, fingernails, and wiped and swiped onto the floor, clothes, notebooks, bags and suitcases.

Perhaps this preoccupation with glitter is also part of wider mainstream girls' worlds where sparkle and shine is pervasive and, more specifically, as Mary Celeste Kearney (2015) argues, functions to signal empowerment, independence and visibility. Kearney proposes the notion of luminosity, or a shimmery presence, to account for "a visual trope [that] has been established in contemporary US girls' media, much of which is distributed internationally and thus has considerable global impact: *Either embodying or surrounded by light, young female characters are stylistically highlighted today in ways that make them visually superior to virtually all else in the frame*" (2015, 264–265, emphasis in original, see also McRobbie 2009). Working with glitter might be a means for the workshop participants to make their futures luminous, to world luminously.

For example, in the collages they made, glitter is often arranged in the shape of hearts or is placed next to a heart with the effect of emphasising it. The collaging activity was divided into two exercises (one for each day the workshops were held on). The first exercise asked participants to note down words significant to their imaginations of presents and futures. One participant drew hearts in red, pink, blue, yellow and orange, which appear at the edges of and in the midst of the words (see Fig. 8.1). Purple and red glitter frames three sides of the name Cleo, spelled out in purple, blue and

---

[5] I also often feel anxious that I do not really address the harms that glitter has on the natural environment, focusing rather on how worlding complicates the boundaries between 'nature' and 'artificial'.

Fig. 8.1 Collage. (Photograph by author)

pink sticky foam letters, and gold glitter circles the largest heart in the top right-hand corner. The hearts alongside the words and other symbols, including the laughing emoji, a sunshine and palm tree, produce a positive and affectionate affective sensation. Hearts also constitute the dot above the 'i' (Lips!) and bump up against the ends of words (Love, America!, #Bermonsey).

Hearts also appear on collages made as part of the second exercise, where the girls were asked to collage their imaginations of the present and future. On one collage, made on an A5 canvas, multicoloured glitter frames the page, and a green and silver heart is placed in the bottom right-hand corner. Glitter has also been shaken into the gaps between cut-out parts of women's body (Sarah Jessica Parker's face and torso, what appear to be knees in patterned trousers, feet in black, block-heeled sandals and eight different pairs of lips) (see Fig. 8.2).

Of significance in both of these examples, as well as other art work made in the workshops, is that glitter hearts are a thing that can be put to work in collaging imaginations of the present and future. In asking the

Fig. 8.2   Collage. (Photograph by author)

girls who participated in the workshops to imagine their presents and futures and then to visualise these imaginations, they selected media images (from the magazines) and materials (from those provided) that most appealed to them. These things might be understood as the most intensely affective, or in Bennett's terms, the most vibrant. Moreover, these things can be understood as positively affective: the glitter hearts indicate love, fondness, tenderness, excitement and/or enjoyment. These things that compose the collage, then, are not mute or passive—waiting for the human in order to be animated. Rather, the things are themselves alive and lively. The glitter hearts that frame, emphasise and/or accompany these things, highlight or make more apparent these affectionate affects. In these ways, the vibrancy of glitter itself and the arrangement of glitter to emphasise vibrant things "make literal the 'shimmering presence'" of contemporary girlhood (Kearney 2015, 269) and do so in a way that is oriented around how the participants imagine their futures (and presents). Put slightly differently, the vibrancy of both glitter and the things surrounded by glitter are future-oriented; they are productive of affection and love now, and these affects are seen as capable as and desirable to endure into the future (Coleman 2008).

Is your glittery thing luminous to you?
Does it produce affection and love, or other less positive or more ambivalent affects?

While the examples of the collages demonstrate the future-orientation of the vibrancy and affectivity of the collages, it is also significant that the process by which the collages were made was also vibrant and full of positive affects. Here, then, I am suggesting that as well as the content of the artwork being important to think with, it is also necessary to consider the methods and conditions through which art is made. The girls seemed to enjoy working with the glitter and found its capacity to get everywhere amusing in the context of moving from the art lesson into other, perhaps more formal, spaces of the school. Such enjoyment might be understood in terms of the sense of foolishness and naivety pointed to by Bennett where the participants became immersed in/with the material, developing a sensory attentiveness to how it might be involved in imagining their futures within the workshop.

The enjoyment of working with the glitter in the workshops might also be understood in terms of Bennett's earlier work on enchantment (2001), which she wants to restore to the condition and experience of modernity. Bennett describes enchantment as "be[ing] struck and shaken by the extraordinary that lives amid the familiar and the everyday" (2001, 4). Moreover, she argues, "[e]nchantment is something that we encounter, that hits us, but it is also a comportment that can be fostered through deliberate strategies. One of these strategies might be to give greater expression to the sense of play, another to hone sensory receptivity to the marvellous specificity of things" (2001, 4). Here, then, glitter 'hits' the girls through its relationality with the workshops. That is, the workshops to collage imaginations of futures might be understood as a 'deliberate strategy' through which the capacity for enchantment is orchestrated. Indeed, the workshops operated through 'the sense of play' and 'hone sensory receptivity to the marvellous specificity of things'. In the case I'm making here, sensory receptivity is honed through the marvellous specificity of glitter. In this sense, while the workshops themselves can be understood to cultivate capacities for enchantment, for the particular participants involved in them, the specific material of glitter intensifies this capacity. Such an understanding of glitter and the workshops can be expanded through how Bennett links her concept of enchantment to wonder, arguing "if enchantment can foster an ethically laudable generosity of spirit, then the cultivation of an eye for the wonderful becomes something like an academic duty" (2001, 10).

In a chapter of the coding of interview data, Maggie MacLure (2013) writes about wonder and discusses 'moments of disconcertion', such as a participant's silence, that were difficult to categorise and incorporate into a coding schema. She describes how her research team "learned to welcome and pause at these moments", coming to understand them as "things that gradually grow, or glow, into greater significance than others, and become the preoccupations around which thought and writing cluster" (2013, 174). These glowing data or "literally hot-spots, [were] experienced by us as intensities of body as well as mind—a kind of glow that, if we were lucky, would continue to develop" (2013, 173). MacLure moves this discussion of the intensive feeling of glowing data into an understanding of wonder. She says,

> Wonder is a liminal experience that confounds boundaries of inside and outside, active and passive, knowing and feeling, and even of animate and inanimate. If I feel wonder, I have chosen something that has "already" chosen me. Wonder in this sense is indissolubly relational—a matter of strange connection. It is moreover simultaneously Out There in the world and inside the body, as sensation, and therefore is distributed across the boundary between person and world. (2013, 181)

MacLure's conception of wonder resonates with the discussion so far in various ways. She characterises that which is difficult or troublesome as requiring her and others to 'pause'—a kind of lingering with that which is tricky to absorb into a system of analysis. Through such pausing, she suggests, certain things begin to take on significance—begin to glow; these things would not necessarily have been anticipated in advance and would, "if we were lucky", develop in their force and importance. This glowing is an intensity of body and mind; a feeling of wonder where borders are confounded and sensation is "distributed across the boundary between persons and worlds". Such wonder may be likened to both the enchantment that Bennett argues may both strike us and be "fostered through deliberate strategies" (such as pausing, re-thinking a coding scheme), and to Bennett's idea of thing-power, where a thing may choose us, may make us feel. Indeed, understood through Hunter and Palmer's definition of worlding as the blending or removing of boundaries, wonder here may world. If methods are performative, enactive and/or inventive of the worlds they study, then the sense of wonder through which "moments of disconcertion" are felt and become clusters for thinking and writing is involved in the worlding of social lives MacLure is studying.

What do you feel about and with your glittery thing?
Did you choose it or did it choose you?
Does it trouble or support your ideas about the world/s?

CONCLUSION: ETHICS AND WORLDING

This chapter has argued and asked you to consider the ways in which materials and affects are involved in worlding. It has argued that worlding is future-oriented. I have framed this understanding of worlding in terms of an ontology of becoming, where 'what is' is processual—always in the process of changing and transforming. I have argued that there is a necessary politics and ethics to such worldings; as researchers, we can ask: what worlds are we involved in making? What worlds do we want to make or make better?

Picking up Bennett's point that "the cultivation of an eye for the wonderful becomes something like an academic duty", I would like to suggest that one way we might address such questions is through developing our capacity to notice those extraordinary yet everyday things that strike us. In many ways, this is not a new argument to make. The aim of much research in the social sciences, arts and humanities is to make the familiar strange and to focus attention on the often unremarked upon but nevertheless remarkable aspects of everyday, ordinary life. Inflected through a new materialist and affect studies sense, what such a project focuses on is the 'cultivation of an eye' for how specific materials and affects are involved in composing and curating 'the wonderful'. Here, I have detailed my noticing of how glitter began to 'glow', what affects it generated in me and others and what it required of me in terms of how I understood research methodologies and methods.

What materials 'glow' for you?
How do you notice them?
Might you be able to further cultivate your 'eye for the wonderful'?

Alongside this cultivation of an eye for the wonderful, there is another mechanism that we, as researchers, might develop further. Bennett argues that wonder and enchantment 'hits us', but also that it is "a comportment that can be fostered through deliberate strategies". I would suggest, then, that part of an 'academic duty' is to consider making specific opportunities through which enchantment and wonder might be engaged and honed. In terms of the politics and ethics of methods in worlding, then, it is important to consider not only which things are enchanting and wonderful but also how things might become affective and sensational in these ways. This demands a commitment to being open to what things might be involved in worlding, how they might do so, and making or curating the conditions through which 'we' might reflect on and experiment with worldings.

I have discussed how the workshops I organised for teenage girls to imagine their futures through art-making functioned, both through their design and an attentiveness to what was unanticipated yet significant—but clearly this is only one, minor, opportunity for an experimentation with methods for worlding. What might become a methodological practice for affect and new materialist studies is a wider experimentation with methods for developing and reflecting on and with the kinds of worlds we want to world and with the possibilities for doing so. This might involve stretching the boundaries of our disciplines, working in inter- and trans-disciplinary ways and with participants (human and non-human), organisations and partners in collaborative and mutually beneficial ways. It might also, relatedly, involve research design that takes seriously the facilitation of an enchanting experience for participants as an ethical obligation alongside the more conventional ethical approvals that universities require. For example, how might we design projects where methods for the cultivation of enchantment and wonder were centrally embedded? Would this necessitate longer, slower projects with space for the opportunity for reflection on and experimentation with enchantment and wonder built in? Would this mean rapid or multiple chances to see what materials are vibrant, for which participants and how? Would the thinking through and design of such projects require a worlding of a specific, and probably different, kind of university and/or institutional understanding of research? How? What happens to a mode of critique concerned with deconstructing the structural reproduction of inequalities and the entrenchment of power relations within such worlding experiments? Is there a way to avoid placing such approaches in an antagonistic dichotomy? These indicative questions gesture towards the intricacies of experimentation with affective methodologies; there is no standard toolbox of methods to take up and use, and the specificities of each project will provoke different responses and indeed different questions. They also gesture towards the potential of affective methodologies to open up the present to other provisional futures, to take seriously our academic duty to experiment with the possibilities of creating more ethical worlds.

What kinds of worlding experimentations might you cultivate and curate?
What worlds would be involved in these worlding experiments?
What materials and affects will be involved?
How will you remain open to the emergence of perhaps unanticipated materials and affects?

REFERENCES

Barad, K. (2007). *Meeting the Universe Halfway: Quantum Physics and the Entanglement of Matter and Meaning.* Duke University Press.

Barrett, E., & Bolt, B. (Eds.). (2012). *Carnal knowledge: Towards a 'new materialism' through the arts.* I.B. Tauris.

Bennett, J. (2001). *The enchantment of everyday life.* Princeton University Press.

Bennett, J. (2010). *Vibrant matter: A political ecology of things.* Duke University Press.

Coole, D., & Frost, S. (eds.) (2010). New Materialisms: Ontology, Agency, and Politics. Durham: Duke University Press.

Coleman, R. (2008). 'Things that stay' feminist theory, duration and the future. *Time and Society, 17*(1), 85–102.

Coleman, R. (2009). *The becoming of bodies: Girls, images, experience.* Manchester University Press.

Coleman, R. (2017). A sensory sociology of the future: Affect, hope and inventive methodologies. *The Sociological Review, 65*(3), 525–543.

Coleman, R. (2020). *Glitterworlds: The future politics of a ubiquitous thing.* Goldsmiths Press.

Coleman, R., & Osgood, J. (2019). PhEMaterialist encounters with glitter: The materialisation of ethics, politics and care in arts-based research. *Reconceptualising Education Research Methodology,* 10(2–3), 61–86.

Coleman, R., Page, T., & Palmer, H. (Eds.). (2019). Feminist new materialist practice: The mattering of method. *MAI: Feminism and Visual Culture,* (4). Retrieved December 17, 2021, from https://maifeminism.com/issues/focus-issue-4-new-materialisms/

Coleman, R., & Ringrose, J. (Eds.). (2013). *Deleuze and research methodologies.* Edinburgh University Press.

Donaldson, K., & Kontturi, K.-K. (2019). Feminist Colour-IN: An aesthetic activism of connection and collectivity. *MAI: Feminism and Visual Culture,* (4). Retrieved December 17, 2021, from https://maifeminism.com/feminist-colour-in-an-aesthetic-activism-of-connection-and-collectivity/

Grosz, E. (Ed.) (1999). *Becomings: Explorations in Time, Memory, and Futures.* Cornell University Press.

Grosz, E. (2010). The untimeliness of feminist theory. *NORA: Nordic Journal of Feminist and Gender Research,* 18(1), 48–51.

Haraway, D. (1988). Situated knowledges: The science question in feminism and the privilege of partial perspective. *Feminist Studies,* 14(3), 575–599.

Haraway, D. (2013). SF: Science fiction, speculative fabulation, string figures, so far. *Ada: A Journal of Gender, New Media & Technology,* 3. https://adanewmedia.org/2013/11/issue3-haraway/

Haraway, D. (2016). *Staying with the trouble: Making kin in the Chthulucene.* Duke University Press.

Hickey-Moody, A. (2013). Youth, Arts, and Education Reassembling Subjectivity through Affect. London: Routledge.

Hickey-Moody, A., & Page, H. (Eds.). (2015). *Arts, pedagogy and cultural resistance: New materialisms.* Rowman and Littlefield.

Hunter, V., & Palmer, H. (2018). Worlding: In a new materialist almanac. Retrieved December 17, 2021, from https://newmaterialism.eu/almanac/w/worlding.html

Jungnickel, K. (Ed.). (2020). *Transmissions: Critical tactics for making and communicating research.* MIT Press.

Kearney, M. C. (2015). Sparkle: Luminosity and post-girl power media. *Continuum,* 29(2), 263–273.

Knudsen, B. T., & Stage, C. (Eds.). (2015). *Affective methodologies: Developing cultural research strategies for the study of affect.* Palgrave Macmillan.

Kontturi, K.-K. (2018). *Ways of following: Art, materiality, collaboration.* Open Humanities Press.

Law, J., Savage, M., & Ruppert, E. (2011). The double social life of methods. CRESC Working Paper, 95.

Law, J., & Urry, J. (2004). Enacting the social. *Economy and Society*, 33(3), 390–410.

Lury, C. (2018). Introduction: Activating the present of interdisciplinary methodologies. In C. Lury, R. Fensham, A. Heller-Nicholas, S. Lammes, A. Last, M. Michael, & E. Uprichard (Eds.), *The Routledge handbook of interdisciplinary research methods* (pp. 1–26). Routledge.

Lury, C., & Wakeford, N. (Eds.). (2012). *Inventive methods: The happening of the social*. Routledge.

Lyon, D., & Carabelli, G. (2016). Researching young people's orientations to the future: The methodological challenges of using arts practice. *Qualitative Research*, 16(5), 430–445.

MacLure, M. (2013). Classification or wonder? Coding as an analytic practice in qualitative research. In R. Coleman & J. Ringrose (Eds.), *Deleuze and research methodologies* (pp. 164–183). Edinburgh University Press.

Manning, E. (2016). *The minor gesture*. Duke University Press.

McRobbie, A. (2009). *The aftermath of feminism: Gender, culture and social change*. Sage.

Nyong'o, T. (2019). *Afro-Fabulations: The queer drama of Black life*. New York University Press.

Renold, E., & Ringrose, J. (2019). Jarring: Making phematerialist research practice matter. *MAI: Feminism and Visual Culture*, (4). Retrieved December 17, 2021, from https://maifeminism.com/introducing-phematerialism-feminist-posthuman-and-new-materialist-research-methodologies-in-education/

Stewart, K. (2007). *Ordinary Affects*. Duke University Press.

CHAPTER 9

Affective Writing Experiments

Signe Uldbjerg and Natalie Ann Hendry

Signe: As a teenager, I loved to write. I wrote for hours every day, in the breaks at school, when I got home in the afternoon and in the evening when my family was watching TV. I wrote everything from diary entries to short stories, poems and three fantasy novels. At the age of 16, I was accepted into a program for young aspiring authors. This was my first encounter with creative writing as a craft that can be taught. Fast-forward 11 years to today, I am using this same craft of creative writing in my PhD work. Reflecting on my own practices of writing as a teenager, I am realizing the impact creative writing and reading had on my early process of shaping my identity and exploring the tabooed elements of life, such as (queer) sexuality, limiting gendered expectations and intimate trauma. I feel certain that creative writing can help people create new meanings in their

S. Uldbjerg (✉)
University of Southern Denmark, Odense, Denmark
e-mail: siu@sdu.dk

N. A. Hendry
The University of Melbourne, Melbourne, VIC, Australia
e-mail: natalie.hendry@unimelb.edu.au

© The Author(s), under exclusive license to Springer Nature Switzerland AG 2022
B. Timm Knudsen et al. (eds.), *Methodologies of Affective Experimentation*, https://doi.org/10.1007/978-3-030-96272-2_9

183

lives—meanings that are both helpful for the writer and certainly interesting insights into affective experiences of coping and living with trauma and other tabooed or marginalized experiences. This assumption has been the basis of my venture into creative writing methods in the context of qualitative research.

Natalie: Making things, creating art and writing were my comforts growing up. I wrote to make sense of the absurd and confusing moments I witnessed. I wrote and drew while waiting in hospital cafeterias that were more familiar to me as my family's mental health issues took over our domestic life. I wrote at the back of my high school English classroom, ignoring lessons, instead listening to CDs on my discman and writing fiction to 'do' theory as I didn't have fancy university words. I struggled to write my dissertation when I returned to academia after years teaching in schools and psychiatric hospitals. I dabbled in journaling again, started writing about grief after family death. I took online writing workshops. I find myself still writing about the same things I was writing about in school in 2000, "like beautiful glass not yet broken" (lyrics from the song 'Electricity' by Something for Kate).

Our reflections touch on some of our attachments to writing as an academic and personal practice. In this chapter, we reflect on writing as an affective method. We consider different and shared methodologies and ideologies behind our various writing experiments and reflect on how writing becomes meaningful for us as academics, activists and feeling bodies. Between us, we have been involved in several research projects using writing—creative writing in particular—as a research method. Recently, we organized workshops in each of our respective countries, Australia and Denmark, focussing on research students' experiences during the international COVID-19 'lockdowns' and public health measures.

Natalie invited graduate research students to participate in digital writing workshops and to write reflections about their workshop experiences. Students joined the workshops from home, via the video platform Zoom, with three and four students in each of the two three-hour workshops. Natalie invited the students to respond to short writing prompts in blocks of five to ten minutes. Students shared either their writing, reflections on writing processes or peer feedback, which was mostly in relation to ideas and concepts rather than writing structure or style. Prompts were different for the two groups and included, for example, descriptive writing of one's room; imagined conversations with people, objects or concepts; or starting sentences with a repeated phase ("I'm trying to …").

The workshops offered space for students to share their experiences and counter their lockdown isolation (see Gomes et al. 2021), albeit in a research-focused format. Natalie's planning was informed by her community education experience and facilitating groups for teaching and research both online and in-person (Hendry 2017) and her personal experience in writing workshops, healing circles and community groups. While there are various approaches to creative writing itself in Australia, particularly following the discipline's institutional growth in the 1980s, there is no one central figure or organization that sparked creative writing as a cohesive tradition (Dawson 2001). While some participants studied communication, none had engaged with writing or digital workshops as a research method.

Signe conducted a similar online workshop at Aarhus University in Denmark. This workshop included two students and worked partly as a pilot study for the workshops in Melbourne. Here, the students read and analysed a literary text, "The Yellow Wallpaper" by C. P. Gilman (2014), and they were encouraged to consider the literary choices of this text when composing their own writing. "The Yellow Wallpaper" is excellent for its descriptions of spaces and making one limited space carry the meaning of broader societal and personal issues. In their writing, the students were asked to describe the room in which they had been working during the lockdown attempting to make this room contain and convey their affective experiences during this time-period.

For this chapter, Signe also draws on her experience conducting two other writing experiments, which were part of her PhD research on victim experiences of digital sexual assault (image-based sexual abuse). The first was a long-term participatory writing experiment, where three young women, who had been victimized by digital assault, were invited to join four workshops where they learned about creative writing, wrote about their experiences and shared and analysed their texts (Uldbjerg 2021b). The second experiment involved digital text conversations, where two young women, also victimized by digital assault, were asked to write narratives of their experiences and afterwards discuss them in private video calls (Uldbjerg 2021a). The second experiment involved individual rather than collective processes and had less focus on learning writing.

These writing experiments drew on a Scandinavian tradition of creative writing that has spread from the Author Schools and is used in writing schools and programmes across Denmark (Lind 2019). This tradition, coming from new criticism, puts the aesthetic expression of the text in focus, and writers are encouraged to work with sensory descriptions to "show-don't-tell" (Llambías 2015); in other words, writers create affective impressions through imagery. All three experiments mixed this tradition with therapeutic writing that addresses the specific situation of using creative writing in a health context or when dealing with sensitive topics (see McNichol 2016; Bolton 2007; Rasmussen 2017).

Together, we have explored different possibilities for doing writing research and writing as an affective and experimental method. This chapter reflects on our reasons for working with creative writing in specific contexts and the knowledge production that writing facilitates. We share "methods [that] need to be open, multiple, uncertain, and also affective or playful, because of the nature of the social world itself" (Coleman 2017, p. 141). Our workshops explore the "not yet known", recognizing this "complexity and multiplicity", albeit in different ways (Gale 2016, p. 249). Natalie explores the collective affects of group-based workshops and how this negotiates therapeutic potential, while Signe focuses on the political and activist potentials of alternative knowledge construction through writing. These interests together help us address the ethics of creative writing as a potentially transformative method.

We first discuss how approaching the workshops as assemblages helps us analyse them as group processes that are potentially therapeutic and as experiments in alternative knowledge creation. Together these threads point to an ethics of change that informs our work. Then, we discuss what kinds of data are produced and what data analysis is required from researchers.

THE WRITING WORKSHOP AS AFFECTIVE ASSEMBLAGE

Gilles Deleuze and Félix Guattari's (1998) concept of 'assemblage' helps us consider how affect emerges and travels in workshop encounters where the 'things' of a group workshop assemblage always exceed the human collective; the affective assemblages of the workshops include, among other things, the texts, the conversations, the bodies, the context and the digital media platforms when the workshops are online. While closely interrogating assemblage and its varied applications is beyond our scope, we draw from Jette Kofoed and Jessica Ringrose (2012) who describe assemblages as "the relationships between bodies and the flows of affect through space and time" (p. 9), emphasizing digital media as parts of social assemblages where "bodies interact with and plug into technological machines" (p. 10).

We use the concept of assemblages to focus on human and non-human bodies in the workshops, how they relate and how affect is circulated and realized in the meetings between them. Here, we understand affect as the intensity of potentials in the meeting between bodies (Thrift 2004) but also in their capacity for individual and relational "embodied meaning making" (Wetherell 2012, p. 5). The workshop becomes an affective assemblage through the interactions of these bodies or 'things' and allows us to include relations, atmospheres and contexts in our data and analyses. We attempt analyses that include, rather than ignore, these affective entanglements.

Online Groups as Assemblages

While assemblages are not synonymous with groups, we use assemblages to attend to how relations emerge through group workshops as a process that includes both the research practice and the data. We understand data as a broad term covering the empirical aspects of our work that become part of the flow of the workshops and our ongoing analyses (Markham and Gammelby 2018).

Group-based writing approaches, as affective processes and assemblages, reflect different cultural histories of creative writing but also different histories of group work such as consciousness raising in feminist political groups or group therapies. We understand the collective encounter of the workshop as an opportunity for collective deep listening, as "a practice of radical empathy" where we make our own experiences available for "compassionate analysis by ourselves and others" (Butterwick and Selman 2000, p. 64). For example, after participating in the Australian workshop on COVID-19, Polly reflected that

> [t]he workshop made sense in a group. We could riff off each other and extend on, counter, and enhance the comments and observations we were making. I like that we didn't have to talk about our research, but *what it felt like being a researcher* constrained by the pandemic in various ways came out through the writing exercises and the subsequent discussion.

Likewise, Molly remarked that "[n]o one exercise stands out, but I got as much from listening and witnessing what others shared. ... [I] loved the collective process of storytelling that emerged." For Shirley, the group enabled "[her to learn] from the other people in the workshop—it's great to bounce around ideas and hear different perspectives and know you are not alone with the things you're struggling with". The process of making your experiences available for others to listen to, and be listened to in return, produced a collective sense of empathy.

Yet deep listening and group empathy is not just a human practice. The workshop assemblage includes laptops, screens, the Zoom platform's interface and sounds; the birds we could hear singing outside one student's window, trees framed in another window that only came into digital focus when a student stepped away from her screen. In an Australian workshop, we 'shared' multiple rooms as we wrote descriptions of them; these mediated entities too became entangled in the affective workshop assemblage. One student, Molly, described how the digital workshop was a "container" for her as she focused on her screen, ignoring other expectations. Others' digital presence through the Zoom interface produced this affective container for Molly and spurred her to share her pandemic struggles with the group. For Hing, doing the workshop online allowed her to "feel safe, [I] am used to being home-bounded after all these months. Of course, in person interaction would allow more pair/side conversations. But I think online workshop allows more flexibility". Screens and the platform mediated, focused and amplified feelings of group security and connection.

However, in the Danish workshop on COVID-19, the students described different, and contrasting, aspects of digital meetings. Hugo wrote:

Behind me is the bed where we sleep and when we have video meetings it is best if the bed is made. ... From this angle, the patterns of light and shadows around the roof rafters, which I usually see every morning, look different. The others don't know what they usually look like. I know, because I look at theirs, if they don't have a blurred background or have added the royal garden in Japan or something like that. My background is the bedroom.

Here, Hugo addresses the intimacy of online meetings talking about how the bed needs to be made, as if he was actually inviting guests into his home, and how his classmates avoid displaying their intimate spaces by using blurred or image backgrounds. Clara, when commenting on Hugo's text, adds:

It can be extremely intimidating. That thing about having to sit in this job-interview like situation. … For me this has been the essence of online teaching, this thing about logging in and then we have this function in Zoom where you can just randomize groups across three of our classes. And it was like, sometimes some people just appear that I have maybe talked to once before in my life, where you are like 'hey, who are you?'

Hugo also noted in one of his texts how it is "exhausting when someone is looking at you all the time". There is a tension between feeling watched, feeling vulnerable when people can see you in your private space and knowing that these people are somehow strangers but yet you are part of the same affective assemblage along with the media platform and how it acts as part of the relations of the assemblage. So, the affective assemblage of the online writing workshop is characterized by collapsing (boyd 2011) otherwise separate social contexts resulting in affective tensions in the mediated meetings between them.

These tensions connect to the feeling of being watched. In Signe's work with digital sexual assault victims, the feeling of exposure is one of the primary everyday aspects of the participants' trauma connected to experiences of shame (Uldbjerg 2020). Shame is regularly theorized in relation to exposure. Elspeth Probyn (2005), for example, describes shame as a consequence of a failed interest, for example to be seen to fail the ideals of a community one is invested in, in other words to have your failure exposed. Similar interests, in, for example, being a good student or a good workshop participant, are present in our writing workshop assemblages and in combination with constant potential exposure through the webcam and the Zoom app; this situation creates affective intensity around the potential of shameful exposure or, alternatively, potential affective solidarity and belonging; how this emerges cannot be predicted prior to workshops.

Group work might risk affective homophily as "similarity that allows for intensity while resisting dissent" (Sundén and Paasonen 2019, p. 3), and assemblages decentre agentic individual humans, but they do not erase how participants individually experienced the workshops. Instead, the workshops illustrated an "affective solidarity" (Hemmings 2012) as applied by Jessica Ringrose and Emma Renold (2016) who discuss feminist groups in UK secondary schools, where over time "individual experiences intra-acted" and were shared within an "affective container" (pp. 230–231) by noticing together. This is not 'group-think', which makes some qualitative researchers shy away from focus group discussions for fear of not getting the 'truth', but rather an attunement towards noticing how sharing hopeless or frustrating experiences together is like being "wrapped in a swirl of 'collective affects'" (p. 231).

THERAPEUTIC POTENTIALS AND LIMITS

While writing together, we were struck by how different Denmark and Australia were in how their participants and their universities made sense of the workshops. While the participants in Signe's workshops would sometimes refer to the writing as therapeutic or 'a bit like therapy', they would never call it therapy or address mental health, unless they were struggling with mental health challenges. Instead, they would describe positive outcomes, referencing sense-making, community or personal and political agency (experiences we address in the next section). In Natalie's notes, she considers how the workshops were shaped by Australia's broader therapeutic culture and psychologization of emotional experiences (see Salmenniemi et al. 2019):

> I frame my workshops as 'not therapy' in a Jungian sense … not tricking participants into revealing a previously-unknown 'unconscious'. But they always feel therapeutic, nourishing, heart-full. We don't have the words to talk about this without drawing on the psy-discourses. Not just comforting or confirming but challenging too in an emotionally satisfying way. What words describe this?

Ffion Murphy and Philip Neilsen (2008) advocate that while there are risks to writing 'therapy' within the discipline of creative writing, these risks are "worth taking: creative writing and writing therapy share common ground". They weave together different approaches that inform writing therapy and creative writing (e.g., autobiography, life-writing, storytelling, journaling) and stress that the *process* of writing is central to writing therapy, rather than the *outcome*. They describe Judith Harris's (2003) work where "creative writing workshops can become healing communities, sites where students learn effective writing, empathy, and a means of recuperation" as well as potential sites of harm (e.g., triggering distressing thoughts). Writing therapy is an orientation to a process that elicits people's experiences, thoughts and feelings in order to motivate reflection or transformation. Natalie mapped her workshops distinct from these therapeutic processes; otherwise, she would need to demonstrate her capacity and psy-expertise to 'manage' participant experiences for her institution's ethics committee. Students were reminded that the workshops were not intended as therapy but were 'experiments'—'What happens when writing together?'

The workshops emerged as 'kind of therapeutic' or 'like-therapy' assemblages. Even though the workshop introduction stressed that the workshops were *not* therapy, it perhaps *oriented* participants towards, rather than away from, therapeutic discourses. Students shared that Natalie's facilitation also co-produced this "sort of like-therapy" orientation. For Sarah, the workshop was intimate and safe, but also welcomed open-ended processes akin to therapy, like engaging with figurative language:

> I was surprised by how intimate it felt very quickly. Even though we were not being asked 'personal' questions directly. Something about sharing connections to a physical place and to objects, allowed people to shift into more figurative spaces. There was also a feeling of safety and trust I guess which I would put down to the facilitation and the preparation which helped us to understand what we were there to contribute even though the experience was novel.

Feeling safe reinforced the therapeutic potential of the workshop as an appropriate space for emotions—some shared, some distinct—even though students were of different ages, ethnicities and family configurations, and from different disciplines.

This like-therapy assemblage also emerged through participants' care towards each other and sense of digitally mediated co-presence, as we discussed earlier. The workshops involved an empathetic, reflective and *synchronous* practice, mediated through screens and platforms. For example, the tension between the workshop being like, but not actually, therapy emerged most clearly when Jas was sharing her writing. From Natalie's notes:

> Jas paused, looked up from reading her writing and into the camera said, 'Sorry to turn this into therapy.' The group all smiled; their faces in boxes in

Zoom's 'gallery' interface. Sharing silence while Jas spoke. Even the birds singing outside Polly's window were quiet (or maybe I did not notice them?).

As a "container" (Molly), the workshops were affective encounters and collective, digitally focused assemblages that produced affective solidarity (Ringrose and Renold 2016). For Australian participants, this therapeutic frame of understanding emerged through dominant therapeutic discourses but was also configured by students' experiences and their shared focus on the workshop-through-the-screen.

But the workshop as 'like-therapy' might also make sense as an impasse. For Ann Cvetkovich (2012, p. 21), "if depression is conceived of as blockage or impasse or being stuck, then its cure might lie in forms of flexibility or creativity more so than in pills or a different genetic structure", including everyday practices and routines that "both accommodate depression and alleviate it" (p. 26). Without labelling these students as depressed, each described feeling exhausted and anxious through the pandemic. The workshops welcomed and accommodated feelings of 'being stuck' during the pandemic and co-produced a creative impasse as synchronous time to write together. The affective solidarity of being stuck *together* offered collective reassurance and, for some participants, freedom from the anxiety of missing research milestones. Students' reflections framed these solidarities as therapeutic, or like-therapy, even as the workshop was not oriented as therapy.

WRITING EXPERIMENTS AND ALTERNATIVE KNOWLEDGE PRODUCTION

Writing workshops as assemblages create a specific kind of affective knowledge and potential affective solidarity. However, focussing on the experimental aspects of writing, other perspectives on knowledge construction also emerge.

Dorthe Staunæs (2016) points to how method experiments can create new realities rather than mirroring and critiquing the existing ones. She calls for an affirmative critique that "may encourage us to strategically design of and analyse a far more performative research apparatus" (p. 67). Similarly, Lisa Blackman (2012) talks about performative methods as "bringing something into being that did not pre-exist the experimental encounter" (p. 184). Hugo, a Danish student from the COVID-19 workshop, elaborates on the constructive potential in writing in this way: "I think it is nice because it is this thing about being able to handle the situation you are in. … When I write, I can test potential situations, and maybe think about how it would be to be someone else in this situation". In Hugo's experience, writing helps him to move beyond himself and construct an alternative perspective, which eventually becomes a way for him to handle his own life. Hugo's reflections show one way in which writing can be an experimental practice: through fictionalization and imagining different realities.

Writing as alternative knowledge construction resonates with the works of practitioners and teachers of creative writing. Dianne Donnelly (2012) claims that knowledge in creative writing is "in the discovery that takes the writer beyond the routines of writing" (p. 123). And in the field of therapeutic writing practices, Kathleen McNichol (2016) claims that conscious self-reflection through writing can result in "a meaningful change in the way that you perceive your own life" (p. 39). For writers, seeing themselves from alternative perspectives can have a therapeutic effect, but for people experiencing stigmatization and marginalization, it can also reshape their sense of self and have political implications.

While the potential for individual change is clear in Hugo's COVID-19 workshop example above, the political potentials are more prevalent in Signe's workshops with victims of digital sexual assault; therefore, those workshops will be the empirical focus of this section. Amalie, a participant in an offline workshop on digital sexual assault, reflects on the collective and constructive process of the writing workshops in this way:

> It was interesting to try and work with it in that way because you often feel very anxious about that they [the assaulting images] are being shared and that feeling of being alone with it. And it is interesting to be able to illustrate it and write about it and try to negotiate the feelings in a way other than just anxiety and try to think of it and express it in a different way than just feeling sick about it. … I also think it was part of participating that I felt like I could use it for something more constructive and others could use it for something, because it has helped me to not just find it meaningless and sad.

Here, Amalie connects the writing processes and the collective workshop space with being able to see things differently and from a perspective where her experiences were not meaningless but could be used constructively to help herself and others. Nancy Naples (2003), working with sexual assault survivors and feminist methods, points to how individual stories are the starting point for working against oppressive expert discourses and creating a more inclusive and diverse movement; in her words: "go[ing] beyond the local expressions of particular experiences to target the process by which such experiences are organized" (p. 167). In this sense, constructing stories that go beyond the hegemonic discourses open the possibility of change by making it possible to rethink the system that listens to some voices while marginalizing others. In the assemblage of the creative writing workshop, such transgressive stories become possible, or even likely, through the taught practices of creative writing, which afford sensual and fictionalized storytelling. In Amalie's case, writing became a way for her to move beyond the feeling of anxiety and loneliness to create an alternative story that did not just concern herself but situated her experiences as part of a larger struggle, thereby expanding the assemblage of the assault situation and of the workshop.

Affective writing experiments' potential as an activist and politically ethical method thereby lies in its ability to create alternative discourses that can be oppositional but most importantly are representational of diverse and in-depth individual perspectives. Here, representation as both an ethical concept and a methodological goal becomes central. In the above, we have already used 'voices' as a metaphor for unique perspectives. This metaphor is unfolded in the work of Carol Gilligan (1982, 2014). She argues for open listening as an ethical approach to research that allows us to question existing truths, listen to the marginalized and overheard voices in our field and thereby include those perspectives that have not been allowed to inform our existing theories. She writes: "We can recognize that even within culture, there are voices that resist culture, and although they may be hushed or hidden at the margins, these voices may hold the power to transform the conversation" (2014, p. 101). For Gilligan, listening is an ethical standpoint more than a methodological intervention. However, when working with subjects that are politically invisibilized or at the same time highly taboo and publicly exposed, methodological interventions are necessary to encourage the kinds of voices that Gilligan aims to hear. This argument resonates with that of Bronwyn Davies (2014) in her work on listening to children. In creating affective art-interventions with children, she argues for 'emergent listening'. Emergent listening in Davies understanding means listening openly for multiple meanings instead of trying to conform meaning to a known status quo:

Emergent listening is demanding. It means not confining oneself to opinion, or to what one has always believed or wanted. It involves the suspension of judgement, letting go of the status quo and of the quotidian lives embedded in that status quo. It opens one up for new ways of knowing and being, actively resisting closure and being curious about the void of any situation. (p. 28)

These approaches are not too different from the kind of deep listening (Butterwick and Selman 2000) described earlier in our chapter; all three approaches offer critical potential for empathy and openness. Just as experimental methods encourage alternative knowledge production for research, listening as an ethical standpoint opens for alternative knowledge production in the ethical—and sometimes political—pursuit of change through representation of diverse voices.

In our experiments, representation and diversity is limited, mostly by the narrow group of people we were recruiting from, the potential exclusion of those who do not feel comfortable with (or capable of) writing and the small number of participants. Therefore, when we talk about representation, we do not refer to broad social representation across categories of identity and belonging. While representation of marginalized and overheard voices, such as those of digital sexual assault victims, is at the core of deep and emergent listening, we refer to in-depth, affective representation rather than broad social representation.

Writing, by virtue of its practices of alternative expression, can become a methodological intervention that makes it possible to hear otherwise silenced voices. By allowing the participants to fictionalize and use poetic language in their texts, these methods encourage production of data that convey feelings over facts allowing for contradictions and represent a turn away from the idea that there is only one true version of a story (Hemmings 2011). Returning to the Danish workshop on COVID-19, Clara realizes this potential of writing, as she reflects on the process of getting beyond the facts in her own writing: "I have to be careful to not write too factually about what is happening to me and the limitations to my life. It might be nicer for a reader to hear about how I experience this weird everyday life which means not seeing anyone socially and sitting here looking into the wall".

WHAT KINDS OF DATA AND DATA ANALYSIS?

Creative writing experiments produce a lot of data—much more than one might expect. Not only are workshops with their focus on learning and feedback time-consuming activities and the creative texts usually very dense with meaning, the process itself also becomes data. The analytical and sometimes participatory space of the workshops adds a meta-level to conversations that stretches beyond data production, the subjects and times of workshops themselves. As affective assemblages, everything in writing workshops is potential data, and analysis begins through the workshop itself. Here, we address characteristics of our data and discuss productive modes of analysis.

Analysing Co-constructed Data

Our writing experiments were collective in the sense of including several participants at the same time and inviting them to discuss and give feedback on each other's texts and ideas. Data emerge through this collective process; taking apart individual responses or writing as if they were individual interviews, ignores how knowledge is assembled through collective sharing. The affective dimensions of workshops respond to the group context and in turn require methods of analysis that engage with this. We might ask how affective solidarity emerges in workshop assemblages? How did participants relate to each other's words, technical glitches or their own bodily feelings?

The workshop itself requires a researcher to be in the mode of analysis alongside modes of listening, facilitating and administering to technical difficulties. Fieldwork notes written during a workshop exercise can change how a researcher might want to introduce the next exercise or modify the order of prompts for a group. Participants too come to analyse their own individual and collective experiences, and in that process of writing-as-reflection encounter emerging themes or concepts.

Workshop plans might change in the moment, as well as the direction of analysis both during and after the workshop. This makes the writing workshop an interesting space for participatory research because it allows for informal conversation structured by the participants' writing rather than the researcher's questions (Borg et al. 2012), and because it is essentially a learning space in which the participants are trained in data production and analysis qualifying their position as co-researchers (Bergold and

Thomas 2012). This format gives time and means to co-analyse and to discuss the research process with the participants, and it allows for intuitive reactions to the specific contexts and events of the workshops, making these relevant as data.

For example, in one of Natalie's workshops, students shared experiences of uncertainty and being 'in limbo'. As it rained outside, they connected the weather changes to their writing about challenges, later shifting to consider what 'sunshine', metaphorically and literally, might be coming their way as the sun outside came through. This exemplifies how approaching the workshops as assemblages—not just in but intertwined with context—can be productive when analysing the co-constructed and processual data of a writing workshop.

Analysing Creative Data

Because participants' words hold conscious aesthetic choices, creative writing texts demand some level of literary analysis. In some of the workshops, participants practised using descriptive metaphors in their writing; analysing metaphors in their texts is relevant to understanding their meaning. When analysing texts, it is important to remember that these texts do not necessarily describe actual real-life events. Instead, participants create and describe fictional scenes and events to express situations they fear or dream of; these situations never actually happened but they are affectively accurate depictions of the participants' feelings, hopes and fears.

For example, a recurring metaphor in the texts and conversations on digital assault was 'the onlooker', referring to the feelings of exposure also described above. In her work in digital sexual assault, Signe used this metaphor in combination with Jean-Paul Sartre's (1943) theorization of the shaming look in order to analyse the participants' experiences of shame and exposure and thereby expand and theorize the insights that the participants already had but struggled to grasp. Here, an analysis of metaphors helped develop affective and conceptual understandings of experiences that had previously been unarticulated but were made tangible through creative writing and the theoretical concept of 'the look' (Uldbjerg 2020).

CONCLUSION: AN ETHICS OF CHANGE

We engage with workshop processes in different ways, where data is both a process and outcome. These processes speak to our different locations, personal histories and writing traditions in Denmark and Australia. Creative writing workshops, as affective assemblages, orient us to an ethics of change; that is, an ethics that is emerging and dynamic. We pay attention to how workshop participants understand themselves as writers (or not), or victims or survivors or something else entirely, or capable and productive students.

We also sense how we move between identities and practices: as facilitators, researchers, activists, practitioners, feminists and community members. This is not straightforward. Some identities bring historical affects and experiences with us into the workshops: joyful curiosity as a researcher, angry energy as an activist. Each identity and practice has its own social, cultural and political aims, even though workshop processes and outcomes are never controllable. Workshops may reveal new realities, ways of listening (deep or emergent) and collective reassurance that relies on the configuration of participants and devices.

Signe has earlier written about an ethics of change in relation to activist methods (Uldbjerg 2021b). Taking inspiration from Shabnam Koirala-Azad and Emma Fuentes's (2009) statement that activist research "provides a hope for change that traditional research and scholarship often lack" (p. 2), Signe notes that keeping the hope for change central to research serves an ethical purpose even when doing research that in less tangible ways becomes part of larger social and political struggles. This ethical approach covers how relations and expectations develop during research and how research becomes part of broader social and political realities, whether within organized movements or everyday resistance and oppositional sense-making.

In all of our experiments, an ethics of change negotiates ethical commitments as they occur through relations in the research assemblage and hard-to-grasp situations. This ethics engages in research that actively works towards affective transformations through personal and collective sense-making. For Natalie, group writing workshops are processes with therapeutic potential because they potentially produce safe spaces to explore change-making possibilities. For Signe, the potential for alternative knowledge production in the workshops relates to necessary social and political change. This ethics of change is a continuous undercurrent in our writing experiments.

Our chapter has explored how

- creative writing workshops are experiments or, for us, affective assemblages towards openness where what emerges is contextual and unfixed. Creative writing workshops are *effective* (perform therapeutic ends or an embodied ethics of change) and *affective* (embodied and relational) as a research method. They orient researchers and participants towards knowledge creation that is collective and group-based but not necessarily homogenizing.
- creative writing workshops, as affective experiments, produce data through and beyond workshops. This urges us to engage in an embedded, participatory, dynamic and, potentially, transformational analysis of assemblage interactions.

Introducing this chapter, we described our own ways into creative writing. Now, it is time to see ourselves out, or more accurately to go out how we came in and return to questions of personal attachments in affective writing research.

Signe: I always stand firmly (perhaps aggressively) behind the writing workshop participants. I am well aware that this stubborn position is an activist more than an academic one (if such a distinction is even possible), but I put them in the vulnerable situation of having their emotional lives and traumatic experiences exposed, and I feel responsible for defending them. I think this brings me to a core condition of working with affective methodologies; it comes with an investment that is personal and precarious and often feels more important than maintaining academic etiquette. To me, 'the juicy stuff' in affective writing as a method is the relationships you can develop with people, even over a relatively short time, when you work together and open up through this very intimate and vulnerable medium of expression that writing can be.

Natalie: Preparing for a workshop evokes responsibility, accountability, an ethical sensibility. This feels like nervousness, holding my breath. Unlike interviewing where the flow is more direct, where I have a clear set of questions, prompts or concerns, what happens in a workshop is often unexpected.

Timing and pacing in a workshop are affective decisions. —I don't know how to explain this. I know when to wait for silence to pass, when I invite others' feedback, when to ask a question. To do this, I need to be present, I watch nods and note taking on the screen. I weave this into my analysis, in the moment, and after. Building relationships and words. Reacting to relationships and words. This chapter cannot write the unexpected and uncontrollable. Holding my breath.

REFERENCES

Bergold, J., & Thomas, S. (2012). Participatory research methods: A methodological approach in motion. *Historical Social Research / Historische Sozialforschung, 37*(4), 191–222. https://doi.org/10.2307/41756482

Blackman, L. (2012). Listening to voices: An ethics of entanglement. *Studies in Qualitative Methodology, 12,* 173–188. https://doi.org/10.1108/S1042-3192(2012)0000012012

Bolton, G. (2007). "Writing is a way of saying things I can't say"—Therapeutic creative writing: A qualitative study of its value to people with cancer cared for in cancer and palliative healthcare. *Medical Humanities, 34*(1), 40–46. https://doi.org/10.1136/jmh.2007.000255

Borg, M., Karlsson, B., Kim, H. S., & McCormack, B. (2012). Opening up for many voices in knowledge construction. *Forum: Qualitative Social Research, 13*(1), Art. 1.

boyd, d. (2011). Social network sites as networked publics: Affordances, dynamics, and implications. In Z. Papacharissi (Ed.), *A networked self: Identity, community and culture on social networks sites* (pp. 39–58). Routledge.

Butterwick, S., & Selman, J. (2000). Telling stories and creating participatory audience: Deep listening in a feminist popular theatre project [Paper presentation]. In *Proceedings of the Annual Adult Education Research Conference.* Vancouver, Canada.

Coleman, R. (2017). Developing speculative methods to explore speculative shipping: Mail art, futurity and empiricism. In A. Wilkie, M. Savransky, & M. Rosengarten (Eds.), *Speculative research: The lure of possible futures* (pp. 130–144). Routledge.

Cvetkovich, A. (2012). *Depression: A public feeling.* Duke University Press.

Davies, B. (2014). *Listening to children: Being and becoming.* Routledge.

Dawson, P. (2001). Creative writing in Australia: The development of a discipline. *TEXT: Journal of Writing and Writing Courses, 5*(1). http://www.textjournal.com.au/april01/dawson.htm

Deleuze, G., & Guattari, F. (1998). *A thousand plateaus: Capitalism and schizophrenia*. University of Minnesota Press.

Donnelly, D. (2012). Creative writing knowledge. In D. Donnelly & G. Harper (Eds.), *Key issues in creative writing* (pp. 116–134). Channel View Publications Ltd.

Gale, K. (2016). Theorizing as practice: Engaging the posthuman as method of inquiry and pedagogic practice within contemporary higher education. In C.A. Taylor & C. Hughes (Eds.), *Posthuman research practices in education* (pp. 242–257). Palgrave Macmillan.

Gilligan, C. (1982). *In a different voice: Psychological theory and women's development* (1993 ed.). Harvard University Press.

Gilligan, C. (2014). Moral injury and the ethics of care: Reframing the conversation about differences. *Journal of Social Philosophy, 45*(1), 89–106. https://doi.org/10.1111/josp.12050

Gilman, C. P. (2014). *The yellow wallpaper*. Createspace Independent Publishing.

Gomes, C., Hendry, N. A., De Souza, R., Hjorth, L., Richardson, I., Harris, D., & Coombs, G. (2021). Higher Degree Student (HDR) during COVID-19: Disrupted routines, uncertain futures, and active strategies of resilience and belonging. *Journal of International Students, 11*(S2). https://doi.org/10.32674/jis.v11iS2

Harris, J. (2003). *Signifying pain: Constructing and healing the self through writing*. SUNY.

Hemmings, C. (2011). *Why stories matter: The political grammar of feminist theory*. Duke University Press.

Hemmings, C. (2012). Affective solidarity: Feminist reflexivity and political transformation. *Feminist Theory, 13*(2), 147–161.

Hendry, N. A. (2017). Social media bodies: Revealing the entanglement of sexual wellbeing, mental health and social media in education. In L. Allen & M. L. Rasmussen (Eds.), *Palgrave handbook of sex education* (pp. 509–526). Palgrave Macmillan.

Kofoed, J., & Ringrose, J. (2012). Travelling and sticky affects: Exploring teens and sexualized cyberbullying through a Butlerian-Deleuzian-Guattarian lens. *Discourse: Studies in the Cultural Politics of Education, 33*(1), 5–20. https://doi.org/10.1080/01596306.2012.632157

Koirala-Azad, S., & Fuentes, E. (2009). Introduction: Activist scholarship – Possibilities and constraints of participatory action research. *Social Justice, 36*(4 [118]), 1–5.

Lind, H. (2019). The mood of writerly reading. *New Writing, 1*(1), 1–15. https://doi.org/10.1080/14790726.2019.1601236

Llambías, P. (2015). *Skrivning for begyndere: om skønlitterær skrivekunst for begyndere – en personlig refleksion*. Gyldendal.

Markham, A., & Gammelby, A. K. (2018). Chapter 29: Moving through digital flows: An epistemological and practical approach. In U. Flick (Ed.), *The SAGE handbook of qualitative data collection* (pp. 451–465). SAGE Publications Ltd.

McNichol, K. (2016). Who am I? Writing to find myself. *Journal of Arts and Humanities*, 5(9), 36–40. https://doi.org/10.18533/journal.v5i9.990

Murphy, F., & Neilsen, P. (2008). Recuperating writers – And writing: The potential of writing therapy. *TEXT: Journal of Writing and Writing Courses*, 12(1). http://www.textjournal.com.au/april08/murphy_neilsen.htm

Naples, N. A. (2003). *Feminism and method: Ethnography, discourse analysis, and activist research*. Routledge.

Probyn, E. (2005). *Blush: Faces of shame*. University of Minnesota Press.

Rasmussen, A. J. (Ed.) (2017). *Læse, skrive og hele: perspektiver på narrativ medicin*. Syddansk Universitetsforlag.

Ringrose, J., & Renold, E. (2016). Cows, cabins and tweets: Posthuman intra-active affect and feminist fire in secondary school. In C. Taylor & C. Hughes, *Posthuman research practices in education* (pp. 220–241). Palgrave Macmillan.

Salmenniemi, S., Nurmi, J., Perheentupa, I., & Bergroth, H. (2019). *Assembling Therapeutics: Cultures, Politics and Materiality*. Routledge.

Sartre, J.-P. (1943). *Being and nothingness: A phenomenological essay on ontology* (1992 ed., H. E. Barnes, Trans.). Washington Square Press.

Staunæs, D. (2016). Notes on inventive methodologies and affirmative critiques of an affective edu-future. *Research in Education*, 96(1), 62–70. https://doi.org/10.1177/0034523716664580

Sundén, J., & Paasonen, S. (2019). Inappropriate laughter: Affective homophily and the unlikely comedy of #MeToo. *Social Media + Society*, 5(4). https://doi.org/10.1177/2056305119883425

Thrift, N. (2004). Intensities of feeling: Towards a special politics of affect. *Geografiske Annaler: Series B: Human Geography*, 86(1), 57–78.

Uldbjerg, S. (2020). Defying shame: Shame relations in digital sexual assaults. *Mediekultur: Journal of media and communication research*, 36(67), 100–120. https://doi.org/10.7146/mediekultur.v36i67.113960

Uldbjerg, S. (2021a). The rhythms of shame in digital sexual assault: Rhythmic resistance and the repeated assault. *First Monday*, 26(4). https://doi.org/10.5210/fm.v26i4.11660

Uldbjerg, S. (2021b). Writing victimhood: A methodological manifesto for researching digital sexual assault. *Women, Gender & Research*, 29(1), 27–39. https://doi.org/10.7146/kkf.v29i2.124893

Wetherell, M. (2012). *Affect and emotion: A new social science understanding*. SAGE.

CHAPTER 10

Problematizing Shame: Affective Experimentation on Social Media

Carsten Stage

Social media can be understood as 'experimental' from the outset. They link people, companies and technologies in complex ways that not only bring together established social formations but also perform, assemble, manipulate, track and extract value from relations, for example, by suggesting that users start communicating, connect with new people or engage in particular groups or with certain types of content. For these reasons, the experimental testing, modification and commercial valuation of new social worlds are at the very core of "the sociality of social media" (Marres and Gerlitz 2018). This chapter presents a partnership-based research project that aims at 'repurposing' social media's potential for assembling social formations around specific issues. This was done by exploring the subject of shame and chronic illness through a participatory research design that invited people with a chronic condition to share their

C. Stage (✉)
School of Communication and Culture, Aarhus University,
Aarhus, Denmark
e-mail: norcs@cc.au.dk

B. Timm Knudsen et al. (eds.), *Methodologies of Affective
Experimentation*, https://doi.org/10.1007/978-3-030-96272-2_10

203

"everyday stories of shame" (Probyn 2004) on or via two social media profiles.[1]

Chronic conditions are most commonly defined as bodily disorders that last more than 12 months and result in functional limitations and/or the need for ongoing medical care. These chronic illnesses and conditions are often described as one of the major health challenges (in terms of treatment costs) facing Western societies (Hvidberg et al. 2020). The chapter investigates the embodied and affective experience of living with one or more of these chronic conditions. As mentioned, it takes a particular interest in the underexplored topic of how, when and why shame is present in the life of people with such conditions and how the public sharing of personal shame stories can help create new affective communities where shame is potentially repoliticized and deindividualized. The chapter seeks to answer the following questions:

1. How is the relation between shame and chronic conditions articulated by the participants taking part in the research experiment?
2. How do the participants perceive the effects and implications of publicly sharing shame stories as part of a research experiment?

The invitations to share stories of shame were distributed on two social media profiles dealing with chronic conditions, but the actual experiences could be communicated in various formats (in comments, via email or in a survey). The idea to conduct the research in this way was conceived and planned together with the three founders and moderators of the Danish peer-led patient community called Kroniske Influencers (Chronic Influencers; KI): Karla Pilgaard (34), Zinna Lautrup (40) and Nanna Marinussen (30). They are all living with chronic conditions like spinal arthritis, heart failure, scleroderma and chronic pain, and established the KI community in 2018. KI aims to provide a public meeting space where people with a chronic condition can share experiences and plan various offline activities (e.g., local coffee meetings), but also a space that communicates knowledge about chronic conditions to the public. The impetus for engaging in this experimental research process was both to crowdsource shame experiences (or experiences of not having felt shame) from a variety of followers as empirical material for research and to create

[1] Large parts of the chapter are also published in a forthcoming journal article that however focuses less on conceptualizing the experimental aspects of the research process.

a week of collective reflection and discussion for the followers of KI's public profiles (approx. 6800 on Instagram and 3600 on Facebook). The research process can be divided into three phases:

1. *Contact and planning*: The researcher and the three founders/moderators met in April 2020 (after an initial contact established by KI) and—after an interaction about shared knowledge interests of the founders and researcher—decided that 'shame' would be a potentially interesting topic for KI, for the researcher and for the followers and that it could be taken up in one of the 'theme weeks' that KI organizes on its social media profiles. After this meeting, the researcher made suggestions for five 'invitation posts' that could be shared on the profiles during the theme week to ask followers to share experiences related to various dimensions of shame and chronic illness. The three founders made smaller suggestions for reformulations that were then accepted. The researcher and the KI founders also discussed a draft of a survey that should be shared at the end of the week to obtain feedback from a wider range of followers and not just those willing to share their stories during the week.

2. *Theme week*: The theme week was held in the first week of June 2020 with five posts, or invitations to share stories, were distributed across the week. A definition of shame as a feeling of being flawed and wanting to avoid the gaze of others was shared in order to create a common understanding of the term. The five posts were each designed to elicit different forms of sharing. The following describes the sharing goals for each of the five posts: (1) memories of particular shameful situations in relation to having a chronic illness, (2) the gazes/people the followers could feel shame in front of, (3) the role of social media in terms of, for example, intensifying or decreasing shame and (4) experiences that have reduced shame. The experiences shared for the first four posts could be communicated in comments on the profiles or via an email to the researcher. (5) On the final day of the theme week, a link to a survey was shared with the dual aim of (a) affording followers the opportunity to share their accounts of (non-)shame if they forgot to do so during the week or did not like the personal exposure involved in writing comments or emails, and (b) hearing the followers' impressions of the theme week. Responses to the 5 invitation posts amounted to 170 user comments on Instagram (87 comments) and Facebook (83

comments), 20 longer emails sent to the researcher, 178 responses to the entire survey and 447 open text answers in the survey.

3. *Evaluation and feedback loops:* After the theme week, the researcher archived all the shared material and processed the material through a thematic NVIVO coding (Braun and Clarke 2006). Preliminary findings established through this coding process were shared and discussed at a meeting with the three founders/moderators in August 2020 and later the same month were presented by the researcher in a live IGTV session (40 min.) on the KI Instagram profile. The collaboration between the researcher and KI will be continued in a recently funded research project based on the early experiences of the initial project process described above.

The ethical problems of staging a public process of sharing shame experiences require consideration (franzke et al. 2020). To ensure that the project was guided by transparency and care, and did not violate the more or less implicit standards of the community, the whole process was planned and discussed with the three founders. Furthermore, the genre of 'theme weeks' dealing with difficult issues (e.g., loneliness) is familiar to the users as this is a recurring format on the KI profiles. What was new was that the communication during the week was used for research. Therefore, all 'invitation posts' were clearly marked with a section about the aim of the research, ethics, anonymization and researcher contact. Consent forms were shared with people who contacted the researcher with stories via email and these were confirmed digitally. All participation in story sharing was explicitly marked as voluntary, and people who wanted to participate more anonymously could take advantage of the survey.

The ethicality of making the process of sharing shame into a public situation could also be questioned, for example, in terms of the effects of public exposure, the risk of imposing shame as an expected response to living with a chronic illness and of providing large platforms with intimate knowledge about their users. The collective and voluntary public sharing of shame stories—and of stories contesting the relevance of shame for the participants' life—was, however, explicitly chosen to experiment with the creation of a more politicizing form of storytelling that could potentially create both *internal awareness* of the collective aspects or social logics of experiences among the followers and *public awareness* of how chronic conditions are experienced and lived with in society. Feedback loops between followers, KI and the researcher were furthermore created through follow-up meetings and live sessions that aimed at ensuring interaction and transparency as KI and the followers had the opportunity to see and comment on how their stories were being processed in a pre-publication research phase.

RESEARCH AS EXPERIMENTAL PROBLEMATIZATION

In describing this chapter's research as 'experimental' I combine and merge various understandings of what constitutes an experiment. I understand the presented research design as experimental due to its participatory approach that caused a less controlled and somewhat unpredictable process (e.g., in terms of who and how many contributed with empirical material) (Markham and Pereira 2019; Probyn 2004). It was also experimental by repurposing already experimental social media platforms (Marres and Gerlitz 2018) to both reveal existing shame dynamics and create the potential for a new social formation that begins to perceive shame as a collective experience, as socially produced and thus as a 'more-than-individual' affective state. In that way the research design also facilitated the-coming-into-provisional-existence of an affective counter-public and thus tested the relevance of a de-privatizing approach to experiences of shame linked to having a chronic condition. Following Britta Timm Knudsen, Carsten Stage and Marianne Zandersen, I thereby understood experimentation as having the capacity to reveal as well as imagine and invent, to make the world knowable as well as to transform or reflect on alternative ways of living with chronic illness (Knudsen et al. 2019).

By taking this approach to research experiments, I also argue that it enacts a process of 'problematisation'. Michel Foucault used the concept of problematization to describe how political processes construct particular obstacles or difficulties as problems to be acted on through interventions and how a specific problematization is not simply a representation of these obstacles. Instead, a problematization "develops the conditions in which possible responses can be given; it defines the elements that will constitute what the different solutions attempt to respond to" (Foucault 1984). 'Problematisation' in this chapter primarily refers to (1) how research experiments make aspects of the world knowable by setting up a particular framework for understanding it, but also (2) how the research process itself might change or affect what is studied due to the experimental setup. In that way 'experimental problematisation' not only enacts the possibility of relevant future intervention (which seems to be Foucault's primary focus) but also tests a particular way of changing the problem—here through publicly sharing an affective state often understood as personal and private. The experiment in this chapter in other words makes it possible both to understand the role of shame for people with a chronic condition (compared to creating knowledge about a problem) and to potentially alter its way of working by revealing its collective and shared dynamics (compared to moving or changing the problem).

This approach to the experiment as method is inspired by Celia Lury's conceptualization of methods as inventive and compositional (Lury 2021; Lury and Wakeford 2012). In *Problem Spaces* (2021), Lury explores how methods are performative in the sense that they do not simply represent 'pre-given' knowledge problems (e.g., how people in a particular life situation feel shame) but also compose situations or 'problem spaces' where problems become visible in certain ways and able to respond to particular knowledge goals. Methods are thus viewed by Lury as "a way of equipping a situation to be a problem" and as producing "sites of engagement" (Lury 2021, p. 19) that twist "problems into processes of problematization" (Lury 2021, p. 48). The five posts shared on the profiles would be a specific methodological example of such a problematization. They repeatedly twist and turn the problem of shame by asking questions about various dimensions of the problem: composing shame as a dynamic or mobile problem (consisting of multiple sub-problems) more than as a stable one through these recurring sequences of engaging the followers of the two profiles. This does not imply that the problem does not exist outside the methodological problem space, but rather that it only becomes 'knowable' through the repetitive problematization enacted through the five posts of the theme week.

By focusing on methods as engaged in the composition of problem spaces, it is also acknowledged that the problem space could always be composed in a different way: "a problem (space) can always be other than it is" (Lury 2021, p. 33). By collaborating with KI, the problem of shame and chronic conditions is, for instance, enacted in very particular way, and even in a way that highlighted for the researcher that the problem investigated was different and more specific than expected. A vast majority of the 178 people answering the survey were female (96%), between 25 and 55 years old (89%), and with a chronic condition linked to the musculoskeletal system (75%) (e.g., various types of arthritis, chronic pain, whiplash syndrome). This transformation of the problem is an effect of the project's attempt to move science into the public (Nowotny et al. 2001) by co-creating empirical material with a large number of profile followers. As such, the research infrastructure (e.g., the social media profiles) and the crowdsourcing of material (letting followers reply to distributed questions) 'produced' a research problem structured by particular patterns in terms of gender, age and types of chronic condition.

Following this I would argue that understanding methods as involved in experimental problematization is a fruitful way of addressing—and experimenting with—how research can both (1) maintain a profound interest in trying to understand social processes with an existence outside the research apparatus and (2) acknowledge its own methodological performativity and productive world-making potentials.

PROBLEMATIZING SHAME

The affective[2] experience of shame relates to a negative exposure of the self and its social failure in terms of living up to social ideals, categories and collective norms in particular contexts. The body in shame feels itself as inferior, unworthy, outside or unacknowledged and as being part of social relations that uphold or produce this negative understanding of "the self in its totality" (Zahavi 2014, p. 208). In existing research, shame is often perceived as a deeper negative affect than, for example, embarrassment and guilt. Embarrassment has been defined as a brief experience of "temporary stupidity" (Billig 2001), while guilt is instead linked to having performed particular actions that have hurt other people or broken a social contract (Nathanson 1987, p. 46). Shame is deeper and more profound as a personal experience than guilt as it is linked less to a sense of *having done something wrong* than to *being wrong* as a subject with a particular identity, body or cultural position.

An influential line of research—particularly within phenomenology— argues that shame can only occur through real or imaginary encounters with derogatory gazes. Jean-Paul Sartre, for example, famously describes shame as a process where the subject feels itself negatively as it becomes an object of the judging gaze of the Other. Shame is "the *recognition* of the

---

[2] I describe shame as an affect and not as an emotion, although these concepts are difficult to distinguish and their relationship has been contested (Leys 2018; Wetherell 2012). Affect is preferred here in order to stress and understand the relationality of shame and to complicate self/world-dichotomies (Ahmed 2004; Blackman 2012)—but not in order to claim that affect is a 'non-cognitive' or 'pre-discursive' state opposed to the more cognitive emotions.

fact that I *am* indeed that object which the Other is looking at and judging. I can be ashamed only as my freedom escapes me in order to become a *given* object" (Sartre 2003, p. 285). As such, shame is understood as an inherently relational experience linked to visual processes of being/feeling looked at or negatively objectified. The gaze of the other can be concrete or imagined. As Dan Zahavi describes it, "the other-as-subject can be present even when the other-as-object is absent" (Zahavi 2014, p. 217).[3] Although the actual encounter with a shaming gaze is often perceived as more painful than imagined ones, the anxiety of meeting that gaze, and various strategies for preventing it, can also come to saturate and structure an entire life even if the actual shame encounter is rare (Mortensen 2020; Wurmser 1987). Shame is furthermore distributed socially according to established hierarchies and norms as some people "are more marked out for shame than others" (Nussbaum 2004, p. 174). The female body has been the object of multiple forms of shaming related to body ideals, sexual assaults, limited notions of proper femininity or motherhood (Shefer and Munt 2019, p. 149). Rita Felski and Sally Munt also argue that class and poverty are crucial sources of shame (Felski 2000; Munt 2007).

Another trajectory of research focuses more on the productive or even constructive aspect of shame. Various work on shame inspired by Silvan Tomkins argues that shame can only exist on the basis on some level of investment (Sedgwick and Frank 1995) and that the "innate activator of shame is the incomplete reduction of interest or joy" (Tomkins 1995, p. 134). You can only feel shame in front of people or agencies whose judgement you care about. In the words of Elspeth Probyn, "without interest there can be no shame. ... It highlights unknown or unappreciated investments" (2005, p. 14). This approach to shame also stresses that shameful experiences can trigger important reflective processes of self-evaluation because the subject becomes aware of its disappointed investments. According to Probyn, shame "is productive in how it makes us think again about bodies, societies, and human interaction" (Probyn 2005, p. xviii) and by indicating a break of connection as well as the desire for connection.

---

[3] This point, despite various theoretical differences, resonates with the Lacanian idea (in *Les quatre concepts fondamentaux de la psychanalyse* [1973]) that individual perception is always mediated by imaginary relationships with the gaze of the other. Processes of *looking* and *being looked at* overlap, and the individual is therefore always both a subject and object of representation.

For Martha Nussbaum, shame is not only painful but also 'constructive' when it becomes a shield towards narcissistic pleasure-seeking (Nussbaum 2004, p. 211). Shame can, however, also be politically productive without redirecting the self towards 'the common good' or ideals of (anti-narcissistic) equality and empathy. This is stressed by research that underlines how shame can become an important vehicle for political mobilization that confronts collective stigmatization. According to Jill Locke, many social movements have the sharing of personal stories of shame and the struggle to obtain 'unashamed citizenship' as a central component (Locke 2016). Sharing stories of shame can produce political collectives through processes that deindividualize shame by revealing it as socially produced and, thus, as an object of collective protest and change more than a strictly personal state of being (Probyn 2004; Shefer and Munt 2019). Here, shame can be converted into collective "shame anger" (Nathanson 1987, p. 254) and, thus, become an affective driver of social mobilization or new "shame formations" (Munt 2017, p. 869) fighting for social justice.

While research on shame has proliferated in various academic contexts, the links between (chronic) illness, health and shame have received less direct attention. Luna Dolezal and Barry Lyons claim that health-related shame should be perceived as an affective determinant of health, thereby stressing that experiences of chronic shame—as opposed to more acute and situational shame experiences—are in themselves harmful and can correlate with health risk behaviour (e.g., alcoholism) (Dolezal and Lyons 2017; see also Woods 2017). They furthermore argue that an increasing focus on personal responsibility in health care can produce shame by turning ill health into an indicator of a lack of individual character and self-control. Following this, they encourage more projects that "explore shame associated with different health problems and in different settings" (Dolezal and Lyons 2017, p. 6). Dolezal elsewhere argues that a more open discussion and interaction about health and shame is a way forward: "Acknowledging and publicly confessing one's shame has a cathartic effect, it dampens its negative affect and shifts the experience towards one of validation and recognition" (Dolezal 2015, p. 575). Rose Richards is also interested in "the othering effect of shame on the nonconforming body" (Richards 2019, p. 270) and explores autoethnographic writing as a way of conveying otherwise invisible or silenced stories of chronic illness and calls for academic (advocacy) work that gives women with chronic illnesses a voice by sharing their experiences (Richards 2019, p. 274).

My analysis draws on this existing research described above by taking an interest in which particular gazes and relations can motivate shame and by focusing on how people with a chronic condition can feel flawed in relation to social norms, hierarchies and categories. Furthermore, the analysis asks how shame is linked to and possibly reveals more positive attachments and how the sharing of everyday stories of shame in public—within the framework of a research experiment—can enable the creation of a social formation that questions shame as private and reframes it as a collective and social problem. Last but not least, the analysis contributes to the relatively limited research on illness, health and shame by offering an account of the shame dynamics of individuals with a chronic condition.

Failing Bodies and Slow Shame

Based on the collected material, shame seems to be a relevant affective quality to investigate. In the survey, 70% indicate that they feel shame in relation to their chronic condition on a daily (30%) or weekly (40%) basis. Looking at the participants' descriptions of what shame is, a majority link them either to the experience of having a body that fails, a body that is slower or weaker than what could be expected or being a burden to society or to a personal social network. Regarding the latter, one participant writes in a Facebook comment, "I feel ashamed for not having a clear purpose or contribution to society".[4] Pertaining to the failure of the body, shame is linked to dysfunction (e.g., not being able to remember, having a disease that could cause premature birth) or mismatches between desired bodily capacities and actual bodily capacities. One participant writes, "I feel ashamed when I don't have the energy to be a mother and therefore have to lie down—in order to find the energy again".

Following the *Rhythmanalysis* of Henri Lefebvre, it could be argued that shame is either produced through (1) destructive encounters between *the biological rhythms of the self* (e.g., cycles of activity, tiredness, rest) and *the social rhythms of others* (e.g., when and how often people are expected to clean the house, pick up their children), or (2) destructive encounters between the *desired* biological rhythms of the self (what I would like to do) and the *actual* biological rhythms of the self (what I am capable of doing) (Lefebvre 1992). These rhythmic or energetic failures seem to cause shame as they put the body at odds with social ideals linked to, for

---

[4] All quotes are translated by the author.

instance, motherhood or personal ideals of what could be expected of a person. Actual encounters of being shamed by concrete others are rarely described in the material and the experience of being condemned is, therefore, mostly explained as imagined. This underlines that the experience of shame relies on envisioning how others look at you and condemn you as you fail collective, but internalized, norms and ideals of how to inhabit social categories in a proper way.

The descriptions of shame as linked to being witnessed during energetic failure point to a somewhat underexplored aspect of shame experiences. They stress that shame is not necessarily linked to a person's affiliation with problematized social categories (e.g., belonging to the 'wrong' ethnic or sexual category), but rather to not living up to the energetic ideals linked to social categories: shame is not shame over being excessive or too much, but rather of being too little, or not alive enough, to inhabit one's categories. This points to how ideals of, for example, being a good citizen or a good mother are also linked to particular expectations to levels of activity, performance and resilience. Following Dolezal, this type of 'slow shame' could be linked to a health care situation where health is increasingly understood as a personal responsibility and where citizens are legitimatized based on their contribution to the social fabric and value production.

The participants in a way describe both how they are too easily affected by their activities and surroundings and how they are not themselves affective enough in terms of making a presence in the world (e.g., in the home, society or workplace). If affect concerns the body's capacities to affect and be affected (Spinoza 1997), then shame is described in affective terms by being related to the body's oversensitive affectedness that drains the body of energy as well as to its lack of ability to affect and give energy to other bodies. Shame is thus explained as the experience of being witnessed as an energetic and affective failure in terms of both too much sensitivity towards the world and too little impact on the world.

Some participants also link the experience of shame to living with an invisible illness that is not present as a sign on the body: the body fails in terms of communicating the lived experience of illness to its surroundings in a convincing way. Or as expressed by a participant: "It is an endless cycle of shame. Once in a while I wish that I had a disease that people could see." The invisibility of illness sets the scene for experiencing various types of failure because the body's surface produces expectations of normal activity levels that must constantly be negated or disappointed due to fatigue: "I feel ashamed when people hear that I have a flex job and then comment: but you look so perky". A different mismatch occurs when knowledge about your illness produces the expectation that you cannot be happy, 'look good' or express joy in public. In other words, social doubt concerning the authentic relation between a person's lived experience of illness and the person's external appearance becomes a source of shame production.

Shame linked to the chronically ill body is also present in the form where the body simply fails in terms of its visible appearance or ability to align with social norms. Two different participants write: "I feel ashamed that I have gained a lot of weight due to the medicine I am taking and have taken" and "Shame is a difficult emotion. I haven't shown my legs to anyone for years." For a third participant, shame is less a question of visual appearance than of not being able to control the body and the symptoms linked to the illness:

I have a diagnosis with symptoms that create shame. I have Ulcerative Colitis. When I have to call and cancel something, or tell friends or my job that I'm late, the honest message could be: "I shit my pants. I have to take a shower and then I'll be there." My message would normally be more moderate than that.

Shame as the Shadow of Loving Attachment

Another shame dynamic, besides shame linked to the failing body and energetic failure, could best be described by returning to Sartre's idea that shame is also relational or produced in front of the gaze of the other. Across the material, various shame-inducing 'gazes' are articulated, but some are mentioned more often than others. One would perhaps think that disapproving gazes were mostly related to authorities like physicians or municipal consultants. And these gazes are also present in the material. The municipal authorities can, for instance, cause shame if they meet the chronically ill with mistrust or with the desire to squeeze him/her into a predefined system: "Feel shame towards the municipal system when I am once again unable to work and I don't fit into any of their boxes". The medical encounter can also induce shame when it does not acknowledge the severity of the condition but instead focuses on (a lack of) motivation: "The hospital doctor keeps on saying that I need to go back to school and has written in my journal that she has 'tried to motivate me to do that'. I don't even have the energy to take a shower more than once a week."

However, a crucial finding in the material is that shame primarily seems to be located in the intimate sphere, stemming from gazes of significant others that the participants love and by whom they want to be loved. Following Probyn, it becomes clear that shame is highly linked to blocked positive interest and disturbed intimate attachment, and that it also reveals the relations in which the participants are invested, for example, being a good partner, parent and friend. In the survey, friends (51%), partner (42%), family in general (41%) and children (37%) are marked as the relations that most often cause shame: the picture is the same across all the comments, emails and survey comments. Institutional and societal authorities are mentioned as important shame-inducing gazes, but children, partner and friends are articulated 3–4 times more often than these authorities. Furthermore, the authorities seem to be linked to a more situational and acute form of shame as described through concrete encounters, while shame in the intimate sphere is described in a more abstract way and as linked to more persistent relational failures.

In terms of failing as a parent, one participant writes: "I would like to be a better mother—a vital and happy mother with the energy to smile and have fun". Another participant describes how she feels shame in relation to her daughter: "because I don't feel that I can be the mother that I want to be and that I think she deserves. I can't live up to my own expectations and the things that I know are best for a child." Shame in relation to parenting is—as shown—connected to failing one's own ideals of how children should be treated and how caring mothers should facilitate a good childhood. Shame in relation to parenthood is highly gendered and related to the ideal of the present, loving mother who is able to provide a loving environment for her children.

Shame towards the partner is described in both abstract and practical terms: one did not play the expected role in the life of the partner in terms of producing a good and happy existence and one leaves the partner with a lot of work and responsibility, which should ideally be shared. Again, the responsibility towards the household is most likely a gendered response, but one of the rare comments of a man in the material also focuses on how his illness leaves the partner alone with a practical burden and blocks his ability to facilitate a home characterized by care, patience and presence: "I feel ashamed that I can't be the father and the husband I want to be. That I'm more absent, grumpy and impatient than I'd like to be. And that I have to leave such a big part of the practical work to my wife." The idea of somehow betraying the hopes and visions of the good life embedded in engaging in an intimate partnership with another person is also repeated in the material: "Feel the biggest shame in relation to my husband as I'm not the fresh and energetic woman he once fell in love with".

An important point, however, is that the family as an institution is not only described as a social formation characterized by love—a love that the subject might worry is not expressed enough—but also by painful rejection, social pressure, harassment and disconnection. One participant explains: "I do not live up to the health norms of my family and I have not been able to do sports and exercise like them. I have gained weight and I am always ashamed when I am visiting my mother because she often comments on it." Another describes that "I often experience being indirectly shamed by my parents. They encourage me not to show my pain to others, or to talk about it, not to ask anybody for help outside my family." A third explains: "I often experience being forgotten by my brother and my parents, and it hurts me so much, so much that I don't have any contact with them at the moment". Finally, a mother writes: "I feel ashamed that my daughter is most likely feeling a lack of self-worth because I have yelled so much at her because of my lack of energy and my pain". These examples underline once again that shame lingers in social relations based on a desire for positive attachment (e.g., feeling loved by your parents or relatives), but that shame as a disturbance of positive attachment can also be embedded in and intensified by more lasting and hurtful family logics.

In terms of the wider network of friends and acquaintances, shame seems to be more linked to being a socially unpredictable individual: someone who has to leave social arrangements early, suddenly lay down on the sofa, postpone or cancel meetings at the last minute, and needs extra arrangements and attention to be able to take part in social life, or to be excused for forgetting important aspects of being a good friend. Participants, for instance, write how they can feel shame when they "forget to write happy birthday to a friend", "have to cancel an appointment", "need constant help for small things", "can't follow" the conversation of friends or leave a social gathering "before planned".

Deindividualizing and Contesting Shame

In the final analytical section, I focus on the participants' engagement with social media, how this relates to shame and the participants' evaluations of making shame a public issue during the research experiment of the theme week. In other words, this section deals with the more inventive aspects of the research experiment and with its potential ability to affect the social problem that it also explores. In doing this, I move away from understanding 'experimental problematization' as a method focused on predominantly trying to represent existing shame experiences among chronically ill people. Instead, I also approach it as a performative method that tries to change what it investigates—here through a process of community storytelling that has social effects that are valuable on their own terms.

According to the material, shame is a dynamic affect both in terms of when/why it occurs and in terms of how it develops over time. In the survey, seven out of ten participants indicate that shame has changed over time and, according to the comments, this change can take many forms. Shame can, for example, increase with the arrival of the chronic condition. However, more participants indicate that shame has decreased, for example, with the arrival of a diagnosis that explains hitherto unresolved bodily weaknesses or as people learn to live with and accept their condition and that they are worthy individuals despite their illness: "I don't feel as much shame as earlier. I think it's because I've settled more in my role. For instance, I felt an enormous amount of shame due to my lack of contribution to society. Now I'm contributing by being a fantastic aunt, friend and a positive person—and that's good enough".

Across the material, (self-)acceptance, the support of partner and network, open dialogue about illness and peer contact/communities are mentioned as the most prominent roads to overcoming or coping with shame.

The participants are—not surprisingly if you take the research design into consideration—active social media users. From survey respondents, seven out of ten indicate that they use social media to communicate or read about illness on a daily or weekly basis; eight out of ten follow the personal narratives of individuals with a chronic condition on social media; and six out of ten engage in patient communities. Reading about others in the same situation as oneself is mentioned as an important way of overcoming shame by 65% of the survey respondents. In relation to the more general role of social media in relation to shame, half of the respondents answer that social media has primarily helped prevent shame, only 1% indicate that social media has primarily produced shame, and three of ten state that social media has both produced and prevented shame.

Of the survey respondents, nine out of ten were aware of the theme week and half indicate that it had been fruitful to follow the week, while one out of four had not followed the week closely, and one out of ten found the week less fruitful. A large majority of the respondents also think that it can have positive effects to share shame stories in public as people did during the theme week. According to the respondents, such initiatives strengthen the community (81% of respondents), facilitate people with chronic conditions coming together to fight shame (69% of respondents) and decrease the level of shame on an individual level by experiencing it as a more collectively shared affect (74% of respondents). Fewer believe that public sharing of shame can have negative effects like producing more shame (4% of respondents) or fixating people in self-victimization (10% of respondents). These numbers appear to indicate that the participants understand the public articulation of shame as a primarily alleviating process that helps build communities and collective resistance against shame. In light of this, one could approach the theme week on the KI profiles as an experiment in building a temporary affective counter-public (Papacharissi 2015; Squires 2002) that comes together in an effort to acknowledge shame as more-than-individual and as intertwined with societal structures and exclusion, and not as an affect that reveals the singular individual as bad or unworthy. As individual stories are shared in public, this sharing achieves a more transformative dimension by creating the basis for articulating a structural critique of how shame is distributed across bodies and for imagining new ways of building collectives around various individual experiences of illness.

However, shame is also politicized on a different level as the theme week allows for this affect to be discussed and contested as relevant for understanding life with a chronic condition. Some participants do not acknowledge that shame is of importance to their life as a chronic patient: "I have a chronic condition full time, 16 physiological diagnoses, and my one-year birthday on disability pension. I'm not in any way ashamed of this, and I'm grateful to be able to take care of and nurture my health and keep the healthcare system running".

Interestingly, it is a recurring strategy among the participants to 'reframe' shame as guilt in order to refute its relevance for the participants. Several of them mention that they do not feel shame in relation to their illness as it is not their fault that they are ill; they cannot be blamed for doing anything wrong and, therefore, do not feel shame. Another type of contestation focuses on how the participants have felt negative affects in relation to illness, but that shame is not the right label for this negativity. This displacement often also implies wanting to disconnect the chronic condition from individual identity. Many types of negative affect are mentioned in the material. Frustration is highlighted most often (eight times), but there seems to be no agreement about which affective alternatives to shame is the most relevant. Bad conscience, insufficiency, fury, guilt, sadness, embarrassment, irritation, loneliness and sorrow are all mentioned between one and four times in the material. Sharing shame stories in public, in other words, also creates the possibility of contesting the relevance of connecting illness to shame in various ways—and possibly also of learning how to overcome shame by watching others who are able to rhetorically push it aside. In that way, the research experiment enables 'shameful storytellers' to assemble in order to repoliticize shame, and it also creates a 'problem space' for articulating voices that reject shame as a relevant framework for understanding life with chronic illness.

CONCLUSIONS

This chapter has presented an affective methodology focused on using 'experimental problematisation' to produce findings both about the shame experiences of people with chronic conditions and about how the experimental research process potentially altered how shame was perceived and approached among the research participants.

In relation to the first type of findings, it was shown that shame revolves around the experience of an affective failure in terms of both being too sensitive (e.g., being exhausted too quickly) and making too little impact on the world (e.g., having to decline normal activities)—a failure that is intensified by the fact that the chronic condition is often invisible and needs constant explanation and justification. Another central pattern is that shame can happen in relation to acute encounters with the gazes of authorities in the health care or employment sector, but more persistent relational failures linked to the participants' children, partner and friends are articulated three to four times more often. Shame thus reveals investments in the ideal of (1) the present, loving mother who is able to provide a caring environment for her children; (2) the practically helpful partner, who is also loyal to shared dreams of the good life; and (3) the predictable and stable friend who does not produce too many social predicaments or problems (e.g., postponement, cancellations, special needs). This underlines that shame stories can also be approached as a repository of affirmative investments articulated through failure: investments in cultural norms and ideals related to the body, motherhood, the household and citizenship—but also that shame is culturally produced in the interface between cultural norms and constraints and the complex lived experience of (vulnerable) bodies.

In relation to the second type of findings, the material seems to underline how collective processes of sharing personal shame stories on social media can exactly create awareness of the cultural and collective dimensions of shame and thus help alleviate the experience of shame as a strictly personal burden linked to the specificities of the self. The analysis showed that seven out of ten participants experience shame in relation to their illness on a daily or weekly basis, but also that shame is a dynamic feeling that changes over time (due to, e.g., the arrival of an explanatory diagnosis). Social media is primarily described as serving a positive role in terms of gaining access to the lived experiences of peers, of decreasing shame and producing a feeling of a shared condition that transgresses personal faults and failures. The theme week on social media was mainly described as fruitful and a large majority indicated that sharing shame stories in public like this could strengthen the community and decrease the level of shame on an individual level. The week also allowed for contestations where the importance of other negative emotions (like frustration) could be stressed. The research experiment thus produced a problem space that both investigated, twisted and turned, and politicized the role of shame for KI's followers.

The presented research experiment is therefore not only valuable in its ability to produce 'socially robust' empirical material for research about shame dynamics in the life of people with chronic conditions, but also through the actual narrative, affective and relational processes it triggers. Bringing research into the public, through a partnership between a researcher and a peer-led patient community, thereby implies that shame among people with a chronic condition is 'problematised' in the double sense of the word: By being addressed as a research problem to be understood through academic knowledge production and by being repositioned as a collective and structural affect more than as an individual experience of affective failure.

Acknowledgements The author would like to thank the participants who shared often painful and intimate details of their life with me and without whom this chapter would not have been possible. Also, a huge thank you to the KI founders for their collaboration and enthusiasm.

REFERENCES

Ahmed, S. (2004). *The cultural politics of emotion*. Edinburgh University Press.
Billig, M. (2001). Humour and embarrassment: Limits of 'nice-guy' theories of social life. *Theory Culture Society,* 18(5), 23–43.
Blackman, L. (2012). *Immaterial bodies: Affect, embodiment, mediation*. Sage.
Braun, V., & Clarke, V. (2006). Using thematic analysis in psychology. *Qualitative Research in Psychology,* 3(2), 77–101.
Dolezal, L. (2015). The phenomenology of shame in the clinical encounter. *Medical Health Care and Philosophy,* 18, 567–576.
Dolezal, L., & Lyons, B. (2017). Health-related shame: An affective determinant of health? *Medical Humanities,* 43, 257–263.
Felski, R. (2000). Nothing to declare: Identity, shame, and the lower middle class. *PMLA,* 115(1), 33–45.
Foucault, M. (1984). Polemics, politics and problematizations: An interview conducted by Paul Rabinow in May 1984. Retrieved December 18, 2021, from https://foucault.info/documents/foucault.interview/
franzke, a. s., Bechmann, A., Zimmer, M., Ess, C., & Researchers, A. o. I. (2020). Internet Research: Ethical Guidelines 3.0.
Hvidberg, Michael F., Johnsen, Soeren P., Davidsen, M., & Ehlers, L. (2020). A nationwide study of prevalence rates and characteristics of 199 chronic conditions in Denmark. *PharmacoEconomics – Open,* 4, 361–380.
Knudsen, B. T., Stage, C., & Zandersen, M. (2019). Interspecies park life: Participatory experiments and micro-utopian landscaping to increase urban biodiverse entanglement. *Space and Culture,* https://doi.org/10.1177/1206331219863312, 1–23.
Lefebvre, H. (1992). *Rhythmanalysis*. Continuum.
Leys, R. (2018). *The ascent of affect*. University of Chicago Press.
Locke, J. (2016). *Democracy and the death of shame*. Cambridge University Press.
Lury, C. (2021). *Problem spaces*. Polity Press.
Lury, C., & Wakeford, N. (2012). *Inventive methods: The happening of the social*. Routledge.
Markham, A., & Pereira, G. (2019). Analyzing public interventions through the lens of experimentalism: The case of the Museum of Random Memory. *Digital Creativity,* 30(4), 235–256.
Marres, N., & Gerlitz, C. (2018). Social media as experiments in sociality. In N. Marres, M. Guggenheim, & A. Wilkie (Eds.), *Inventing the social*. Mattering Press.
Mortensen, S. U. (2020). Defying shame. *Mediekultur,* 36(67), 100–120.

Munt, S. (2007). *Queer attachments: The cultural politics of shame*. Ashgate.

Munt, S. (2017). Argumentum ad misericordiam: The cultural politics of victim media. *Feminist Media Studies*, 17(5), 866–883.

Nathanson, D. (1987). A timetable for shame. In D. Nathanson (Ed.), *The many faces of shame*. The Guilford Press.

Nowotny, H., Scott, P., & Gibbons, P. (2001). *Re-thinking science: Knowledge and the public in an age of uncertainty*. Polity Press.

Nussbaum, M. (2004). *Hiding from humanity. Disgust, shame, and the law*. Princeton University Press.

Papacharissi, Z. (2015). *Affective publics: Sentiment, technology, and politics*. Oxford University Press.

Probyn, E. (2004). Everyday shame. *Cultural Studies*, 18(2–3), 328–349.

Probyn, E. (2005). *Blush: Faces of shame*. University of Minnesota Press.

Richards, R. (2019). Shame, silence and resistance. How my narratives of academia and kidney disease entwine. *Feminism and Psychology*, 29, 269–285.

Sartre, J.-P. (2003). *Being and nothingness: An essay on phenomenological ontology*. Routledge.

Sedgwick, E. K., & Frank, A. (1995). Shame in the cybernetic fold: Reading Silvan Tomkins. In E. K. Sedgwick & A. Frank (Eds.), *Shame and its sister: A Silvan Tomkins reader*. Duke University Press.

Shefer, T., & Munt, S. (2019). A feminist politics of shame: Shame and its contested possibilities. *Feminism and Psychology*, 29(2), 145–156.

Spinoza, B. d. (1997). *Ethics part III, Online article, Project Gutenberg*.

Squires, C. (2002). Rethinking the black public sphere: An alternative vocabulary for multiple public spheres. *Communication Theory*, 12(4), 446–468.

Tomkins, S. (1995). Shame-humiliation and contempt-disgust. In E. K. Sedgwick & A. Frank (Eds.), *Shame and its sister: A Silvan Tomkins reader*. Duke University Press.

Wetherell, M. (2012). *Affect and emotion*. Sage.

Woods, A. (2017). On shame and voice-hearing. *Medical Humanities*, 43, 251–256.

Wurmser, L. (1987). Shame: The veiled companion of narcissism. In D. Nathanson (Ed.), *The many faces of shame*. The Guilford Press.

Zahavi, D. (2014). *Self and other: Exploring subjectivity, empathy, and shame*. Oxford University Press.

CHAPTER 11

Affective Experiments: Card Games, Blind Dates and Dinner Parties

Sophie Hope

This chapter introduces a practice-based methodology that uses convivial methods for researching socially engaged art: dinner parties, blind dates and a card game. I outline and analyse specific aspects of this socially engaged, participatory artistic research practice, which I have been using to research histories, politics and economics of socially engaged arts practices. My methodology is qualitative, action-oriented, practice-based, dialogical and participatory. In essence, I am experimenting with socially engaged practice to research the broader infrastructures and discourses of socially engaged practices (as a painter might use painting to research histories, methods and theories of painting). By socially engaged art I mean a broad range of artistic practices that overlap with community arts, political activism and social justice movements. I hope these methods may be of interest to other artists, researchers and cultural workers who aim to embed critical thinking and action into their practices to understand it better.

S. Hope (✉)
Birkbeck, University of London, London, UK
e-mail: s.hope@bbk.ac.uk

© The Author(s), under exclusive license to Springer Nature
Switzerland AG 2022
B. Timm Knudsen et al. (eds.), *Methodologies of Affective
Experimentation*, https://doi.org/10.1007/978-3-030-96272-2_11

223

As a practice-based scholar of socially engaged art for the last 20 years, I still find myself frustrated with the lack of time and space to think and reflect on the processes, promises and politics of the practices I am engaged in. To ease this frustration, I have been experimenting with ways to facilitate discussion on these issues as part of my research practice. There are often funding-led pressures to present exaggerated positive accounts of the impacts of socially engaged art and research. I, along with others researching in this field, have found that there are often difficulties in speaking about failure in conversations with peers, funders, employees or clients in formal contexts (Belfiore 2009; Clift et al. 2021; Hope 2020; Jancovich and Stevenson 2020; Wong 2019). Rachel Blanche and Anthony Schrag hosted a series of workshops in 2019, for example, to explore the 'failure of participation', pointing to a "dependency on the 'positive' successes of participatory arts" that has led to a lack of criticality due to pressures to ensure its continued financial survival (Blanche and Schrag 2020, para. 2). Leila Jancovich and David Stevenson (2020, p. 4) in their related research on failure also refer to how "the fear of being blamed for failures, or being perceived as a failure professionally, reduces risk-taking, encourages uncritical reporting". They found that social learning and structural change are "far less likely … if cultural professionals keep telling themselves publicly that they are delivering success".

In the company of these critical voices, I wanted to find ways to collectively unpack what, why and how we were doing what we were doing, without the pressure to agree to a single narrative of events or ignore experiences of awkwardness, failure and conflicting agendas as they were quietly swept under the carpet. The methods I have co-devised and present here aim to provide time and space for evaluative, reflective work that is not under pressure to promote positive impact but encourages discussion on disappointments, failures and uncertainties, based on the premise that there are different perspectives around the table. I wanted to find ways to understand these often unspoken aspects of the practices and explore what they might be able to tell us about the conditions in which we were working and perhaps will prefer to work in the future. As a participatory, socially engaged method of research, each of the approaches I present here focuses on a scenario with a set of parameters and timeframe for the discussion, which people are invited to step into and draw on their own experiences in response to and in relation to others in that scenario. The people engaging in these methods have a shared experience they are (re)uniting over. Participants are invited to spend time remembering, reflecting and dwelling on these shared moments, with no expectation that they need to reach an agreed testimony of events. The methods are devised to encourage conflictual, non-aligned stories to emerge. The convivial, performative, intersubjective aspects of the methods have gone some way to enable critical accounts of shared experiences in a way that holds onto their polyvocal complexity.

I focus here on the methods themselves, rather than the content produced by the methods. What happens between people in these staged convivial encounters, and how and why might they offer ways to encourage experiments in embodied criticality as research? As is often the case with practice-based research, I have become as interested in the methods of critical enquiry as I have in the data they produce. This chapter is focused on my methodology and what I have learnt about these staged encounters, specifically their limits. The three methods are *1984 Dinners* about art and politics in the year 1984; *Blind Dates* for people who have been partners on the same art project but who have never met and *Cards on the Table*, which invites people working on the same project to critically reflect on their ideals, discourses and agendas. These methods have evolved over a period of 15 years, following other iterative research experiments such as Critical Friends (Hope 2015), Performative Interviews (Hope 2020) and Social Art Maps (Donini and Hope 2016; Druiff and Hope 2015), all of which attempted to re-imagine the way we talk about, share and research motives, agendas and conflictual experiences of socially engaged arts practices.

After outlining these three approaches in more detail, I position the research in a broader conceptual framework of embodied criticality that allows us to sit with the complexities of the practice rather than attempt to look at experience from a distance or dig deep for a verifiable truth. I explore how these convivial interventions allow us to hold on to and appreciate the polyvocal, conflictual and contradictory experiences of the same event. I point to how a foregrounding of the framing of the research (such as dinner, date, card game) encourages playful interactions that allow a way into a tricky conversation. The bodily, facial, emotive responses and interactions around the table are elevated as significant as speech, calling for a broader appreciation of vocality as an in-situ form of reflection and analysis amongst those conversing. I then explore the ways in which these methods are performative in that they invite people onto a stage (blind date, dinner table, card game) where subjectivities are in formation, through a process of listening and responding to their peers. Co-ordinates, conventions and questions allow for an unpredictable exchange to occur, but one which encourages personal experiences to be considered in relation to broader structural and infrastructural concerns of art, politics and economics. In the final section I explore the intersubjective and affective aspects of these convivial methods and the difficulty in cracking open an accessible space for dissensus amongst peers.

Methods

I have taken my cue from approaches to art and social science that question the boundaries of their own disciplines, question the authority of the artist/researcher and challenge assumptions and power relations of what it means to create critical knowledge. Judith Butler, in her essay "What Is Critique? An Essay on Foucault's Virtue" (2004), writes that "the primary task of critique will not be to evaluate whether its objects—social conditions, practices, forms of knowledge, power, and discourse—are good or bad, valued highly or demeaned, but to bring into relief the very framework of evaluation itself". My research asks: How do we do this critical thinking together and in the process question the assumptions around critical thinking? The construction of the enquiry is brought into focus in a way that aims to encourage critical reflection of the infrastructures of the subject under discussion as well as the method for getting to that point.

I have been developing a practice that is self-reflexive, critical, co-authored and open to interpretation, and this has its roots in elements of community arts practices as well as feminist and queer approaches to researching, where the researcher becomes more self-reflexive and the participants of the research become recognised as co-constructors of the work. Through the methods I outline below, I am trying to explore ways of holding a space for the complexities of experience, different agendas and ideologies to be spoken and heard. Key to these methods is a question about how territories of memories and narrative fictions of recent histories are created and re-interpreted across generations and geographies. These exercises in oral history are never neutral but imbued with the performance of recollecting that goes on around the table. The dinner/blind date/card game are settings for the creation of multiple versions of events from different perspectives, depending on who is present and what and how they choose to recall in that moment.

1984 Dinners as a research method stems from my archival research into the Greater London Council (GLC) from 1981 to 1986 and the relationship between the left-wing metropolitan council and their support of activist, feminist, anti-racist, overtly political art groups and actions at the time. Through a brief exercise in time travel I wanted to explore the tactics and practices of artists/activists working in the margins of institutionalised culture during the Conservative government of the 1980s. On September 29, 2011, I hosted the first *1984 Dinner* with six invited guests who were active politically and artistically in 1984, in my studio in Deptford, London, to discuss art and politics during that period. As a way of researching an area of recent history that is relatively undocumented, I wanted to use the method of choosing one year to focus my research. Taking inspiration from the 1991 Jim Jarmusch film *Night on Earth* which tells the story of five taxi drivers in five different cities on one night and Jean-Michel Rabaté's history of literature in his book *1913: The Cradle of Modernism* (2007), I wanted to take a slice in time and explore what was happening in very different places to different people at that time. I chose 1984, not just with Orwell's spectre in the background, but because it was a period when the GLC was midway through its socialist project in a Conservative Britain. As I was seven years old in 1984, I was interested in how I can translate and re-interpret events I did not experience first-hand and consider what we can learn from these approaches for our practices today.

Following the initial dinner, I went on to co-host 1984 dinners in Singapore (in 2014 with Terence Chong), Melbourne (in 2014 with Marnie Badham and Bern Fitzgerald), Johannesburg (in 2014 with Gabi Ngcobo, Rangoato Hlasane, James French, Sara Hallatt and Monique Vajifdar) and Montevideo (in 2016 with Ana Laura Lopes de la Torre and Gonzalo Vicci). The resulting audio extracts are housed on a website (Hope 2011–2016). Each location was chosen because of the shared research interests of my fellow co-hosts and the contexts in the 1980s in each of the locations, such as the work of the theatre group Third Stage in Singapore, which led to their arrest in 1987; the developing critiques of funding of community arts in Australia; the aftermath of the 1982 *Culture and Resistance Festival* in Gaborone, Botswana, which brought together South African exiled cultural workers in the struggle against apartheid (members of Medu Arts Ensemble, the organisers of the festival were killed by the South African Defence Force in 1985) and in Uruguay the first democratic elections since the dictatorship were being held in 1984.

The discussions were framed by the same menu of questions placed on the tables about the frictions and conflicts that existed at the time among artists, the institutional support structures and funding they tapped into, how they made a living and what they think of the context now in relation to 1984. These questions led to discussions on the ideals and desires for political and social change they were actively working towards at the time. I sat (with the co-hosts) at the table, but we mainly remained silent, acting as hosts, serving food and drink, checking that audio recorders were on, and listening. This convivial format reunited people who had not necessarily had a conversation reflecting on these experiences since they had occurred. As these were informal group discussions, they were asking each other questions, responding, reacting, re-telling from their own perspectives. Listening back, there is a soundscape of memories of the same time across different geographies and political contexts amongst people who thought their actions were going to change the world.

Cards on the Table (*COTT*) is a card game I developed from 2016 to 2021 with Ania Bas, Siân Hunter Dodsworth, Sophie Mallett and Henry Mulhall (2021). Prior to developing the card game, I had co-facilitated a series of workshops that brought participants, artists and curators/commissioners/producers together who had worked on recently completed socially engaged art projects (Druiff and Hope 2015; Donini and Hope 2016). We facilitated conversations and created timelines together of the projects on long pieces of paper based on the diverse perspectives of those sitting around the table. This process enabled us to compare and contrast different starting points, sticking points and end points of a process, acknowledging the crossovers and departure points as everyone around the table remembered shared events differently. *COTT* expands on this method by turning the format of reflection into a game. The cards contain selected anonymous quotes from interviews with community organisers, artists and cultural organisations supplemented with quotes from the recordings of subsequent *COTT* games. *COTT* is a timed game for between three and eight players. Players choose quotes from their dealt hand and speak about their experiences of the project using that quote as a prompt. There are also theme cards (such as administration, agency, reputation and power) and keyword cards (including words such as honest, slow, boundaries, look hard, push, exploitative and frank), which set a framework for the discussion and prompt other ways to tackle the subject. The game can be played between people who are working on the same project to encourage them to think and talk critically together before, during and after a project. There are many assumptions that are made about the language used between people working on the same project, and this game cracks open some time and space to find out more about the agendas and experiences behind the language being used. The game is being played in different contexts in the UK such as part of public art commissioning processes, socially engaged art forums, local authorities, community development projects and artist-led support networks.

The *Blind Date* method is a dialogical encounter for two people who have worked on the same project but have never met to have a conversation with each other without the researcher present. This stems from an invitation by an arts organisation in 2018 to carry out research into partnerships on a specific project. When it transpired that many of the partners on the project had not met, I put people in touch via the format of an online or in-person dialogue. People were invited to meet together in pairs in person or via Skype (pre-pandemic, this was a more common online platform than Zoom) and given a set of questions to guide their conversation. Each partner received a pack in the post that included friendly guidance on getting ready for their conversation, herbal tea and a chocolate treat. Each encounter was introduced by my colleague Alice Whithers, recorded and transcribed. The findings from *Blind Dates* were presented in a document that included extracts from the conversations, reflections on meanings of partnerships and a manifesto for partnership working (Hope and Withers 2018). Both *COTT* and the *Blind Dates* methods are currently being used in a European research project looking into meaning and experiences of co-creation in arts projects and organisations (Be Part n.d.).

EYE-ROLLING AND YAWNING: EMBODYING CRITICALITY

I am suggesting here that critical reflection is important and has the potential to be opened up as a process to people beyond the artist/researcher. I am emphasising the significance of criticality to counter assumptions about the positive properties and impact of participation and empowerment. What role can critical reflection play in intervening in the ideals we hold dear, and why would anyone sign up for this? In the experimental scenarios discussed here, moments of reflection have cracked open assumptions and long-held beliefs, leading people to question motives, agendas and expectations. This does not always happen, of course, but they have provided occasions for this reflection-on-action whilst in-action; in the thick of projects, practices and complexities and compromises of living.

But what does it mean to critically reflect? It can imply that there is an underlying, uncorrupted meaning that some critical digging and deconstruction can unearth. Irit Rogoff (2006) points out that "there is a serious problem here, as there is an assumption that meaning is immanent, that it is always already there and precedes its uncovering" (para. 3). Rather it is in the practice. Rogoff suggests that it is by "inhabiting a problem rather than by analysing it" and engaging in these messy encounters with each other that critical knowledge emerges and is felt; "meaning is not excavated for, but rather, ... it takes place in the present" (Criticality section, para. 1). She suggests an evolution from criticism, through critique towards criticality: "[W]e have moved from *criticism* which is a form of finding fault and of exercising judgement according to a consensus of values, to *critique* which is examining the underlying assumptions that might allow something to appear as a convincing logic, to *criticality* which is operating from an uncertain ground of actual embeddedness" (Rogoff 2006, Criticality section, para. 1).

This latter approach, she writes, is "a state from which one cannot exit or gain a critical distance, but which rather marries our knowledge and our experience in ways that are not complimentary" (Criticality section, para. 5). Benjamin Noys (2017) calls for a return to critique (in a way that tallies with Rogoff's notion of criticality) that "involves being very close and very deep, in the sense of recognising and being immersed within the forms of capitalist value and state power" (p. 304). Lynne Keevers and Leslie Treleaven (2011) use the metaphor of diffraction, which "encourages managers and practitioners to not only reflect on what has been done but to also map the effects of their practices and interventions" (p. 518). They take the notion of diffraction from Donna Haraway (2004) who describes it as a "mapping of interference", where "the effects of difference appear". It is a metaphor that "speaks to entanglements, relationalities, co-production and the effects of intra-actions" (Keevers and Treleaven 2011, p. 509). It could be that the food, cards and blind date packages are the objects through which a diffracted way of reflecting on the effects and affects of these experiences occurs. Looking back in order to address what we are feeling and experiencing now and what can be done next have been features of these methods. One participant, for example, mentioned during the first *1984 Dinner* how this exercise acted as "reiterative inspiration" in terms of reflecting where we are now in relation to our previous histories.

Both Noys and Rogoff question the notion of critical distance and the objective position it occupies, rather they highlight the potential for negativity in awkward encounters when reflecting with others. My research paradigm is firmly rooted in this non-positivist, reflexive and situated position. I am interested in exploring how embedded and embodied approaches to research are also spaces for criticality. Haraway suggested "a doctrine of embodied objectivity that accommodates paradoxical and critical feminist science projects: Feminist objectivity means quite simply situated knowledge" (Haraway 1988, p. 581). This contests the notion of the objective researcher reliant on a professional distance, remaining unaffected by and not influencing their research. Magdalena Nowicka refers to Gillian Rose's argument (Rose 1997, p. 315) that we "should consider knowledge produced in research encounters as co-constitutive, emerging in relation to each other in the process of negotiation between the participants and researcher's identities and positions" (Nowicka 2019, p. 27). The feminist researcher, as I understand it, is embodied in a research process of permanent partiality (Haraway 2004, p. 31). Following bell hooks, critical paradigms are forever shifting as "we are constantly changing positions, locations, that our needs and concerns vary, that these diverse directions must correspond with shifts in critical thinking" (hooks 1990, p. 111). My methodology acknowledges that the voice has a body, that the body holds experience. Brandon LaBelle (2014), for example, explains how "language and voice are thus bound to the fact of our social experiences, which come to fundamentally shape our mouths" (p. 8). Reading the work of Haraway, hooks, Rogoff, Nowicka and LaBelle have helped me to develop and reflect on the emerging methods as they develop and adapt through practice.

What do these convivial methods provoke, allow for and capture that other research methods might not? In a formal interview situation, the interviewee may tell the interviewer what they think they want to hear—providing a kind of fiction. Sociologist Barbara Sherman Heyl has remarked on the problematic power relations of the interview: "for some respondents, the research interview may not be an appropriate place to 'tell all'" (2001, p. 376). If power relations exist in all encounters, rather than expecting people to 'tell all', how can research encounters such as the ones I am experimenting with acknowledge the different ways we tell versions of ourselves and foreground the research methods' performative, affective, subject-forming capacity? How can the research process itself hold the messiness, conflict and uncertainty of working in a participatory, collective way? The three methods I present here construct scenarios for people to reflect on converging but perhaps clashing experiences of shared moments.

Specifically, I suggest the convivial, affective (social, informal, playful) framing and staging of the methods provoke critical insights into the structural and infrastructural conditions of the practices under discussion. Each of the methods has created a scenario for a conversation to occur that would not necessarily have happened otherwise. In a related piece of research, Bernadette Lynch's *Whose Cake Is It Anyway?* (2009) used forum theatre techniques to reflect on partnership working between staff of galleries and museums and community partners. She found that use of drama to re-enact experiences, feelings and concerns meant the group were able to tackle subjects that otherwise would have been perhaps more difficult to engage with. This sideways, non-confrontational, conversational approach amongst peers allows a different way into quite difficult topics that might not be tackled in other less convivial situations such as work meetings, research interviews or public panels. They have become spaces where the interplay between structure and agency are played out, where conflicting opinions and voices coalesce.

I am suggesting that awkward conversations have been made more possible by the convivial gestures of the game, blind date care packages and welcoming dinner party atmosphere, but these props do not cover up the fact that participatory research environments are contested and group dynamics are very much alive and present. Participatory, convivial methods may offer different formats for reflection, but they are not in themselves more ethical approaches to research. Bill Cooke (2001) draws on social psychology to critique participatory development and the assumptions that participation is a good thing, instead he suggests that all acts of interventionist participation are laden with ideologies and assumptions played out in the unfolding group dynamics. He distinguishes between participation as empowerment as an end and participation as a means to develop more effective development. Both rely on a neocolonialist distinction between insiders and outsiders: them and us. By thinking through analyses of group dynamics, he cites the problems with researching with others and how the dynamics of the group can affect what is said and done and what is not. Cooke's focus is on participatory development, but the methods I am describing here also involve a 'participatory intervention' where I as an outsider set up and stage the encounter, where "the very presence of the interventionist changes things" (Cooke 2001, p. 103).

Analyses of talking, dialogical exchange and polylogue conversations often prioritise the words that are spoken between the guests and yet we are also responding, reacting and communicating in other bodily and vocal ways. What is happening to the reactions, faces, bodies of those not speaking around the card table or dinner? What role does listening play on the part of the other participants in the research and do these methods invite a particular mode of listening that requires interaction and response from those present?

Oscar Rantatalo and Staffan Karp (2016) refer to the role of the other in an audience of peers "who were largely passive, listening and interacting non-verbally through micro-cues, such as nodding or small signs of recognition with the individual engaging and sharing her reflections verbally with a group of peers" (p. 718). Their research explores collective aspects of critical reflection in the context of police training in Sweden. They developed three different aspects of collective reflection: polylogue, dialogue and specular reflection. If I apply these to the methods under discussion here, for example, to *Cards on the Table* and *1984 Dinners*, they involve a combination of specular reflection episodes in which individuals are "verbally reflecting through monologues or storytelling" in front of an audience of peers who "primarily listened with attention but without interrupting or actively participating in the story" (p. 718). These methods also involve informal polylogue collective reflection where "competing narratives of group members interplay in a fluid and multivoiced manner" (p. 715). The *Blind Dates* method is based on dialogue, a type of "peer-to-peer sharing of experiences and interpretation" that involves "a relatively structured back-and-forth form of reasoning" (p. 717). Rantatalo and Karp state that "learning through collective reflection can, on a practical level, be characterized as a messier and more unstructured process than the metaphor of 'dialogue' suggests" (p. 721). The methods here promote a combination of these communicative approaches where the contributions of those taking part might overlap or never touch the others present. Someone performing a specular presentation can result in no visible or vocal empathy or recognition, or it might prompt a ripple of consensual laughter around the table.

LaBelle refers to Donald Meltzer's "theatre of the mouth" where the mouth is a stage "upon which a number of essential performances are enacted" (LaBelle 2014, p. 9): "it is fundamentally a site of conflict, and from which we may learn the skills for negotiating—through acts of singing, burping, and laughing". He refers to the "script that preceded us" as directing our "oral imaginary" (p. 9). How do secretions, dialects, silences, jargon all swill around and influence our sonorous encounters in a meeting with other artists, researchers, funders, collaborators, participants, community groups, activists, curators? Both Adriana Cavarero and LaBelle call for a wider interpretation of vocality beyond speech. Cavarero relocates the voice in "the uniqueness of the one who emits it" (Cavarero 2005, p. 24), drawing attention to the ways "vocal emission and acoustic perception" are deeply connected to "the fleshy cavity that alludes to the deep body, the most bodily part of the body ... the vocal emission 'comes out of a wet mouth and arises from the red of the flesh'" (p. 4). She takes vocality as an object of study that "concerns an analysis of the voice that avoids the traditional privileging of its relationship with language" (p. 12). Quoting Roland Barthes, the voice's 'grain' is "the materiality of the body that springs from the throat, there where the phonic metal is forged" (p. 15). "The task of the voice", she writes, "is therefore to be a pathway, or better, a pivotal joint between body and speech" (p. 15). While vocality could be recorded and analysed (images of facial expressions from Charles Darwin's 1872 *The Expression of the Emotions in Man and Animals* come to mind), the affect of these bodily, more-than-speech reactions during the dinners, dates and card games are also analysed synchronously, in situ by those sitting around the table. Research is held in facial expressions, eye movements and body languages as they inform and reflect the knowledges being produced.

In a related example, Lynne Froggett has developed a psychosocial methodology using a visual matrix method as an alternative to the focus group, to "develop an analysis of the cultural significance, value and impact of artworks based on the public's experience, rather than their effects on the economy and environment" (Froggett et al. 2015). It involved a group of between 6 and 35 people selected by the researchers silently looking at visual material for 10 minutes, then group discussion in a snowflake pattern for 40 minutes (participants were not directly facing each other) followed by a facilitated plenary discussion and final reflection on the method itself. What I appreciate about this approach is that it acknowledges how the use of props (e.g., the visual material) grounds and focuses attention, allowing memories, thoughts and associations to come to the surface. The researchers found that tired stereotypes or assumed knowledge are not foregrounded as much as they often are in focus groups on the same topics. These experiments using a visual matrix, card game, dinner or blind date encourage hidden, unspoken or forgotten experiences to re-emerge into that space triggered by the props, staging and setting for the conversation. The direction in which the participants sit; the way the chairs are organised, facing each other; scattered chairs, to the side, opposite each other; eyes closed or open—all have a part to play in the way people speak, listen and interact. Experimenting with the direction of eyes and ears and how they relate to each other become a significant element of these convivial methods—partly stage-managed and partly impromptu depending on how the participants use the spaces. An awareness of the context, layout, introductions, participants, and getting to know each other through the process and finding out from each other more about the contexts they are/were working in are revealing and in each of the cases has solicited new insights and reflections that would perhaps otherwise go unsaid.

Through the dinners, card game and dates, it is possible to draw attention or at least acknowledge these broader soundscapes in the moment of the encounter, bringing into relief the framing of the research/evaluation itself. In listening back, we can learn to train our ears to place speech in the background and turn up the environmental sounds and the other movements and sounds mouths make. By facing each other, those present can see the expressions of those around them. This is also a process of placing the sounds and words in the broader socio-political context—re-rooting and embodying them, refusing to extract and codify them from afar. Les Back is also interested in this shift from being concerned only with 'voice' to an attention to soundscape and sound image (Back 2014). He refers to Murray Schafer's book *The Tuning of the World* (1977) and the idea of "slowing down modes of analytic attention—to take seriously the soundtrack of the social background". This would mean taking seriously the sounds of the streets, the clinking of dinner plates, the shuffling of cards, the 'micro-vocables' (the er, um, and uh; LaBelle 2014, p. 132), the pauses and interruptions, and also the bureaucratic infrastructures in which the conversations were taking place—turning up the dial on the budgets, audits, reporting and policy frameworks of the projects under discussion. As well as being audio recorded for review and further analysis, the games/dates/dinners are also sites where new knowledges are produced depending on the dynamics of the encounters themselves. They are processes that open the research process to multiple interpretations, drawing attention to the mode of research itself and the way we listen to each other and understand not only what people think has happened, but how it has made them feel and the different ways this is expressed.

PERFORMATIVE, CONVIVIAL ENCOUNTERS

While complaints, uncertainties and negativity may be more easily expressed informally amongst friends, reflection with colleagues you work with (such as managers, clients and funders) might require a presentation of self that preserves one's reputation. While the conviviality suggested by the language and conventions of games, food and dates might introduce an element of informality into these environments, these are still risky sites of potential judgement, discipline and reputational damage. Putting on a positive, confident front is a matter of professional survival. While the guidelines for participation in these methods are made explicit (e.g., timings, menu of questions), group dynamics are unpredictable. For example, unspoken rules about table manners are not always shared; dinner guests drift off into small talk with their seated neighbours; the language on the cards is hard to read for some non-native English speakers; the timings of the game are sometime ignored; one of the partners on a blind date might do most of the talking and not ask the other person any questions back. Not participating, not being able to be critical, self-censorship and exclusion are all happening despite these methods of conviviality attempting otherwise. How do moments of criticality slip through, how are grievances aired in contexts where it is difficult to speak out?

There is an element of theatricality to the dinners, card games and blind dates, as with any encounter, but the invitation to eat together, play a game or meet a relative stranger perhaps highlights the performativity of these meetings, inviting guests to play along if they wish. Erving Goffman has written on the "presentation of self" and how "a performer may be taken into his own act, convinced at the moment that the impression of reality which he fosters is the one and only reality" (Goffman 1959, p. 86). Judith Butler has contested the idea of an already existing subjective agency that freely chooses to act; rather the subject is formed through the performative process (Butler 1997). Subjectivities are not pre-existing or self-determined acts of agency lying dormant, waiting to be analysed or awakened by researchers and artists; rather, subjectivity is formed through the performative act itself. Which versions of ourselves are we putting forth, and what do our broader 'mouthing practices' reveal about our feelings in these contexts? How are subjectivities being formed through these research encounters?

Many artists and researchers have played with the performative aspects of dialogical encounters, developing these exchanges as embodied acts of presentation of self, reflexivity and collective analysis of situations. Australian artists Change Media, for example, have developed a card game called *What Privilege?* that used their "notice, disrupt and reframe methodology" to explore "how power and privilege [supremacy thinking] arise in our daily interactions" and "examine our shared values, highlight existing community resistance and rehearse acts of solidarity" (Tallstoreez Productionz 2020). The cards invite players to identify with characters such as Caterer, Gatekeeper, Moderator, Curator (there are 50 types). Each card also labels a value associated with it and act of violence that this character could perpetrate. I played an earlier prototype of this game and appreciated the way it gave us tools to reflect on aspects of our roles, belief systems and ideologies that would be difficult to tackle head on. By taking on the role of dinner guest, card player, blind date participant, there is a shield or mask implicit in the invitation—you can still come as you are, but the format provides a stage on which you can play your part. This invitation to socially interact, flirt, argue, play, compare, disagree are conventions of the convivial formats themselves. Through these interventions you are invited to express a critical relationship with the value systems we usually take for granted. The performed element adds an aesthetic layer of drama and absurdity to the research process. Through listening and exchange, the methods ask us to question our own assumptions and the harm we may be doing by having an unwavering and unquestioning approach to the work we are doing. This may allow us to create ways of interpreting and discussing experiences and potentially changing the way we work. The menu of questions at the dinner table, timed turn-taking in the card game and invitation to a blind date encourage different voices to come together. People can share as much or as little as they want as these methods disrupt the usual formats where the loudest and most articulate get heard. The cards, dates and dinners are visible constructions where the apparatus of the research is made obvious. As Judith Butler (1997) has explored, one's subjectivity and agency are created through these performative acts, drawing attention to the different possibilities of interaction and interpretations of the interview format itself as a site where the subject performs itself into being.

The mode and aesthetics of the invitation, the settings and facilitation all have an impact on how, who and why the resulting encounters play out in the way they do. Nowicka (2019) insists that "ethical reflection on the co-production of conviviality in research must be an element of every project that describes itself as convivial" (p. 29). This might involve transparency as to who was invited, how decisions were made, what the financial arrangements are (who is paid what): "who is entitled to participate in particular encounters—and on which terms?" (p. 28). Making visible the social psychological dynamics, as well as the research paradigm in which these encounters are set up is based on the idea that knowledges are partial, compromised, socially constructed, embodied and complex and therefore any interpretation of these exchanges needs to take this on board.

INTERSUBJECTIVE, AFFECTIVE ENCOUNTERS

If one of the characteristics of these methods is that they foreground the performative aspects, another element worth reflecting on is the underlying intersubjectivity of the research encounter. This can be described as the ability to empathise with someone else's position in a way that might shift your own perspective. This can come from self-critical participation in a conversation or practical event that opens the possibility to empathise with others in a way that may shift one's own perspective and experience. It implies an empathetic sharing of divergent, contradictory and perhaps conflicting meanings of the same experience. Cavarero refers to breathing, for example, as "a profound communication of oneself, an exchange in which one inhales the air that the other exhales" (Cavarero 2005, p. 31). This reciprocal intersubjectivity relates to Grant Kester's theory of a dialogical aesthetics that "requires that we strive to acknowledge the specific identity of our interlocutors and conceive of them not simply as subjects on whose behalf we might act but as co-participants in the transformation of both self and society" (Kester 2004, p. 79). Taking Bakhtin's notion of the work of art as a conversation, Kester develops a case for dialogic art that goes beyond avant-garde aesthetic criteria based on criticality, disruption and rupture and instead looks at the transformative potential of an aesthetics based on reciprocity and collaborative encounters. The staging and framing of the card game, dinner format or blind date, for example, momentarily suspend other logics and logistics to reclaim some unproductive, discordant, informal reflection. If all encounters are understood as affective, relational and intersubjective, the card game, dinner and blind date arrangements promote interaction and monologues, dialogues and polylogues that present, respond and interact depending on the people around the table and the subject under discussion. I suggest the framing of the conversation as performative and playful permits a different type of conversation to occur that there may not otherwise be time for.

Nowicka (2019) suggests "participants and the researcher affect each other not only as producers of knowledge, but also as empathic humans capable of engaging with the positions of others" (p. 27). She refers to how convivial aspects of the research encounter "have the potential for personal transformations and becoming through relational engagements with the positions and knowledge of the self and the other" (p. 27). Referring to the *1984 Dinners* method, Tim Waterman and Ruth Catlow (2016) suggested that it is the conviviality of the dinner party format that allowed "greater veracity in memory, as participants jog memories and reconstruct events". They suggest "[t]he commensality provides a series of failsafe mechanisms that stop participants from rhapsodising, romanticising, or grandstanding in the process of recalling events" (Waterman and Catlow 2016). It is perhaps the informality of the exchange between people that means they cross-reference and contradict, remembered events in tandem and on different tracks. While the participatory methods do not aim for veracity, they are a chance to speak and be heard—in all sorts of manners—in contexts where marginalised voices and practices are silenced or ignored.

The card games, dates and dinners draw on people's memories, cross referencing experiences, generating empathy and disagreements that have an impact on their ways of working, thinking and relationships to their work. Conflictual consensus or 'dissensus' (Mouffe 2000) may be a way of understanding this conflation of the concepts of individual and communal structures in moments of collective critical reflection. Chantal Mouffe identifies an agonistic struggle as one where principles are agreed but interpretations of them differ and coexist: a "struggle between different interpretations of shared principles, a conflictual consensus: consensus on the principles, disagreement about their interpretation" (Miessen 2007, para. 3). I relate the practice of agonism to intersubjectivity as it involves empathy towards and respect of the other (recognising different subjectivities) as well as acknowledging that it is these differences rather than the need to overcome them that constitutes democratic society (Laclau and Mouffe 1985). Ben Gidley in his reflections on his own participatory research methods calls for "forms of conviviality and cohesion that have space for contention" (Gidley 2019, p. 137). Nowicka (2019) also reminds us that "to see situations through the lens of *analytical conviviality* means to see them as equally 'peaceful and conflictual', and to make the relational dependence of people the focus of research" (p. 22). This is about creating scenarios that do not attempt to overcome difference but encourage and respect divergent experiences of the same moments to be shared. In the case of the card game and blind dates, they offered evaluative interruptions to the project management and delivery of participatory arts programming, where the agendas and topics come from the shared experiences of those present. They involved small attempts at slowing down, taking stock and looking inwards and around as we inhabit and hold intersubjective positions of self and other. Given the performative and intersubjective nature of these relational and affective forms of research, the conversations went in all sorts of directions. There was a safety net in the format of the encounter, which means that while self-censorship and reputation management was still present, there was an openness to the process that meant experiences of failure, uncertainty, misunderstandings and not-knowing were given permission to be aired and shared.

CONCLUSIONS

The dinners, dates and card game have been, and continue to be, used and adapted in different contexts underpinned and shaping a diverse range of research questions, from exploring meanings of co-creation, experiences of cultural partnerships and histories of art and politics in the 1980s. They form part of a growing toolbox of creative commons licensed participatory research methods that promote critical thinking entwined with practical experiences of socially engaged arts practices, embracing the diverse experiences and agendas of all those involved (artists, funders, participants, curators etc.), as well as those on the edges (non-participants). While the methods I have introduced here emphasise the learning and exchange in the moment of the encounter, I am often the one setting the framework, devising the research questions, pressing record, doing some solitary analysis and writing up the results. Artist and writer Lea Kantonen raises the issue of power in her essay on shared expertise in fieldwork, writing that the participatory researcher "strives towards a close relationship with members of the community, and formulates the knowledge both by listening to them and by relating to the traditions of the academic institutions" but "only she is rewarded for her accomplishments in the academic community" (Kantonen 2008, p. 184). Gidley (2019) argues that "the political economy of academic knowledge production blocks collaborative research and convivial tools" (p. 124). Sociologist Kip Jones suggests that research material does not need 'academically analysing' but instead can be left open to interpretation so that the reader becomes part of the process (Jones 2006, p. 79). Barbara Sherman Heyl also acknowledges that "researchers have considerable control over the 'reporting' and the outcome, while still striving to empower the respondents through respectful listening" (Heyl 2001, p. 376). This re-framing of a collective or collaborative process as one that privileges the individual artist or researcher is perpetuated through the forms of dissemination that validate academic or artistic work (such as conferences, exhibitions and book chapters, such as this one).

There are telling moments when the method of research is brought into question, such as at the end of the *1984 Dinner* in Johannesburg when one of the guests asked why it had taken "some English lass" to get them talking to each other. A debate followed between the guests about whether this mattered and that there were in fact already examples of people talking in this way. Similarly, at the end of a *COTT* game, the players questioned the need for yet another artist-facilitated game when all they needed was some unstructured time to chat. These reflexive moments raise questions as to where and how criticality is not just facilitated but also allowed to reflect on the methods of facilitation and assumptions of the researcher. Self-censorship, pauses and non-participation are equally telling in these constructed scenarios for reflection. While there is a move to understanding critical distance as embodied, how deep can these methods go in the difficult work of questioning the ideological roots and research frameworks that piggyback desires for participation and criticality?

Because the methods I am referring to invite people to slow down to consider past or current events, my focus is on what Donald Schön (1983) refers to as reflection-on-action, rather than reflection-in-action. I suggest that intersubjectivity in research encounters that involve other people listening and responding to each other (not the researcher) might provide opportunities for different kinds of reflection-on-action. This is significant in terms of opening the research process to learn from and think with others, not in an extractive way, but in a diffracted way that folds back into the practices around the table. Here, critical reflection is not done at a distance, rather the space is created for awkward, agonistic encounters to be shared from experience. They offer approaches to reflecting on our own privileges, assumptions and agencies in relation to those we are opening up to and with, where the assumptions around the table can be questioned and re-considered. I invite you to use the tools, adapt the methods and wallow in the messiness that experiments in convivial, embodied criticality can conjure up.

REFERENCES

Back, L. (2014). Tape recorder. In C. Lury & N. Wakeford (Eds.), *Inventive methods: The happening of the social* (pp. 245–260). Routledge.

Bas, A., Hope, S., Hunter-Dodsworth, S., Mallet, S., & Mulhall, H. (2021). *Cards on the table.* Retrieved December 20, 2021, from https://www.cardsonthetable.org/

Belfiore, E. (2009). On bullshit in cultural policy practice and research: Notes from the British case. *International Journal of Cultural Policy*, 15(3), 343–359.

Be Part. (n.d.). *Be part homepage.* Retrieved 16 September 2021 from https://beyondparticipation.eu/

Blanche, R. & Schrag, A. (2020). *Why are we talking about failure?* The failure of participation. Retrieved December 20, 2021, from https://the-failure-of-participation.com/

Butler, J. (1997). *Excitable speech: A politics of the performative.* Routledge.

Butler, J. (2004). What is critique? An essay on Foucault's virtue. In S. Salih & J. Butler (Eds.), *The Judith Butler reader* (pp. 302–322). Blackwell.

Cavarero, A. (2005). *For more than one voice: Toward a philosophy of vocal expression.* Stanford University Press.

Clift, S., Phillips, K. & Pritchard, S. (2021). The need for robust critique of research on social and health impacts of the arts, *Cultural Trends*, 30(5), pp. 442–459. https://doi.org/10.1080/09548963.2021.1910492

Cooke, B. (2001). The social psychological limits of participation? In B. Cooke & U. Kothari (Eds.), *Participation: The new tyranny?* (pp. 102–121). Zed Books.

Donini, S. & Hope, S. (2016). *Social art map: Mapping four art commissions in Swale & Medway, North Kent.* Retrieved December 20, 2021, from https://sophiehope.org.uk/wp-content/uploads/SAM-Web-Copy-v3.pdf

Druiff, E. & Hope, S. (2015). *Social art map: An in-depth study of 5 art commissions from 3 perspectives.* Retrieved December 20, 2021, from https://sophiehope.org.uk/wp-content/uploads/social-art-map-A1-sign-off.pdf

Froggett, L., Manley, J. & Roy, A. (2015). The visual matrix method: Imagery and affect in a group-based research setting. *Forum: Qualitative Social Research* 16(3).

Gidley, B. (2019). Failing better at convivially researching spaces of diversity. In M. L. Berg & M. Nowicka (Eds.), *Studying diversity, migration and urban multiculture: Convivial tools for research and practice* (pp. 123–140). UCL Press.

Goffman, E. (1959). *The presentation of self in everyday life.* Penguin Books Ltd.

Haraway, D. (1988). Situated knowledges: The science question in feminism and the privilege of partial perspective. *Feminist Studies*, 14(3), pp. 575–599.

Haraway, D. (2004). The promises of monsters: A regenerative politics for inappropriate/d others. In D. Haraway (Ed.), *The Haraway Reader* (pp. 63–124). Routledge.

Heyl, B. S. (2001). Ethnographic interviewing. In P. Atkinson, A. Coffey, S. Delamont, J. Lofland & L. Lofland. (Eds.). *Handbook of ethnography*. Sage.

hooks, b. (1990). *Yearning: Race, gender, and cultural politics*. South End Press.

Hope, S. (2015). Cultural measurement on whose terms? Critical friends as an experiment in participant-led evaluation. In L. MacDowall, M. Badham, E. Blomkamp & K. Dunphy (Eds.), *Making culture count: The politics of cultural measurement. New directions in cultural policy research*. Palgrave. https://doi.org/10.1007/978-1-137-46458-3_18

Hope, S. (2011–2016). *1984 Dinners*. Retrieved December 20, 2021, from https://1984dinners.sophiehope.org.uk/

Hope, S. (2020). Unfinished business: Performative interviews as a method for expressing failure in the socially engaged art job. *Conjunctions: Transdisciplinary journal of cultural participation, 7*(2), 1–14. https://doi.org/10.7146/tjcp.v7i2.119748

Hope, S., & Withers, A. (2018). *A partner in every port: Exploring the meanings of partnerships in the 2017 Floating Cinema Tour*. UP Projects.

Jancovich, L., & Stevenson, D. (2020). Editorial. *Conjunctions: Transdisciplinary Journal of Cultural Participation, 7*(2), 1–8. https://doi.org/10.7146/tjcp.v7i2.121812

Jarmusch, J. (1991). *Night on Earth*. [Film]. JVC Entertainment, et al.

Jones, K. (2006). A biographic researcher in pursuit of an aesthetic: The use of arts-based (re)presentations in "performative" dissemination of life stories. *Qualitative Sociology Review, 2*(1), pp. 66–85.

Kantonen, L. (2008). Shared expertise in fieldwork, research process, artistic presentation and representation. *Geist,* 11,12,14, pp. 182–196.

Keevers, L. & Treleaven, L. (2011). Organizing practices of reflection: A practice-based study. *Management Learning,* 42(5), 505–520. https://doi.org/10.1177/1350507610391592

Kester, G. (2004). *Conversation pieces: Community and communication in modern art*. University of California Press.

LaBelle, B. (2014). *Lexicon of the mouth: Poetics and politics of voice and the oral imaginary*. Bloomsbury.

Laclau, E., & Mouffe, C. (1985). *Hegemony and socialist strategy: Towards a radical democratic politics*. Verso.

Lynch, B. (2009). *Whose cake is it anyway?: A collaborative investigation into engagement and participation in twelve museums and galleries in the UK*. Paul Hamlyn Foundation.

Miessen, M. (2007). *Articulated power relations – Markus Miessen in conversation with Chantal Mouffe*. Retrieved December 20, 2021, from https://16beavergroup.org/articles/2007/09/29/articulated-power-relations-markus-miessen-in-conversation-with-chantal-mouffe/

Mouffe, C. (2000). *The democratic paradox.* Verso.

Nowicka, M. (2019). Convivial research between normativity and analytical innovation. In M. L. Berg & M. Nowicka (Eds.), *Studying diversity, migration and urban multiculture: Convivial tools for research and practice* (pp. 17–35). UCL Press.

Noys, B. (2017). Skimming the surface: Critiquing anti-critique. *Journal for Cultural Research*, 21(4), pp. 295–308.

Rabaté, J-M. (2007). *1913: The cradle of modernism.* Blackwell Publishing.

Rantatalo, O. & Karp, S. (2016). Collective reflection in practice: An ethnographic study of Swedish police training. *Reflective Practice*, 17(6), pp. 708–723.

Rogoff, I. (2006). 'Smuggling' – An Embodied Criticality. eipcp.net. Retrieved December 20, 2021, from https://xenopraxis.net/readings/rogoff_smuggling.pdf

Rose, G. (1997). Situating knowledges: Positionality, reflexivities and other tactics. *Progress in Human Geography*, 21(3), pp. 305–320.

Schön, D. (1983). *The reflective practitioner: How professionals think in action.* Basic Books.

Schafer, M. (1977). *The tuning of the world.* Random House Inc.

Tallstoreez Productionz. (2020). *Change media.* Retrieved December 20, 2021, from http://www.changemedia.net.au

Waterman, T. & Catlow, R. (2016). Dining at a distance: Performing the commons across time and space. *p-e-r-f-o-r-m-a-n-c-e*, 3(1–2). http://www.p-e-r-f-o-r-m-a-n-c-e.org?p=2668

Wong, S. (2019). *Beside engagement: A queer and feminist reading of socially negotiated art through dialogue, love, and praxis.* [Doctoral dissertation, University of Wolverhampton]. Open Repository of University of Wolverhampton. https://wlv.openrepository.com/handle/2436/622274

Wind as an Elementary Attraction: An Avant-Garde Experiment on the West Coast of Jutland, Denmark

Britta Timm Knudsen

This chapter presents a media-induced experience of a landscape and its climatic and atmospheric distinctiveness with the wind in the leading role as an important local resource along the West Coast of Denmark. As a natural agent and force, wind already plays an important role in the region's economy, and the region plans to excel at renewable energy and in the experience economy, which already includes numerous leisure and open-air sports facilities involving wind (surfing, windsurfing, stand-up paddling [SUP], wakeboarding, fishing, sailing etc.), as well as the newly opened (2020) Theme Park for the Forces of Nature situated just outside Ringkøbing. Thus, wind is discursively positioned as an economic resource and a strongly instrumentalised form of energy. Likewise, wind in its extreme forms—such as hurricanes and storms—is a strong driver of

B. Timm Knudsen (✉)
School of Communication and Culture, Aarhus University,
Aarhus, Denmark
e-mail: norbtk@cc.au.dk

B. Timm Knudsen et al. (eds.), *Methodologies of Affective
Experimentation*, https://doi.org/10.1007/978-3-030-96272-2_12

245

floods. In the past, the wind used to cause many shipwrecks, and it now causes increasing coastal erosion owing to the frequent storms and precipitation caused by climate change. In this chapter, wind is framed in a way that goes beyond discursive and dramatised understandings, being regarded as an atmospheric factor, omnipresent and barely noticeable, an elementary, everyday phenomenon. Through a pair of virtual reality glasses, wind also reveals its qualities as a perfect non-human attractor and place-performer (Coleman and Crang 2003), if we grant its experiential and seductive capacities (Lew and Cartier 2004; DeLanda 2006; Sandvik 2010), which appeal to both locals and part-time residents (Gravari-Barbas and Guinand 2017). My avant-garde experiment goes beyond social relations and examines the connective capacity of digital media—here, virtual reality (VR) with a focus on human-nature relations and entanglements—and asks how to enchant the everyday and add a sense of mystery and renewed affective intensity to mundane phenomena (Knudsen et al. 2019). Was it even possible to attract audiences to an experience of wind? Was it possible to have a deep experience of wind as an invisible, fleeting element through an apparently distracting technology such as VR? Would an enhanced sense of the ecological environment prove to be the main outcome of the whole experience? These were some of the key questions that were posed before the experiment.

Methodologically, this case study and the whole *Rethinking tourism to a coastal city: Design for new engagements* (2016–2019) research project—apart from field studies, mapping and assembling strategies and interviews—was based on interventionist and participatory approaches in the form of design experiments, research by design, laboratories for testing prototypes and provotypes, and key approaches for gathering data and testing research findings (Hauberg 2011; Glanville 2014; Roggema 2017).

I begin by introducing readers to the West Coast of Denmark as a tourist destination, before considering wind as a signifier in this area. The primary theoretical framework is the avant-garde aesthetic that we find in French author Georges Perec's space-oriented experiments. This chapter will show how this aesthetic was deployed in an interactive wind installation and how the whole set-up was assembled and then experienced by about 150 residents and tourists in August 2018.

Ringkøbing-Skjern: A Tourist Destination

Geographically speaking, Ringkøbing-Skjern is the largest municipality in Denmark, covering 1489 square kilometres. It has about 57,000 inhabitants. The area's topography is distinctive, dominated by a large fjord and the North Sea coastline, which is characterised by sand dunes that are crucial for the region's natural attractiveness and the outdoor activities that take place here (such as surfing, windsurfing, wakeboarding, swimming, sailing, fishing, hiking, bicycling and searching for amber). The topographical features of the area—ample space, the iconic scenery along the coast and the vast meadows surrounding the fjord—are used in a tourist brand called Ringkøbing-Skjern: Realms of Nature (The Municipality of Ringkøbing-Skjern, Plan and Development Strategy 2015).

Ringkøbing-Skjern Municipality is the fourth most-popular tourist destination in Denmark and the second most-popular coastal destination. The total number of overnight stays at RSK was 3,524,248 in 2020, reflecting a steady growth of 16% since 2008.[1] More than 6 million Germans visit the West Coast every year. Most tourists to Ringkøbing-Skjern rent one of the 10,000 summer cottages available along the coast.[2] Seventy-five per cent of them are German, many returning to the same location for decades, and even for generations.[3] Ringkøbing-Skjern Municipality, in partnership with the other municipalities on the West Coast, has outlined a strategy for the future. This strategy places a new focus on cultural and urban activities in the area, the aim being to achieve a 3% increase in overnight stays and a 4% increase in consumption related

---

[1] "Om Partnerskab for Vestkystturisme." Retrieved December 21, 2021, https://www.vestkystturisme.dk/media/1678/arbejdspapir-2-udvikling-og-forbrug.pdf

[2] These figures do not reflect the large number of domestic tourists who own a second residence in this area, which still represents 61% of the total number of tourists who are temporary summer residents. This distinction between temporary resident-owners and temporary resident-tenants is solely a market-driven perspective that regards ownership as the (only) legitimate claim on land and excludes other forms of capital, such as social and cultural parameters. If we determine that tourists and permanent residents engage in polytopical living, this would blur the implicit distinction between domestic and foreign tourists: they appear more equally positioned with respect to having knowledge of, and emotional claims on, the land.

[3] VisitDenmark. 2016. "International markedsføring af Danmark som rejsemål: Notat med fokus på kulturoplevelser." https://slks.dk/fileadmin/user_upload/0_SLKS/Dokumenter/Kommuner_Plan_Arkitektur/Turisme/International_markedsfoering_og_kultur.pdf

to travel to and tourism in the area.[4] Some stakeholders in Ringkøbing-Skjern want tourism to increase in order to generate more revenue and jobs, but also to stop the general trend of negative settlement in rural areas, in particular along the West Coast of Jutland. Statistics show a 2–5% decline in settlement in Ringkøbing-Skjern Municipality in the period from 2008 to 2017, and a dramatic 50% increase in abandoned houses in rural areas over the last 15 years throughout Denmark (Kristensen et al. 2017).

In the research project *Rethinking tourism to a coastal city: Design for new engagements* (2016–2019), the interdisciplinary research group's aim[5] was to shift the focus from the coastal area's demand side to its supply side, using a series of subtle site-specific interventions to accommodate both residents and tourists. A focus on the supply side entailed that we chose to study the co-creation between nature, locals and part-time locals (tourists and summer-cottage owners who spend two to three weeks a year in their summer cottage) using a set of prototype interventions in which we tested new scenes of engagements between these stakeholders. A number of interventions were conducted at different locations in the municipality. For instance, war films were screened on bunkers left behind after the Second World War; industrial waste was recycled to build benches and chairs in one of the coastal towns; wilderness bathtubs were installed in significant industrial zones in order to let tourists and locals savour a wild experience; and part-time locals were invited to describe their strong attachment to certain places in a digital guide book.

My project on the performative potentials of wind was conceived in collaboration with two artists—Lise Autogena and Joshua Portway—and it (im)materialised as an outdoor data visualisation of wind in the form of a VR-artistic installation that may have resembled a scientific laboratory from the perspective of the bystanders. Our site-specific experiment to visualise wind took place near one of the most iconic heritage sites in Ringkøbing-Skjern Municipality: the 53-metre tall Lyngvig Fyr lighthouse, erected in 1906. The experience was individual, rather long and

---

[4] "Om Partnerskab for Vestkystturisme." Retrieved December 21, 2021, from https://www.vestkystturisme.dk/media/1782/udviklingsplan-for-vestkysten.pdf
[5] Our project was a collaboration between the key partners: Ringkøbing-Skjern Municipality, the Aarhus School of Architecture and Aarhus University, as well as additional partners including Ringkøbing-Skjern Museum, Powers of Nature, VisitAarhus, and Danish Coastal and Rural Tourism.

Fig. 12.1 The two artists Joshua Portway and Lise Autogena at the left side of the experimental site; the technological set-up and a participant having the wind experience in the middle of the dunes at Lyngvig Fyr, Hvide Sande. (Image by author August 2018)

meditative, giving everyone the time to explore the movements of wind through VR glasses at their own pace (Fig. 12.1).

Multiple Methods

In my research I used different methods in the various phases of my project. The first exploratory phase was primarily made up of 22 qualitative, semi-structured interviews with wind users in the area, with data being generated during the summer and autumn of 2017. The interviewees were selected according to their professional or lay interest in (and experience of) wind. They included wind turbine engineers, coastal protection personnel, nature guides, windsurfers, cyclists, sailors, meteorologists and German part-time locals. I also held a range of informal talks with tourists in the area.[6]

---

[6] I have translated the interview excerpts that I use in this chapter.

The second phase was an assemblage (DeLanda 2006) and prototype design phase that provided an opportunity for research through design, based on input from the first phase. As I needed to add artistic designer skills, I invited two London-based artists to join the project and design a prototype of a wind experience, based on my research and their own mapping of the area.

The third phase involved testing the artistic prototype design in the chosen area. The design, a data visualisation of wind, was placed in the dunes about 50 metres from the sea. The defined area covered about eight square metres and was symbolically enclosed by an open tent. The test equipment consisted of a small table, a VR headset, two beamers, a huge computer, cables and us—the artists and me as a researcher. Through the VR headset, the virtual reality application visualised the physicality of the wind by making the airflow visible as it swirled and eddied around the shapes of the dunes. The test took place on August 13–14, 2018, at Lyngvig Fyr, Hvide Sande, and had elements of a research by design process (Stappers et al. 2014; Zimmerman and Forlizzi 2014), as there were some adjustments to the experience during this process, in particular with a view to facilitating the use of the VR headset and the beamers. The data that the test produced consisted of first-hand testimony and brief discussions with the audience after each experience. As mentioned earlier, about 150 people tried out the prototype during the test period.

Wind as a Signifier

It is well-known that tourists move towards the sun, which is called heliotropism (Martin 2005). The wind has never been regarded as equally important as a tourist attraction (Martin 2005), but this seems to be changing significantly, and increasing numbers of recreational activities are now based on wind. Ringkøbing-Skjern on the West Coast of Jutland has focused a good deal on the presence of wind and rough weather in the region. For instance, the region refers to itself as Cold Hawaii and has 31 registered surfing spots on the West Coast for windsurfing, surfing, kitesurfing and SUP.

Many of the leisure activities carried out on Ringkøbing Fjord and in the nearby sea depend on the wind. Wind is also an important resource for Ringkøbing-Skjern's economy, as seen in the planned location of 20 wind turbines offshore, along the coastline of Holmsland Klit, the 40-kilometre long and 1–2-kilometre wide peninsula of dunes separating Ringkøbing

Fjord from the North Sea. The preservation of the dune landscape and the hollows behind the dunes has high priority in the management of the area. The splendid dune landscape and the spectacular views of the sea are regarded as highlights of any visit to the area, and they are preserved by the Danish Nature Agency, as well as by the landowners who own summer cottages in the area. Quite a lot of management effort goes into preserving the constantly moving and changing coastline, and this is done by implementing a whole range of coastal protection procedures (e.g., dredges that pump sand from the seabed onto the beach to prevent the inevitable erosion of the coastline by the wind and current), some of which disturb the tourist gaze (Urry 1999), while many of the locals are pleased with all this activity because it generates income for the small community. One of the primary findings of our project was that tourists and locals take different sides in the conflict that the placement of the offshore wind turbines cause. Not all tourists are fond of undisturbed sunset views, not all locals are crazy about the area's wind turbine venture and the economic reasoning behind it, and many tourists enjoy the performative aspects of the industrial harbour (and also the performative fishermen posing as 'authentic' fishermen, even though fishing in the area is fully industrialised) and its heavy machinery and regard the industrial skyline of Hvide Sande as part of the area. It should be emphasised that the cultivation of untouched horizons is done more by part-time landowners and the tourism industry than by tourists and full-time locals themselves.

Wind as a signifier is a contested attraction. As a resource, it sparks conflict. Everybody seems to agree that capturing energy with wind turbines is a good, green idea, but placing 41 turbines quite close to the shore (the closest are four kilometres from land) has generated anger and protests from landowner associations, the tourism industry and nature protection associations. The offshore wind turbine park called Horns Rev 3 has currently been delayed, as new environmental investigations are required to document any damage to the natural environment and also because of the local protests mentioned above. But the offshore wind turbine farm—Scandinavia's largest—opened in August 2019, but at a significant distance from the shore (24–40 kilometres). Wind, especially too much of it, alters flora and erodes landscapes, with sometimes devastating consequences, as when storms and category 4 hurricanes in 1981, 1983 and 1999 flooded dykes and eradicated entire colonies of birds at Tipperne in Ringkøbing Fjord, one of Europe's most important wading bird sanctuaries of 2900 hectares of land. But wind also has strong experiential qualities. As a mobile force, its effects are obvious for yachts and all kinds of surf-related activities. Wind also produces the fascinating spectacle of storms, which both locals and tourists enjoy watching because "nature appears untamed" (this was a recurrent statement in the data). As a natural resource, it is a carrier of salt, which enters bodies, making them healthier and "able to breathe better" (German tourists, two couples in their 50s). The role that humans play in the present extreme weather incidents is rarely mentioned in my data, but a longing for the kind of wild nature that is a scarce resource in Europe (European Environment Agency 2020) is mentioned often.

Wind is an everyday companion at the coast, and locals exploit it as an important economic resource and as a very important green resource that could secure renewable forms of energy in the future. Tourists regard the wind primarily as an agent of health with purifying powers, and everyone recognises its capacity for moving leisure technologies forward and caus-ing catastrophes and spectacular visions of untamed nature.

But wind is also a kind of infra-ordinary although omnipresent feature of the landscape that locals currently overlook or find annoying. A recur-rent observation made by my interviewees from the area was that wind in the area is noticeable only when it is not present. The absence of any wind at all contrasts with the normal meteorological conditions. As one former resident of the area noted, "You normally get it [the wind] in your face. It's always windy out here, dammit" (woman, 20–25 years old).

The Infra-Ordinary and Omnipresent Wind

Taking my point of departure in the everydayness of wind, I wanted to dig deeper into the concept of ordinariness and have been inspired by the concept of the infra-ordinary, from the avant-garde aesthetic of the 1960s (Gruhn 2019).

The concept of the infra-ordinary comes from the French author Georges Perec, who used artistic endeavours to approach raw reality with-out resorting to its common understandings and framings. In the after-math of the death of the author/artist proclaimed by leading poststructuralist thinkers such as Michel Foucault, Jacques Derrida and Roland Barthes, art in the 1960s attacked essentialist conceptions of art-work and emphasised that all subject matter could be the basis of art, which transgressed distinctions between fine art and low art as well as incorporating many elements of everyday culture, including commodities, of which Warhol's endlessly repeated objects (the portraits of Marilyn Monroe, and Campbell's soup cans) are iconic examples. Objects that had been found somewhere (metro tickets, toilet bowls, half-eaten apples) were featured in museum exhibitions as an attack on the imagined inherent qualities of art objects. The Fluxus movement—probably the most radical of the avant-garde forms—focused on processes, interactions, events and performances with various degrees of audience involvement. Fluxus took an interest in everyday actions, gestures and tones, which were often expressed through interrelated media or through various art forms: music, installations, poetry and visual arts.

A focus on wind in itself as an everyday object, and the question of how to enchant it through processes and interactions, was key to my wind experiment. Georges Perec was interested in the immediate perception of the world and in ways of rendering this perception artistically. This endeavour is seen in many texts that investigate the world of things, and a range of spaces (e.g., rooms, streets, Parisian locations, the world and the universe) became the centre of interest (Perec 1965, 1974). The literary process did not involve narration about places and interrelationships between things and characters. Instead, the intention was to describe things and spaces meticulously, in order to get closer to the ordinary and the infra-ordinary as it forms the backbone of existence: "What happens every day and that which returns every day, the banal, the everyday life, the obvious, the commons, the ordinary, the infra-ordinary, background noise, the routines, how to document all this, how to question it, how to describe it" (Perec 1989, p. 11). The infra-ordinary contrasts with the scandalous and the spectacular (Ørum 2003, p. 141), and Perec looks for the "endotique", defined as "that which is confronted directly in its sensuous quality without detours". To look for the infra-ordinary and render it through endotique descriptions is to examine how small, everyday routines and the descriptions of those routines interact: "Describe your street and yet another street and compare them. Pile up the content of your pockets and ask yourself about the provenance, use and future of the objects you find there. Ask about small spoons, and look at how people compose text messages, where and when" (Perec 1989, pp. 12–13). Through endotique descriptions, allowing the insignificant and the unimportant to 'speak', Perec hoped to let the disorder and the messiness (but also the accidental beauty) of the everyday appear. In concrete terms, Perec's search for the endotique encompasses both formal fieldwork strategies and self-inflicted playful tactics in documenting the activity with the least possible interference from the writer.

Endotique descriptions of the infra-ordinary aim to go beyond the usual discursive and narrative patterns, hierarchies and frameworks of understanding, to experience—momentarily—the radical and immediate presence of the object world. When Claude Burgelin writes that Perec "is fascinated by the strange alchemy that produces something new from the identical" (Burgelin 1988, p. 211, my translation), this is a result of closely registering infra-ordinary phenomena according to pre-established formal rules and rendering this registration in ways that wake the sensibility of the ordinary things around us and the overlooked features of our everyday lives. To see them anew so to speak. This strategy aims to bring an unexpected, troubling and enchanting density into our banal, everyday lives.

As a category, the infra-ordinary—omnipresent and unnoticed at one and the same time—is interesting with respect to the field of tourism, which normally cultivates escapism and extraordinariness, although this has been challenged by studies that show that all travel also encompasses everyday life and routines (Larsen 2008; Haldrup and Larsen 2010). Another characteristic of wind at the West Coast is that it is a natural phenomenon that is encumbered with a lot of data: wind speed, direction of the wind that prognostically foresees how it will behave in the near future and with particular affordances to support or destroy nature and infrastructures such as the production of energy, the fishing industry, the locks and more (Peters 2015, p. 30). The installation aimed at getting closer to a phenomenological exploration of the wind was not supposed to supply the viewer with data but rather let the viewer encounter wind as a natural phenomenon in itself.

In my case, the wind experiment, the heavy and bulky technology of the VR glasses served as an enhancing mediator between landscape and bodies and increased the experience of closeness to the now-visible wind, which provided the landscape with new layers and dimensions. The interaction design was the tool we used not only to mediate the invisible aspects of the omnipresent and unnoticed element but also to reveal the wonders of the everyday. New materialist theories, in particular Jane Bennett's academic scholarship on the enchantment, wonder and vibrancy of (ordinary) things, were a source of inspiration (Bennett 2001, 2010). Bennett cites a counter-perspective to the well-known disenchantment thesis of modern life we have inherited from Durkheimian sociology. She seeks to induce an experience of the contemporary world, "a world of inequity, racism, pollution, poverty, violence of all kinds—as also enchanted—not a tale of re-enchantment but one that calls attention to magical sites already here" (Bennett 2001, p. 8). Bennett, like Perec, is interested in the everyday and the familiar, and she stresses that enchantment exists amid the familiar, as encounters with everyday marvels that strike us with great intensity. Like Perec, she emphasises formal tactics to "learn to be affected" by the everyday (Latour 2004), as attention to these encounters is something that can be cultivated through play, and by attuning one's sensory receptiveness to the marvellous specificity of things (Bennett 2001, p. 4). The term 'enchantment' is defined as a 'moment of pure presence' and wonder that although one's affect alternates between shocked surprise and a certain amount of fear, because one's default sensory-psychic-intellectual dispositions are disrupted, ends with joy taking over and with a sense of fulfilment, plenitude, liveliness, being 'tuned-up' and recharged (p. 5).

Closely related to the enchantment thesis is the concept of non-human charisma developed by geographer Jamie Lorimer, which draws attention to affect in understanding environmental ethics (Lorimer 2007). Non-human charisma is a gift of grace capturing the specific, enchanting character of a charismatic being (Lorimer 2007, p. 915). Based on ethnographic case studies of different species conservation programmes for insects in the UK, and in particular the interspecies encounters between amateur as well as professional conservation experts and species in nature, Lorimer proposes three forms of charisma according to the affordances of humans (these are often technologically enhanced) as well as the affordances of non-human actors. Differences in visibility, colour, size, speed and degree of movement are perceived in the encounters between non-humans and humans: ecological charisma qualifies the space rhythms (p. 917) of humans and non-humans with the ideal of 'becoming wind' for the humans in the encounter in my case. Aesthetic charisma attribute to the visual impact and the affections triggered in the specific encounters with the humans, and corporeal charisma assign to the visceral becomings involved in tuning in to another species over a longer period of time.

Basically, wind is air, which is one of the four elements from which all forms emerge: fire, earth, water and air. The dynamic relationships of these elements with human bodies and their affective moods were conceptualised in medieval times as fluids connected to internal organs: for fire, yellow bile (anger) is tied to the liver; for earth, black bile (melancholia) is tied to the spleen; for water, slime/mucus (phlegm) is tied to the brain; and for air, blood (the sanguine) is tied to the heart (Stefánsson 2009).

Attuning bodily to the wind (Massumi 2009) means aligning with one of the basic environmental elements using VR as an immersive environment. Facilitating an experience of openness to the world—in this experiment, the world of wind—beyond or besides its instrumental and economic uses—*might* make visitors receptive to environmental concerns in subtle ways. In Jane Bennett's words, "To begin to *experience* the relationship between persons and materiality more horizontally [meaning without a prior hierarchy between human and non-human actors] is to take a step towards a more ecological sensibility" (2010, p. 10).

The overarching purpose of the art installation was to immerse participants even deeper into the landscape and to connect to invisible and unnoticeable layers of the natural environment on the one hand, while using VR neither as an information-saturated device nor as a medium to narrate or dramatise a situation on the other. The installation gave participants space and time to investigate phenomenologically and to attune rhythmically to the visible airflows of wind swirling and eddying around the shapes of the dunes. The technological set-up in the experiment thus allowed the participants to experience the speed and movements of the wind. One of the interesting outcomes of the experiment was that the human experience was partly one of becoming weightless (feeling lighter, zero gravity) and partly one of a sharpened awareness of the socio-technical assemblage and its constituent parts, which many people were either attracted to or repelled by. I will come back to these points in my concluding remarks.

ASSEMBLING THE EXPERIENCE OF THE OMNIPRESENT BUT INFRA-ORDINARY WIND

The 53-metre tall Lyngvig Fyr lighthouse is locally considered the entrance to the experience of the Danish West Coast: the lighthouse area is a site that locals and tourists visit on summer evenings to gaze at the sunset. According to John Durham Peters, it is necessary to see media as "ensembles of nature and culture" (Peters 2015, p. 49) that add ontological status to the semiotic approach to media as meaning producing devices: "A medium must not mean but be" (p. 14). In parallel to the wilderness bathtubs that were considered as part of the site-specific nature by users, our experiment was also considered part of nature. The two artists produced outdoor data visualisations of wind. A whole range of technologies, authorities, institutions, local entrepreneurs and materiality were involved.

We had to get permission to install the temporary test-bed in the protected dunes from the coastal directorate (a huge challenge) and the landowners along that part of the coast (Ringkøbing-Skjern Museum). As it is close to the industrial harbour and the many coastal protection activities, the local people are already used to and already enjoy the performative qualities and vibrancy of heavy technology, to which we added drones, a computer screen, cables, a VR headset, a noisy generator that we displayed in the dunes, a tent, a couple of chairs and a table. The non-human actors that played roles in the project were climatic factors such as rain (which is why we had a tent) and wind. The wind was quite strong during the test period, which suited our experiment perfectly but also constituted a challenge because it threatened to blow our equipment over. We had to dig four poles into the sand to reinforce the tent and the four devices that ensured communication between the computer and the VR headset. We had to ask for help from a strong local handyman, who helped to plant the poles more deeply into the sand. Sand was the third problem, getting in everywhere, destructive to computers; and the sun eventually destroyed the very expensive pair of VR goggles because they did not tolerate direct sunlight. In other words, nature itself, the very setting of our immersive experience, also played the intriguing role of antagonist during the project's test period.

Even though our tent was a discreet sandy colour, the presence of heavy equipment in this protected area was perceived as alien and immediately prompted either curiosity or repulsion. Some people demonstrated quite a hostile attitude in not wanting to interact with the unusual set-up in the dunes. Some people clearly shunned the installation and reacted directly to its unfamiliarity, while others—young people and the locals who had heard about our presence via local media—were more attracted by it. The intention was to superimpose a digital model of the wind conditions in the landscape and to let people immerse themselves in that simulation while they were in the real environment, open to sounds and smells from the physical landscape, resulting in a mixed virtual-real-world experience. The installation was designed to investigate this technology's capacity at this specific site, for each individual testing it, and also to let users explore and discover the capacities of this digital technology at their own pace and in their own way (DeLanda 2006, p. 19).

The wind installation invited solitary meditation. While wearing the headset, the test persons were expected to use the beamers to enter the

Fig. 12.2 A glimpse of how the wind formations were represented through the VR glasses in a rather moon-scape-like landscape having the recognisable shape of the dunes at Lyngvig Fyr. (Photo still of a video, courtesy of the artists)

wind fluctuations and to transport themselves to a more interesting place (virtually, of course), into stronger wind patterns (Fig. 12.2).

Each person took about ten minutes for their exploration. Some would have taken longer (but we had unfortunately a timeline to respect), but some could not get rid of the annoying headset quickly enough and even said they felt dizzy, uncomfortable and under surveillance during the experience (a couple of German women in their 40s). It was possible for relatives, friends, colleagues and the researchers/artists to follow the person experiencing the wind on the computer screen, which displayed what the test person could see through the VR glasses. There was ongoing dialogue. For example, we could intervene if a test person wanted help with the beamers, and we were able to give advice about catching a swirling wind formation.

The representational layer of the experience was a black and white, naked, desert-like landscape with similar shapes to the physical landscape at Lyngvig Fyr. Most of the test persons recognised it, although the lighthouse itself was not represented, and although the sea was black instead of blue, which provoked many comments. The wind was represented as short lines of light, swirling around. The two beamers were in the frame of the glasses. The one on the lower right-hand side of the picture frame is detectable, which allows one to enter the wind flow. Using the beamer on the right allowed the test person to beam themselves virtually to an interesting wind spot outside the few square metres of the tent.

We decided to use virtual reality (glasses that are connected to a computer, limiting the physical experience to a few square metres) instead of the mobile technology of augmented reality (transportable glasses) because augmented reality glasses to track outdoor environments in rural areas were simply not available at the time of our experiment. That being said, virtual reality offers a universe in which you can immerse yourself to the point of body oblivion and the feeling of zero gravity. This is why so many people described the landscape as a moon landscape. Virtual reality (VR) can be defined "as the use of a computer-generated 3D environment—called a virtual environment (VE)—that one can navigate and possibly interact with" (Guttentag 2010, p. 638). A VR experience can be defined by its capacity to provide physical immersion and a psychological presence. On the reality-virtuality continuum, our wind experiment could be characterised as semi-immersive as sound, smell and tactile sensations from the real world entered the virtual reality experienced through the headset. On the other hand, some of our users hardly spoke at all and seemed fully immersed in the virtual world, in particular those who were most familiar with experiences of virtual reality.

To collect wind data with a view to developing software, our project built a detailed 3D model of a section of the coastline, using drone photogrammetry and ground-based photogrammetry. Computational fluid dynamics were applied to simulate the movement of air at 11 on the Beaufort scale, indicating a wind speed of about 30 m/s (violent storm conditions). Originally, the simulation of air movement was planned to correspond to the real-world wind conditions, but in order to reduce expenses and man-hours, we used one violent storm simulation, regardless of the actual wind conditions, even though this ran counter to our wish for authenticity in terms of correspondence between the actual and virtual wind conditions. However, we found that on quiet days (of which there were few in our test period), this discrepancy did not matter much. Our choice indicated an inherent dramatisation of the simulated wind conditions, but it did not feel inappropriate, probably, in part, because this location triggers many strong wind memories in users' bodies.

The experiment enables us to claim that there was a four-fold enhancement of the dunes below Lyngvig Fyr. Mapping the site using drone photogrammetry was the first step in creating a wind simulation of the site.

Second, experiencing the landscape virtually and really through the head-set was another enhanced way of being in the landscape. Looking at the screen of the control panel (the huge computer) was a third level of experience. Even though the experiment addressed users' solitary investigation of wind formations, the fact that audiences were able to watch made the experience open to a more collaborative interaction mode (Wakkary et al. 2012, p. 222). Some people gave valuable advice, and some gave advice to a 'lost' spouse. Fourth, all the scenery was definitely a point of interest, and its unexpected oddness was an attraction in its own right (Fig. 12.1).

Interaction between users and virtual information is an essential aspect of various forms of immersive reality. Mafkereseb Kassahun Bekele and colleagues distinguish between six types of interface for augmented, virtual and mixed-reality systems: tangible, collaborative, device-based, sensor-based, hybrid and multimodal interfaces respectively (Bekele et al. 2018, pp. 7–10). I do not intend to go into detail about these interactive affordances and will only note that our VR experiment used a device-based form of interaction that employed two joysticks: one for beaming yourself out of the confined space of the physical tent and another for entering the wind formations by moving the joystick around to catch the wind. It soon became evident that these two kinds of handheld interactive affordances favoured those participants who were experienced gamepad and joystick users (the younger participants and those with professional expertise).

Quite a few of the users (myself included) needed some time to adjust to the fact that physical movement in the real world (manipulating the joystick in all directions) was necessary to make things happen in the virtual world. On the other hand, the sensation of estrangement that one experiences when the dual perspective of inside/outside is directly perceptible was one of the side-effects of this experiment for users unfamiliar with VR experiences. One exclaimed, "It's odd that I can't see my feet" (German tourist in her 40s), when describing the phenomenological distance experienced with a mixed-reality design. In spite of the demographic differences (age, gender, profession) that certainly affected our experiment in terms of its technological aspects, we can say—unsurprisingly—that more younger individuals than older ones seemed familiar with the affordances of the technology, and more younger participants than older ones were fascinated with the *how* rather than the *what* of the experiment. We invited an entire class of students (11 years old) who were studying science, and they were all fascinated by the technological side of the experiment. Others—also the elderly (aged 60+) members of our test audience—just regarded VR as a medium for experiencing the infraordinary wind. Some members of this group (e.g., an experienced local sailor, a woman in her 80s) stayed with the experience for at least 20 minutes, completely fascinated, without showing any particular interest in the relationship between the wind and the software (Fig. 12.3).

The preliminary conclusion I draw from the preceding paragraph is that we must add the technological side of the VR experience to the attraction of our experiment, engaging younger audiences and persons with a professional interest in the software aspect of this experiment, in parallel with their experience of the elementary wind. If we consider the effects of the installation in naturalising media and mediatising nature in an effort not to distinguish between man-made craft and nature, the project was a success. One important finding was that the immersive quality of the VR—the annulment of the visible aspects of the test persons'

Fig. 12.3 A natural sciences school class of 11-year-old students participated in the wind experiment and they followed closely from behind the scenes what the participant on stage was experiencing. In the background towers the lighthouse Lyngvig Fyr. (Image by author August 2018)

bodies—produced different affective reactions in the users. Some felt that they had been left at the mercy of the surveillance gaze of the other (us? the tech-giants?) and expressed a sense of unease and dizziness. Secondly, quite a few of the participants were silent, focused and immersed in the wind world, reluctant to 'translate' their experience into common language. Pursuing the enchantment experience further into non-human charisma, the ecological charisma perceived as experiences of similarities and differences in space-time rhythms with wind as a non-human actor seems to be crucial. The speed and the rapidly changing movements of the wind in all directions constituted the visual basis of the VR set-up. The rhythmic attunement we detected in participants was divided into two phases: at first a remarkable slowness prevailed, which could be read as a bodily attunement to the difference in rhythm between the human and the non-human actor in the set-up: "Enchantment includes, then, a condition of exhilaration or acute sensory activity. To be simultaneously transfixed in wonder and transported by sense, to be both caught up and carried away, enchantment is marked by this odd combination of somatic effects" (Bennett 2001, p. 5). The affective reaction to the mediated wind translated into an awe-struck "frozen" condition of the body. This frozen-ness did not seem to be caused by the fact that the technological set-up only allowed the test persons to move within a limited space. It is more likely that the arrested movement was an affective reaction to the mediated wind: concentration, wonder and joy. The rhythmic dissonance between the swirling wind and the arrested body translates into joy, fascination and quiet contemplation as far as we could see. Thirdly, wonder, awe and the praise of the "miracle" were detected in the test persons' many "wows" and also in their silence, and when urged to express themselves they used the term 'magic'. When a German tourist (a man in his 40s) solemnly exclaimed, "Oh, I feel as though I'm standing in the middle of creation itself", it had at least the triple meaning of an experience of (1) the wind becoming visible as a result of the whole data visualisation design, (2) a digital network that makes this happen, and (3) the fact that this experiment connects the test persons to wind as a primary natural force that predates human intervention.

Concluding Remarks

Our experiment was definitely a success in terms of perceiving the wind in ways that were not based on economic and instrumental aspects. Contrary to urban prejudices, it was possible to carry out a workable avant-garde artistic experiment in a rural area. The key here is to think site-specifically. The site-specific features that our experiment resonated with are the heavy technological infrastructures in the harbour areas at Hvide Sande, in the form of industrial fishing boats, containers and so forth, and the coastal protection 'gear'. Onshore and offshore wind turbines are also part of the industrial infrastructure of Ringkøbing-Skjern Municipality. The tech-heavy, unpolished dimensions of the experiment belong to the area and seem crucial for its success.

One of the other highly important outcomes of the experiment was that when offering sufficiently interesting local attractions, it is possible to overcome the traditional divides between locals and tourists, whether those are part-time locals or domestic or foreign guests. Our experiment did not divide people according to national stereotypes or chauvinist logics. Age, gender, profession, lay expert skills and interests weighed more heavily than the traditional distinction between tourists and locals. This made it possible to intervene in subtle ways in the local region and attract publics encompassing both locals and non-locals at the same time.

The wind, sky, sea, sand, sun, dunes, lighthouse, VR glasses, computer screen, tent, cables, generator, humans, all these factors and even more were part of the crafted and natural environment of the experiment. All these agents of creativity combining the various natural, technological and artistic forces in the set-up were at play in the intervention: "I feel as though I'm standing in the middle of creation" has many meanings and points to cultural, technological and natural forces. The experiment seemed to encourage a will to immerse yourself in the technological set-up as a mediated wind-experience in the midst of the physical wind. What we wanted to do was to take Bennett's view on enchanting encounters—joyful encounters—instead of moral obligations to be able to cultivate ethical behaviour in general. Tuning bodies into the care of the landscape was the underlying aim of the project, but this goal was overshadowed by an openness towards creativity in general cultivated through the wind experiment.

Acknowledgements I am deeply thankful for the collaboration with the artists Lise Autogena and Joshua Portway on the wind installation without whom the experiment would not have been possible. Thank you as well to the locals, part-time locals and tourists to the area who were eager to take part in the fun.

264   B. TIMM KNUDSEN

REFERENCES

Bekele, M. K., Pierdicca, R., Frontoni, E., Malinverni, E.S., & Gain, J. (2018). A survey of augmented, virtual and mixed reality for cultural heritage. *ACM. Journal on Computing and Cultural Heritage*, 11(2), 1–36. https://doi.org/10.1145/3145534

Bennett, J. (2001). *The enchantment of modern life: Attachments, crossings and ethics*. Princeton University Press.

Bennett, J. (2010). *Vibrant matter: A political ecology of things*. Duke University Press.

Burgelin, C. (1988). *Georges Perec: Les contemporains*. Seuil.

Coleman, S. & Crang, M. (2003). *Tourism: Between place and performance*. Berghahn Books.

DeLanda, M. (2006). *A new philosophy of society: Assemblage theory and social complexity*. Bloomsbury.

European Environment Agency (EEA). (2020). *State of nature in the EU: Results from reporting under the nature directives 2013–2018*. No 10. Retrieved December 21, 2021, from https://www.eea.europa.eu/publications/state-of-nature-in-the-eu-2020

Glanville, R. (2014). Researching design and designing research. *Design Issues* 15, pp. 80–91.

Gravari-Barbas, M., & Guinand, S. (Eds.). (2017). *Tourism and Gentrification in Contemporary Metropolises. International Perspectives*. London, New York: Routledge.

Gruhn, E. (2019). Music from plastic butterflies, a disassembled grand piano and flying eggs. In 1962, the fateful Fluxus movement emerged in Wiesbaden and It continues to attract worldwide attention to this day. *SchirnMag*. Retrieved March 24, 2020, from https://www.schirn.de/en/magazine/context/2019/big_orchestra/fluxus_in_wiesbaden_big_orchestra/

Guttentag, D. A. (2010). Virtual reality: Applications and implications for tourism. *Tourism Management*, 31, pp. 637–651.

Haldrup, M., & Larsen, J. (2010). *Tourism, performance and the everyday: Consuming the Orient*. Routledge.

Hauberg, J. (2011). Research by design: A research strategy. *Architecture, Design and Conservation*, 5, pp. 46–56.

Knudsen, B. T., Stage, C., & Zandersen, M. (2019). Interspecies park life: Participatory experiments and micro-utopian landscaping to increase urban biodiverse entanglement. *Space and Culture*. https://doi.org/10.1177/1206331219863312

Kristensen, N., Kolodziejczyk, C., & Wittrup, J. (2017). *Nedrivninger af huse of fremtidige nedrivningsbehov i Danmark*. VIVE, The Danish Center for Social Science Research.

Larsen, J. (2008). De-exoticizing tourist travel: Everyday life and sociality on the move. *Leisure Studies* 27(1), pp. 21–34.

Latour, B. (2004). How to talk about the body? The normative dimension of science studies. *Body & Society* 10(2–3), pp. 205–229.

Lew, A. A., & Cartier, C. (Eds.). (2004). *Seductions of place: Geographical perspectives on globalization and touristed landscapes.* Routledge. https://doi.org/10.4324/9780203645796

Lorimer, J. (2007). Nonhuman charisma. *Environment and Planning D: Society and Space,* 25, pp. 911–932.

Martin, B. G. (2005). Weather, climate and tourism: A geographical perspective. *Annals of Tourism Research,* 32(3), pp. 571–591.

Massumi, B. (2009). Of Microperception and Micropolitics. An Interview with Brian Massumi. *Inflexions: A Journal for Research – Creation,* 3. Retrieved March 3, 2020, from http://www.inflexions.org

The Municipality of Ringkøbing-Skjern, Plan and Development Strategy. (2015). *Realms of nature, #pladspladsplads,* Retrieved March 3, 2020, from https://www.youtube.com/watch?v=-ubgyuhnP74

Ørum, T. (2003). Det infra-ordinære. In M. Sandbye & K. Petersen (Eds.), *Virkelighed! Virkelighed!. Avantgardens realisme* (pp. 133–169). Tiderne Skifter.

Perec, G. (1965). *Les Choses: Une histoire des années soixante.* René Jullard.

Perec, G. (1974). *Especes d'Espaces.* Galilée.

Perec, G. (1989). *L'infra-ordinaire.* Seuil.

Peters, J. D. (2015). *The marvelous clouds: Toward a philosophy of elemental media.* University of Chicago Press.

Roggema, R. (2017). Research by design: Proposition for a methodological approach. *Urban Science,* 1(1), p. 2. https://doi.org/10.3390/urbansci1010002

Sandvik, K. (2010). Crime scenes as augmented reality: Models for enhancing places emotionally by means of narratives, fictions and virtual reality. In B. T Knudsen & A. M. Waade, (Eds.), *Re-investing authenticity: Tourism, place and emotions* (pp. 138–153). Channel View Publications.

Stappers, P. J., Visser, F. S, Keller, I. (2014). The role of prototypes and frameworks for structuring explorations by research through design. In Rodgers, P., & Yee, J. (Eds.) *The Routledge Companion to Design Research* (pp. 163–174). Routledge.

Stefánsson, F. (2009). *The four elements.* In *Symbolleksikon.* Retrieved October 19, 2021, from https://symbolleksikon.lex.dk

Urry, J. (1999). *The tourist gaze.* Routledge.

Wakkary, R., Desjardins, A., Muise, K., Tanenbaum, K., & Hatala, M. (2012). Situating the sociability of interactive museum guides. In E. Giacardi (Ed.), *Heritage and social media: Understanding heritage in a participatory culture* (pp. 217–238). Routledge.

Zimmerman, J., & Forlizzi, J. (2014). Research through design in HCI. In J. S. Olson & W. A. Kellogg (Eds.), *Ways of knowing in HCI* (pp. 167–189). Springer, e-book.

CHAPTER 13

The Tombstones that Cried the Night Away: An Allegory

Phillip Vannini and April Vannini

In a far and cold land at the southern edges of the world there was a very large cemetery full of tombstones that couldn't sleep at night. Some nights the tombstones would stay up to talk until the sun rose, sharing stories about the day that just passed. Other nights they would tell each other tales and memories of times long gone. On some nights the chatter would fade out and turn into whimpering sounds, laments, and crying.

On some cold nights, the tears the tombstones cried would freeze. Strong winds would carry the frozen tears away, and sometimes they would drift onto creeks and rivers and lakes and drift far away. As they drifted, some of those frozen tears would eventually meet others that had washed away before, sometimes clustering together and forming large icy banks at the end of valleys and fjords around the cemetery.

P. Vannini (✉) • A. Vannini
Royal Roads University, Victoria, BC, Canada
e-mail: Phillip.Vannini@RoyalRoads.ca

267

The tombstones had been there for longer than anyone could remember. Some people say the tombstones were there even before any people were alive at all. Others believe the tombstones were a memorial the mountains had themselves built to remember the lives of animals that had died. Though many different people had different ideas as to how the tombstones came to be, no one knew for sure who had put the tombstones there, who really rested there, how the poor souls who rested there had died, or even whether they were actually dead.

Regardless of who or what had died there, the tombstones seemed to have a livelihood of their own. Tombstones the world over tell stories about lives, but these tombstones told especially vivid and unusual stories about life. Those who cared to take the time to listen to them marvelled at how the tombstones could tell so many stories, feel so many things, and cry so many tears.

Some of the people who knew them well could even swear the tombstones could move and change shape. One day they would be in one place, another day—maybe a year or two later—they would be in another place a few metres away from where they once were. One day they might appear frail, dirty, and weary, and some time later they would look tall, mighty, and imposing. Then there were tombstones that somehow disappeared. One night they would be where they had always been. The next morning they would be gone, with no one the wiser as to where they had gone and whether they would ever come back.

Among all the tombstones there was one that many people say had been there the longest. Its name was Perito Moreno, but everyone knew it by just Perito. In actuality, Perito may or may not have been there longer than a few others, but it carried the air of someone who knew a thing or two about the cemetery and its history. Everyone who came to the cemetery knew where Perito was, and hardly anyone walked in and out of the cemetery without seeing Perito. Perito knew this and enjoyed it. It knew that its shape, its size, and the way that its materials had been sculpted to give it form were a thing of beauty. And so it always enjoyed it when visitors went out of their way to look at it and marvel. But for all of its narcissistic and sociable tendencies, Perito had a dark and sad side too, a side it did not like to talk about much.

No one understood Perito's dark side better than a lonesome tombstone laying in a far corner of the cemetery, a corner where hardly anyone ventured. That tombstone was known as Upsala. Upsala was at the very western edge of the cemetery. It was a very large and old stone that enjoyed being left alone all day long and all night long. Upsala had become ill over the years and it hated being unable to sleep at night when the other tombstones would talk loud and whine until morning time. Upsala, however, knew Perito well and while it didn't always understand why Perito enjoyed the visitors' attention so much, it held Perito in high regard. Perito was only one of a few tombstones that Upsala trusted and quietly revealed its own sorrows to.

The other tombstone that Upsala was very close to was a tall and colourful gravestone by the name of Spegazzini. Like Perito, Spegazzini was in a central area of the cemetery, and many of the visitors who entered the grounds would see it on their way in or on their way out. But like Upsala, Spegazzini deeply enjoyed peace and quiet. In fact, Spegazzini envied Upsala very much and wished it could move next to Upsala, where few visitors could venture. The busyness, the traffic, the litter that sometimes visitors would leave behind made Spegazzini very upset, and on some days it was barely able to cope with it all. On the darkest and saddest nights Spegazzini's tormented lament could be heard at the far edges of the cemetery, and over the years only Upsala had seemed to find a way to console Spegazzini.

"Everything will be alright one day," Upsala would tell Spegazzini, "these visitors will leave us alone one day. They will become ill from my very same sickness and maybe even die away, but we will outlast them, we will still be here, long after they're gone, perhaps weaker but alone, peaceful, and free."

This kind of talk would upset Perito. "Nonsense!" Perito would protest. "The visitors will always be with us, and we will learn to enjoy their presence, indeed we must, or else we will be the ones who will perish!" Perito's attitude upset some of the others, but they still respected it for Perito was their Elder after all. And so these quarrels would go on and on, night after night, in between stories, memories, banter, and daydreaming.

One night, neither a particularly dark nor a cold one, when the moon was high and the stars faint in the presence of her bright light, a new voice was suddenly heard. It was a mighty voice, seemingly coming from as far away as the night itself.

"Who is this speaking?" wondered Viedma, an old cenotaph who thought she knew everyone. "Could it be Mayo?" asked Spegazzini incredulously. "We haven't heard from Mayo in a long time!" "No, it's someone else," said Upsala, "someone we don't know." The night stood still for an hour or two, the winds themselves muted by their very own curiosity. Then the voice spoke again.

"My name is Brüggen," the far tombstone said, sounding raspy and cold. "I have been listening to you whine on and on for the last few years, and I have had enough of you!"

"The nerve of this foreigner!" uttered Spegazzini in indignation.

"Who are you, and where are you?" Upsala wondered, feeling somewhat smitten with the foreigner's strong presence.

"My name is Brüggen but some people call me Pio XI. I am one of the mightiest tombstones in the entire world," the far stony monument spoke with a mighty roar, "in fact I am so big that I can speak to you even from far, far away, and unlike you I am still growing."

"Well, what do you want, Brüggen?" Spegazzini protested.

"I want you to quit whining!" Brüggen roared. "Stand up for your rights, don't just sit there and cry a river, do something!"

A chorus of confused chatter ensued. Who was this tombstone? What did it really want? Why was this any of its business? And so on. Perito had not yet spoken a word, but it was listening closely to the buzz. In fact, Perito had not spoken a word that entire evening and night. It felt tired from a long day but deep down it was also starting to feel as though ordinary fatigue wasn't the real reason why it felt that way. Just that very morning a group of visitors, one like many before, had arrived on the grounds of the cemetery. They came from a land far away called America. There were four of them: an older couple and their adult child, accompanied by her husband. They spoke loudly and felt no shame in speaking publicly about their private affairs. They were so loud that Perito couldn't help but hear their every word. They yammered and chattered about their daily lives back home and went on and on about the wines they had enjoyed the night before their visit to the cemetery. The red and the white wines, the dry and the sweet, the bold and the fruity. And how they paired with meats, and with cheeses, and with fish. And how they reminded them of this and that wine, of this and that place they had visited before, and on and on. What conversation to be had in a cemetery! Perito thought, how disrespectful. And so what Brüggen said touched a raw nerve for Perito.

"What rights?" Perito suddenly rebutted Brüggen. "We have no rights."

"You do!" Brüggen responded. "We all do, but our visitors won't respect us until we rumble, until we scream, until we all create some kind of movement together, until we show them that we are alive!"

Spoken to mostly anyone else those words would have caused a big roar of laughter. "Tombstones?" "Alive?" "That's ridiculous!" "Tombstones symbolize death." Just about anyone else would have chuckled in disbelief. But not them. Not the tombstones of that faraway land. They knew they were alive. They knew tombstones exist in order to tell stories. They had always known the grounds where they rested hosted life in its myriad forms, not death. After all, their tears, cried night after night, had always been nothing but signs of their will to be alive.

"Everyone who comes to visit us will be scared if we tell them we're alive," cried Perito, "and no one will ever come back."

"That's the idea," replied Brüggen. Just about anyone else would have chuckled in disbelief. "Show them you are alive. Speak loudly and they will hear you. And eventually they will learn to respect you."

Brüggen told everyone how much it hated when visitors showed up and spoke loudly in its proximity or when they ate greasy food in its proximity. But most of all Brüggen hated it when visitors forgot it was alive. A tombstone is never dead, Brüggen would always tell those who cared to listen, for it embodies the lives of the spirits who dwelled therein. Some of the people who knew Brüggen well had learned to treat it as a person, as someone who was alive. And so Brüggen had people to share stories with, people with whom it had developed a deep kinship since time immemorial, people who had learned to listen and show respect.

As the night went on, Brüggen spoke at length to Upsala, Spegazzini, Perito, and all the others. It told them stories about itself, the Lands around them, and the relationships it had with some of its recurring visitors. The tombstones listened to its stories in silence, enchanted by its knowledge, and impressed by its resolve. When night turned to dawn, Brüggen bade farewell and pleaded with its new friends to quit crying their nights away. "Stand up for yourselves!" Brüggen admonished them.

The morning sun rose and with it the winds. The winds pushed a few clouds towards the ocean, and soon the skies turned sapphire. But a storm was brewing inside the tombstones' souls. Spegazzini barely had a chance to snooze a few minutes when the first group of visitors arrived. They came from lands far away, just like visitors before. And like so many others before them they only seemed interested in taking photographs of themselves with Spegazzini in the background.

How lucky Upsala was, Spegazzini thought. No one ever woke Upsala up in the morning with loud boats like it always happened to Spegazzini. How strong Brüggen was, Spegazzini thought, how brave it was to remind everyone that it was alive, that it was owed respect. Brüggen's words on greasy foods in particular had struck a chord with Spegazzini. All of the boats that brought visitors ashore reeked of grilled meats and cheap wine, and there were no odours that Spegazzini hated more. The noise, the odours, the visitors' narcissism, their ignorance, the lack of respect; it was all suddenly too much to bear. Any other day Spegazzini would have just tried to sleep. It would have just tried to put up with it all. Spegazzini would have just taken it all in and waited patiently to vent its frustrations with friends at night-time. But not that day. Not after Brüggen's words.

"Perito!" Spegazzini rumbled. Silence. "PERITO!" Spegazzini shrieked once again, this time louder, scaring some of the visitors and their boats away.

"Spegazzini?" Perito wondered. "What is it? Why are you calling me in the middle of the morning, can't you see I'm busy?"

"Busy with what?!" Spegazzini retorted. "Get a hold of yourself! Let's get these ignorant visitors away from here!"

"What?!" Perito whimpered, sounding unsure.

"Spegazzini is right, buddy," Upsala suddenly spoke, "enough is enough."

"Upsala? You too?" Perito wondered. "What is going on this morning?"

"You reek of cheap whiskey Perito, and every day you smell worse and look the worse for wear," said Spegazzini. "It's time to put an end to all of this."

Perito did smell funky. As part of a strange ritual, groups of visitors had gotten into the habit of drinking small amounts of whiskey while they visited the grounds near Perito. They would even take some of the smaller frozen tears cried by Perito and dip them in their plastic cups to make their cheap liquor cooler. Perito deeply hated this, but it had always thought this was just the way visitors enjoyed themselves in its presence and that it should just let it be.

"Speak!" Spegazzini implored Perito. "Say something! And you too Upsala!"

Upsala had deep wounds of its own. Over the last few years, it had gotten sicker and sicker, largely as a result of warm weather. Out in the far edges of the cemetery where she lived, the winds and temperatures had gotten warmer and warmer and that had greatly stressed Upsala's mind and body. Year after year Upsala looked thinner and weaker, and less capable of enjoying life. Though it was never known to be caring and social, her separation from her long-time companion Bertacchi had taken a profound emotional toll.

"Upsala, please, now!" Spegazzini pleaded. "Now or never!" As Spegazzini implored Upsala, a tear streamed down, hitting the ground on which it stood. Moments passed, and then another large tear fell down, dripping to the earth with such force that the few visitors who had lingered thus far immediately ran away in fear.

Upsala was usually unconvinced by emotional pleas, but today everything was different for it too. It almost seemed to stand up taller and straighter, as if to puff its chest, as it let out a large whipping crack of a scream that echoed with sickening force all around. If the birds and the trees could describe it, they would say the sound was so sinister that it seemed to be less that of an angry soul and more that of a spirit that had finally broken in half. Alas, Upsala lived so far away that only a very, very few visitors seemed able to detect it.

But it was then, the very moment that Upsala's scream went unheard by humans, that everything changed. Miles and miles away from its good friend Upsala, but close to its agony, Perito Moreno heard Upsala's pain loud and clear. Perito had tolerated the visitors' chatter. It had coped with the stinky booze. It had put up with boats full of insensitive visitors, day after day. Surely Perito enjoyed their attention, but it was ever more and more sick of their disrespect. But at that moment it all came to an end. Perito would not tolerate seeing Upsala in pain anymore. "Tell them you're alive!" Brüggen's words rang in Perito's ears. "Stand up for your rights!"

And so Perito shook. This was no twitch. It was no flick, or whip, or crack. The shake was a guttural convulsion so deep and so mighty that the entire cemetery trembled. The shake was so frightening that the visitors tossed their cameras and started running away. In fact, the seism was so shockingly strong that a good chunk of Perito's body broke off, causing aftershocks and tsunamis so powerful that the entire world turned. The big ole tombstone wasn't dead after all, and now everyone knew it.

But Perito, Upsala, Spegazzini, and all the tombstones around them weren't done. As the echo of Perito's movement ceased, Upsala turned around and called upon the tombstones that laid far south and far, far north. As it turns out, they had spoken before, many years ago, and made a solemn promise to each other, swearing to keep it forever.

"It is time," Upsala sombrely told its southern and northern friends. "Now, many of our human visitors finally know we're alive."

Upsala paused, her voice breaking, choked with torment.

The time has come for us to no longer be shy, to no longer be quiet. Our voices will be heard and so we must speak louder and louder every day. I have been dying of a slow death. And so have you. All of you. Humans are drowning in our sorrows, in our pain melting away day after day, and yet they are doing nothing about it. It is they who view us as nothing but tombstones. It is they who have long refused to recognize we have always been alive. It is they who have been oblivious to our vitality. And it is they who will die off eventually, stilled by their carelessness, entombed by their unwillingness to move, frozen by their inability to be sensitive to other forms of life.

Upsala paused for a moment, caught a deep breath, and uttered its final call: "Let us be quiet no more. Let our stories be loud and clear, and heard by all."

ETHNOGRAPHIC ALLEGORY AS AFFECTIVE EXPERIMENT

The affective experiment you have just read is an *ethnographic allegory*. We define an ethnographic allegory as a literary device meant to share a moral, insight, or lesson by way of replacing a subject of ethnographic research with a different subject without revealing who or what the original subject is, why the replacement took place, and what the "true" connection with ethnological reality is. The purpose of an ethnographic allegory is to mean one thing but say another. The point in doing so is to present a complex reality, allow the readers to more closely relate to ethnographic subjects, and lead readers to re-envision a reality they previously took for granted. Because our text is explicitly intended to be allegorical, this is not an ethnographic allegory in the sense proposed by James Clifford (1994) who argued that all ethnographic writings can be read as allegories. Now, even though explaining the meanings of one's own allegories is a neither elegant nor necessary thing to do, it is valuable to spend a few words discussing how our allegory came to be and what its value as an affective experiment is.

Ethnographic Allegories as Method

An ethnographic allegory is a writing experiment that does not require any atypical data collection procedures. As an experimental literary device, it comes to life through the act of writing an ethnographic story by consciously following allegorical conventions and through a trial and error process in repurposing those conventions towards ethnographic objectives. At the very least, the method of writing an ethnographic allegory entails the following:

1. Thinking of a complex idea or lesson we want to share with readers and employing a fictional narrative based on ethnographic material to convey that idea or lesson.
2. Replacing real-life characters with fictional characters.
3. Replacing real-life events and experiences with events and experiences that are creatively adapted to allow for interaction and dialogue among the fictional characters.
4. Ensuring that real-life characters and real-life events and experiences are never revealed within the allegory.
5. Enabling readers to read between the lines by giving them cues so they can arrive at an intended meaning, without however making matters too obvious for them.
6. Creating a story that stands on its own through characters that are credible and relatable and through plots that have a strong central narrative.

It is important to emphasize that ethnographic allegories are not made up; they must be based on true stories collected in the field. Our allegory, for example, is based on actual fieldwork we conducted as part of a multisite project focused on the social ecologies of natural heritage and the cultural meanings of wildness. As part of that project, we travelled to Los Glaciares National Park in the winter of 2018–2019. We spent a few weeks in the two hubs of the park, the towns of El Chalten and El Calafate, both located in the Patagonian province of Santa Cruz, Argentina. There we conducted 13 interviews with individuals who taught us about the mountains and the glaciers—individuals like business owners, guides, glaciologists, estancia owners, mountaineers, biologists, and local historians. We also travelled throughout the park extensively, at times as part of package day tours and at times accompanied by guides with whom we talked during extensive walk-along interviews.

Moved by the desire to strengthen ecological protection and heritage conservation while simultaneously recognizing the interconnectedness of culture and nature, of social life and wildlife, of people and their environments, our research unfolded not just in Los Glaciares National Park but altogether in 20 UNESCO World Heritage sites inscribed as natural or mixed. Our fieldwork introduced us to individuals and collectives who live, work, enjoy, protect, study, develop, and live off such sites. By telling their stories, actions, and experiences, our various writings challenge our readers to rethink the idea of wildness, to reimagine the relations between natural and cultural heritage, and re-envision the rapport between nature and culture (Vannini and Vannini 2021). Throughout three years of ethnographic fieldwork and travel we conducted approximately 300 interviews and explored a vast web of old and innovative conservation policies, exploitation and development schemes, and diverse understandings of what natural heritage and wildness mean.

Throughout our interviews we treated our informants as experts, guides, and teachers. Nigel Thrift (2004, p. 81) writes that non-representational theory is "an attempt to change the role of academics by questioning what counts as expertise and who has that expertise." This for us entailed rethinking the value of our research as a type of co-production with our interlocutors "through which the researcher and the researched are resituated or repositioned in the world and thereby are engaged in remaking the world through the process of their encounters" (Greenhough 2010, p. 48).

It is upon acts of noticing—based on our "modest witnessing" (Haraway 1997, p. 269) of multiple relations and multiple species—that our analysis and arguments, as well as our narratives, were built. In our writings we prefer not to take the approach of drawing out themes and categories from the data in order to ascertain what is common. Instead of writing about what is "typical," we focus on fragments of our encounters that generated new ideas, activated new imaginings, affected us more intensely, and astonished us. In doing so, throughout our project we have created affective experiments including ethnographic allegories such as the one above, as well as etho-ethnographic fables (Vannini and Vannini 2020a), geo-stories (Vannini and Vannini 2020b), and more (Vannini and Vannini 2021).

Ours is a logic built on singularities, not generalities. Rather than based on abstraction and generalization, our writing is driven by the infinite capacity that a multiplicity of relations has for generating new ideas and for making our world more, not less, complex (Greenhough 2010; Hinchcliff 2010). This is a partial analytic based on the possibilities open by conjunctions such as *and*, rather than the definitive certainties of what *is* (see Deleuze 2001). Our writings are therefore often a collection of radical ideas, lessons, arguments, epiphanies, and transformative events not meant to be judged for how they resemble a sample or represent a population or how they approximate reality, but rather to be valued for what they do next, what they generate and activate, and how they invent "new relations between thought and life" (Thrift 2004, p. 82).

In light of this, we view the literary genre of allegories as an experiment intended to enliven our data, to emplace ethnographic material, and to inspirit more-than-human geosocial assemblages. On the surface, assemblages, such as glaciers as inanimate objects, are not immediately "alive" in the sense that humans, animals, and plants are. But in Patagonia several of our research participants taught us otherwise. Through numerous conversations we learned that glaciers move frequently by shrinking or expanding in relation with climate and their own trajectories. Glaciers make sounds—haunting at times, we were told—as they creak, crack, shift, and fracture. Glaciers also calve regularly as well, sending large chunks of ice to the waters underneath. At times those calving events are massive and spectacular and draw large crowds. Other times Patagonian glaciers break up into small pieces that float as icebergs down Lake Argentino and Lake Viedma. These are stunningly beautiful icebergs that some of our research participants viewed as forms of art and nature's own self-expression. Therefore, with our allegory we have enabled glaciers to express themselves, to interact with one another and with us, to feel emotions, and to affect us through their actions and their stories.

Brüggen is a glacier found inside Los Glaciares National Park. But in the allegory Brüggen speaks and acts much like one of the Canadian glaciers discussed by Julie Cruikshank (2007). As Cruikshank articulates on the basis of her ethnographic research in the Yukon Territory with the Kluane First Nation, glaciers are able to listen, feel, and share stories as well. For the Kluane First Nation glaciers are not inanimate objects but ancestors whose bodies are inspirited by relations with human and animal companions. We ourselves conducted interviews with members of the Kluane First Nation as part of our fieldwork in Kluane National Park in September 2016. There we learned about ways in which glaciers are alive. These teachings about their vitality pushed us to question and ultimately problematize Western binary oppositions between inanimate and animate objects, and people and things. These teachings were in the back of our mind in Patagonia as we experienced a dramatically different glacial atmosphere. The contrast between the glaciers became the basis of our allegory.

An allegory is a simple and well-recognized literary trope that allows non-human characters to speak, act, and feel in human-like ways. In this sense an allegory is a simple way to enliven more-than-human lives, to present an alternate and subjunctive reality. We chose to present glaciers as tombstones in order to underline the fact that while they may on the surface seem lifeless, they are in fact lively entities. While tombstones symbolize death, in other words, they tell stories about life and affect us. In the allegory, as tombstones make their vitality known by speaking and ultimately by breaking apart, their stories begin revealing their suffering. In the end, as they break apart and flood the lands around them, they remind us of human mortality and the finitude of our species in the context of climate change.

The glaciers' stories also reveal something else that we observed regularly throughout our fieldwork in Argentina: the ways they are commodified by the tourist industry. Our observations of tourists' behaviour on site (the picture-taking, the constantly distracting conduct, the consumption of food and liquor, etc.) stand in sharp contrast to what goes on in Kluane National Park, where hardly any one ventures out on glacial fields. This is how eventually Kluane becomes a source of inspiration in the allegory, albeit through Brüggen's character, by raising the consciousness of the Patagonian glaciers and invoking their rebellion. Needless to say, all the characters presented in our allegory are named after actual glacier names, and some of their personality characteristics are also generated in direct relation to their size, shape, remoteness, and role in the tourist industry.

Ethnographic Allegory as a More-than-Human Way of Sharing Knowledge

The purpose of an ethnographic allegory, like we said, is to reveal a lesson or insight. In a recent essay on geophilia Jeffrey Cohen (2015, p. 19) urges us to think about how "the lithic inhabits the secret interiors of the earth." The lithic refers to rock, but the argument can be easily extended to glacial ice; it too inhabits the "secret interiors" of our planet and it too urges us to think about inhabitation of the lifeworld in different ways. In light of this we characterize our allegory as an attempt to reveal the vitality of more-than-human life as embedded in and emanating from glacial beings and becomings.

Allegories like ours call attention to geosocialities (Pálsson and Swanson 2016): the discrete entanglements of the earth with multiple forms of life.

Geosocialities are not only material, organic meshworks of geological and biological lives, but also entanglements of the multiple sensibilities inherent in those forms of life. Examinations of geosocialities are sensitive to issues of distributed agency, the vibrancy of materials, vitality, and affect. As Gisli Pálsson and Heather Anne Swanson (2016, p. 155) put it, "[G]eosocialities ... attend to the intertwinings of bodies and biographies with earth systems and deep time histories." Writing about geosocialities demands an experimental approach that stimulates reflections on nonlinear geologic time scales and on how human and non-human lives are enmeshed in relations that exceed the limits of present time and space.

Of course, geosocial beings like glaciers do not speak human languages, and the writing of allegories inevitably results in putting words in their mouths. Making glaciers tell stories through human words could be viewed as an anthropomorphic act or maybe even as a juvenile way of sharing knowledge. But the real issue is not that inanimate objects cannot speak. Rather the issue is that many of us humans are unable to attune ourselves to non-human experiences. Let us then for a moment pause the usual scientific attitude driven by binary ontologies that stipulate what is and what is not. And let us instead cultivate a speculative ontology that asks what else could life be and how else it could be expressed.

So, what could non-human beings like glaciers say? What could they share with us humans if we cared enough to listen? Like animals, glaciers, mountains, rocks, and other so-called inanimate entities can speak, in a way, but not every human knows how to listen. Indigenous people have made this point before. The Cree people of eastern James Bay, for example, teach us that animals communicate regularly and clearly with their hunters but only insofar as their relationships are based on respect and trust (Berkes 2012). Inuit and Blackfoot people have similar knowledge and obligations to fulfil towards animals (Little Bear 2012; Schmidt and Dowsley 2010). First Nations peoples in the Kluane region, Cruikshank (2007, p. 142) tells us, believe that the mountains and glaciers around them are part of "a sentient landscape that listens and responds to human indiscretion." And so do countless other Indigenous people around Canada and the world who share their knowledge through their memories and their stories.

These non-Cartesian, non-Western worldviews teach us that non-human beings have spirits, are intelligent, are sentient, and are aware of people's behaviour towards them. Western human exceptionalism, however, denies non-humans the subjectivity and capacity to communicate in order to legitimize their subjugation to human will. But in doing so Western worldviews go even farther: by denying alternate ontologies and silencing Indigenous ways of knowing they render Indigenous peoples and their Lands "irrelevant to the modern world" (Cruikshank 2007, p. 258). In fact, Western scientists even often degrade the value of Indigenous knowledge by labelling it as allegorical and therefore inferior to the literary devices utilized by positivist science and Western epistemologies.

Nevertheless, advances in more-than-human epistemologies and ontologies are now beginning to show how non-human beings are communicative, sentient, and intelligent. For example, in a recent book Belgian philosopher of science Vinciane Despret (2016) argues that animals could share with us many interesting and insightful stories about our shared lifeworlds if only we, humans, learned to ask the right questions. Throughout her book Despret listens to animals' perspectives about issues of concern to both them and us and shares through fables. We ourselves have written etho-ethnographic fables as experiments through which we can attempt to attune ourselves to animals' ontological perspectives and experiences (see Vannini and Vannini 2020a). Just like such fables, ethnographic allegories are experimental narratives that transcend the neutral and dispassionate limitations of anonymous bodies of humans talking about non-humans and denying them the capacity to express themselves (see; Despret 2016).

Allegories of the kind we presented here are also inspired by the development of multi-species ethnography (e.g., see Kirksey and Helmreich 2010; Kohn 2013; Ogden et al. 2013; Van Dooren and Rose 2016). Multi-species ethnography is "ethnographic research and writing that is attuned to life's emergence within a shifting assemblage of agentive beings" (Ogden et al. 2013, p. 6). Within multi-species ethnography more-than-human beings are intended as a multiplicity of organisms in relation with one another, relations through which life as a whole is animated. Unbounded by the notion of organic bodies, or by inanimate-animate boundaries, multi-species ethnographers aim to reconsider the notions of nature and society, thus decentring the role of humans and opening the doors to alternate ontologies and epistemologies, as well as to novel styles of knowledge representation (Ogden et al. 2013; Van Dooren and Rose 2016). In this way multi-species ethnography becomes less solely about ethnos and more about a diffused more-than-human corporeality that emerges through a kinship among humans, animals, elements of the landscape, and the plant world—a kinship that is "materially real, partially knowable, multicultured and multinatured, magical, and emergent through the contingent relations of multiple beings and entities" (Ogden et al. 2013, p. 6).

CONCLUSION: ETHNOGRAPHIC ALLEGORY AS EXPERIMENTS IN SHARING AFFECTIVE RESPONSIBILITY

Affective experiments are often thought of as mere transgressions of conventional scholarly representations. Transgressions are extremely valuable tools to be used in the dismantling of canons, conventions, and expectations, but their importance is reduced if we think of them as simple exercises in playfulness or creative trial and error. A different way to think about transgression is to remind ourselves of the established historical value and the traditional relevance of some kinds of experiments.

Allegories, for example, have been around for a long time. Their stylistic conventions have long been recognized and accepted by countless audiences, and their sharing has proven over time to be an effective way of disseminating oral history, knowledge, and moral values. Though nowadays we might view an allegory as a transgression from the current dominant ways of sharing knowledge, from a broad scale, historical perspective allegories are not so much experiments, but rather traditional ways of teaching. The value of allegories as affective experiments in the current times lies therefore not so much on their innovativeness or transgressiveness, but rather in their immediate recognizability and acceptance by large and different audiences.

Allegories are unique affective "experiments" whose current genesis—indeed rebirth—is characterized by a recognition of failure. This is the kind of failure writers experience when they realize that our collective understanding of a subject is limited, that our ability to convey affect is short of the ideal, and that no full explanation of a subject is possible. Allegories, in fact, are narratives driven not so much by the will to explain, but rather by a will to leave something unexplained. So, whereas a conventional way of writing might conceptualize, interpret, and explain, an allegory metaphorizes, leaves open to interpretation, and reveals the limits of explanation. In this sense an allegory is not so much a transgression, but a regression: a return to a world self-conscious of its limitations, and a homage to an attitude marked not so much by the desire for certainty (the "what is"), but rather by the pursuit of possibility (the "what if").

Allegories have at times been silenced and marginalized by Western scientific epistemologies and ways of sharing knowledge. It would be a mistake, indeed yet another colonial act, to "rediscover" them and claim that their use is an original practice. Allegories and the epistemologies and ontologies on which they rely have long predated our own experimental practices. So, in a sense, while these kinds of affective experiments do allow us to envision new futures, they also invoke old traditions and often forgotten ways of how to cope with the limits of our knowledge and the contingencies of moral codes.

Allegories in general are typically driven by a moral imperative. Ethnographic allegories as well should recognize their responsibility in raising awareness about critical issues. Ethnography and qualitative research in general are not always driven by a moral imperative, however. At times ethnography is treated by social scientists as a mere research method: a system of procedures and techniques for collecting, analysing, and presenting data. While we understand why this is sometimes the case, we believe that ethnography and ethnographers can play a greater role in the public sphere by better understanding its public education value and by becoming more committed to its affective responsibility.

By affective responsibility we mean a moral obligation to exercise the affective capacity of ethnographic knowledge. Unlike most other social scientific research methods and strategies, ethnographic knowledge and ethnographic storytelling can move people. Ethnographies can affect people due to the intimacy, vividness, and personable value of their narratives. Ethnographic stories can provoke change. But ethnographic storytelling can only affect audiences if storytellers recognize their moral responsibilities and understand the affective power of the tools at their disposal. Ethnographic writing that is dispassionate, politically uncommitted, formal, distant, quasi-objective, and pretentiously rigorous fails to recognize its affective responsibility. Ethnographic writing that is passionate, morally committed, narrative, performative, intimate, personable, and resolutely experimental is writing that embraces its moral responsibility.

We view ethnographic allegories as an example—one of many—of affectively responsible writing. For us allegories are affective experiments of thought. They are speculations, mystifications driven by curiosity and possibility. They are a "what if" asked in order to shock, to unsettle, to animate a moment of doubt, to enliven the possibility of what else something might be. These are ordinary affects, in the language of Kathleen Stewart (2007), committed to speculation, impact, and the power of the subjunctive. Ordinary affects are "the varied, surging capacities to affect and be affected that give everyday life the quality of a continual motion of relations, scenes, contingencies, and emergences" (Stewart 2007, pp. 1–2).

Allegories largely derive their affective power by use of the subjunctive mood. The use of the subjective mood is a non-representational strategy "directed at making ethnographic representation less concerned with faithfully and detachedly reporting facts, experiences, actions, and situations, and more interested instead in making them come to life, in allowing them to take new and unpredicted meanings, in violating expectations" (Vannini 2015, p. 119). The subjunctive mood is potential, hypothetical, and conditional. It is intended to animate, not to invent, a pluriverse of knowledges. It is a writing style intended to provoke: to enliven what things could be and what they could become through performance, possibility, and imagination.

Throughout our fieldwork on natural heritage and wildness we have learned to reimagine ecology. Ecological science is conventionally viewed as a branch of biology concerned with spatial and temporal patterns of the distribution of organisms in ecosystems. The people who have taught us about their places and their Lands, especially Indigenous people, have pushed us, in their own ways, to reimagine ecology as a meshwork of relations, an affective ecology "that is attuned to openness to being transformed by the world" (Singh 2018, p. 2). Affective ecologies are political entanglements that can help us think of relations as alive, open to change, mutually interdependent, and based on the equality of all its constituent members. As Neera Singh (2018, p. 3) writes, "thinking in terms of affective ecologies inspires and enables an ecopolitics rooted in care for the material world not as 'impersonal nature at a distance' but from a lived-in or kin-centric ecological perspective."

In such an ecology, as countless Indigenous teachings remind us, respect for the personhood of all members of more-than-human kinships is of quintessential importance (Kimmerer 2013). Many of the stories shared by Indigenous people have morals that teach about respect. Just like stories do, ethnographic allegories can help us come to terms with the affective responsibility of storytellers. Allegorical writing of the kind presented in this chapter therefore embraces an ethic of respect towards all beings, including those presumed to be inanimate. This affective experiment enables us to go beyond the mere celebration of biodiversity and to transcend the limitations of dispassionate biological science. It calls upon us to relate emotionally to other beings, other species, other forms of life and to recognize their inherent right to being respected and being alive.

REFERENCES

Berkes, F. (2012). *Sacred ecology*. Routledge.

Clifford, J. (1994). On ethnographic allegory. In S. Seidman (Ed.), *The postmodern turn: New perspectives on social theory* (pp. 205–228). Cambridge University Press.

Cohen, J. (2015). *Stone: An ecology of the inhuman*. University of Minnesota Press.

Cruikshank, J. (2007). *Do glaciers listen?* UBC Press.

Deleuze, G. (2001). *Pure immanence: Essays on a life*. Introduction by Rajchman, J. Zone Books.

Despret, V. (2016). *What would animals say if we asked the right questions?* University of Minnesota Press.

Greenhough, B. (2010). Vitalist geographies: Life and the more-than-human. In Anderson, B. & Harrison, P. (Eds), *Taking place: The promise of non-representational theories* (pp. 37–54). Routledge.

Haraway, D. (1997). *ModestWitness@Second_Millennium. FemaleMan©_Meets_OncoMouse™*. Routledge.

Hinchcliff, S. (2010). Working with multiples: A non-representational approach to environmental issues. In Anderson, B. & Harrison, P. (Eds), *Taking place: The promise of non-representational theories* (pp. 303–320). Routledge

Kimmerer, R. (2013). *Braiding sweetgrass: Indigenous wisdom, scientific knowledge and the teachings of plants*. Milkweed Editions.

Kirksey, E. & Helmreich, S. (2010). The emergence of multispecies ethnography. *Cultural Anthropology, 25*, 545–576.

Kohn, E. (2013). *How forests think: Toward an anthropology beyond the human*. University of California Press.

Little Bear, L. (2012). Traditional knowledge and humanities: A perspective by a Blackfoot. *Journal of Chinese Philosophy, 39*, 518–527.

Ogden, L., Hall, B., & Tanita, K. (2013). Animals, plants, people, and things: A review of multispecies ethnography. *Environment & Society, 4*, 5–24.

Pálsson, G., & Swanson, H. (2016). Down to Earth: Geosocialities and geopolitics. *Environmental Humanities, 8*, 149–171.

Schmidt, J., & Dowsley, M. (2010). Hunting with polar bears: Problems with passive properties of the commons. *Human Ecology, 38*, 377–387.

Singh, N. (2018). Introduction: Affective ecologies and conservation. *Conservation and Society*, 16(1), 1–7.

Stewart, K. (2007). *Ordinary affects*. Duke University Press.

Thrift, N. (2004). Summoning life. In Cloke, P., Crang, P., & Goodwin, M. (Eds.), *Envisioning human geography* (pp. 81–103). Arnold.

Van Dooren, T., & Rose, B. (2016). Lively ethnography: Storying animist worlds. *Environmental Humanities*, 8, 77–94.

Vannini, P. (2015). Enlivening ethnography through the irrealis mood: In search of a more-than-representational style. In Vannini, P. (Ed.), *Non-representational methodologies: Re-envisioning research* (pp. 112–129). Routledge.

Vannini, P., & Vannini, A. (2020a). What could wild life be? Etho-ethnographic fables on human-animal kinship. *GeoHumanities*, 6, 122–138.

Vannini, P., & Vannini, A. (2020b). Attuning to wild atmospheres: Reflections on wildness as feeling. *Emotion, Space & Society*, 36: 1–14.

Vannini, P., & Vannini, A. (2021). *Wildness: The vitality of the land*. McGill-Queen's University Press.

CHAPTER 14

Activating Limit as Method: An Affective Experiment in Ethnographic Criminology

Christina Jerne

In September 2018, I started a research project that, at the time, aimed to study a Danish gang called Loyal to Familia (LTF). Armed with curiosity and inexperience, I chose to carry out the project at the Centre for Global Criminology, Copenhagen University, which was established to bring together scholars who were keen on investigating methodologically innovative approaches to crime and criminalisation. I was confident that I had made the best possible professional alliance to tackle the practical and ethical challenges of carrying out a study on such a covert and defiant group. But literally one day after I began the project, the gang was banned by the Danish police. Identifying as part of this particular group or collaborating with any of its members would lead to penalty. If carrying out an ethnographic study of minority gangs as a white woman was already a challenge, I thought, this was the end. How would I get access to something so forcefully criminalised and politicised?

C. Jerne (✉)
University of Copenhagen, Copenhagen, Denmark
e-mail: chje@anthro.ku.dk

© The Author(s), under exclusive license to Springer Nature Switzerland AG 2022
B. Timm Knudsen et al. (eds.), *Methodologies of Affective Experimentation*, https://doi.org/10.1007/978-3-030-96272-2_14

287

It turned out that this eventful hindrance would turn my work upside down and actually in many ways facilitate my research process. Several gang members appealed the provisional law, initiating a legal process against the state on the legitimacy of the ban. Among other things, in practice this meant that the massive labour of tracing the contours of the field, that is, of finding relevant informants,[1] clues and documents was outsourced to the lawyers, and that, at least to begin with, I could simply sit down and take notes in a warm courthouse room.

More broadly, this limit placed by the act of criminalisation and the consequences this event had on my research led me to start thinking about the possibilities offered by limitations in research processes and the epistemological quandaries they present for world-making, whether practical, conceptual, or ethical.

In a sense all research aims to find, challenge, investigate, or push limits within a given field of knowledge. The question mark itself punctuates that which is not known, thus revealing the limits to what is known and delineating a particular trajectory of discovery. And once one embarks on that path of discovery, one will inevitably encounter many limitations that will ramify into new questions, relations, and ideas. Some of these limitations may be set by others, for example, when one is not granted access to some contacts or information, or when one does not have sufficient resources to carry out an experiment in a laboratory. Others are (consciously or not) set by oneself. For instance, when one decides what (not) to wear for an interview, which words to use, and which questions to ask interlocutors, but also, which findings to reveal or hide, or which format to publish them in. Managing these limits and learning to negotiate them are not only fundamental research skills, but also productive sites of knowledge.

The question I explore in this chapter is, then: what happens if one activates limits as a methodological tool rather than an inherent premise or side-effect of a research process? I argue that while limits do not necessarily translate to emotional or cognitive awareness, all moments of discovery are traceable back to the experience of limits. That is, that limits are necessary but not sufficient ingredients for knowledge formation. By actively making the limit explicit one may discover, reveal, or ally oneself to a novel perspective or empirical detail.

---

[1] Fifty-nine witnesses and many audience members.

My contribution to this book is therefore to experiment with the methodological affordances of limits through the classical Spinozian approach to affect (Spinoza [1677] 2001). If all bodies have certain dispositions to movement and rest at a given point in time (what Spinoza calls *modes*), then an affect is an alteration of this mode of being resulting from the encounter with another body (both in extension and in thought). I thereby understand a limit as a particular kind of affect, that is, not as a disposition, but as an occurrence that diminishes or temporarily halts one's capacity to act. I argue that putting the occurrence under the magnifying lens, rather than treating it as a by-product or an inevitable but rather insignificant step in a research process, is generative of a different type of knowledge— of an affectively driven process of learning.

The first part of this chapter introduces my understanding of the relationship between limit and affect. After clarifying this connection, I exemplify how I have actively used these types of affects within the specifics of my criminological research via three different modes of relation: *outside-out*, *outside-in*, and *inside-out*.[2] More specifically, *outside-out* refers to limits that are independent of you, that occur and affect bodies within a given field which you observe. The experiment, in this case, implies a method of registering the occurrence of affects and tracing what they move in the world (Knudsen and Stage 2015, pp. 8–10). *Outside-in* refers to limits that are directed by others but that directly affect your personal behaviour in the research context. This technique thus involves actively tracing the way you are affected and affect a given empirical or conceptual limit and therefore requires a heightened level of reflexivity. Conversely, *inside-out* refers to limits you find within yourself, be they conceptual, practical, or corporal, and how you negotiate, challenge, or project these upon a given field. Finally, a last mode of relation is *inside-in*, which refers to the limits you discover within yourself and how you relate to them in your own process of becoming. This last type of inquiry will not be addressed for reasons of space and genre but is certainly one that is also highly relevant for affectively inspired research.

---

[2] Although the "outside" world and our "inner" worlds are inextricably linked, and thus cannot be seen as isolated or impermeable vacuums, I find that marking the analytical distinction between *what you* and *what something that is not you* moves in the world to be beneficial for thinking about methodological questions such as agency, causality, positionality, scale, and dependency.

Using these modes of relation as filters is an experiment in the episte-mological sense, that is, it affords the mobilisation of a specific course of thought and/or action in a research process before, during, or after the occurrence has unfolded. Although they are inspired by a criminal topic, which in itself resides at the limit of a given culture (Tonkonoff 2014), these analytical tools are elastic enough to be useful to other, less explicitly edgy topics of inquiry. However, the way I unpack them here pertains to my own style of discovery, that is, ethnography.

Affect, Limit, and Crime in Particular

If an affective occurrence is an encounter between bodies that either decreases or increases their capacity to act, then a limit is a particular example of an affective relation where one of the bodies is arrested, or somewhat decreases its capacity to act, in conformity with the particular configuration of relations of "speed and slowness" that composed it prior to the affective occurrence. In other words, a limit is something that forces one to somehow shift a specific course of action, movement, or thought: a red traffic light, a travel restriction, a loss in internet connection, a drop in blood sugar, a rejection. In Spinozian terms, a limit might be under-stood as a recoiling change of *mode*, as an alternation of a specific manifes-tation (both in extension and in thought) of what he calls "substance" (Spinoza [1677] 2001, p. 3). In this sense, we might think of limits as passions rather than actions.

The difference between passions and actions is that the first are exter-nally caused, whilst the second are caused by the body in question. Spinoza conceptualises affects as sad passions when they act upon the body and decrease its capacity to act. Indeed, as Bradley Robinson and Mel Kutner remind us (2019, p. 115), the Latin root of both "passion" and "passive" is *pati*, meaning *to suffer*. Affects are always accompanied by ideas the body has of these affections. In the case of passions, we are in the presence of what Spinoza calls inadequate ideas, as the body is passive and thereby confused, disoriented, overwhelmed, and incapable of apt rationalisation. When it is the body that acts in a way that increases its affective capacity, we enter into the realm of joyful affects, which, coupled with conscious reflection, can better lead us to true knowledge or what he calls "ade-quate ideas".

The methodological impetus that I am suggesting is a thought experi-ment. By activating limits, that is, by consciously reflecting over passions or instances where the body has been acted upon, we can move further away from inadequate ideas and closer to adequate ideas or "active joys", thereby actively shaping and adapting to the affective shift. I want to stress, however, that the distinction between adequate and inadequate ideas does not imply a true or false epistemological binary. In Spinoza's universe, consciousness is in fact merely transitive; it only carries informational value on the passage from less potent totalities to more potent ones (Deleuze 1988, p. 21). And what is more, this information is always confused and distorted. So what I am stimulated by is the humbleness of the Spinozian posture that admits that the human mind is in itself limited, but that it is through making an active effort to relate to the ideas one has of affections that one can perfect, refine, and improve one's own awareness of the world and, consequently, one's power to act upon it. A joyful ethical stance implies an ongoing, conscious, and active effort to "learn to be affected" (Latour 2004).

The invocation of the term "limit" leads me to another related but different term, that is "limit experience", most commonly associated with the work of Georges Bataille ([1944] 1988; [1957] 2001), but also, among others, to Michel Foucault, Maurice Blanchot, and Jacques Lacan. The limit experience is a particular instance whereby the subject reaches such a level of affective intensity that it becomes something other than itself, "so that it may arrive at its annihilation or dissociation" (Foucault 1991, p. 27). Some classical examples of such levels of excess include madness, mysticism, crime, drug use, sacrifice, and sado-masochism.[3] These moments, which lie at the paradoxical encounter between self-annihilation and self-expansion (Jay 1995, p. 159), afford particular opportunities for the transformation of the subject's mode of relating to the world and are thus worthy of attention by those interested in the methodological potentials of affective thinking. However, despite being conceptually connected to the affective occurrences I shall describe, these extremes are not the kind of experiences I focus on in this chapter. Therefore, I will from here on distinguish between the "experience of limit" and the "limit experience".

It is not by chance that I am inspired by the topic of limits at this specific point in my life. Working with gangs has caused me to spend several years in the company of marginalised youth who practise a violent form of identity politics, which actively seeks recognition and voice (Jerne

---

[3] These themes were also flamboyantly explored by the Australian new-wave/rock band INXS.

forthcoming). The quest for sovereignty (Kuldova 2019), palpable in gang behaviour, provokes disgust, rage, fear, or fascination in public opinion, and in me. The ways gangs assert their presence onto the urban space therefore prod at what society considers to be tolerable or too transgressive (in Danish *grænseoverskridende*, which literally means limit-crossing) and thus worthy of punishment. Thus in a sense, I have spent the past two and a half years investigating processes of boundary-making and breaking from the point of view of gangs, the social contexts they inhabit, and, of course, myself.[4]

In hindsight, therefore, limits and affects seem to be a rather straightforward analytical choice, one that I might have benefited from consciously embracing at the onset of this study. But then again, the premise of the experimental method is that it "gives unknown answers to questions that the experimenter is not yet ready to formulate clearly" (Roepstorff 2011, p. 139). Indeed, as Sergio Tonkonoff capably illustrates (2014), crime itself demarcates the boundaries of a given social order and its subjects at a specific point in time. Per contra, crime is also the limit against which that very same culture measures, mirrors, and moulds itself continuously. This is why the theme of limits is implicitly traceable in much criminological literature, from the classics to the more contemporary examples (e.g., Tarde 1890; Durkheim 1895; Malinowski 1926; Becker 1963; Bataille [1957] 2001; Kuldova 2019). Building on these insights, yet also moving beyond the specifics of criminology, I seek to illustrate a more explicitly methodological use of limits in a research process. What follows are in fact some practical examples of the shift in perception obtainable by actively prioritising one's attention to limits and what they move in general, rather than a theory of the relation between limits and crime in particular. The experimental aspect thus consists in the method of actively tracing the learning process, of revealing the epistemological alterations that occur in the knower,[5] such as the generation of novel questions or the attunement to aspects of the field that were inaccessible or invisible before the research posture became focused on limits.

---

[4] I am grateful to Ceren Özselçuk for bringing this to my attention.

[5] A method that George Marcus (2010) classifies as having a relational aesthetic (see also Roepstorff 2011).

Outside-Out: Witnessing the Making of Crime

The banning of LTF is a historic judicial event in Denmark. First of all because, being issued as an administrative ban, it effectively entered into force before it was passed as a law, thereby challenging the separation of powers. It is indeed not the first attempt to ban groups that are deemed harmful and violent. One successful precedent was the temporary banning of a Danish section of the First International (*Den Internationale Arbejderforening for Danmark*) in 1873. More recently, the government attempted (but failed) to ban other groups such as the Islamic organisation Hizb ut-Tahrir and the Outlaw Motorcycle Clubs (OMCs) Hells Angels and Bandidos. The ban on LTF, now a law, successfully and permanently denies the freedom of association—a constitutional right—to a specific group, thereby setting a legal precedent for a faster, more tailored approach to arrest the movement of groups that are deemed dangerous. Moreover, this ban marks an important passage towards a more collective definition of crime (and connectedly, its criminalisation) that until now has been comparatively individual-based in the context of Denmark.

Had it not been for this eventful limitation, I would probably not have learned about the history of Danish criminalisation that I summarised above, nor would I have been so exposed to the broader political conflict in which this particular gang was inscribed. Indeed, if crime comes to be through a political process (Malinowski 1926), then how to better study the process if not in its relation to a highly technical judicial process? As Howard Becker reminds us, in order to understand criminal subcultures, we must investigate not only the criminals themselves, but the legal and political authorities that construct these subcultures (Becker 1963). The courtroom fieldwork I had the opportunity to carry out as a result of this ban indeed shifted my perspective because it brought me directly into the very arena where the terms of the social limit were debated, negotiated, and investigated. Importantly, the activity of tracing the contours of the crime (i.e., what exactly was considered socially harmful) allowed me to reveal the many contact points between the criminals and the incriminators, showing me that they are co-constitutive forces.

This became increasingly evident to me through the highly symbolic and representative modes of assertion employed by both the gang and the executive/legislative forces. Indeed, one of the reasons that this particular gang had caught my attention was its attempts to colonise different international territories through a rather forceful communicative campaign operated through events, raids, and the use of logos. In a similar fashion, the ban on LTF prohibited, above all, the performance of belonging to this collective in the public space. Eight of the ten guidelines the police follow to enforce the ban have to do with the display of signs that are indexical to the group (tattoos, movement in the public space, clothes, logos, use of social media, and more). This confirms a general tendency within legislative approaches that seek to curb the movement and existence of violent gangs to incriminate "radical" signs rather than acting on criminal acts and infringements (Standing 2006).

Although one of the primary aims of the case was to verify whether the group, as such, promoted violence, the vast majority of the proof presented and the interrogations I witnessed regarded the use of clothes, tattoos, and the use of titles and ranks. Alternatively, the group was defined based on criteria such as having a common calendar (meetings and events) and a membership payment system based on rank—both markers that imply the institutionalisation of a group, rather than being something violent per se. Thus, one of the prime lines of argumentation for whether or not this group was to be regarded as a harmful social unit was its degree of formalisation and how it represented itself outwards.

What struck me was the parallel development of this logic within LTF. LTF is one of many examples of a neighbourhood-based ethnic minority group that grew and began to self-identify as a gang in the late 2000s. At that point in time, OMCs monopolised the drug market, so a series of conflicts began between OMCs and youth groups, culminating in 2008, when Hell's Angels' support group AK81 shot openly against a group of minority Danes. Later that year, Hell's Angels published the *Jackal Manifesto* (Nielsen 2008), which denounced these groups on the basis of ethnoracial and cultural arguments. Despite the fact that these groups are increasingly hybrid in composition, more than 20 years later, the ethnic divide continues to linger in group self-identification and common tongue: OMCs represent majority Danes, while gangs the minority.

Minority gangs, like LTF, often oppose majority culture by mimicking it. Throughout the trial, I had the possibility of tracing the genealogy of dress in the gang, as we spent much time examining clothing. The underlying assumption was that uniforms and shared symbols are an essential constitutive feature of an organisation. Yet this was not always the case for LTF. Initially, they did not wear a uniform. It was not until after the conflicts with the OMCs that they began to wear cotton T-shirts and hoodies with their group name, and not until 2013 that they began to militarise their dress by wearing bullet-proof vests, according to one policeman. In other words, they only started dressing and performing a "we" in the same fashion as OMCs, once they were interpellated as their criminal other.

One testimony was striking in this regard. The police had managed to confiscate 109 leather vests that LTF had ordered. The tailor declared that when the order was made, he asked for specifications on what they should look like. The gang member answered: "make them as big as the ones the rockers[6] have". Size was not the only parameter they used to conform themselves to the legitimate criminal form. The classification of rank, geographical belonging, and internal relations were also marked in the same manner that biker organisations do (Fig. 14.1).

Later on, I found out that these hierarchies were often quite irrelevant in the everyday praxis of many minority gangs or, at least, that much effort went into seeking to enforce them as they were not always representative

Fig. 14.1 Sketch of a vest made in the courtroom by author

[6] "Rockers" is an emic term for members of OMCs.

of the actual configuration of powers within the group. Other more spontaneous hierarchies were formed around the lines of age, charisma, and personal skills. In other words, the formalisation of the organisation, both in its internal structure and in its representation, emerged in an effort to be considered worthy of opposition—to oppose the hegemonic forces in their own aesthetics and language. The affective register here expressed in the typical criminal combination of admiration/abjection is fortified through repetition and mimicry performed by the legislators, who seek out familiar criminal signs, as well as the gang members, who reproduce and appropriate the very same signs. This confirms that affective signs intensify through repetition and slippage, regardless of their actual coherent link to a referent object (Ahmed 2003, p. 123).

This incoherence between sign and signifier, or better, the overriding power of signs, became apparent to me in the very process of tracing the way the social limit was constructed in court. Here I learned to uncover some of the inherent premises for what legitimates sociality in Denmark and thereby also what can be considered a "true" (criminal) group. The first being the institutionalisation and explicit allocation of roles in a group setting. The second is the use of indexes to distribute and govern bodies in the public space. These norms are asserted by both the gang and the law enforcers, in a show of force. In Tonkonoff's words (2014, p. 3): "the radical otherness of crime sometimes consists of the exacerbation of the very values that dominate the culture in rule; sometimes of (sub)cultural configurations that defy this cultural hegemony by opposition."

Recording the details of an affective occurrence at such a scale, the legal arrest of the movement of a specific group of bodies, constituted an occasion to trace the contours of this opposition. Observing the process of territorialisation (Deleuze and Guattari 1987, p. 314), in other words the "making" of crime, showed me how criminal groups and law-enforcement bodies affect and are affected by one another in ways that are not easily separable.

Outside-In: Reading Censorship

In 2020, the police estimated that there are 1242 gang and OMC members in Denmark, of which 378 (30%) are in prison on a monthly average (DKR 2021). Therefore, prison constitutes an important space of socialisation for gangs (Reed 2003) and has been another central field site for this research. Although the Danish criminal authorities were generally inclined to collaborate, their high level of professionalism entailed that I underwent the long bureaucratic screening procedure for researchers seeking to work in prison. In what follows, I unpack some of the ways these external limits affected my behaviour in the seven months of negotiating my access to prison. Differently from the previous case, these limits emerged directly out of my personal relationship with the executive body: the penal institution that had direct power over and affected my access and specific movement.

The first limit I had to respond to was the active censorship of the term LTF in my research proposal. The authorities told me that it was important that I did not address the inmates by their group name (LTF) for two reasons. The first, technical, reason was that since the group had been banned, agreeing to participate in a study on LTF would imply admitting one's connection to the group, making this an illegal and thus punishable action. So although the authorities were trying to help me by pointing me towards prisons with a high concentration of "they who must not be named", I had to hold my tongue. We could speak *of* them as such, but I could not speak *to* them as such. Second, they said that they did not wish to strengthen and reinforce the group's identity by calling it by its name. I later found that the prison authorities had developed the praxis of keeping the groups physically separated from one another, in an effort to avoid conflict and to protect the prison staff. This implied that the different groups would spend a very long period of time together in difficult conditions, making prison a time for in-group bonding. Yet it seems that language was considered a more powerful group-making force than the physical distribution of bodies. But by whom?

The fact is that the ban was a highly political act emanating from the Minister of Justice's aim to put down a firm fist against a particular group that was highly present in the media. None of the prison staff or police I worked with found this law useful in curbing gang violence. Instead it made life more difficult in the everyday life of policing; for example, they told me that it became more challenging to identify gang members on the street given that they no longer used their identifying markers, which in turn caused an increase in stop-and-search of random ethnic minorities. It also fortified the allure of the group; as the only group that could not be named, its criminal status was accrued and its affective force intensified through repression (Ahmed 2003, p. 120). In fact, prohibition is a specific kind of negation, which in linguistic terms is a citation, an essentially affirmative act. For negating something implies that it must first be included into the symbolic order (Lacan 1954) and then, in this case, prohibited. Despite the police and guards' awareness of this, they were bound to act in accordance with the law and, thus, in denial of their own common sense. The exposure to these contradictions in the approaches to collective identity making and breaking taught me much about the complexity of the disciplining of collective bodies and the many layers of power inherent in the punitive system I was learning to navigate.

After abandoning the word "LTF", I finally traversed what I thought would be the most difficult barrier: the formal approval of my research and my pass to access prison. At this point, the officer told me that I was welcome to come into the prison of interest, on the condition that I got an invitation from a detainee.

How could I get an invitation to an interview from a detained gang member whom I had never met and who did not have access to any communication means, you wonder? I was granted permission to announce my project on a poster, which the authorities promised to hang up in the various communal eating areas of the prison. If they were interested, they could then tell the staff who would be responsible for contacting me—a long shot.

I started off with a multimedia announcement. I designed the poster using images of carefree young men riding in a car, and I included references from famous gangster films and music that are popular in those subcultures. I also used wording that took seriously the economic organisation of gangs as a type of enterprise. I did this to be honest about my own true research intention, which was not to study the illicit or criminal aspects of these groups, but more their way of being together and benefitting from one another. I also thought this might motivate them to participate in a conversation that was not centred around their criminal precedents, of which they were constantly reminded by everything that surrounded them.

I also wrote that the study's findings on gang economies could also ultimately help researchers better understand the difference between other forms of criminal economies such as triads and mafias. I chose to include this comparison because I knew that gang members were often very interested and knowledgeable about other forms of organised crime. I knew that gang members also often admired these more structured international organisations and speak of themselves in a belittling tone in relation to these ("We are small fish" or "We are nowhere near the honour of mafia men"). I did not want to legitimise their actions, but as I had a very small space of manoeuvre to capture their attention, I had to hit all the potential topics of interest.

But the poster bounced right back at me. The first reaction I got was the order to remove the wording "organised crime is a very successful international enterprise that makes up about 3.6% of global GDP". They said that they were afraid that this would be misinterpreted by the prison *staff*, and it might provoke them. This surprised me, as I had thus far only thought of the inmates' sensibilities. What I had forgotten was that I also had to win the sympathies of the staff, who are important actors in prison and who had to mediate between me and the detainees—again, another reminder of how multiple the punitive system is. In trying to imagine what else could rankle the staff, I experimented by sending back a renewed version that took away any element of success in the entrepreneurial framing of organised crime, adding the term "criminal", which I thought might resonate with them more directly. "Research on organised crime", I wrote, "has long focused on the criminal aspects of these groups. But organised crime is also an enterprise." I also removed the subcultural references to film and music. I thought this more "serious" framing might be more to the liking of an imaginary prison guard.

But this was not enough. This version too bounced back, this time with the request to remove the picture of the young man cruising around in his car, without any explanation. I did not inquire about the reason, to avoid asking more of this censor. But I interpreted this censorship as being connected to the affective tone. This representation of organised crime was carefree, youthful and thereby desirable, in other words, the opposite of what the rehabilitation facilities sought to communicate about that lifestyle. In truth I do not know why this photo was censored, but the way I experienced this limit led me to return a very bland, solely textual poster. And indeed, it finally passed the test. Clearly I was learning to be affected by the censorship, learning to relate to the institutional body that I (and my interlocutors) had to navigate.

Although the poster unsurprisingly did not grant me a single invitation from the inmates, the process through which it was censored, the various limits set by the authorities as to what I could and could not communicate, is a rich source of knowledge about the penal system in question. Although this study was not about criminal justice systems, this information was valuable for my work. It taught me about the sobriety of the institutional atmosphere and the norms the gangs I studied were exposed to on an everyday basis. This also better prepared me for the interactions

I eventually had in prison, which I finally managed to access via other channels. Moreover, while getting access is most commonly spoken of as a skill or a situation one must learn to navigate in order to get closer to knowledge, I have illustrated how instead the process of getting access can instead also in itself be the source of knowledge. And the material traces of this source of knowledge consisted in this case in a rich archive of a lengthy censorship process, which allowed me to trace the development of my own framing of the gangs in relation to the limits and reactions of the institutional bodies that I encountered.

INSIDE-OUT: MOVEMENT IN AND OF THE FIELD

One of the first field visits I carried out was a guided walking tour of the neighbourhood of Nørrebro, which has been one of the stages for minority gang conflicts in the past 15 years. Although the boundaries of urban marginality have become increasingly porous (Wacquant 2008, p. 51), the government has included parts of this neighbourhood in the so-called Ghetto Plan: a set of policies that seek to curb crime through a more forceful "integration" of marginal groups, via territorially differentiated legislation, cultural surveillance, and, in some instances, forced displacement to reduce intra-ethnic contact within designated housing areas (Regeringen 2018). Thereby the area of Nørrebro represents an important setting for the politics and territorialisation of ethnic minorities and gangs from many perspectives. In these final examples, I illustrate how I became aware of my own prejudices about the relationship between the neighbourhood and its inhabitants. In particular, I will share some insights I gained about my own assumptions about space, place, and identity by paying attention to how I moved. And particularly what happened when I began transforming what Spinoza calls passions into actions (Spinoza [1677] 2001), that is when I started to actively affect and move the field rather than only being moved by it.

Ghettotours is a tourism initiative taken by a local youth centre, called RCYN, that aims to break the stigma around the so-called ghetto areas and give local youth ownership over their homes by making them tour guides. The fact that this tour was already available to the public meant that I could simply pay to be moved through space and be affected by my interlocutors' narrative filter, without having to negotiate my presence. As the tour was guided by several people, it also allowed me to conduct rich place-based interviews with the participants (Riley and Holton 2016) that gave me a fantastic overview of the youth's relationship to different sites, objects, and materialities, as well as my and the other tourists' frames of reference.

At the end of the tour, I tried to exchange numbers with several of the guides, but they were cautious and told me that I had to ask the youth centre's leaders for permission, as they were minors. So I met the very caring and professional leaders of the centre, who thoroughly interviewed me about my research, ensuring that my intentions and practices were non-harmful. Although they did not give me the numbers of the guides, they allowed me to volunteer at the youth centre for about a year. Soon enough, I realised that my own teaching experience in tourism and experiential design was a valuable resource for the centre, so together with another employee, I curated a course called Ghetto Tours, Vol. II. We trained the guides in designing, presenting, and curating a new, improved version of the tour that they could sell to the public.

Teaching this course has been one of the biggest challenges of my teaching career. Besides being a very diverse group of students, both in age and in educational level, the very aim of the course was unusually split. On the one hand, I wanted to give the students some useful aesthetic, political, and design tools that they could use for their tour. On the other, I wanted to gain as much knowledge as possible about their own experience of living alongside organised crime and the so-called ghetto in general. This meant that I tip-toed for months and tried to make the course more about general form than specific content. I was far more interested in learning what they wanted out of the tour than in teaching them what I knew. My inner modernist social-scientist limit began sounding loudly: "Do not mould artificially; observe the raw data as it unfolds naturally!" For a while I adhered to this inner limit, even though I grew increasingly suspicious of it. In fact, I have a general tendency to do action research, and to some extent, all my research has been characterised by conscious interventions on the field. So why was this voice holding me back from relaxing into my usual mode of intervention, and what was it telling me? In hindsight, I realise that I thought[7] I could not intervene before I knew enough. Apparently years of feminist action research had not fully undone the positivist limits that had been successfully implanted throughout my social science training: because I was in their physical territory, their buildings, their neighbourhood, I thought I had to continue to be moved by

---

[7] As if I wasn't already intervening!

them, as I was a foreign body who had to limit herself to observe, register the occurrences through an objective scientific gaze.

It was not until the end of the course that I realised how wrong I was, when I thought I had figured out much of what I could know about young ethnic minorities living in the vicinity of Danish gangs. It happened at the point where I moved the field quite drastically. In fact, we had organised "bait" that would keep the young motivated and ensure their participation: a free one-week study trip to Sicily. We went on a cultural exchange with a youth group in Palermo, AddioPizzo Travel, that was also curating tours in the context of organised crime heritage.

As soon as we got off the plane, the group started to self-identify as Danish. "Us Danes aren't used to this weather." "These pastries are far too sweet for a Dane like me." The stark contrast with this new place made them constantly reflect and comment on their own identity. Indeed, as Alison McIntosh and Anne Zahra note (2007), tourism is a cultural encounter, not just with the local population, but with one's own. Needless to say, this was an incredible gift for me, researching Danish ethnic minorities, one that I had not foreseen the potency of. In this case, the identity they related to was not the minority citizen in Denmark, which they always referred to back home, but it was the more general "Danishness" that came to the front as their own. Through the encounter with the other, they affirmed themselves not as the minor other, but instead began representing themselves as the majority other. It was as if the contrast towards the new context to which they were minorities reduced or temporarily suspended the difference they perceived towards the majority they usually related to.

Because I am part Sicilian, I was part of the other they were visiting, which gave me another set of advantages. My connection and knowledge of the place increased my authority, and my role as a teacher became more central than my role as a researcher investigating them. Our roles were reversed. They were also tourists now, which took away much of the inhibition from their curiosity. The questions they asked about Sicily in general and organised crime in particular gave me a lot of insight into their own knowledge and preconceptions. Per contra, I shared much of my personal life and networks with my informants over the course of the week. Not only because we spent all day together, but also because they started to recognise me as part of "them", in that I too was a Danish ethnic minority. This levelling out gave me the confidence to finally ask difficult questions.

The formal activities we organised with our hosts also allowed the guests to ask and answer the local youth's difficult questions. One of the many workshops we organised was centred around the genre of difficult heritage and was framed around the question of what it was like to live with and talk about organised crime. Filtering the self-reflection onto the main focus of my research worked wonders in this setting. First of all, the formalised conversation made it easier to keep the attention of the young restless bodies that would much rather go around exploring and having fun on their own. They listened, focused, and answered out of politeness to the hosts, who had put a great deal of work into presenting their own reflections in a language that they were not confident in. The first-hand experiences of the Sicilian tour guides also provoked strong reactions in the Danish group. In the discussions that followed, both groups gave personal accounts of what they had witnessed and how they negotiated their ethical choices in their everyday lives.

For now, it suffices to highlight that I learned more about life in the so-called Danish ghetto during our one week stay in Palermo than I did in the first year of fieldwork in Copenhagen. Learning came from the intervention, rather than being a prerequisite to it. By moving the bodies and immersing the field in new stimuli, I learned about its boundaries, its openings, and its differences and similarities to Palermo. This limit only became apparent after the deterritorialisation of the group occurred, so it was not a conscious choice as such. However, in hindsight, I realise that my own inner conception of the "field" was bound to a particular physical space, and thereby, my idea of *where* I could know about it was too. By displacing the field, I radically modified the group's behaviour and, also, my own interaction with it. This suggests the epistemological power of mobile methods (Büscher et al. 2011; Sausdal and Vigh 2019), not only intended as moving *with* the field and being affected by it as I did with the initial tour I went on, but actually actively moving *the* field and radically affecting it.

PRACTICAL SPECULATIVE AFFIRMATION

The various thought experiments I have reconstructed all emerged from asking this question: what if one puts the affective occurrences that temporarily reduce one's capacity to act, that is the limits one encounters in a research process, at the centre, rather than at the periphery of knowledge generation? The short answer is a more relational understanding of the world.

A longer answer would of course require expansive elaborations of the short ethnographic examples I have gathered for the purpose of illustrating this methodological impetus. But what all of these have in common is a heightened focus on the various ways in which persons, places, objects, and, of course, the researcher herself are intertwined, how they are affected and affect others within the field.

On the one hand, I have illustrated how this experiment has helped me discover and reveal novel empirical perspectives or details that escaped me: for instance, how following the making of a legal limit shifted my perspective from one gang to the more general relationships between criminal organisations, law enforcement, and the social norms that both sides reproduce and challenge at a given point in time. This insight indirectly suggests the epistemological and political importance of letting go of approaches to crime and its prevention that operate in social vacuums that, for instance, treat criminals as isolated individuals with inherent qualities that need to be removed or added.

But this experiment also led me to a heightened self-awareness of my own assumptions, behaviour, and trajectory of discovery. Focusing on affective encounters that went *outside-in* taught me about the contours and intricacies of an institutional setting I would work in for a long time and trained me to respond to it and make myself more attuned to it. This not only increased my power of acting with it, but it also made me aware of my own learning process. This reflexive aspect is even more pronounced in the last example, where I revealed some epistemological preconceptions I had as a researcher and the immense richness that came from "accidentally" letting go of them. Moreover, the insights that came from actually moving a field to another site highlighted that a field is not materially rooted to a place in a manner that is materially fixated, but that the relationship between people and place also travels and transforms in movement.

Overall, the method of tracing one's encounters with limits allows for the construction of an *archive* of one's ways of relating to the field of study, as well as one's own processes of knowledge formation. Having these traces might make it more difficult to forget one's positionality while making it easier to trace where and how one affects and is affected. Activating limits is a practical exercise in speculative affirmation, one that leaves traces, and that therefore also affords the potential for more ethical research practices.

Acknowledgements This project has benefitted from the support of Carlsberg Foundation (Grant number CF17_0871) and the European Research Council (Grant agreement ID: 725194). I am grateful for the feedback received from colleagues from the Centre for Global Criminology and the editors of this volume on earlier drafts of this chapter.

REFERENCES

Ahmed, S. (2003). Affective economies. *Social Text 79*, 22(2), 117–139.

Bataille, G. (1988). *Inner experience* (L.A. Boldt, Trans.). State University of New York Press. (Original work published 1944).

Bataille, G. (2001). *Eroticism* (M. Dalwood, Trans.) Penguin Books. (Original work published 1957).

Becker, H. S. (1963). *Outsiders: Studies in the sociology of deviance.* Free Press Glencoe.

Büscher, M., Urry, J., & Witchger, K. (Eds.). (2011). *Mobile methods.* Routledge.

Deleuze, G., & Guattari, F. (1987). *A thousand plateaus: Capitalism and schizophrenia* (B. Massumi, Trans.). University of Minnesota Press. (Original work published 1980).

Deleuze, G. (1988). *Spinoza: Practical philosophy* (R. Hurley, Trans.). City Lights Books.

Det Kriminal Preventiv Råd (DKR). (2021). Bander og rockere i tal. Retrieved January 17, 2021, from https://dkr.dk/ungdomskriminalitet/bander/bander-i-tal/

Durkheim, E. (1895). Criminalité et santé sociale. *Revue Philosophique, 39*, 148–162.

Foucault, M. (1991). How an 'experience-book' is born. In *Remarks on Marx: Conversations with Duccio Trombadori* (R. J. Goldstein & J. Cascaito, Trans.) (p. 27). Cited in Jay, M. (1995). The limits of limit-experience: Bataille and Foucault. *Constellations, 2*(2), 155–174.

Jay, M. (1995). The limits of limit-experience: Bataille and Foucault. *Constellations, 2*(2), 155–174.

Jerne, C. (forthcoming). The diversity of solidarity economies: Transactions and property in Danish minority gangs. *Economy and Society.*

Knudsen, B. T., & Stage, C. (2015). Introduction: Affective methodologies. In B. T. Knudsen & C. Stage (Eds.), *Affective methodologies: Developing cultural research strategies for the study of affect* (pp. 1–22). Palgrave Macmillan.

Kuldova, T. (2019). *How outlaws win friends and influence people.* Palgrave Macmillan.

Lacan, J. (1954). Réponse aux commentaires de Jean Hyppolite sur la "Verneinung" de Freud. In J. Lacan. (1966). *Écrits* (pp. 381–399). Seuil. Cited in Evans, D. (1996). *An introductory dictionary of Lacanian psychoanalysis* (p. 18). Routledge.

Latour, B. (2004). How to talk about the body? The normative dimensions of Science Studies. *Body & Society*, 10(2–3), 205–229.

Marcus, G. E. (2010). Contemporary fieldwork aesthetics in art and anthropology: Experiments in collaboration and intervention. *Visual Anthropology*, 23(4), 263–277.

Malinowski B. (1926). *Crime and custom in savage society*. Rowman & Littlefield.

McIntosh, A.J., & Zahra, A. (2007). A cultural encounter through volunteer tourism: Towards the ideals of sustainable tourism? *Journal of Sustainable Tourism*, 15(5), 541–556.

Nielsen J. J. (2008). *Sjakal Manifestet*. Hells Angels MC Danmark. Retrieved May 28, 2020, from https://hells-angels.dk/en/sjakal-manifestet-2008/

Reed, A. (2003). *Papua New Guinea's last place: Experiences of constraint in postcolonial prisons*. Berghahn Books.

Regeringen. (2018). Ét Danmark uden parallelsamfund: Ingen ghettoer i 2030. Retrieved June 6, 2020 from https://www.stm.dk/multimedia/2018_t_Danmark_uden_parallelsamfund.pdf

Riley, M., & Holton, M. (2016). Place-based interviewing: Creating and conducting walking interviews. In *SAGE research methods cases*. https://doi.org/1 0.4135/9781446273050155595386

Robinson, B., & Kutner, M. (2019). Spinoza and the affective turn: A return to the philosophical origins of affect. *Qualitative Inquiry*, 25(2), 111–117.

Roepstorff, A. (2011). Eksperimentel antropologi. *Tidsskriftet Antropologi*, 63, 137–152.

Sausdal, D., & Vigh, H. (2019). Anthropological criminology 2.0: Ethnographies of global crime and criminalisation. *Focaal: Journal of Global and Historical Anthropology*, 85, 1–14.

Spinoza, B. (2001). *Ethics* (W.H. White & A.H. Stirling, Trans.). Wordsworth. (Original work published 1677).

Standing, A. (2006). *Organised crime: A study from the Cape Flats*. Institute for Security Studies.

Tarde, G. (1890). *Penal philosophy* (R. Howell, Trans.). Transaction Publishers.

Tonkonoff, S. (2014). Crime as the limit of culture. *Human Studies*, 37(4), 529–544.

Wacquant, L. (2008). *Urban Outcasts: A Comparative Sociology of Advanced Marginality*. Polity Press.

INDEX[1]

---

[1] Note: Page numbers followed by 'n' refer to notes.

Printed by Printforce, United Kingdom